THE
ULTIMATE
ENCYCLOPEDIA
OF
TENNIS

THIS IS A CARLTON BOOK

Copyright © Carlton Books Ltd, 1998

First published in 1998 by Carlton Books Limited

This revised edition first published in 2006 by Carlton Books Limited

10 9 8 7 6 5 4 3 2 1

A CIP catalogue record for this book is available from the British Library

ISBN: 1 84442 157 0
ISBN 13: 978 184442 157 2

Project editor: Chris Hawkes
Project art direction: Diane Spender
Picture research: Justin Downing
Production: Sarah Schuman
Design: Paul Cooper

Printed and bound in Dubai

Carlton Books Limited
20 Mortimer Street
London W1T 3JW

Author acknowledgments:
The author would like to thank Alan Little and staff at the Wimbledon Lawn Tennis
Museum Library; Henry Wancke for providing the section detailing Davis and Fed
Cup nations, Alan Trengove, Dennis Cunnington, the International Tennis Federation,
the United States Tennis Association and the Deutscher Tennis-Bund.Federation, the
United States Tennis Association and the Deutscher Tennis-Bund.

THE
ULTIMATE
ENCYCLOPEDIA
OF
TENNIS

THE DEFINITIVE ILLUSTRATED GUIDE TO WORLD TENNIS

John Parsons

Updated by **Henry Wancke**

CARLTON
BOOKS

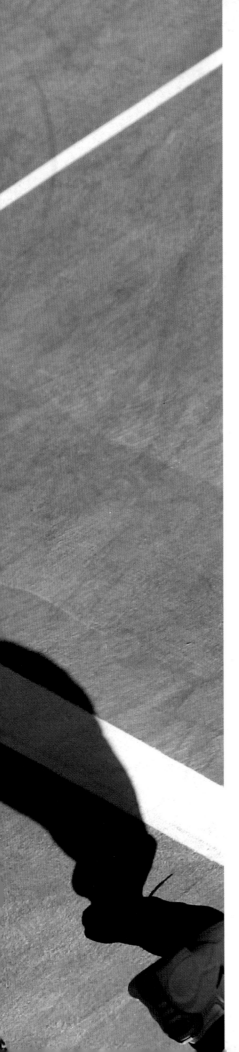

CONTENTS

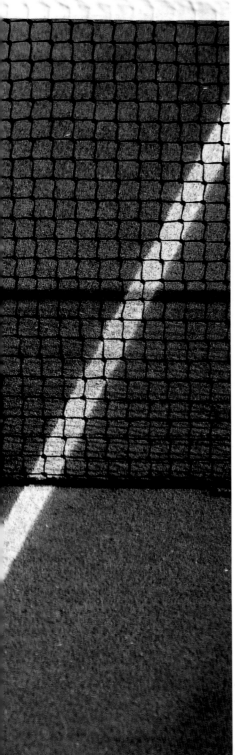

INTRODUCTION

The old theatrical style cry used to be "Anyone for tennis?" Now, when one looks around the world at the vast numbers who play this beguiling game, which transcends all geographical and age boundaries, it is more a case of "Everyone for tennis".

Over the last 40 years since leaders at Wimbledon and the Lawn Tennis Association in Britain most of all, at last convinced enough delegates in the rest of the world to vote for Open tennis, the way the game has grown and flourished has been spectacular.

Even the mini slump in the United States, which has been evident in recent years, needs to be kept in perspective, for it is only a decline for what was an extraordinarily high peak in the mid-1970s. If anything the most worrying aspect for Americans is that in both men's and women's tennis, their players, with one or two exceptions, no longer dominate the scene in the way which many had come to expect.

In turn, though, that reflects how the cream at the top of both the men's and women's ranking lists is spread over a much wider list of nations, so any loss for the United States is a gain for the rest of the tennis world.

The Ultimate Encyclopedia of Tennis not only reflects that in a major section detailing the record 134 countries which entered the Davis Cup in 2005, but tells in words and pictures, how a game which was born almost by accident on a lawn in the middle of England, now involves and intrigues countless millions.

It was once claimed by Philippe Chatrier, former president of both the French Tennis Federation and the International Tennis Federation, that tennis was one of the few sports which catered for its converts, in an active and competitive way, from the cradle to the grave. The enormous range of opportunities for youngsters from as young as five to start learning the rudiments of the sport, coupled with the phenomenal growth of the veterans game, with rankings for the 85s and over in some countries, suggests that what he said was true.

Much of this book naturally focuses on the players, past and present, the places and the events which automatically write themselves into sporting history. Names such as Suzanne Lenglen, Fred Perry, Don Budge, Rod Laver, Billie Jean King, Chris Evert, Martina Navaratilova, John McEnroe, Jimmy Connors and Peter Sampras, Steffi Graff through to Roger Federer, Rafael Nadal, Serena and Venus Williams, Kim Clijsters and Martina Hingis of today. There are pen pictures of almost 200 of the best players throughout the years, plus features on the four Grand Slams and other major competitions and some of the most famous tennis venues.

The book also looks at the commercial and showbusiness side of tennis, the evolution of modern rackets, the changes in playing styles and recalls the extraordinary incidents, some serious, some amusing, which fill the cupboard of tennis memories. Like the game itself, *The Ultimate Encyclopedia of Tennis* aims to provide something for everyone.

THE ORIGINS OF THE GAME

It is said that when Queen Elizabeth I was being entertained at Elvetham in Hampshire by the Earl of Hertford that after lunch at about three o'clock, ten of his servants were ordered to hang up lines on the lawn, squaring out what we see now as the form of a tennis court, for recreational purposes said to be "to the great liking of her Majesty".

The birth of lawn tennis can be traced back to 1858, when Major Henry Gem, a solicitor and clerk to the magistrates in Birmingham, and Major Walter Clopton Wingfield, a member of the Honourable Corps of Gentlemen-at-Arms at the court of Queen Victoria, marked out a lawn in Edgbaston, Warwickshire, and called it a tennis court. Until the first lawn tennis club was formed in nearby Leamington in 1872, the only game generally known as tennis was what the French called *jeu de paume*, because it was originally played with the hand, and what was called real tennis in Britain, court tennis in the United States and royal tennis in Australia.

Some historical references suggest that a form of lawn tennis can be traced back many centuries. There is evidence that a similar type of outdoor game existed in AD 500 and that its roots could be found in Egypt and Persia. The fact that the earliest mention of the game in English history occurs in ecclesiastical manuscripts lends credence to the belief that tennis began in an abbey cloister – hence the characteristic design for a real indoor tennis court of a sloping roof round three sides, with pillars supporting it and a hatch (grille) in one corner.

Sport of kings

Whatever the truth of the matter, tennis was certainly a royal game during the reign of Louis X of France (1314–16) and quickly grew in popularity. Contests were held and large fortunes staked on the outcome in palaces throughout much of Europe – indeed a chill which Louis is said to have caught from drinking an urn of ice-cold water immediately after a strenuous game was thought to have contributed to his death. Charles VIII (1483–98), son of Louis XI, was another king to die as a result of playing real tennis, though not quite so directly. He apparently struck his head on the lintel of the door leading to the court and never recovered.

There is mention of a woman called Margot playing real tennis in Paris in 1427. It was even said that she was better than most men at hand-ball,

TENNIS *at Windsor Castle during the reign of Henry VIII*

from which the name *jeu de paume* was derived. The first mention of it in England is in statutes forbidding it and encouraging other activities such as archery, but Henry V (1413–22) is said to have become a convert after receiving a gift of carefully stitched tennis balls "stuffed with good hide and wool wadding" from the French Dauphin.

Not that he and his courtiers totally appreciated the gift. They took it to be a boastful, provocative gesture and promptly began preparing for the Battle of Agincourt in 1415.

Modern lawn tennis probably owes a great deal to the Battle of Agin-

HENRY VIII *was reputed to be an excellent player*

ANNO · ETATIS · SVÆ · XLIX ·

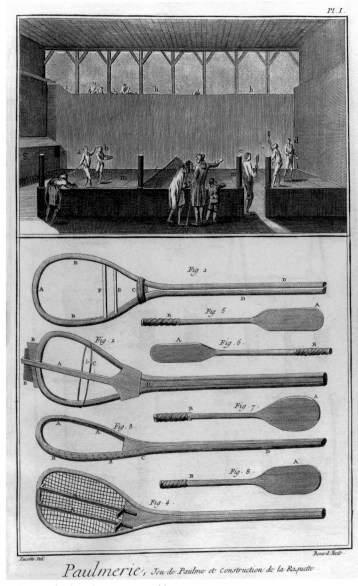

Paulmerie, Jeu de Paulme et Construction de la Raquette.

A COURT *for* jeu de paume *and* le racquette

best-known venues for real tennis in England. There is also evidence of real tennis having been played out of doors in Elizabethan times.

Courts of Europe

The sport was by no means confined to France and Britain. During the sixteenth century it was highly popular in most of Europe, especially Spain, Italy, Switzerland and Brussels, and there were courts dotted right through Germany and what was then the Austrian Empire. There were also courts in Prague and, until 1866, there was certainly one in St Petersburg.

By the middle of the seventeenth century the game was being played in New York, where it still thrives today. The passions which it aroused seemed to be uniform the world over. The highly emotional Italian painter Caravaggio is said to have worked himself into such a frenzy, while playing a match in Rome in 1606, that he killed his opponent and had to flee.

Lawn tennis

In time, though, real tennis, which still needed a wider social acceptance for it to become a leading sport, spawned the new game of rackets – which in turn led to the introduction of squash rackets – first played at Harrow School in the 1880s and made possible to some extent by the same early technical advance which also helped Major Gem and Major Wingfield to start developing lawn tennis. For it was around then that inventors learned how to make a rubber ball which would bounce – not least on grass.

Major Wingfield's new version of the game no longer required an elaborate, expensive indoor court. The court was designed in the shape of an hourglass, wider at the baseline than at the net, narrowing from 30ft (3ft more than today) to 21ft, while the length was 60ft, 18ft shorter than the present dimension. The height of the net was set at 4ft 8in and, according to illustrations published at the time, it was clearly meant to be the same in the centre as at the sides. Major Wingfield is reputed to have used a much lower net, barely 2ft high, while he was still experimenting with adaptations in the late 1860s before he applied to

patent his "New and Improved Court for Playing the Ancient Game of Tennis", which he called "Sphairistike", in 1874. It was during the negotiations for the patent to be issued that Wingfield, who was not happy about the way the name was being abbreviated to "Sticky", seemingly decided that lawn tennis would be a more appropriate description.

Sets of Major Wingfield's game cost five guineas (£5.25) and comprised balls, four rackets and sufficient netting to make up a court. The popularity of the game grew so rapidly that it quickly surpassed croquet – which was a national game, especially for the aristocracy – on vicarage lawns and became one of the first sports in which it was deemed acceptable for women to participate. Indeed, while tennis was still in its infancy consideration was given as to whether, in women's (or ladies' as they were called then) matches, the ball should be allowed to bounce twice on their side of the court because of the added handicap they suffered from trying to move swiftly in long dresses, often with heavy petticoats underneath or even a bustle at the back. Documents from the time indicate that ladies, when given the option, politely but firmly declined, although two bounces are allowed in the game today in the case of wheelchair tennis, which has spread dramatically in recent years and achieved outstanding levels of competitive skill, stamina, courage and international acclaim.

Ground rules

As the popularity of lawn tennis grew, so entrepreneurs began to cash in with their own, slightly modified versions of the game and it soon became evident that some order needed to be imposed. The Marylebone Cricket Club, in its capacity as the governing authority of rackets and real tennis, suggested that their tennis committee should draft universal rules for all lawn tennis. The meeting, in public, was convened at Lord's early in 1875 and on May 24 the new code was issued.

The code decreed that a tennis court should be 30ft wide at the base (still 3ft longer than now) and 78ft long, which it remains today. The ser-

court. During such times, the English captured Prince Charles d'Orléans who, like his father and grandfather, was a devoted exponent of the game. Indeed, when Louis XII was on the French throne (1498–1515), there were said to be no less than 40 courts in his home town of Orléans, with the popularity of the game spreading well beyond the nobility. Meanwhile Prince Charles spent 25 years in various prisons in England until, after protests from the French, he was transferred to the care of a certain John Wingfield who, unlike most gaolers of that era, decided that Charles d'Orléans should be allowed to resume his pastime at Wingfield Castle. That was in 1435. In 1873 it was a direct descendant of that gaoler, Major

Walter Wingfield, who revived and began to modernize the sport to make it suitable to be played by both sexes out of doors.

Henry VIII (1509–47) was reputed to be an excellent player. There were four courts at his Palace of Whitehall, which he wrested from Cardinal Wolsey, and one in St James's Palace, which he built for Anne Boleyn, although the story goes that even as the poor lass was being chopped down by the executioner he was happily engaged playing tennis elsewhere. The most famous of all the courts which can be traced back to the amorous monarch are those which were the first to be built at Hampton Court Palace. These and the Queen's Club in London remain two of the

vice court was drawn to a distance of 26ft from the net, rather than from the baseline. The service had to be delivered with one foot outside the baseline and was required to drop between the net and the service line of the court diagonally opposite to that in which the server stood. Under Wingfield's original rules, all serves were from one side only. This meeting also reaffirmed the belief that all the rules should be the same for women as for men.

Although the code was approved by all those present, it was not long before amendments were being made. In 1878, largely because of experience gained during the first Wimbledon in 1877, the height of the net was reduced to 4ft 9in at the posts and 3ft at the centre. Two years later the posts, which were originally 7ft high and 24ft apart, retaining the hourglass appearance of the court, were

reduced to 4ft, and in 1884 they were reduced once more to 3ft 6in, the height they are today. The changes were made so quickly that it is difficult to trace much reliable evidence that the original MCC code was ever applied, except possibly in a handicap match reported to have been played at Cambridge in June 1875. At this stage, too, most balls remained bare, with no covering of the rubber. Only after a letter from J.M. Heathcote appeared in *The Field* in December 1874, saying that he had found it beneficial to cover lawn tennis balls with white flannel, which not only made them bounce better but made them easier to see and to control, did covering become common.

Croquet vs. tennis

Yet while tennis was undoubtedly thriving and had already spread to the United States, it was its adoption by

the All England Croquet Club at Wimbledon, as it was then, which was to ensure it became more than a passing fashion. In 1875, Henry Jones, though principally a croquet enthusiast, proposed, as a member of the committee, that the All England Croquet Club should broaden its horizons and introduce the new sport of lawn tennis. It was approved at the annual meeting and a membership fee of two guineas (£2.10) was agreed which would cover both sports. Two years later lawn tennis had taken such a hold that the annual meeting agreed to incorporate it into the name of the club, which then became the All England Croquet and Lawn Tennis Club. Today, of course, it is the All England Lawn Tennis and Croquet Club.

Hard though it may be to believe now, there have been a few occasions during its history when the most famous lawn tennis club in the world

has been short of funding. Indeed it was partly because of the need to generate extra revenue in its first three years to meet an increase, first from £50 to £75 and then from £75 to £100, on the rent for the four acres of its original home adjoining the old London and South Western Railway line near Worple Road in Wimbledon that the introduction of a tennis section was mooted in the first place.

The Championships

By 1877 the financial picture was again looking gloomy. The pony roller which was needed more for the croquet lawns than for the tennis courts was in need of repair, but the money was not available. It was then that Henry Jones put forth another proposal. Why not organize a lawn tennis event for all-comers? Mr J.H. Walsh, who as editor of *The Field* had played a significant part in the for-

A TENNIS *garden party in the Gay Ninetees, depicted in this printing by Hy Sandman*

HERBERT LAWFORD *and Ernest Renshaw in the 1881 Wimbledon semi-finals*

mation of the club, liked the idea and persuaded his proprietors to support it by providing a silver challenge cup worth 25 guineas. Incidentally, he it was who had donated the original pony roller to the club, when it was formed at a meeting in the offices of *The Field* in 1868, in return for the election of his daughter as a member. On Monday July 9, 1877, The Championships, as they are known the world over, were born.

Not that the opening tournament took place without teething problems. Deciding to stage a tennis event was one thing. Producing an acceptable set of rules was quite another. The committee of the All England Croquet and Lawn Tennis Club was still unhappy about the outcome of the MCC deliberations and some of the rules which had been laid down. At the same time, a prolonged debate was being maintained in the press on the relative merits or otherwise of the scoring in rackets and tennis respectively. Other issues which needed to be settled – the height of the net, the position of the service line and whether to allow a first-serve fault – were still being discussed, and not always without rancour. The All England offi-

cials decided to appoint a sub-committee to frame rules for the conduct of The Championships.

It was resolved that the court should be rectangular, rather than hourglass shape, 26 yards long by nine yards wide, with the net being suspended from posts placed 3ft outside the court. Much more controversial at the time was the decision to adopt tennis rather than rackets scoring in its entirety. It was also agreed that there would be the allowance of one service fault without penalty, whether the ball dropped into the net, did not clear the net, landed in the wrong court or went beyond the service line. All those decisions have undoubtedly stood the test of time, despite occasional campaigns to limit players to one serve or reduce the size of the service court, a change last made in 1880 when it was reduced from 26ft to 21ft in an attempt to combat serving power.

Other decisions taken at the time which have been altered with the benefit of experience include the necessity for the server always to have one foot outside the baseline until the ball has been struck. This rule has been subject to change more than once, and

the original version would be welcomed back again today by quite a few. Also considered, but rejected, was the serve which dropped in after hitting the net and which was to be considered as good. Yet the most spectacular rule introduced by those pioneers in 1877, which clearly did not stand the test of time, was that the net should be fixed at 5ft at the posts and 3ft 3in in the centre, severely limiting the opportunities, especially in doubles, to hit winning passing shots down the lines. Five years later it became the height we know today, 3ft 6in at the side and 3ft in the middle.

Keeping score

The origins of the scoring system are far more difficult to pin down than the antecedents of the game itself. The points system is probably based on the quarters of the hour. In that case 15 and 30 are easy to understand, but why 40? Most tennis historians tend to agree that it was originally 45, but eventually became shortened in its usage to 40. As for "love", there are two commonly expressed theories. One is that the term stems from the French word *l'oeuf* (egg), which symbolizes nothing or zero inasmuch as

almost everything in life begins to take shape from an egg; the other theory, favoured by literary scholars, is that it was derived from sayings such as "not for love nor money".

Similarly the derivation of the word "tennis" in English has been the subject of considerable research. Way back at the end of the last century, the French ambassador to the United States, J.J. Jusserand, who was a frequent member of what President Theodore Roosevelt called his "tennis cabinet", undertook to solve the puzzle. The customary belief is that the word tennis is derived from the French *tendre*, meaning "to hold". The theory is that in olden days the server called out "tendre" as a means of advising his opponent that he was ready to serve. The idea is given credence from research carried out some years ago in Brussels where the use of the word "attendez" offered the same message.

These days when there is so much concern about the dominance of power in the game, especially in men's tennis, it is fascinating to discover that there was similar anxiety at the end of the first Wimbledon 119 years ago. Henry Jones decided to carry out an analysis of all the scorecards and concluded from the high proportion of service games won that the service was

AMBASSADOR, *Jules Jusserand*

far too powerful for the long-term good of the game. Three remedies were suggested. One was to heighten the net in the middle, another was to do away with first faults and the third was to move the service line closer to the net. The majority of players, we are led to believe, favoured limiting players to one serve. The All England Club, with typical foresight, realized that this might make the game seem too difficult for those who had not played before. They opted instead for reducing the size of the service court to 22ft.

The first Wimbledon

From 22 players competing in 1877, each of whom paid £1.05 for the right to enter, the number increased to 34 for the second staging of Wimbledon a year later, when an overarm serve was reputedly introduced by A.T. Myers and the number of spectators watching the final more than tripled from 200 to about 700. Meanwhile the game was beginning to find favour in other parts of Britain. The first recorded doubles competition, one year before Oxford University provided the trophy and staged what is now regarded as the first Wimbledon men's doubles – or four-handed championship, as it was called – was played in Scotland in 1878. The first championships for women were held in Ireland in 1879 and remain the oldest event for women in the world.

Curiously enough the earliest Wimbledon champions were not so obviously excited about their success as their modern counterparts are. Recalling his 1877 victory as the first Wimbledon champion, Spencer Gore wrote three years later: "That anyone who has really played well at cricket, (real) tennis or even rackets will ever seriously give his attention to lawn tennis, beyond showing himself a promising player, is extremely doubtful for in all probability the monotony of the game, as compared with the others, would choke him off before he had time to excel in it." R.F. "Frank" Hadow, the second champion, was equally dismissive. Rather than stay to defend his title, he returned to Ceylon to continue his career as a tea planter.

United States

Opinions differ widely as to how the game first began to take root in the United States. It is generally accepted that the credit should go to Mary Outerbridge, a member of a prominent Staten Island family who, during a visit to Bermuda in 1874, watched members of the British garrison playing lawn tennis and was so enchanted that she bought from them a net, two rackets and a set of balls to take home with her. More than a century later the eminent British tennis historian Tom Todd revealed that he had discovered that a Dr Wright of Boston should be given the credit for having introduced tennis to the United States at least some months earlier. And in 1974 American historian George Alexander produced evidence which suggested that the first recorded tennis match there had not been in Massachusetts or even New York, as one might suppose, but in the wilds of Arizona in 1874, thanks to the wife of an army captain, Ella Wilkins Bailey.

No one will ever be quite sure who was responsible. The likelihood is that all three, and possibly others no one knew about at the time, were involved in introducing the game to

the Americans at more or less the same time. Whoever it was, judging by the way their children, grandchildren and now great-great-grandchildren have taken up and often dominated the game since, they are clearly owed a major debt of gratitude.

International championships

Lawn tennis spread with remarkable speed during the rest of the nineteenth century, particularly throughout the old British Empire. Although the first Australian national Championships did not begin until 1905, which was also the first year of Australia as a separate nation, the game had been taking hold steadily for more than a decade before that, with the first Victorian Championships taking place in 1880. Two years before that tennis was already being established in Panama. In 1881, there was a tournament in Durban, the forerunner of the South African Championships which were launched 10 years later. New Zealanders claim that their first lawn tennis club began operating as early as 1875.

The spread of the game throughout Europe began with British players taking it first to their spring retreats

in the resorts of the French Riviera, Dinard or Le Touquet. There are records of the Decimel Club, founded in Paris in 1877, as being the first tennis club in France, five years before the Racing Club was established which in turn organized the first international championship in France in 1889. The French National Championships started two years later but, until 1925, the event now known as the French Open at Roland Garros was limited to French citizens. The German Championships were launched in 1893.

Yet while lawn tennis was undoubtedly played first in Britain, the first national governing body was established in the United States. The United States Tennis Association (formerly the US Lawn Tennis Association) was founded in 1881. The Lawn Tennis Association, the ruling body for the game in England, Scotland and Wales, was formed seven years later in 1888, with the International Lawn Tennis Federation, now the International Tennis Federation, coming into being in 1913, by which time the game that began on a Warwickshire lawn in 1858 had spread worldwide. It shows no sign of stopping now.

INDOOR TENNIS, *as far back as 1881, in New York*

TENNIS AROUND THE WORLD

From its lowly beginnings, the game of tennis has now grown into a mass-participation, multi-billion-dollar business covering all corners of the globe. From the largest countries in the world to the smallest, tennis has become more than just a highly popular pastime.

Afghanistan

AFGHAN LAWN TENNIS ASSOCIATION

Tennis survives amongst some of the population despite the country being ravaged by internal turmoil.

Albania

FEDERATA SHOIPETARE E TENSIT
Founded: 1985
No. of Players: 280
Clubs: 7
Courts: 28

Historically tennis dates back to 1935 when it was introduced by students returning from France. The sport's development suffered under communism, but retained a foothold in the country which is now being fostered under the management of the national association which has set up an administrative structure and calendar. In 1996, the Albanian Tennis Federation beacme an associate member of the International Tennis Federation and joined the European Tennis Association.

Algeria

FÉDÉRATION ALGÉRIENNE DE TENNIS
Founded: 1962
No. of Players: 10,000
Clubs: 53
Courts: 160

Birthplace of Tarik Benhabiles and Françoise Durr, a former French No. 1 who rose to become world No. 3 in 1967. Algeria, who list just 2,820 licensed tennis players, have developed a strong junior programme and have 2,059 youngsters on their books. Became an associate member of the ITF in 1963, progressing to full membership in 1965. Entered the Fed Cup for the first time in 1997, but has been a regular competitor in the Davis Cup (1976–78; 1980–94). Algeria is now established as one of the stronger African tennis nations.

American Samoa

AMERICAN SAMOA TENNIS ASSOCIATION
Founded: 1985
No. of Players: 100
Clubs: 10
Courts: 25

Affiliated to the USTA, the island was the site of the first South Pacific Junior Championships in 1983. To ensure Olympic participation, American Samoa joined the International Tennis Federation as an associate member in 1986.

Andorra

FEDERACIO ANDORRANA DE TENIS
Founded: 1986
No. of Players: 100
Clubs: 2
Courts: 43

Better known as a tax haven where many top players have settled. Became a full member of the International Tennis Federation in 1997, but while they currently host an ATP Tour Challenger tournament, they have not participated in either Fed Cup or Davis Cup competitions.

LLEYTON HEWITT *continues Australia's fine tradtion of producing great tennis players*

Angola

FEDERAÇAO ANGOLANA DE TENIS
Founded: 1983
No. of Players: 500
Clubs: 10
Courts: 40

Despite the continuing effects of war, the standard of tennis is good with several players established at the ITF/SATA training centre based in South Africa at Ellis Park, Johannesburg. As an associate member of the ITF, Angola are ineligible to play either Fed Cup or Davis Cup.

Antigua

THE ANTIGUA AND BARBUDA TENNIS ASSOCIATION
Founded: 1982
No. of Players: 1,200
Clubs: 8
Courts: 102

Small Caribbean island which can thank its colonial ancestry for its tennis tradition

Argentina

ASOCIACION ARGENTINA DE TENIS
Founded: 1921
No. of Players: 2,500,000
Clubs: 235
Courts: 3,500 outdoor; 70 indoor

British immigrants building Argentina's railroads at the turn of the century are credited with establishing tennis there. Now the sport's popularity is second only to soccer, with an estimated 7.5 per cent of the population playing the game. The AAT plays a dominant role in the development of the game in South America and, not surprisingly, many top international players have emerged including Guillermo Vilas, Gabriela Sabatini and more recently Guillermo Coria. Currently 32,000 are licensed with the national body.

Regular entrants in both international team competitions, first entering the Fed Cup in 1964, reaching the semi-finals on three occasions (1985, 1986 and 1993). Made their Davis Cup debut in 1923 and were beaten finalists in 1981.

Armenia

ARMENIAN TENNIS ASSOCIATION
Founded: 1937
No. of Players: 150
Clubs: 5
Courts: 48

and good standards. Recent Davis Cup (1996) and Fed Cup (1977) entrants.

Following the break-up of the Soviet Union, the Armenian Tennis Association was reconstituted in 1992 and despite it having just one club, 50 courts and 1,200 players – of whom only 14 are licensed at senior level – Sargis Sargisan emerged to make the world's top 50 on the ATP Tour.

Entered the Davis Cup competition for first time in 1997, and the Fed Cup a year later.

Aruba

ARUBA LAWN TENNIS BOND
Founded: 1954
No. of Players: 400
Clubs: 7
Courts: 41

Former Dutch colony in the Caribbean with an affinity for the sport.

Australia

TENNIS AUSTRALIA
Founded: 1904
No. of Players: 560,000
Clubs: 2,200
Courts: 20,000 outdoor; 100 indoor

One of the "big four" nations in tennis with a very strong history in the sport, the governing body was originally formed in 1904 to allow Australia (then Australasia, as it also included New Zealand up to 1922) to compete in the Davis Cup.

A founding member of the ITF, they host the first major Grand Slam championship of the year, the Australian Open, and have produced many of the world's top players including Rod Laver, Margaret Court Smith, John Newcombe, Evonne Goolagong Cawley, Lew Hoad and, more recently, Pat Cash, Mark Philippousis and Pat Rafter.

On the administrative side, Australian Brian Tobin was elected in 1991 to the presidency of the ITF, where he has contributed to the growth of the game internationally, retiring in 1999.

Their long tradition in the game is being upheld by 3.2 per cent of the population who actively participate – of whom 130,000 are licensed – and

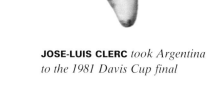

JOSE-LUIS CLERC *took Argentina to the 1981 Davis Cup final*

AUSTRALIA'S *John Newcombe, world No. 1 in 1974 and winner of five Grand Slam singles titles*

the sport's national future is safe-guarded with 300,000 juniors coming through in the background.

Champion nation in both major international team championships, Australia have captured the Davis Cup – which they first entered in 1905 – on 26 occasions. They were inaugural entrants in the Fed Cup (1963), which they have won seven times.

Austria

OSTERREICHISCHER TENNISVERBAND
Founded: 1902
No. of Players: 400,000
Clubs: 1,756
Courts: 6,317

The national federation, a founding member of the ITF, was originally founded by a group of 21 clubs in the days of the Austro-Hungarian monarchy. Play then was limited to the cities and the aristocracy, and the game only started enjoying public recognition in the 1930s through the exploits of Franz Wilhelm Matejka and Hermann Artens. The national body was dissolved when Germany annexed the country, but reconstituted immediately after the war. The sport's popularity increased in the 1970s and currently 6.3 per cent of the population is estimated to be playing. As the nation's fourth-largest sporting body, the Austrian federation can count on 142,000 licensed players plus 52,648 juniors.

The sport is enjoyed great national success thanks to Thomas Muster – who briefly rose to be world No. 1 in 1996 – and the national teams' successes in the international competitions where both teams made the semi-finals of their respective events in 1990.

Azerbaijan

AZERBAIJAN TENNIS FEDERATION
Founded: 1956
No. of Players: 170
Clubs: 5
Courts: 25

Former member of the Soviet Union; the ATF is a full member of the ITF, but so far has not competed in either the Fed Cup or the Davis Cup.

The Bahamas

THE BAHAMAS LAWN TENNIS ASSO-CIATION
Founded: 1961
No. of Players: 500
Clubs: 4
Courts: 195

Long tradition in the sport thanks to their colonial background. Recently completed the construction of their National Tennis Centre and can now claim a close association with the ITF who have based their registered office, ITF Ltd, on Bahamian soil. The BLTA has 280 licensed players with Roger Smith being the most famous.

Since 1989, the Bahamas have been a regular competitor in the Davis Cup zonal competition, reaching the Qualifying Round for the World Group in 1993. Apart from 1994, they have also competed regularly in the Fed Cup zonal events from 1990.

Bahrain

BAHRAIN LAWN TENNIS FEDERATION
Founded: 1981
No. of Players: 600
Clubs: 20
Courts: 200

First introduced by the expatriate communities, the sport is growing fast under the guidance of the BLTF which has established a strong youth pro-gramme, under the supervision of some imported, top-quality foreign coaches. First played in the Davis Cup in 1989, but so far have not competed in the ladies' Fed Cup competition.

Bangladesh

BANGLADESH TENNIS FEDERATION
Founded: 1972
No. of Players: 10,000
Clubs: 400
Courts: 500

Became active after the War of Liberation in 1971 and, despite their poverty, they have established their own National Tennis Centre at Ramna Green. A full member of the ITF, the BTF is extremely active in the junior game which augurs well for the future. Have enjoyed Davis Cup competition at zonal level since 1986, but have not yet competed in the ladies' Fed Cup.

Barbados

BARBADOS LAWN TENNIS ASSOCIATION
Founded: 1948
No. of Players: 1,000
Clubs: 9
Courts: 121

While the game was played on private courts since its earliest days, it was not until 1948 that the Barbados LTA was established to look after the sport's development. A recent full member of the ITF, the BLTA now competes in the zonal competitions of the Davis Cup and Fed Cup.

Belarus

TENNIS ASSOCIATION OF THE REPUBLIC OF BELARUS
Founded: 1992
No. of Players: 1,000
Clubs: 0
Courts: 180

A former Soviet Union state with a strong tennis tradition dating back to 1924, Belarus, since gaining independence in 1991, have quickly gained international recognition thanks to their top player, Natasha Zvereva, and their exploits in the Fed Cup where they made the World Group in 1994. In the Davis Cup where they have competed since 1994 at zonal level, they made the semi-finals in 2004.

The amalgamation of six regional and 24 city tennis organizations

NATASHA ZVEREVA *of Belarussia reached No. 5 in singles in 1989*

brought about the establishment of the national association which has 1,700 licensed players.

Belgium

ROYAL BELGIAN TENNIS FEDERATION (FÉDÉRATION ROYALE BELGE DE TENNIS)
Founded: 1902
No. of Players: 214,515
Clubs: 950
Courts: 5,800

A founder member of the ITF, the Royal Belgian Tennis Federation was first established in 1902 as the Belgian League of Lawn Tennis and brought together 12 clubs, some 20 years after the first club was established in Kortrijk. The association became the Belgian Tennis Federation in 1914 and in 1930 received the Royal accolade. The Federation evolved into two separate divisions in 1979 in order to cater separately to the Flemish and French-speaking communities.

The tennis-playing population is strong, with two per cent of Belgians actively playing the sport, 181,652 of them being licensed players.

Belgium have been represented in the Davis Cup since 1904 when they lost out in the Challenge Round to the British Isles. They have also been instrumental in establishing the Fed Cup as one of the inaugural nations in 1963, making the semi-finals in 1997 and thanks to Kim Clijsters and Justine Henin-Hardenne, winning the trophy in 2001.

Belize

BELIZE TENNIS ASSOCIATION
Founded: 1910
No. of Players: 125
Clubs: 6
Courts: 15

A small former British colony in Central America; the BTA has sent youngsters to compete at the Orange Bowl and can proudly claim that all their players are licensed or registered.

Benin

FÉDÉRATION BENINOISE DE LAWN TENNIS
Founded: 1963

Currently very active in developing the game, Benin in West Africa made their Davis Cup debut in 1993 at zonal level, but have yet to compete in the ladies' Fed Cup. Have established their own National Tennis Centre.

Bermuda

BERMUDA LAWN TENNIS ASSOCIATION
Founded: 1967

The island is credited with being the launching pad for the establishment of tennis in the United States, a claim made by the main club on the island, which is the only club outside of the US to be affiliated to the USTA.

The BLTA recently gained full membership of the ITF and currently organizes a challenger event. Recently started to compete in international team competitions, making their debut in the Davis Cup in 1995 and the Fed Cup a year later.

Bhutan

BHUTAN TENNIS FEDERATION
Founded: 1976

An associate member of the ITF.

Bolivia

FEDERACION BOLIVIANA DE TENNIS
Founded: 1937
No. of Players: 2,400
Clubs: 26
Courts: 144

Without government support, the development of the sport has been dependant on the goodwill of the club members who originally banded together to establish the national federation. The federation has received assistance from the ITF's Development Fund which has given many of their juniors a chance to compete abroad and consequently help the sport's growth.

The nation's first taste of international competition came in 1971 with their first foray into the Davis Cup. They returned in 1975 and, apart from a couple of other breaks, have competed regularly since then. However, their biggest contribution to the Davis Cup was the introduction of the "altitude" rule preventing Davis Cup competition in "thin air" above a certain level, which resulted in the exclusion of their capital, La Paz, as a possible venue. Santa Cruz is now their major tennis centre, where they hold a number of challengers and satellites. Bolivia also hosts the Condor De Plata for juniors on the South American circuit.

In the Fed Cup, Bolivia have competed regularly since 1991.

Bosnia/ Herzegovina

TENNIS ASSOCIATION OF THE REPUBLIC OF BOSNIA AND HERZEGOVINA
Founded: 1950
No. of Players: 980
Clubs: 26
Courts: 94

Historically, tennis here dates back to 1928, though the national association was not established until 1950. At present 26 clubs are affiliated, with 455 registered players. The association was recognized internationally when the country became independent from Yugoslavia in 1992.

Many of the tennis facilities which were destroyed during the civil war are being restored with grants from the ITF, which in turn is allowing the federation to pursue a positive development programme, including international entry at zonal level into both the Davis Cup (1996) and the Fed Cup (1997).

With a national tennis centre at Juzla and 270 licensed juniors, the sport's national governing body is well on track with its tennis development programme, which also includes the staging of major events at Sarajevo and Zenica.

GUSTAVO KUERTEN *of Brazil, a surprise French Open winner in 1997*

Botswana

BOTSWANA LAWN TENNIS ASSOCIATION
Founded: 1956
No. of Players: 450
Clubs: 14
Courts: 92

Traditionally tennis was seen as a sport for the elite, which could well account for the mere 92 courts available in the country. However, following independence in 1966, the national association established a strong junior programme in the early 1970s. Botswana are represented in both the Davis Cup and Fed Cup competitions, having entered the former for the first time in 1996, and the latter a year earlier.

Brazil

CONFEDERAÇAO BRASILEIRA DE TENNIS
No. of Players: 1,000,000

One of the oldest national associations in South America, Brazil is an amalgam of 13 state federations and now has 4,300 licensed players. They have been a member of the ITF since 1930, but only established their national governing body in 1950.

Brazil first competed in the Davis Cup in 1932, and have since taken part regularly since 1957. They have also competed in the Fed Cup, reaching the semi-finals on their debut in 1965.

Brazil's most famous player, Maria Bueno, won Wimbledon in 1959, 1960 and 1964, resulting in a postage stamp being issued in her honour. More recently, Gustavo Kuerten sprang to international prominence following his surprise 1997 French Open victory.

British Virgin Islands

BRITISH VIRGIN ISLANDS LAWN TENNIS ASSOCIATION
Founded: 1983
No. of Players: 120
Clubs: 1
Courts: 25

The BVILTA, despite a lack of public facilities, is very active in promoting the game within schools. The association was originally set up by a group of just 13 enthusiasts.

Brunei Darussalam

BRUNEI DARUSSALAM LAWN TENNIS ASSOCIATION
Founded: 1967
No. of Players: 1,282
Clubs: 9
Courts: 70

Joined the ITF as an associate member in 1984 with a view to establishing the Brunei Junior International Tennis Tournament. Originally the national association was set up to organize tennis in the area and so become involved internationally. The junior event was the first realization of that ambition, which now sees them also competing in the Davis Cup and they entered the Fed Cup for the first time in 1996.

With 1,282 licensed players the game is still in its infancy. Nevertheless, the recent completion of a magnificent National Tennis Centre will help to promote it further.

Bulgaria

BULGARIAN TENNIS FEDERATION
Founded: 1930
No. of Players: 1,010
Clubs: 72
Courts: 651

The game was introduced to the country in 1896 by diplomats who established the first tennis club. It was not until 1930 that the BTF was set up, the year that they joined the ITF.

The sport became more popular after the 1939–45 war, when Bulgaria started to participate in international events like the Balkan Games and the King's Cup. Also regular competitors in the Davis Cup and Fed Cup. The latter provided them with their best international result when the team of Katerina and Manuela Maleeva, led by mother Yulia

KATERINA MALEEVA *helped to put Bulgarian tennis on the map*

Berberian, reached the 1985 semi-finals.

Joining the ETA in 1977, BTF now hosts a series of international events.

Burkina Faso

FÉDÉRATION BURKINABE DE TENNIS
Founded: 1970

Formerly Upper Volta; the federation is very active.

Burundi

FÉDÉRATION DE TENNIS DU BURUNDI
Founded: 1993

Joined the ITF in 1993 and is still developing.

Cambodia

THE TENNIS FEDERATION OF CAMBODIA
Founded: 1985

Former French colony with a tradition in tennis; birthplace of Patricia Hy-Boulais who reached No. 28 in the world rankings in 1993.

Cameroon

FÉDÉRATION CAMEROUNAISE DE LAWN TENNIS
Founded: 1966

Best known as the birthplace of former French No. 1 Yannick Noah, who was discovered by Arthur Ashe and went on to achieve a world ranking of 3 in 1986, having won the French Open in 1983.

Except for 1993, they have competed regularly in the Davis Cup; 1997 saw their first entry in the Fed Cup.

Canada

TENNIS CANADA
Founded: 1890
No. of Players: 1,441,000
Clubs: figures not available
Courts: 4,100 outdoor; 600 indoor

Interest in the game first manifested itself shortly after the Canadian Confederation in 1867 with the first club establishing itself in Toronto around 1878. Not long afterwards, the game spread to the West Coast and these days 5.1 per cent of the population play.

In those early days Canada produced some excellent players and made the final round of the Davis Cup in 1913, failing to get past the US to meet the British Isles in the Challenge Round. Latterly they have achieved better results in the Fed Cup which they have contested since 1963, culminating in a semi-final appearance in 1988 at Melbourne.

A year earlier they successfully hosted the Fed Cup in Vancouver, making the quarter-finals. Also well known for their Canadian Opens which interestingly switch between Toronto and Montreal, one year Toronto hosts the men's tournament and Montreal hosts the women's, swapping the following year.

For the present it is better known as Britain's, Greg Rusedski's, country of origin.

Cape Verde

FEDERAÇAO CABO-VERDIANA DE TENIS
Founded: 1986
No. of Players: 300
Clubs: 6
Courts: 15

Portuguese-speaking islands in the Atlantic; starting to become involved at international level.

Cayman Islands

TENNIS FEDERATION OF THE CAYMAN ISLANDS
Founded: 1973
No. of Players: 600
Clubs: 1
Courts: 150

Despite 150 courts being available, the TFCI has just one affiliated club. This reflects the background of the sport on the islands, which has evolved around the tourist industry. Earlier, it had been played only on private properties.

MARCELO RIOS *of Chile, the first South American to make world No. 1*

Central African Republic

FÉDÉRATION CENTRAFRICAINE DE TENNIS
Founded: 1990

An associate member of the ITF.

Chile

FEDERACION DE TENIS DE CHILE
Founded: 1920
No. of Players: 10,000
Clubs: 250
Courts: 968

Representing 14 states in the country, the national federation is one of the more advanced in South America, where the sport, with 5,000 licensed players, is second in popularity only to soccer.

The country's strong traditions have been reflected at international level by the former success of players such as Luis Ayala, Jaime Fillol and Hans Gildemeister. Currently Marcelo Rios, who ended 1997 in the world's top 10, ranks as one of the top sportsmen in the country. His popularity rose further when he displaced Pete Sampras as the world's No. 1 player by defeating Andre Agassi to win the 1998 Lipton Championship in Florida.

Success has also been achieved in the Davis Cup competition, in which they have participated since 1928, with their 1976 team making the final only to lose out to Italy. Participation in the Fed Cup has not been as regular.

China,
People's Republic of

TENNIS ASSOCIATION OF THE PEOPLE'S REPUBLIC OF CHINA
Founded: 1956
No. of Players: 500,000
Clubs: 20
Courts: 2,450 outdoor; 50 indoor

Tennis is a sport which, despite having 500,000 players, does not rank highly in the country with the world's largest population. On the other hand the potential is considerable, with the 2008 Beijing Olympics looming and Yan Zi and Zheng Jie winning the 2006 ladies doubles.

The national association, having joined the ITF in 1938, represents 29 regions with 2,800 licensed players and regularly sends teams to compete in the Davis Cup and Fed Cup events, featuring in the former from 1924 and the latter since 1981.

SHI-TING WANG, *winner of six WTA tour titles for Chinese Taipei*

Chinese Taipei

CHINESE TAIPEI TENNIS ASSOCIATION
Founded: 1964
No. of Players: 500,000
Clubs: 3,520
Courts: 3,480 outdoor; 20 indoor

Chinese Taipei became a full member of the ITF in 1970 when the organization was known as the Republic of China Tennis Association; it was changed to the CTTA in 1981.

With 2.4 per cent of the population admitting to being players, the CTTA has 950 licensed competitors. The best known is Shi-Ting Wang who reached 26 on the women's world rankings in 1993.

Regular competitors in both the Davis Cup and Fed Cup competitions, the CTTA have hosted events at all levels and was instrumantal in establishing the Asian Tennis Federation back in 1964.

Colombia

FEDERACION COLOMBIANA DE TENIS
Founded: 1932
No. of Players: 10,000
Clubs: 210
Courts: 2,476 outdoor; 10 indoor

Tennis in Colombia dates back to 1906 when Colombians introduced it having sampled the sport on their travels. Nowadays the national association hosts many international events at various levels having joined the ITF in 1934.

As a nation they have participated in both the Fed Cup and Davis Cup.

Comores

FÉDÉRATION COMORIENNE DE TENNIS
Founded: 1985

Island off Africa where the sport is growing. Recent associate member of the ITF.

Congo

FÉDÉRATION CONGOLAISE DE LAWN TENNIS
Founded: 1962
No. of Players: 800
Clubs: 27
Courts: 63

With 27 clubs and 63 courts catering to the needs of 800 players, the Congo achieve reasonable results at international level within Africa. Standards are expected to improve further thanks to an active junior programme. Have competed regularly since 1991 in the Davis Cup, but only once in the Fed Cup (1992).

Congo,
Democratic Republic of the

FÉDÉRATION CONGOLAISE DÉMOCRATIQUE DE LAWN TENNIS
Founded: 1984

Formerly Zaire, they have the potential to be one of the strongest tennis nations in Africa. The national association was first formed in the early 1970s and reconstituted in 1984, and comprised of local tennis organizations, tennis clubs and individual members. Current development has been hindered by the country's internal political problems.

Cook Islands

COOK ISLANDS TENNIS ASSOCIATION
Founded: 1947
No. of Players: 800
Clubs: 30
Courts: 30

The CITA has developed over the years in close association with New Zealand, but is now establishing its own identity, having created strong inter-village tennis competitions for 30 clubs and 800 players, which represents four per cent of the population.

Costa Rica

FEDERACION COSTARRICENSE DE TENIS
Founded: 1964
No. of Players: 6,960
Clubs: 13
Courts: 87

Despite being founded in the 1960s, it was not until the national association reorganized itself in 1978 that it was able to reaffiliate to the ITF in 1984.

The association, which has 450 licensed players, has established one of the best junior events in the world, known as the Coffee Bowl. In international competition, they have only recently started to participate in the Davis Cup (from 1990) and the Fed Cup (1992).

Côte D'Ivoire

FÉDÉRATION IVOIRIENNE DE TENNIS
Founded: 1969
No. of Players: 5,000
Clubs: 17
Courts: 400 outdoor; 6 indoor

A former French colony, Côte D'Ivoire have a strong tradition in tennis with 2,300 players licensed to the national association. It has established a very active junior development programme and, since 1986, has been a regular entrant at zonal level of the Davis Cup. They have yet to compete in the ladies' Fed Cup.

Croatia

CROATIAN TENNIS ASSOCIATION
Founded: 1922
No. of Players: 3,105
Clubs: 155
Courts: 1,820

Croatia experienced their first taste of tennis in 1880 thanks to the British. They hosted their first international competition in 1911, but it was not until 1922 that they set up their national association. Now they stage the Umag championship, which is one of the major stops on the men's ATP Tour.

Croatian tennis came to the fore during the civil war through the exploits of Goran Ivanisevic, who rose to be world No. 4 in 1996.

They have competed in the Fed Cup since 1992, entering the Davis Cup for the first time a year later, and winning the trophy in 2005.

Cuba

FEDERACION CUBANA DE TENIS DE CAMPO
Founded: 1925

Tennis was first played in Cuba at the turn of the last century, gaining in popularity during the early 1920s. One of the strongest tennis nations in the Caribbean, Cuba played in the Davis Cup twice before establishing their national association in 1925.

The Cuban Tennis Federation recently built a National Tennis Centre for the Pan American Games. Regular participants in the Davis Cup, Cuba made the World Group in 1993. They have also started playing in the Fed Cup more regularly since their first entry in 1992.

Cyprus

CYPRUS TENNIS FEDERATION
Founded: 1951
No. of Players: 2,500
Clubs: 12
Courts: 54

Played in 1912 by the British administration, it was not until 1960, following the island's independence, that the sport became popular amongst the Cypriot community.

The sport has expanded and facilities improved thanks to the activities of the CTF and the expanding tourist industry. Many international events are staged there at junior, challenger and satellite level and the island has recently entered a team in the Fed Cup, having participated in the Davis Cup since 1985.

Czech Republic

CZECH TENNIS ASSOCIATION
Founded: 1906
No. of Players: 20,208
Clubs: 969
Courts: 5,040

Czech tennis has a long tradition dating back to the fifteenth century, as confirmed by the survival of a "*chameber*" for ball games in the Prague Castle and the two-court indoor complex in East Bohemia. Czech history also reveals that a grass court existed at Bonrepos while another court – made of Czech garnets – was built in Trebenice.

The Czechs were also the first Middle European country to stage a tournament – in 1879 in East Bohemia, two years after the first Wimbledon.

It was not until 1906 that the Czech Lawn Tennis Association was

HANA MANDLIKOVA

established by seven clubs. These increased to 18 clubs in 1918 as the national governing body became the Czechoslovak Tennis Association on the formation of Czechoslovakia.

The CTA joined the ITF in 1921 and in 1993 was divided into two separate organizations as the country itself reverted to its former Czech and Slovak boundaries. The CTA, with 12,000 licensed players and 2,500 juniors, is based at the National Tennis Centre in Prague, originally built to host the 1986 Federation Cup.

As a tennis nation, they have been successful at both the Fed Cup (five-time champions) and the Davis Cup (champions in 1980 and World Group semi-finalists in 1996) thanks to a string of international players including Jan Kodes, Wimbledon champion in 1973, Ivan Lendl, Miloslav Mecir, Martina Navratilova and Hana Mandlikova.

Denmark

DANSK TENNIS FORBUND
Founded: 1920
No. of Players: 3,407
Clubs: 304
Courts: 1,750

Formed in 1920 as the Danish Lawn

CROATIA'S *Ivan Ljubicic led his nation to Davis Cup glory in 2005*

Tennis Association, the national body became the Danish Tennis Association in 1974 and is now the fifth-largest sport governing body in the land. The country's first tennis club was established in 1883, and that was followed by the staging of their first tournament in 1889. One could say the DTA was slow in coming together, especially as Danish tennis players have competed regularly at the Olympics since 1900, but they are regular participants in both international team competitions – in the Davis Cup since 1921 and the Fed Cup since 1963.

Djibouti

FÉDÉRATION DJIBOUTIENNE DE TENNIS
Founded: 1978

A full member of the ITF; have not played in the Fed Cup, but have

competed in the Davis Cup at zonal level.

Dominica

DOMINICA LAWN TENNIS ASSOCIATION
Founded: 1960
No. of Players: 170
Clubs: 2
Courts: 5

A full member of the ITF and active on both Fed Cup and Davis Cup fronts at zonal level despite poor tennis facilities, though plans are in hand for a National Tennis Centre.

Dominican Republic

FEDERACION DOMINICANA DE TENIS
Founded: 1929

ANDRES GOMEZ *of Ecuador who pulled off his greatest win at Roland Garros, winning the French Open in 1990, aged 30*

With a seven-million-plus population, the standard of tennis is genuinely good. The country hosts a number of men's and women's satellite events as well as being the home base for the COTECC (Confederacion de Tenis de Centroamerica Caribe).

Regular participants in the Davis Cup since 1989 and the Fed Cup a year later.

Ecuador

FEDERACION ECUATORIANA DE TENIS
Founded: 1967
No. of Players: 1,000
Clubs: 80
Courts: 500 outdoors; 15 indoors

Tennis is very much centred in Guayaquil where the federation has erected a National Tennis Centre. Traditionally a strong tennis nation which has produced a good string of top players including Pancho Segura and Andres Gomez.

Good record in the Davis Cup, having beaten the United States and Britain once, and regular competitors in the Fed Cup since 1992.

EGYPT'S *Ismail El Shafei*

Egypt

EGYPTIAN LAWN TENNIS FEDERATION
Founded: 1920
No. of Players: 30,000
Clubs: 96
Courts: 451

Despite just 1,500 licensed players, Egypt have a long tradition with the game and have produced players of international standing like Ismail El Shafei, as well as hosting several international events. Active Davis Cup participants, Egypt will be remembered for their defeat by Britain on Wimbledon's No. 1 Court in 1996, the last occasion the famous show court was used.

El Salvador

FEDERACION SALVADORENA DE TENIS
Founded: 1949
No. of Players: 2,500
Clubs: 25
Courts: 121

The most improved and progressive tennis nation in Central America, now hosting satellites and with an excellent development programme. The federation has established tennis as the second most popular sport in the country, behind soccer.

Tennis was first introduced in 1919 by the then president of the country,

Dr Alfonso Quinonez, who established an affinity for the sport while being educated in Europe. It remained a sport of the elite until 1952 when the first junior competitions took place. In 1960, the first serious attempts were made to establish a national association, but it was not until 1980 that it finally became fact. With 890 licensed players, the Salvadorean Tennis Federation competes regularly at zonal level in both the Fed Cup and Davis Cup competitions.

Equatorial Guinea

EQUATORIAL GUINEA TENNIS FEDERATION
Founded: 1992

Tennis here is in its infancy

Estonia

ESTONIAN TENNIS ASSOCIATION
Founded: 1922
No. of Players: 2,620
Clubs: 42
Courts: 208

Estonia have a high standard and good facilities with a tennis history allegedly dating back to 1913, when their first tournament was organized. The Estonian Tennis Association came into being in 1922 and joined the ITF 12 years later.

In 1940 the country was overrun by the Soviet Union who became reliant on Estonian players for their national team. Following independence in 1991, Estonia have 880 licensed players and have become a regular competitor in the Fed Cup.

Ethiopia

ETHIOPIAN LAWN TENNIS FEDERATION
Founded: 1972
No. of Players: 10,000
Clubs: 45
Courts: 248

Despite their hardships, Ethiopia have a tennis heritage which is reflected in a general standard of play

that has seen 4,500 players register with their national body. Currently the Ethiopian LTA is making good progress with its development, entering the Davis Cup competition for the first time in 1995 and the Fed Cup the following year.

Fiji

FIJI LAWN TENNIS ASSOCIATION
Founded: 1934
No. of Players: 3,500
Clubs: 25
Courts: 65

With a strong junior development programme, Fiji, where the ITF/OTF Pacific Oceania Training Centre is based, have been very successful at the Pacific Oceania Championships. Tennis on the islands was originally the sport of expatriates, who introduced it in 1907 when the first Fiji Championships were held.

The Fiji LTA was formed in 1934 when competitive play became possible in all areas of the main island as communications improved. Unfortunately the association was restricted to Europeans only and as a result the Indian Lawn Tennis Association was formed in the 1940s, later becoming known as the Dominion Lawn Tennis Association.

In 1978 the Dominion LTA merged with the Fiji LTA, under which banner the game is now administered for all. In 1985 they became associate members of the ITF and currently 190 players are licensed with the association.

Finland

SUOMEN TENNISLIITTO
Founded: 1911
No. of Players: 3,608
Clubs: 210
Courts: 1,550

Introduced in 1911 in Turku, tennis in Finland has grown substantially with 3.9 per cent of the population enjoying the game and 21,852 actually licensed.

Finland joined the ITF 18 years later and competed in the Davis Cup for the first time in 1928, making the fourth round in 1980. In Fed Cup competition, having made their debut in 1968, a quarter-final appearance in 1993 is their best-ever performance.

Despite a keen interest in the sport, Finland have only staged one major international event which was back in 1977.

France

FÉDÉRATION FRANÇAISE DE TENNIS
Founded: 1920
No. of Players: 1,075,025
Clubs: 8,748
Courts: 33,353

Hosts of the world's greatest clay court championships, the French Open at Roland Garros (the second leg of the Grand Slam), France have a long tradition in the sport which was first played in the country in 1886, with the formation of their first club, Société des Sports de L'Ille. Two years

later a tennis committee was set up at the Union des Sociétés Françaises de Sports Athlétiques, which was followed in 1891 by the country's first national tournament. This was restricted to men, the women's equivalent following in 1897.

In the interim the famous Tennis Club de Paris where the first two indoor courts were built (Boulevard Exelmans), was established.

But it was not until after the First World War, in 1920, that 61 clubs met to set up the Fédération Française de Lawn Tennis which became the FFT in 1976 as the word "Lawn" was dropped.

In 1928, Stade Roland Garros was built to provide a suitable venue to stage major events like the Open, but also to accomodate the offices of the French Federation.

The federation itself was transformed during Philippe Chatrier's term as president, from 1972. This involved not only the revitalization of a flagging Open, but also regenerating interest in the game, forcing French tennis back as a major player on the world stage. Chatrier was also elected president of the ITF in 1977, and successfully held the post for 14 years.

As the sport grew, with licensed players at one stage reaching 1.5 million, and clubs increasing from 300 in 1924 to over 10,000 in 1997, so did the French results on the international scene, with the emergence of Yannick Noah, Henri Leconte, and Guy Forget, each of whom played a part in winning the Davis Cup in 1991 and 1996. France also won the cup in 2001 thus reviving the glory days of the 1920s and 1930s, when they held the trophy for six conxecutive years with the "Musketeers" – Jean Borotra, Toto Brugnon, Henri Cochet and René Lacoste. The 1920s is also the era remembered for the exploits of the great Suzanne Lenglen, who is considered to be amongst the most exciting and successful players ever to have played the women's game.

France participated in the inaugural Fed Cup, winning the trophy in 1997 and 2003.

JEAN BOROTRA, *one of the French "Four Musketeers"*

Gabon

**FÉDÉRATION GABONAISE
DE TENNIS**
Founded: 1988
No. of Players: 1,000
Clubs: 10
Courts: 100

An associate member of the ITF.

Gambia

GAMBIA TENNIS ASSOCIATION
Founded: 1938

Despite records showing the sport was first played in 1928, it was not until the 1950s that it was popularized. That, however, proved short-lived and courts fell into disrepair as tennis management crumbled in the 1960s. A new administration came into being in the 1980s and the game now has a solid foundation and is showing reasonable growth.

Georgia

GEORGIAN TENNIS FEDERATION
Founded: 1992
No. of Players: 954
Clubs: 15
Courts: 133

Former Soviet Union state and birthplace of Alex Metreveli, the best Soviet player of the 1960/early 1970s who made the Wimbledon final in 1973. They compete in both Davis Cup and Fed Cup competitions at zonal level.

Germany

DEUTSCHER TENNIS BUND E.V.
Founded: 1902
No. of Players: 1,901,968
Clubs: 10,185
Courts: 50,483

With the rise of Boris Becker and Steffi Graf, Germany's influence in the world of tennis increased dramatically during the 1980s and 1990s.

Historically, the national governing body – not formed until 1902 despite the fact that for the previous 10 years the country had been staging the International Championships of Germany – was a founding member of

AMELIE MAURESMO *of France plays a powerful backhand in the US Open*

the ITF in 1913 with Dr Hans Otto Behrens acknowledged as the first president of the world governing body.

The two World Wars disrupted the German organization, which then had to be readmitted twice to the ITF, first in 1927 and later in 1950. In 1991 the unification of East and West Germany resulted in the DDR's tennis association merging with the DTB and this has meant a massive internal restructuring. Tennis is classed as one of the nation's top sports with a varied and successful league structure, plus a positive junior programme.

The contribution made to tennis by Germany was acknowledged by the ITF with the introduction of the Grand Slam Cup which, from 1990, was staged annually in Munich.

Germany have been extremely successful at Davis Cup and Fed Cup levels, having won the men's international team event on three occasions

(1988, 1989, and 1993) and the women's equivalent twice (1987 and 1992).

Ghana

GHANA TENNIS ASSOCIATION
Founded: 1909
No. of Players: 8,000
Clubs: 88
Courts: 205

Acknowledged as one of the stronger tennis nations in West Africa with a very active federation who can proudly claim that 95 per cent of their tennis-playing population are licensed players. The federation is nurturing some good youngsters and can be expected to improve on their results in the Davis Cup, which they have played at zonal level since 1988.

Great Britain

**THE LAWN TENNIS
ASSOCIATION**
Founded: 1888
No. of Players: 48,535
Clubs: 2,600
Courts: 35,200

The birthplace of lawn tennis, a game invented in 1873 by Major Walter Clopton Wingfield in Natelyd, Wales. Originally enjoyed as a social garden game, its popularity grew to such levels that it became necessary for a governing body to be set up in 1888 when The Lawn Tennis Association was founded.

The lack of a national prefix acknowledges the status of the country which introduced the game to the world. But in fact it is not the oldest national governing body. That distinction is held by the USTA, which was established seven years earlier as the United States National Lawn Tennis Association.

Nevertheless the LTA went on to produce the first set of rules for the game and in 1923 handed the copyright of those rules to the ITF.

As a founder member of the ITF, Britain are one of the big four, thanks to the establishment of Wimbledon – the third leg in the Grand Slam series – as the premier tennis event in the world.

Historically Britain have made many major contributions to the game internationally, including the inauguration of the Davis Cup in 1900 and the Fed Cup in 1963. But perhaps most important, following the invention of the game, is the way Britain finally forced the acceptance of professional players, thus ending the "amateur" days. So, in 1968 at Bournemouth – the first tournament to include both amateurs and professionals – the Open era of the sport began, resulting in the creation of a multi-million-dollar industry.

In Davis Cup competition, Britain have won the trophy on nine occasions, mainly in the early years of the event when the country "included" Ireland and competed as the British Isles, until separation in 1923. Their greatest Davis Cup triumphs were recorded between 1933 and 1936, with victories over France,

USA (twice) and Australia. These wins coincided with the years of Fred Perry's domination (the last Englishman to win Wimbledon). Britain have never won the Fed Cup, though they have made the final on four occasions.

With a strong tradition in the sport, despite the general lack of success at international level over the years, Britain continues to stage a series of top-quality events in keeping with the nation's status in the sport. But while the fortune and the standing of the British game look to be improving with the successes of Tim Henman, Greg Rusedski and more recently Andy Murray, the LTA continues in its efforts to lift the national game further.

The introduction of a player registration scheme in the 1980s has attracted 55,322 into the scheme.

Greece

HELLENIC TENNIS FEDERATION
Founded: 1939
No. of Players: 32,000
Clubs: 220
Courts: 1,118

A keen and active organization with 12,000 licensed players, hampered by lack of facilities. Founded in 1939 by 49 clubs, the Hellenic Tennis Federation's activities were expanded in 1946 to include the national team's participation in international events – resulting, in 1960, in Nicky Kalogeroupoulos making the world's top 16.

In 1969 the Greeks, in just their second year of Fed Cup competition, hosted the event in Athens. In the Davis Cup, Greece first competed in 1927 and have been regular contestants, apart from a 14-year absence, from 1949.

Grenada

GRENADA TENNIS ASSOCIATION
Founded: 1973
No. of Players: 300
Clubs: 2
Courts: 35

An associate member of the ITF.

Guam

TENNIS ASSOCIATION OF GUAM
Founded: 1973
No. of Players: 600
Clubs: 6
Courts: 30 outdoor; 1 indoor

Acknowledged as the centre of tennis in the north Pacific, Guam can count on 160 licensed players.

Guatemala

FEDERACION NACIONALE DE TENIS DE GUATEMALA
Founded: 1948
No. of Players: 4,000
Clubs: not known
Courts: 100 outdoor; 2 indoor
A good tradition in tennis, reflected by the number of international events at both satellite and junior level which the federation has hosted.

Have played at zonal levels in both Fed Cup and Davis Cup, the former since 1992 and the latter since 1990 and joined the ITF in 1960.

Guinée Conakry

FÉDÉRATION GUINÉENNE DE TENNIS
Founded: 1980
No. of Players: 1,500
Clubs: 6
Courts: 25

Former French colony which are actively competing in regional competitions and one of the few countries in the enviable position of having all their players licensed. Though the association was originally founded to administer both table tennis and tennis, its functions are now separated. The tennis federation became affiliated to the African Tennis Federation in 1980 and the ITF in 1985.

Guyana

GUYANA LAWN TENNIS ASSOCIATION
Founded: 1933
No. of Players: 300
Clubs: 11
Courts: 48

Part of the Caribbean, for sports purposes, with an active national governing body.

Haiti

FÉDÉRATION HATIENNE DE TENNIS
Founded: 1950
No. of Players: 500
Clubs: 6
Courts: 100

The sport was introduced to the island in the 1920s, but the national association was not established until 1946 when three private clubs formed the FHT. An associate member of the ITF since 1975, the FHT gained full membership in 1986, entering the Davis Cup for the first time in 1988 with a team including Ronald Agenor, then world ranked in the 50s. Haiti has not competed in the Fed Cup.

Honduras

FEDERACION HONDURENA DE TENIS
Founded: 1989

RONALD AGENOR, *although born in Morocco, played for Haiti following his parents move to the island*

Have only recently begun to participate in international events. They host a satellite tournament having recently completed the erection of a National Tennis Centre.

Hong Kong

HONG KONG TENNIS ASSOCIATION LTD
Founded: 1909
No. of Players: 35,000
Clubs: 41
Courts: 700 outdoor; 6 indoor

One of the older national governing bodies, established during colonial days, the HKTA is a founder member of the East Asian Tennis Association. Incorporated as a limited company in 1984, it has been extremely active in the Far East, establishing one of the top international events of the area.

With 5,166 licensed players there, tennis remains a popular activity and national teams enter both the Davis Cup and Fed Cup.

Hungary

MAGYAR TENISZ SZOVETSEG
Founded: 1907
No. of Players: 5,400
Clubs: 214
Courts: 3,700

Records show that the first tennis match in Hungary was played in 1881, followed two years later by the establishment of the first tennis club. In 1907, 15 clubs banded together to set up the MTS which then affiliated itself in 1909 with the governing body of Britain to establish the first international tennis body. This eventually culminated in the founding of the ITF in 1913.

Hungary played the Davis Cup for the first time in 1924 and made the World Group in 1994, having made the semi-finals of the European zone on four previous occasions.

Their most successful international player in recent years was Balaz Taroczy who reached the world's top 15 during the early 1980s, following the success of the Hungarian team in winning the King's Cup, now known as the European Cup, in 1976.

In Fed Cup terms, Hungary have

VIJAY AMRITRAJ, *led India to the Davis Cup final in 1974*

competed most years since 1963, reaching the quarter-finals in 1985.

Iceland

ICELANDIC TENNIS ASSOCIATION
Founded: 1987
No. of Players: 821
Clubs: 6
Courts: 16

While the Icelandic Tennis Association is comparatively young, the recent completion of a purpose-built indoor centre shows a determination to make up for lost time.

The game was played during the 1920s and 1930s when several national championships were held. Unfortunately interest in the sport then evaporated and it was not until 1980 that it re-emerged, the ITA being

founded seven years later. The association now has 1,000 licensed players and has entered teams in both the Davis Cup and Fed Cup since 1996.

India

ALL INDIA TENNIS ASSOCIATION
Founded: 1920
No. of Players: 300,000
Clubs: 1,500
Courts: 10,000 outdoor; 4 indoor
India first enjoyed the delights of tennis at the turn of the 20th century, establishing their national governing body eight years later. Originally set up as Lawn Tennis of India, it first evolved into the All India Lawn Tennis Association before finally being shortened to All India Tennis Association in 1984.

The name changes reflected

changes in administrative responsibilities, resulting in the current system whereby clubs affiliate direct with district associations which, in turn, are affiliated to the state associations which make up the AITA. Through that organization an incredible 299,700 players are categorized as licensed, which represents 99.9 per cent of the tennis-playing population.

India entered the Davis Cup competition in 1921 and have made the final on three occasions, losing to Australia in 1966, conceding a political "anti-apartheid" walk-over to South Africa in 1974 and losing to Sweden in 1987.

Much of the game's early development was provided by the patronage of princely states, such as Baroda and Mysore. They had the privilege of the East India Company bringing coaches from England who, unfortunately, just played tennis with the princely families rather than teach.

Two families have contributed greatly to the growth of the sport in India over recent years, both through success on the world stage. They are Ramathan Krishnan and his son Ramesh, plus the Amritraj brothers, Vijay, Anand and Ashok. Currently Sania Mirza is their main flagbearer.

INDONESIA'S *Yayuk Basuki*

ISRAEL'S *Amos Mansdorf, winner of six ATP Tour titles*

Indonesia

INDONESIAN TENNIS ASSOCIATION
Founded: 1935
No. of Players: 138,000
Clubs: not known
Courts: 1,680 outdoor; 45 indoor

The game has developed strongly over recent years, especially on the women's side, following the success of Yayuk Basuki who reached 21 in the world rankings during 1995, and the quarter-final placings achieved by the Fed Cup team in both 1974 and 1991.

With strong traditions emanating from their Dutch legacy when tennis was administered by the Algemene Nederlandsch Indische Lawn Tennis Bond, Indonesia took control of their own destiny in 1934 when the ITA was founded.

They have now established a strong ladies satellite circuit which attracts many Europeans trying to build computer points.

Iran

TENNIS FEDERATION OF ISLAMIC REPUBLIC OF IRAN
Founded: 1937
No. of Players: 12,000
Clubs: 120
Courts: 500 outdoor; 27 indoor

Quite active, especially in Davis Cup terms, having competed reasonably regularly since 1959. Iran have entered the Fed Cup only once, in 1972.

Iraq

IRAQI TENNIS FEDERATION
Founded: 1959
No. of Players: 500,000
Clubs: 50
Courts: 50 outdoor; 25 indoor

Tennis was introduced mainly by the occupying armies of the Second World War, the oil companies operating in the Gulf and students returning from overseas studies.

The establishment of the national governing body in 1959 proved a major step forward as it has effectively developed the game further, especially among women. They have yet to compete in the Fed Cup, but have participated in the Davis Cup, making their debut in 1983.

Ireland

IRISH LAWN TENNIS ASSOCIATION
Founded: 1895
No. of Players: 50,000
Clubs: 200
Courts: N/A

The Irish Tennis Association was formed in 1895 and was part of the British LTA until separation in 1923 when it also affiliated to the ITF.

A regular entrant in both the Davis Cup and Fed Cup competitions, the ILTA also includes Northern Ireland. Ireland have a long tradition in the sport which is epitomized by the Fitzwilliam Club in Dublin, venue for many an international event over the years.

Israel

ISRAEL TENNIS ASSOCIATION
Founded: 1946
No. of Players: N/A
Clubs: N/A
Courts: N/A

Tennis in the region was originally established in 1936 by the British Mandate of Palestine who continued to administer the sport until the formation of the Israel Tennis Association in 1946. The first courts were laid by the Menorah Society, from which small beginnings the sport slowly grew in appeal.

Even before the establishment of the ITA, national championships were held regularly since 1940, from which time licensed players have grown to a total of 4,900.

Israel competed for the first time in the Davis Cup in 1949, a year after the establishment of the State of Israel and a year before the ITA became a full member of the ITF.

Since that date Israel have been regular competitors, qualifying for the World Group in 1986. Shlomo Glickstein and Amos Mansdorf are the two players who have emerged to help put Israeli tennis on the world map in recent years.

In the women's game they have also made substantial strides and have been regular Fed Cup participants since 1970.

Italy

FEDERAZIONE ITALIANA TENNIS
Founded: 1910
No. of Players: 157,493
Clubs: 2,933
Courts: 10,278

Officially the Federazione Italiana Tennis came into being in Florence during 1910, but in fact it filled the gap left by the original body, the Federazione Italiana Lawn Tennis, based in Rome, which was disbanded in 1900 having been set up five years earlier to pull together a few main city clubs for the purposes of running the National Individual Championships.

After World War II the federation resumed its activities based in Milan, moving in 1958 to Rome, the home of the Italian Open at Foro Italico, the country's major event which attracts a top international entry.

In 1964, the federation set up their first national tennis centre for boys, adding one for girls in 1980. Italian tennis has been at the forefront of the game for many years. A number of their players have established themselves at international level and their representative teams have competed well in both Davis Cup and Fed Cup competitions, winning the former in 1976.

Jamaica

JAMAICA LAWN TENNIS ASSOCIATION
Founded: 1925
No. of Players: 5,000
Clubs: 50
Courts: 2,000

The Jamaican LTA has a very active development programme based on a sound tradition established through the sport's original colonial connections. They currently host a number of events at all levels and compete regularly in the zonal competitions of both Fed Cup and Davis Cup events, having joined the ITF in 1937.

Japan

JAPAN TENNIS ASSOCIATION
Founded: 1921
No. of Players: 5,000,000
Clubs: 680
Courts: 39,800 outdoor; 200 indoor

With 10 per cent of the players licensed, the JTA is one of the more active national governing bodies of the region. Players from Japan competed at Wimbledon and in the Olympic tennis event (where they won two silver medals) the year before they established the JTA in 1921, affiliating themselves to the ITF in 1926. They first competed in the Davis Cup in 1921, going all the way to the Challenge Round where they lost to the USA.

The sport suffered during the Second World War when the JTA was disbanded, coming back into being in 1946 and regaining its ITF affiliation in 1950.

They underwent a major reorganization in 1980 which has provided them with their current impetus and seen their women players emerge strongly on the world stage, the more recent being Ai Sugiyama and Nadko Sawamatsu.

They have been regular competitors in both the Davis Cup and Fed Cup, hosting the latter on three occasions when it was played in its original week-long format. They are also the hosts of many of the top junior international events and, as a nation, have supplied the main sponsorship company of the main international team events, as well as the junior ones.

Jordan

JORDAN TENNIS FEDERATION
Founded: 1980
No. of Players: 3,000
Clubs: 4
Courts: 57 outdoor; 10 indoor

Relatively new organization concentrating on the development of facilities and juniors. Historically the region has a tradition in the game going back to its Palestinian heritage, when the game was played in the region by Arab students who took it up while abroad.

At international level they have consistently played in the Davis Cup since 1989, but not in the Fed Cup.

Kazakhstan

KAZAKHSTAN TENNIS FEDERATION
Founded: 1991
No. of Players: 4,000
Clubs: 10
Courts: 168 outdoor; 14 indoor

Former member of the Soviet Union just establishing themselves on the international scene through the Davis Cup and Fed Cup competitions.

Kenya

KENYA LAWN TENNIS ASSOCIATION
Founded: 1922
No. of Players: 600
Clubs: 40
Courts: 150

Established as a result of expatriate interest in the game, the KLTA still relies on the club facilities set up by the colonists. With no public courts the development of the game is somewhat hindered, but every effort is being made to facilitate progress, and junior development is a priority.

Kenya used to host a lot of events before the Open era. But they have only participated twice in the Fed Cup, and, following two appearances in the Davis Cup back in the 1970s, have become regular entrants since 1986. Kenya (a member since 1934) has been benefitting from ITF grants and has become an integral part of the East and Central African circuit.

Kiribati,
Republic of

KIRIBATI TENNIS ASSOCIATION
Founded: 1979

An associate member of the ITF.

Korea,
Democratic People's Republic of

TENNIS ASSOCIATION OF THE DEMOCRATIC PEOPLE'S REPUBLIC OF KOREA
Founded: 1945

An associate member of the ITF.

Korea,
Republic of

KOREA TENNIS ASSOCIATION
Founded: 1945
No. of Players: 2,000,000
Clubs: not known
Courts: 10,000 outdoor; 100 indoor

Regular competitors in both Davis Cup and Fed Cup events. Korea have pursued an active programme of development which has seen the establishment of the Korea Open Tennis Championships plus the introduction of veterans' tennis in 1987 – the year before they staged the Seoul Olympics which witnessed the return of tennis to the Games as a full sport.

Kuwait

KUWAIT TENNIS FEDERATION
Founded: 1967
No. of Players: 850
Clubs: 25
Courts: 95 outdoor; 5 indoor

Introduced by expatriates attached to the oil industry, the game has grown sufficiently for the KTF to

LARISA NEILAND,
formerly of Russia but now, through marriage, representing Latvia

compete consistently in the Davis Cup at regional level.

Kyrghyzstan

KYRGHYZSTAN TENNIS FEDERATION
Founded: 1992

Former member state of the Soviet Union which are only just starting to find their feet in tennis.

Latvia

LATVIAN TENNIS UNION
Founded: 1929
No. of Players: 371
Clubs: 41
Courts: 279

Latvia were introduced to tennis in 1903, but it wasn't until 1929 that the sport was organized under the banner of the Latvian Tennis Union, which affiliated itself to the ITF in 1937.

The occupation of Latvia by the Soviet Union brought to an end the individual authority of their Tennis Union, but this was reinstated in 1991 following the break-up of the communist regime, as was the affiliation to the ITF.

Now expanding rapidly, the LTU has organized a number of international events at satellite and challenger level and is represented in both Fed Cup and Davis Cup competitions. Their best-known player is Larisa Neiland, who reached the top 16 on the women's ranking in 1988, but is possibly better known as a doubles player.

Lebanon

FÉDÉRATION LIBANAISE DE TENNIS
Founded: 1945

Lebanese tennis has been greatly affected by the events which have torn the country apart. In earlier times, tennis flourished with the International Tennis Championships of Lebanon, staged in Beirut, providing an excellent focal point for the game in the region between 1947 and 1974.

Lebanese tennis teams have recently returned to international competition at Fed Cup (1993) and Davis Cup (1992) level.

Lesotho

LESOTHO LAWN TENNIS ASSOCIATION
Founded: 1920
No. of Players: 227
Clubs: 9
Courts: 33

An associate member of the ITF, the LLTA numbers 24 licensed players on its registry.

Liberia

LIBERIA TENNIS ASSOCIATION
Founded: 1987

An associate member of the ITF.

Libya

JAMAHIRIYA TENNIS FEDERATION
No. of Players: 8,640
Clubs: 505
Courts: 108

An associate member of the ITF.

Liechtenstein

LIECHTENSTEINER TENNISVERBAND
Founded: 1968
No. of Players: 650
Clubs: 7
Courts: 29

The first club was established in 1918 in the capital Vaduz and, as the only club in the country for 50 years, could be reached by simply writing to The Tennis Club, Liechtenstein! A name change to Tennis Club Vaduz followed when other towns set up their own clubs, and in 1968 the national governing body was founded.

With 700 registered players and 8.3 per cent of the population categorizing themselves as players, the Liechtensteiner Tennisverband is the largest sports association in the country.

In 1988 the LT joined both the ITF and ETA and has been competing at zonal level in both the Fed Cup and Davis Cup since 1996.

Lithuania

LITHUANIA TENNIS UNION
Founded: 1930
No. of Players: 310
Clubs: 35
Courts: 140

The game was first played here at the turn of the 20th century, but it was not until 1919 that the first club was established. As the sport grew in popularity, the national association followed in 1930. However, Lithuanian tennis was overrun by the Soviet Union in 1940. Following independence in 1990, the LTU are working to re-establish their country on the international scene.

With that objective in mind, the LTU entered the Fed Cup for the first time in 1992 and the Davis Cup two years later – both at zonal level – and revived their "President's Cup" as an international event in 1994, at their new national tennis centre, "Karolina" in Vilnius.

Luxembourg

FÉDÉRATION LUXEMBOURGEOISE DE TENNIS
Founded: 1946
No. of Players: 4,036
Clubs: 55
Courts: 269

The Grand Duchy of Luxembourg has a long tradition in the game stretching back to 1900 when it was played strictly for leisure and social purposes.

The first clubs were established in the 1920s, but it was not until 1946 that they joined forces to found the national governing body. Three years later the FLT joined the ITF, and in 1975 became a founding member of the ETA.

The sport is very popular, having grown dramatically over the last 20 years as regards clubs and their membership, with 3 per cent of the population classified as active players and 2,751 registered with the FLT, who also have a strong junior registered membership totalling 1,159 youngsters. Not surprisingly, therefore, Luxembourg have been represented in Davis Cup competition since 1947 and the Fed Cup from 1972.

Macedonia

FORMER YUGOSLAV REPUBLIC OF MACEDONIA – MKD
FYR MACEDONIAN TENNIS ASSOCIATION
Founded: 1993
No. of Players: 458
Clubs: 17
Courts: 79

The Macedonian Tennis Association was first established as an individual organization within the Yugoslav Republic in 1950. On the break-up of the Republic, the MTA became an independent organization in 1993 and inherited a major part of the sport's tradition in Yugoslavia.

With four major clubs adopted as National Tennis Centres, Macedonia have set their sights on expanding their international events. As a full member of the ITF, the MTA has entered teams in both Fed Cup and Davis Cup competitions since 1995.

Madagascar

FÉDÉRATION MALAGASY DE TENNIS
Founded: 1979
No. of Players: 3,000
Clubs: 60
Courts: 300 outdoor; 4 indoor

A minority sport in the country, with just 350 players registered to the FMT. At international level they have only competed once in the Fed Cup (1995) and have yet to make their debut in the Davis Cup.

Malaysia

LAWN TENNIS ASSOCIATION OF MALAYSIA
Founded: 1921
No. of Players: 100,000
Clubs: 200
Courts: 5,000 outdoor; 15 indoor

A member of the ITF since 1937, they first sampled Davis Cup competition in 1957 and 1958, returning to the event following a five-year absence to become regular participants, except for 1980. Currently 60,000 players are registered with the national body, though players have yet to emerge on to the world stage.

Malawi

LAWN TENNIS ASSOCIATION OF MALAWI
Founded: 1966
No. of Players: 1,000
Clubs: 15
Courts: 50

Following their independence from the Federation of Rhodesia and Nyasaland, the LTA of Malawi was formed in 1966. The association's activities are centred around the town of Blantyre though programmes encouraging participation are promoted nationwide.

Maldives

TENNIS ASSOCIATION OF THE MALDIVES
Founded: 1983

An associate member of the ITF.

Mali

FÉDÉRATION MALIENNE DE TENNIS
Founded: 1963

The national governing body was conceived in 1961, but failed to gain recognition for some years as the sport was the exclusive prerogative of the white population. Despite these early setbacks, tennis grew in popularity during the 1980s and now rates as one of the country's top four sports.

Malta

MALTA TENNIS FEDERATION
Founded: 1966
No. of Players: 1,450
Clubs: 20
Courts: 55

Britain's links with Malta provided the initial impetus for the establishment of the sport on the island, when the British services, the Maltese Sports Federation and independent clubs were the administrators of the game.

This changed in 1966 when the Malta LTA was set up and the organization affiliated itself to the LTA in

RAFAEL OSUNA, *the brilliant Mexican who was tragically killed in an air crash*

Britain. This connection was severed in the mid-1980s with the MLTA joining the ITF in 1986 and the ETA three years later, eventually changing its own name to the Malta Tennis Federation in 1994.

With a successful tourist industry, Malta's many hotels and clubs provide excellent tournament facilities for visitors. The MTF are now regular participants in the Fed Cup and Davis Cup, entering both for the first time in 1986, and have 900 licensed senior players plus 250 juniors registered.

Marshall Islands,
Republic of

MARSHALL ISLANDS TENNIS FEDERATION
Founded: 1996

An associate member of the ITF.

Mauritania

FÉDÉRATION MAURITANIENNE DE TENNIS
Founded: 1989

An associate member of the ITF.

Mauritius

MAURITIUS LAWN TENNIS ASSOCIATION
Founded: 1910
No. of Players: 1,300
Clubs: 21
Courts: 116

Another country which traces its tennis history back to British forces who established tournaments on the island as far back as 1893. In 1910 a group of players gathered as a committee, with the meeting subsequently being seen as the inauguration of the Mauritius LTA.

In 1950, a visit by Jean Borotra, one of the French "Musketeers", provided the sport with an invaluable lift which helped draw attention to the game and its facilities. Visits over the years by other well-known players have reinforced that view, ensuring a continuing positive growth.

Mexico

FEDERACION MEXICANA DE TENIS
Founded: 1952
No. of Players: 200,000
Clubs: 421
Courts: 3,235 outdoor; 78 indoor

Despite 16,589 players being registered with the FMT, the sport's popularity lags well behind that of soccer.

Nevertheless, Mexico have played a major part in the development of the sport, especially in the re-introduction of tennis to the Olympic Games, by including tennis as a demonstration event in Mexico City in 1968.

Regular competitors in both the Davis Cup and Fed Cup, in the latter competition they have scored some memorable wins over countries like Australia and the US.

Their greatest player was Rafael Osuna who died tragically in a plane crash in 1969 while returning victorious from a Davis Cup tie against Australia. Champion of the US in 1963, Osuna was also twice doubles champion at Wimbledon, in 1960 and 1963.

Micronesia

FEDERATED STATES OF MICRONESIA LAWN TENNIS ASSOCIATION
Founded: 1995

An associate member of the ITF.

Moldova

TENNIS FEDERATION OF THE REPUBLIC OF MOLDOVA

Founded: 1953
No. of Players: 205
Clubs: 12
Courts: 65

Tennis was introduced into Moldova with the establishment of the national federation in 1953, all attributed to the Russian coach Natalia Rogova.

Currently the federation is focusing on establishing an international event within Moldova's borders and ensuring their youngsters receive as much experience overseas as possible to help build a strong game within the Republic. A team has been entered in the Davis Cup since 1995.

Mongolia

MONGOLIAN TENNIS ASSOCIATION
Founded: 1990
No. of Players: 450
Clubs: 5
Courts: 15 outdoor; 3 indoor

An associate member of the ITF where all players are licensed.

Monaco

FÉDÉRATION MONEGASQUE DE TENNIS
Founded: 1927
No. of Players: 2,300
Clubs: 4
Courts: 23

The Principality staged their first championships of Monaco in 1897, but it was not until 1927 – two years before the national association was established – that the foundations were laid for the Monte Carlo Club, where the championships, probably the most important clay court event of the year behind the French Open, are now played.

The creation of the FMT not only brought together the four clubs within the Principality, but allowed Monaco to enter the Davis Cup where they have competed regularly since 1929.

As a tax haven, it is the official residence for many of the male international players, as well as being the headquarters of the ATP Tour.

HIRCHAM ARAZI, *Morocco's most talented player in recent years*

Montserrat

MONTSERRAT TENNIS ASSOCIATION
Founded: 1985

An associate member of the ITF since 1985.

Morocco

FÉDÉRATION ROYALE MAROCAINE DE TENNIS
Founded: 1957
No. of Players: 35,000
Clubs: 110
Courts: 500 outdoor; 4 indoor

Morocco's national governing body was originally known as the League of Moroccan Tennis and was affiliated to the French Tennis Federation.

In 1956 the call for separation was made and the following year the Royal Moroccan Tennis Federation was not only born, but they were immediately elected as a full member of the ITF.

A strong development policy has been pursued over the years, with the federation concentrating more on Davis Cup competition than the ladies' Fed Cup where they have only competed twice in 29 years.

Currently Hicham Arazi is their best tennis ambassador, having climbed as high as No. 38 in the world rankings by the end of 1997 and having secured some impressive and notable victories in the process.

Mozambique

FEDERAÇAO MOCAMBICANA DE TENIS
Founded: 1979

The creation of the FMT in 1979 received full support from the country's government despite the fact that the federation had no clubs affiliated to it – nor any registered members. A year later, the FMT received further support as it became an associate member of the ITF.

From 20 players in 1979, Mozambique have concentrated on creating educational coaching programmes which have seen the sport grow to respectable levels over the last two decades.

Myanmar

MYANMAR TENNIS FEDERATION
Founded: 1949
No. of Players: 10,000
Clubs: 450
Courts: 800

An associate member of the ITF.

Namibia

NAMIBIA TENNIS ASSOCIATION
Founded: 1930
No. of Players: 2,200
Clubs: 52
Courts: 180

An associate member of the ITF with 1,900 registered players.

Nauru

NAURU TENNIS ASSOCIATION
Founded: 1992
No. of Players: 2,000
Clubs: 5
Courts: 8

An associate member of the ITF with 593 licensed players.

Nepal

ALL NEPAL TENNIS ASSOCIATION
Founded: 1954

TOM OKKER, *the Dutchman who collected 31 titles during the 1970s*

Private courts, constructed back in 1900, provided the initial facilities for the game in Nepal, which formalized itself with royal patronage into the All Nepal Tennis Association in 1954. A year later the association staged its first tournament in Kathmandu with help from the International Club which became a regular feature on their calendar.

In 1971, ANTA joined the ITF and a solid programme of coaching has seen the standard of play rise with teams and players participating at tournaments overseas.

Netherlands

KONINKLIJKE NEDERLANDSE LAWN TENNIS BOND
Founded: 1899
No. of Players: 685,683
Clubs: 1,776
Courts: 10,781

Founded in an Amsterdam cafe in 1899, the governing body of Dutch tennis has nurtured the game well over the ensuing years and established it as the second most popular sport in the country, with 8.5 per cent of the population enjoying the game.

Of that percentage, 727,000 have registered with the association, making it one of the most successful tennis organizations in Europe. Unfortunately, success at international level has been limited with just two players winning singles titles at Grand Slam level: Kea Bouman the ladies' title at the 1928 French Open and Richard Krajicek the men's title at Wimbledon in 1996. In between those two achievements, Tom

Okker, known as the "Flying Dutchman", and Betty Stove were the country's best-known players, the latter losing the 1977 Wimbledon final to Britain's Virginia Wade.

In the team events, the Dutch reached the final of the Davis Cup in 1925 where they lost to France. The men's team also made the final of the King's Cup in 1968 while the ladies made two semi-final appearances in the Fed Cup.

Currently the Dutch host top-level tournaments on the professional circuit at Amsterdam, Rotterdam and Rosmalen.

Netherlands Antilles

NETHERLANDS ANTILLES TENNIS ASSOCIATION
Founded: 1941

A full member of the ITF.

New Zealand

NEW ZEALAND TENNIS INC.
Founded: 1886
No. of Players: 1,300,000
Clubs: 700
Courts: 3,200 outdoor; 100 indoor

Based in the capital, Wellington, New Zealand Tennis Inc. – originally established as the NZ LTA in 1886, making it the second-oldest national tennis association in the world – oversees the most popular participant

sport in the country with 37.7 per cent of the population involved in some level of participation.

During the early years, New Zealand combined with Australia to compete in the Davis Cup as Australasia. This partnership came to an end in 1921. New Zealand's participation became irregular and dependent on finance until 1959, from which date they have never missed a year. They have also been a regular entrant in the Fed Cup from 1970.

Their best-known player in recent years was Chris Lewis, a surprise Wimbledon finalist in 1983, while Anthony Wilding, four-time Wimbledon champion between 1910 and 1913, remains the country's most successful international player. New Zealand currently plays host to both men's and women's

tournaments as pre-Australian Open warm-up events.

Nicaragua

FEDERACION NICARAGUENSE DE TENIS

An associate member of the ITF.

Niger

FÉDÉRATION NIGÉRIENNE DE TENNIS
Founded: 1988
No. of Players: 300
Clubs: 15
Courts: 35 outdoor; 1 indoor

An associate member of the ITF with 150 licensed players.

NEW ZEALAND'S *Chris Lewis was a surprise Wimbledon finalist in 1983*

Nigeria

NIGERIAN TENNIS FEDERATION
Founded: 1927

Though the game was the prerogative of the elite and privileged few when it was first played in the country in 1904, the NTF can now count on a registered membership of 4,000 players. The dominance of Europeans in Nigerian tennis ended in 1954 when two Nigerians emerged to contest the final of the All-Nigerian Open tournament.

Nigeria have not competed in the Fed Cup, but have established themselves since 1986 as regular entrants in the Davis Cup, following three previous appearances in the 1970s.

Northern Mariana Islands

NORTHERN MARIANA ISLANDS TEN-NIS ASSOCIATION
No. of Players: 2,300
Clubs: 160
Courts: 750

An associate member of the ITF with 175 registered players.

Norway

NORGES TENNISFORBUND
Founded: 1909
No. of Players: 2,300
Clubs: 160
Courts: 750

The national game dates back to 1887 when the rules of tennis were first printed in Norwegian and the English vice-consul attempted to set up the first club. The national association eventually came about in 1909 when representatives from five clubs met in Oslo to found the Norwegian LTA.

Notwithstanding a short four-month outdoor season, Norwegian tennis has grown from 90 clubs in 1950 to the current level, with some 27,000 players, of which 2,300 are registered. Currently statistics show tennis to be the tenth most popular

sport in the country.

Molla Mallery, an Olympic bronze medallist in 1912 and eight times a winner at Forest Hills, remains their most successful player.

Keen participants in the Davis Cup since 1928, a founding nation of the Fed Cup in 1963 and three times semi-finalist of the King's Cup in the 1950s.

Oman

OMAN TENNIS ASSOCIATION
Founded: 1986
No. of Players: 2,000
Clubs: 18
Courts: 100 outdoor; 1 indoor

A full member of the ITF with 400 licensed players.

Pakistan

PAKISTAN TENNIS FEDERATION
Founded: 1947
No. of Players: 4,000
Clubs: 70
Courts: 500

Regular participants in the Davis Cup since 1947 becoming an ITF member two years later.

Panama, Republic of

FEDERACION PANAMENA DE TENIS
Founded: 1964
No. of Players: 2,500
Clubs: 14
Courts: 125

A full member of the ITF since 1972.

Papua New Guinea

PAPUA NEW GUINEA LAWN TENNIS ASSOCIATION
Founded: 1963
No. of Players: 2,200
Clubs: 18
Courts: 36

An associate member of the ITF with 1,860 licensed players.

Paraguay

ASOCIACION PARAGUAYA DE TENIS
Founded: 1920
No. of Players: 5,000
Clubs: 25
Courts: 450 outdoor; 10 indoor

Regular participants in the Davis Cup since 1931; the national governing body has a registry of 1,200 licensed players.

Peru

FEDERACION DE TENIS DEL PERU (TENIS PERU)
Founded: 1930
No. of Players: 8,000
Clubs: 65
Courts: 350

Regular participants in the Davis Cup since 1933; the Peruvian Tennis Federation claims 8,000 licensed players.

Philippines

PHILIPPINE TENNIS ASSOCIATION
Founded: 1946
No. of Players: 1,000,000
Clubs: 581
Courts: 462 outdoor; 118 indoor

Despite a long tradition in the sport and Davis Cup competition since 1921, the PTA's list of registered players totals 520.

Poland

POLSKI ZWIAZEK TENISOWY
Founded: 1921
No. of Players: 2,500
Clubs: 161
Courts: N/A

The Polish Lawn Tennis Association was established in 1921 when a number of clubs and divisions were created to satisfy a demand which had grown since the game's introduction in 1896; that year also saw the rules of the game translated into Polish.

The first Polish championships took place in 1921 and while the sport declined during World War II, it was revived in 1945 under the new regime. A change of name to the Polish Tennis Association followed and

the PTA then rejoined the ITF in 1973, becoming a member of the ETA in 1977.

Regular participants in the Davis Cup from 1925 and the Fed Cup since 1974, Poland's best-known player in recent years is Wojtek Fibak, who is credited with single-handedly reviving Polish tennis in the late 1970s and early 1980s.

Portugal

FEDERAÇAO PORTUGUESA DE TENIS
Founded: 1925
No. of Players: 12,438
Clubs: 355
Courts: 2,050

Established in 1925, the FPT oversees the national game through 13 regional associations accounting for 6,848 registered players.

Regular participants in the Davis Cup since 1925 and the Fed Cup since 1968.

Puerto Rico

PUERTO RICO TENNIS ASSOCIATION
Founded: 1959
No. of Players: 40,000
Clubs: 40
Courts: 500

A group of like-minded individuals, having originally met in 1952 to enjoy a game of tennis, carried their enthusiasm forward to become, in 1955, the Puerto Rico Lawn Tennis Association, which soon after was affiliated with the USTA as a district. This status was changed in 1967 and within a few years the association was being accepted into the various tennis and Olympic organizations in the area.

In 1980, the Puerto Rico Tennis Association, as it had became known, was elected to the ITF and since 1992 has been competing at zonal level of both the Davis Cup and the Fed Cup.

Paraguay is better known, however, as the birthplace of Gigi Fernandez, who won Olympic gold with namesake, Mary Joe Fernandez, in Barcelona in 1992.

RUSSIA'S *Maria Sharapova preparing to serve*

Qatar

QATAR TENNIS AND SQUASH FEDERATION
Founded: 1984
No. of Players: 3,800
Clubs: 24
Courts: 81 outdoor; 12 indoor

A full member of the ITF with 667 registered players, Qatar made their Davis Cup competition debut in 1992, but are yet to participate in the Fed Cup. Qatar's recent admission on to the ATP Tour has pushed Doha into the forefront as an attractive stop for the pro players enroute to the Australian Open.

Romania

FEDERATIA ROMANA DE TENNIS
Founded: 1929
No. of Players: 19,090
Clubs: 158
Courts: 920

Romania trace their tennis roots back to the days of Major Walter Wingfield as tennis was introduced by diplomats and students returning from studying abroad shortly after the game became established in Britain.

The first clubs were founded in Bucharest and Calatzi in 1898. Shortly thereafter, the game spread into most towns and cities. In 1912 a Lawn Tennis Committee was formed within the Romanian Federation of Sports, and following the First World War the committee organized the country's first international championship in 1922, which was also the year Romania made their Davis Cup debut.

A separate national governing body was set up in 1929 which, with government support during the post-war years, stimulated the sport successfully.

Romania have reached the Davis Cup final on three occasions, losing out to the USA in 1969, 1971 and 1972. The latter final, in Bucharest, was one of the most exciting contests the country had witnessed, involving their best known players, the charismatic Ilie Nastase and Ion Tiriac. Tiriac went on to become one of the game's (and Romania's) greatest entrepreneurs.

In Fed Cup competition, Romania have competed since 1973 with a quarter-final appearance their best result.

Russia

ALL RUSSIA TENNIS ASSOCIATION
Founded: 1975
No. of Players: 12,000
Clubs: 200
Courts: 4,800

The game was already being played in Russia in the late 1870s, with 1878 being adopted as the official birthdate of the sport since it was then that St Petersburg published the *Manifesto on the All-Round Development of Lawn Tennis in Russia*. A year later the country's first tennis club was created.

The growth of the sport crystal-lized in 1908 with the formation of the All-Russian Union of Tennis Clubs following the previous year's successful launch of their national championships. The Union then progressed the game further and was one of the founding members of the ITF before it was forced out of existence by the Bolshevik revolution in 1917.

Russian tennis was forced to take a back seat as the Soviet Union took control and promoted the game on behalf of all their satellite republics as the All-Union Tennis Section, rejoining the ITF in 1956.

In 1975 Russian individuality was reactivated with the formation of the Russian Tennis Federation which was allowed a minor role under the overall umbrella of the sports bodies of the USSR – including membership of the ETA in 1977.

Perestroika in 1989 saw the rise of the All-Russian Tennis Association which, after 18 months, successfully merged with the RTF to become the game's sole national body.

Davis Cup competition was ignored until 1962, since when they have been regular participants, making the final twice, eventually capturing the title in 2002.

They have also been more than reasonably successful in the Fed Cup event with two appearances in the final, in 1988 and 1990 and winning in 2004 and 2005.

In 2004 Russia nearly made a clean sweep of the ladies Grand Slam titles (Anastasia Myskina, French Open; Maria Sharapova, Wimbledon; Svetlana Kuznetsova, US Open)

RUSSIA'S *Olga Morozova, Wimbledon finalist in 1974*

while Marat Safin joined Yevgeny Kafelnikov (French Open 1996 and 1999) as a Russian male Grand Slam winner (US Open 2000, Australian Open 2005).

Rwanda

FÉDÉRATION RWANDAISE DE TENNIS
Founded: 1984
No. of Players: 1,500
Clubs: 9
Courts: 40

An associate member of the ITF.

St Kitts and Nevis

ST KITTS LAWN TENNIS ASSOCIATION
Founded: 1962

An associate member of the ITF.

St Lucia

ST LUCIA LAWN TENNIS ASSOCIATION
No. of Players: 300
Clubs: 5
Courts: 50

A full member of the ITF with 300 licensed players, the island has yet to compete in either the Davis Cup or Fed Cup competitions.

St Vincent and the Grenadines

ST VINCENT AND THE GRENADINES LAWN TENNIS ASSOCIATION
Founded: 1972

An associate member of the ITF.

San Marino

FEDERAZIONE SAMMARINESE TENNIS
Founded: 1957
No. of Players: 500
Clubs: 5
Courts: 19

Founded in 1957 to promote the development of the game within the country, the San Marino Federation established its own National Tennis Centre in 1988, and staffed it with well-known coaches. The project absorbs much of the federation's finances, but they have been well rewarded as their junior players are now making an impression on the international front.

San Marino have competed annually in the Davis Cup since 1993 making their debut in the Fed Cup four years later.

Saudi Arabia

SAUDI ARABIAN TENNIS FEDERATION
Founded: 1956
No. of Players: 30,000
Clubs: 82
Courts: 470 outdoor; 8 indoor

Saudi Arabia joined the ITF in 1961 and have never competed in the Fed Cup, but recently (1991) became a regular entrant in the Davis Cup, having played twice previously in the mid-1980s.

Senegal

FÉDÉRATION SÉNÉGALAISE DE TENNIS
Founded: 1960
No. of Players: 1,500
Clubs: 25
Courts: 130

Dominated by the French from its inception in 1960, and despite joining the ITF a year later, the Senegal Tennis Federation cast off the "elitist" mantle in 1976 which had hindered the overall development of the sport. Currently the federation has 900 players registered.

Concentrating on programmes for juniors and coaches, the Senegalese game has benefitted greatly with their players doing well in African competitions. In international team competitions they have been regular participants at zonal level in the Davis Cup since 1984. Entry in the Fed Cup has been a bit more erratic, with only five appearances since 1982

Seychelles

SEYCHELLES TENNIS ASSOCIATION
Founded: 1955
No. of Players: 100
Clubs: 1
Courts: 20

Tennis in the Seychelles can thank some keen enthusiasts who, in 1955, literally carved a court out of the wooded terrace behind the island's only secondary grammar school for boys. The students who learned their tennis on that court continued playing there into their adulthood, and eventually became the tennis committee in 1961.

More courts were built to provide the necessary impetus to widen the sport's appeal and from the initial Seychelles College Tennis Club evolved the Seychelles Tennis Association which now promotes the game amongst the islanders.

Sierra Leone

SIERRA LEONE LAWN TENNIS ASSOCIATION
Founded: 1965

An associate member of the ITF since 1987.

Singapore

SINGAPORE LAWN TENNIS ASSOCIATION
Founded: 1928
No. of Players: 50,000
Clubs: 65
Courts: 1,000 outdoor; 4 indoor

Singapore have competed in the Fed Cup regularly since 1993, having

MIROSLAV MECIR, *a brilliant player who became Olympic champion in 1988*

made their debut in 1989, and in the Davis Cup since 1984

Slovakia

SLOVAK TENNIS ASSOCIATION
Founded: 1928
No. of Players: 3,500
Clubs: 203
Courts: 1,210

The first courts appeared in Bratislava between 1880 and 1890, but it was not until 1910 that a tournament was officially held. Following the establishment of the Czechoslovak Republic after the First World War, tennis was not considered a major sport in the Slovak territory until 1968 when the Slovak Tennis Association gained responsibilities for its own region.

The STA has concentrated on developing the game at junior level and can thank their best-known player, the 1988 Olympic champion Miloslav

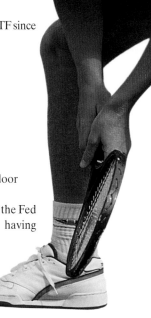

Mecir, for his support in this area.

The independent Slovak Republic did not resume Davis Cup competition until 1994, reaching the final in 2005. No similar success in Fed Cup.

Slovenia

SLOVENE TENNIS ASSOCIATION
Founded: 1940
No. of Players: 1,800
Clubs: 90
Courts: 2,750

The country's first international tournament was held in 1910, but tennis never established itself as a national sport. In 1940, the Slovene Tennis Association was set up in Maribor but, again, no positive development was undertaken until the break-up of Yugoslavia in 1991 when the STA became an independent body in its own right.

Positive programmes are now in place and already some 1,313 players have registered with the governing body, who are now establishing their own national tennis centre.

In international competitions, entries into both the Davis Cup and Fed Cup have regularly been made since the early 1990s.

Solomon Islands

SOLOMON ISLANDS TENNIS ASSOCIATION
Founded: 1993
No. of Players: 70
Clubs: 0
Courts: 6

An associate member of the ITF which boasts 12 licensed players.

Somalia

SOMALI TENNIS ASSOCIATION

An associate member of the ITF.

South Africa

SOUTH AFRICAN TENNIS ASSOCIATION
Founded: 1991

JOHAN KRIEK, *one of the many South Africans who adopted US citizenship to pursue their careers*

No. of Players: 90,000
Clubs: 2,100
Courts: 38,000 outdoor; 4 indoor

Historically, tennis in South Africa goes back to 1873, making it one of the first countries to take up the sport, courtesy of English settlers.

It became very popular with both sexes and by 1881 was being played in most of the major towns. This progress culminated in 1891 with the first South African National Championships at Port Elizabeth, the country's accepted centre of tennis. There, in 1903, agreement was reached between four of the major provinces to form the South African Lawn Tennis Union. Ten years later SALTU became a founding member

of the ITF and for many years contributed to the growth of the sport internationally.

The apartheid policy pursued by the government eventually saw South Africa as a nation estranged from the rest of the world and boycotted on every sporting front. Their banishment covered the years between 1978 and 1992, a period which saw many of their sporting heroes leave the country and take citizenship elsewhere in order to be able to pursue their careers.

Players who were "forced" to follow that route are Kevin Curren and Johan Kriek, while Frew McMillan and Bob Hewitt, who in the 1960s dominated the doubles scene, represent the previous generation before

apartheid became internationally recognized for the scandal it was. More recently Wayne Ferreira made the world's top 10 before retiring in 2004. On the women's tour, Amanda Coetzer was his counterpart retiring at around the same time.

Before 1972, South Africa entered the Davis Cup on a sporadic basis in accordance with available funds, becoming champions in 1974 when India, objecting to apartheid, conceded the final.

In the Fed Cup, South Africa were one of the original countries to support the innaugural event in 1963, winning the trophy in 1972 when they hosted the event.

Following the abandonment of apartheid, and the establishment of a new multi-racial governing body, South Africa was welcomed back into the tennis fraternity and quickly regained a place as one of the world's foremost sporting nations. In tennis terms, the South African team rose to the World Group within a few years – a feat they also achieved in the Fed Cup, though their ladies currently languish in Group One.

Spain

REAL FEDERACION ESPAÑOLA DE TENIS
Founded: 1909
No. of Players: 88,000
Clubs: 1,000
Courts: N/A

Spanish tennis is very much centred on Barcelona. It was there that the first tennis clubs were established and provided venues for the first championships in 1904, under the auspices of the Lawn Tennis Association of Barcelona, an affiliate of the LTA in London.

In 1909 the first national association was formed when clubs met to found the Lawn Tennis Association of Spain. This was changed, five years later, to the Royal Lawn Tennis Association of Spain. Another name change to the Spanish Tennis Federation came about in 1935 with the word Royal (or Real) being reintroduced in 1957. Spain was also a founding member of the ITF in 1913.

While the national sport is administered from Barcelona, which with Madrid is the home of the country's top clubs, tennis can be said to have blossomed thanks to the tourist trade for most courts are either attached to hotels or privately owned on the coasts of Spain.

Spanish tennis has become a stalwart of the international game over the last decade, with Spain able to count at least 16 nationals in the men's top 100 led by Carlos Moya, Sergi Bruguera, Juan Carlos Ferrero, Rafael Nadfal, the Sanchez brothers, Carlos Costa and others. Previously their best-known players were Manolo Santana (1966 Wimbledon champion) and Manuel Orantes.

Arantxa Sanchez-Vicario raised the profile of Spanish women with her French Open titles in 1989 and 1994, plus the US Open in 1994, as did Conchita Martinez, who won the 1994 Wimbledon crown defeating Martina Navratilova in the process and denying her a record 10th victory. The two women also formed the nucleus of Spain's winning Fed Cup team between 1991 and 1995.

In Davis Cup terms, only recent results have been as positive with championship victories in 2000 and 2004.

Sri Lanka

SRI LANKA TENNIS ASSOCIATION
Founded: 1915
No. of Players: 4,000
Clubs: 65
Courts: 350

Introduced by the British, tennis has a long tradition in Sri Lanka and can even claim a Wimbledon champion, tea-planter P. F. Hadow, who won the singles in 1878. The island's first national championships were staged in 1908 and were dominated in those early days by the colonial administrators.

Originally established in 1915, the Ceylon Lawn Tennis Association was restyled the Sri Lanka Tennis Association to reflect not only the new name adopted for the island, but also the disappearance of lawn courts.

Sri Lanka have competed in the Davis Cup since 1953 and in the Fed Cup since 1990.

Sudan

SUDAN LAWN TENNIS ASSOCIATION
Founded: 1956

As a full member of the ITF, Sudan have participated in both international team competitions, albeit only in 1974 for the Fed Cup. They have been regular entrants in the Davis Cup since 1994.

Surinam

SURINAAMSE TENNISBOND
Founded: 1936
No. of Players: 2,000
Clubs: 13
Courts: 17

An associate member of the ITF.

Swaziland

SWAZILAND NATIONAL TENNIS UNION
Founded: 1968

An associate member of the ITF.

Sweden

THE SWEDISH TENNIS ASSOCIATION
Founded: 1906
No. of Players: 7,700
Clubs: 565
Courts: 4,500

The Swedish Tennis Association was founded in 1906 and has long ties with Swedish royalty. It was in fact King Gustav V, known as "Mr G", who introduced tennis to the country in 1878.

In 1901 the "Kungens Kanna", an annual handicap competition, was held, a year after the country's first National Championships were organized.

Swedish players won Olympic medals in 1908 and 1912, but the public popularity of the sport was not really created until 1920, when Sweden first participated in the Davis Cup. The King's Cup, a European equivalent of the Davis Cup, was launched through Swedish initiative in 1936. This competition was taken over by the ETA in 1976 and run as the "European Men's Team Championships" (or European Cup). A women's version was launched in 1986.

The popularity of tennis – the STA now has 6,750 registered players – increased even further with the appearance of Bjorn Borg, whose record remains one of the best in the

CARLOS COSTA, *one of the Armada of Spaniards who have come to the fore in the last decade*

ROGER FEDERER *of Switzerland expertly returns a backhand*

modern era. A string of excellent players followed Borg, amongst them Mats Wilander and Stefan Edberg, all helping to increase Sweden's stature in the world game which in turn was further enhanced by six Davis Cup victories plus five other final appearances.

Teams have appeared regularly in the Fed Cup since 1964, but regrettably the women's game has never been able to live up to the standard set by their men.

Switzerland

SWISS TENNIS (SCHWEIZERISCHER TENNISVERBAND)
Founded: 1896
No. of Players: 51,255
Clubs: 1,010
Courts: 3,906

Five clubs originally met in 1896 to form the Swiss Tennis Association which has been extremely active in recent years in creating good programmes for their 54,900 registered players.

With some of the best facilities available, Swiss Tennis now stages a number of international events on both professional tours and can thank Martina Hingis, the former world No.1 and holder of five singles Grand Slam titles, for raising the profile of the Swiss game. Previously Jakob Hlasek and Mark Rosset, the

1994 Olympic champion, carried that responsibility which resulted in them reaching the Davis Cup final in 1992. Now that mantle has passed to Roger Federer, the current world No.1 and holder of nine masters.

Basle, Switzerland, is the headquarters of the European Tennis Association (ETA), which was founded in 1975 to foster the development of tennis in Europe. The ETA is recognized by the ITF as a regional association.

Syrian Arab Republic

SYRIAN ARAB TENNIS FEDERATION
Founded: 1953
No. of Players: 2,000
Clubs: 85
Courts: 118 outdoor; 16 indoor

Originally set up to administer both table tennis and tennis in 1953 – when the first court was laid by the Syrian graduates of the American University in Beirut – the Syrian Federation for Table and Lawn Tennis split up in 1964 and the SATF emerged.

With 1,200 licensed players, tennis has often featured in the region's many Pan-Arabian competitions. Syria became an associate member of the ITF in 1970 and were elevated to full membership in 1984. Davis Cup competition followed a year later, with the Fed Cup left until 1994.

Tajikistan

NATIONAL TENNIS FEDERATION OF THE REPUBLIC OF TAJIKISTAN
Founded: 1992
Played the Davis Cup in 1997 but not the Fed Cup.

Tanzania

TANZANIA LAWN TENNIS ASSOCIATION
No. of Players: 300
Clubs: 0
Courts: 70

An associate member of the ITF.

Thailand

THE LAWN TENNIS ASSOCIATION OF THAILAND
Founded: 1927
No. of Players: 40,000
Clubs: 88
Courts: 500 outdoor; 10 indoor

Tennis in Siam can be traced back to 1899 when His Serene Highness Prince Pithayalongkorn laid a tennis court on his return from England. Not surprisingly, the royal family have been strong supporters of the game and the most prestigious trophy for their national championships, inaugurated in 1903, was presented by the Crown Prince in 1909.

The growth of the sport was such that in 1927 the national governing body was set up and, at the Palace of Prince Pithayalongkorn, the Lawn Tennis Association of Siam was born, with Prince Pithayalongkorn elected chairman.

Joining the ITF in 1936, Thailand (as it was now known) played in the Davis Cup for the first time in 1958 and are now regular entrants, as they are in the Fed Cup following initial sporadic appearances from 1979.

Togo

FÉDÉRATION TOGOLAISE DE TENNIS
Founded: 1955
No. of Players: 1,500
Clubs: 8
Courts: 40

Though the association was originally established in 1955 simply as Togo District Tennis, with just four clubs, four courts and 50 members, a successful youth programme during the 1960s pushed the game into the national psyche and, from those humble beginnings, the Fédération Togolaise de Tennis evolved. It now counts on 1,330 licensed players.

Togo have not competed in the Fed Cup, but have regularly done so in the Davis Cup since 1970.

ANDY RODDICK *of the USA unleashes one of his powerful forehands on the run*

Tonga

TONGA TENNIS ASSOCIATION
Founded: 1959
No. of Players: 700
Clubs: 12
Courts: 60

An associate member of the ITF with 700 licensed players.

Trinidad and Tobago

THE TENNIS ASSOCIATION OF TRINIDAD AND TOBAGO
Founded: 1951
No. of Players: 700
Clubs: 34
Courts: 80

The islands' colonial background is credited with the introduction of tennis into the community, the first club being established in Trinidad's Port of Spain in 1883. The club has become one of the pioneers of the sport and in 1912 hosted the first local championships. Much was done to bring the islands together and in 1951 Tobago and Trinidad set up their national Lawn Tennis Association. With contributions from national and local governments, facilities are becoming available for all levels of society.

The LTA of Trinidad and Tobago has entered teams in both the Davis Cup and the Fed Cup since 1990.

Tunisia

FÉDÉRATION TUNISIENNE DE TENNIS
Founded: 1954
No. of Players: 30,000
Clubs: 45
Courts: 503 outdoor; 3 indoor

In the 1960s, the Tunisian Tennis Federation set up a school to train players for the 1967 Mediterranean Games. The success reaped there, and at other competitions during the following decade, helped create a public awareness which the federation has capitalized on. National teams have competed in the Davis Cup from 1982 and the Fed Cup since 1992.

Turkey

TURKIYE TENIS FEDERASYONU
Founded: 1923
No. of Players: N/A
Clubs: N/A

While the Turkish Tennis Federation was established in 1941 it is accepted that tennis was played by minority groups as far back as the 1920s. Public acceptance of the sport has been slow despite strong youth programmes and the targeting of the game amongst schools.

International competition has been limited; the first year that Turkey entered the Davis Cup was 1946 and a women's team debuted in the Fed Cup as recently as 1991.

Turkmenistan

TURKMENISTAN TENNIS ASSOCIATION
Founded: 1992

An associate member of the ITF.

Uganda

UGANDA TENNIS ASSOCIATION
Founded: 1948

Entered Davis Cup team in 1997 but have yet to compete in the Fed Cup.

Ukraine

UKRAINIAN NATIONAL LAWN TENNIS FEDERATION
Founded: 1946
No. of Players: 966
Clubs: 28
Courts: 520

Ukrainian tennis dates back to 1910, but it was not until after the Second World War that sport as a whole came alive in the region, with tennis led by the Dynamo Tennis Club.

The 1980s witnessed a number of junior players emerge, amongst them brother and sister Andrei Medvedev and Natalya Medvedeva. It is also the birthplace of Larisa Savchenko, who subsequently became Latvian through marriage.

The Ukraine contributed greatly to the Soviet Union's Davis Cup and Fed Cup campaigns, competitions in which they now participate in their own right.

United Arab Emirates

UNITED ARAB EMIRATES TENNIS ASSOCIATION
Founded: 1982
No. of Players: 2,000
Clubs: 60
Courts: 310 outdoor; 10 indoor

Established in 1982, the UAETA has pursued a policy of improving tennis standards by concentrating on coaching within schools in many cases through the importing of foreign coaches and the staging of exhibition matches. The policy's success can be measured by the fact that since 1993 the association has been able to field a team to compete in the Davis Cup zonal competitions. So far, though, no Fed Cup team has been entered.

Unites States of America

UNITED STATES TENNIS ASSOCIATION
Founded: 1881
No. of Players: 11,158,000
Clubs: 6,800
Courts: 234,000

The most successful tennis nation in the world and the first nation to try to standardize and organize the game, leading to the establishment of the United States National Lawn Tennis Association in 1881, making it the world's oldest tennis governing body.

Shortly after its formation, the first US National Championships were staged which eventually became the fourth leg of the Grand Slam, and the US Open when the professional era arrived in 1968.

In the interim, the USNLTA underwent many changes, and adopted new events. It established the Davis Cup competition in 1900 by issuing the British Isles with the first-ever challenge in what was to become the widest and most prestigious of annual sporting competitions.

In 1923 the Wightman Cup for ladies was born, with the donor of the Cup hoping the event would become their equivalent of the men's Davis Cup. This never materialized as the event remained a private annual battle between Britain and the USA until it was discontinued in 1990.

In 1920 the governing body dropped the "National" tag from its title, joining the ITF in 1923, 10 years after the international body had been founded. The final change of name came about in 1975 when "Lawn" was dropped for the governing body to become the USTA.

With 4.3 per cent of the population listing tennis amongst their activities, it is not surprising that they can maintain a steady stream of talented players to dominate the game for decades on end. Also, with the depth of talent that they can draw on, the USA have seldom been off the top step of the winners' rostrum in both Davis Cup and Fed Cup competitions. The former they have won 31 times, losing in the final on 29 other occasions, while in the ladies' event they have scored 17 wins with nine other final appearances. Currently Andy Roddick keeps the stars and stripes flying in the top ten as the women's game awaits a new star to emerge.

US Virgin Islands

VIRGIN ISLANDS TENNIS ASSOCIATION
Founded: 1973
No. of Players: 400
Clubs: 29
Courts: 80

Set up in 1973, the Virgin Islands Lawn Tennis Association – dropping the word "Lawn" from its title in 1980 – was also a district within the USTA. The association's main objective was to unite different organizations and establish a common goal amongst all the main islands which make up the US Virgin Islands.

Uruguay

ASOCIACION URUGUAYA DE TENIS
Founded: 1915
No. of Players: 4,300
Clubs: 32
Courts: 143

Montevideo has been the mainstay of Uruguayan tennis, with the majority of clubs based there. With 900 licensed players, the association has concentrated on junior programmes and established some strong circuits for them.

Internationally Uruguayan teams have competed regularly in the Davis Cup since 1931 and in the Fed Cup since the early 1970s.

Uzbekistan

TENNIS ASSOCIATION OF REPUBLIC OF UZBEKISTAN
Founded: 1992
No. of Players: 5,000
Clubs: 20
Courts: 160 outdoor; 8 indoor

A full member of the ITF with 570 licensed players. Uzbekistan only recently entered the international competitions, the Davis Cup from 1994 and the Fed Cup a year later.

Vanuatu

FÉDÉRATION DE TENNIS DE VANUATU
Founded: 1990
No. of Players: 150
Clubs: 3
Courts: 14

An associate member of the ITF.

Venezuela

FEDERACION VENEZOLANA DE TENIS
Founded: 1926
No. of Players: 135,000
Clubs: 315
Courts: 1,065

The first tennis club in Venezuela was established by an Englishman in 1890; the Venezuelan Central Railway Tennis Club. Tournaments started to be played in 1910, though some of the private courts were conversions of a variety of villa patios, producing unusually shaped areas. Eventually, on the formation of the governing body in 1926, standardization was achieved including the translation of the rules into Spanish.

The first national championship was held in 1927 but, more interestingly, the association established an inter-club competition based on the Davis Cup format which ran until 1940.

In 1957 Venezuela entered the Davis Cup proper for the first time and, following some interesting junior initiatives, the Federation built their own National Tennis Centre in Caracas.

Vietnam

VIETNAM TENNIS FEDERATION
Founded: 1989

An associate member of the ITF.

Western Samoa

WESTERN SAMOA LAWN TENNIS ASSOCIATION
Founded: 1955

An associate member of the ITF.

Yemen

YEMEN TENNIS FEDERATION
Founded: 1902
No. of Players: 300
Clubs: 0
Courts: 50 outdoor; 2 indoor

An associate member of the ITF with 300 licensed players.

Yugoslavia

TENIS SAVEZ YUGOSLAVIJE
Founded: 1922
No. of Players: 2,500
Clubs: 120
Courts: 345 outdoor; 45 indoor

The Yugoslav Tennis Federation was formed in 1922 in Zagreb and a Yugoslav team has competed in the Davis Cup since 1927. However, with the break-up of Yugoslavia, the national team was suspended from all international competition in 1991. On the removal of UN sanctions the teams were reinstated and continue to play in both the Fed Cup and the Davis Cup.

Zambia

ZAMBIA LAWN TENNIS ASSOCIATION
Founded: 1975
No. of Players: 2,000
Clubs: 40
Courts: 245

As a full member of the ITF, Zambia have competed in the Davis Cup from 1990, but have yet to participate in the Fed Cup.

Zimbabwe

TENNIS ASSOCIATION OF ZIMBABWE
Founded: 1904
No. of Players: 15,000
Clubs: 96
Courts: 600 outdoor; 1 indoor

A long tennis tradition was established during the country's colonial days as Rhodesia. This continues under the new Zimbabwe administration. They have competed in the Fed Cup and the Davis Cup since 1963.

THE GREAT

The four Grand Slam tournaments – the Australian Open, French Open, Wimbledon and the US Open – are the highlights in the tennis calendar, closely followed by the ATP and WTA Tours, the Davis Cup, Fed Cup and the Olympics. Between them they involve around 3,000 full-time professional players in what has become a multi-million-dollar sporting business.

MARTINA HINGIS, *the youngest player to successfully defend a Grand Slam title*

AUSTRALIAN OPEN

From a humble start at the Warehousemen's Ground in Melbourne's Albert Park, home to the Australian motor racing Grand Prix, the Australian Open is now very firmly an equal partner in the quartet of the Grand Slam tournaments which outshine all others in the eyes of the players, as well as the public. Yet even as recently as the early 1980s, by no means all the top players wanted to travel to Australia over the Christmas holiday and the policy of staging the men's and women's tournaments in different months soon lost its appeal. There were events in other parts of the world, most notably in Japan and Germany, which were keen to press their claim for Grand Slam status – if necessary by replacing Melbourne.

Then during 1983 Australian

officials put together a commercial and presentation package which not only halted Melbourne's decline but began the transformation which has made the Australian Open one of the most envied sporting events in the Southern Hemisphere.

Bringing together the men's and women's tournaments again – and offering prize money which was no longer quite so far removed from the rewards being provided at Wimbledon, the French and the US Open – was obviously one vital factor. But the move from Kooyong to a magnificent new home capable of staging sporting and other entertainment events, next door to the famous Melbourne Cricket Ground in the centre of the city, was the other.

Kooyong, for all its countrified charm, suddenly found that, like For-

TOURNAMENTS

1934 Miss J.HARTIG...
1935 Miss D.ROUND
Miss J.HARTIG...
1937 Miss N.WYNNE...
1938 Miss D.M.BUH...
1939 Mrs W.ESTACO...
1940 Miss N.WYNNE...
1941... COMPETITION
1946 M... N.BOLTON...
... N.BOLTON...
1948 M... N.BOLTON...
...(U.S.A)...
...8-Miss L.BROUGH(U.S.A)...
1951 Mrs N.BOLTON (VIC)
1952 Mrs M.LONG (N.S.W)

LEW HOAD, *a great champion and a much-loved character*

est Hills in New York, it could no longer cope with the increased number of players in two 128-player draws, to say nothing of escalating crowds and media. The move was not made without much heart-searching, especially as it meant changing the surface from grass, on which the tournament had been played for 80 years. Initially there was strong support for an artificial grass surface but ultimately Reebound Ace, a synthetic hard court, was chosen. The surface is said to be fine most of the time but "murderous", according to the players, when the temperature soars and the heat burns into the soles of their shoes and their feet.

The new centre, originally called Flinders Park but changed in 1996 to Melbourne Park on the instruction of leading City fathers who felt Melbourne should get greater worldwide recognition for their contribution to the financing of the project, was opened in 1988. Today it not only has a new name but is set within wonderfully landscaped grounds where, between matches, picnickers can sunbathe on the grass. And the crowds, which have grown year-on-year, reached a 550,550 record in 2006 when an emotional Roger Federer beat surprise finalist Marcus Baghdatis, the first Cypriot to reach a Grand Slam final, in four sets. In 2006, too, Martina Hingis, the youngest player to successfully defend a Grand Slam title back in 1998, made a welcome return to the circuit after a three year absence, reaching the quarter-finals in the year Amelie Mauresmo made her own breakthrough by winning her first major.

Everything involving the Australian Open now is a far cry from those early days when just 17 players from only three of the states took part in the men's singles. At that time the tournament was called the Australasian Championships and it was twice held in New Zealand – in Christchurch in 1906, and six years later in Hastings. Otherwise, it travelled round all the mainland capital cities of Australia before settling in Melbourne in 1972.

The impetus to form a national association had arisen not so much to facilitate a national championship as the growing belief that Australia should join the band of nations competing for the Davis Cup. Under its rules, a nation could only compete if its team was under the jurisdiction and organization of a national association. It was when New Zealand officials said they were eager to support such a move that a meeting was convened in Sydney, in September 1904, and the Australasian Lawn Tennis Association was formed.

Even with players of the calibre of Norman Brookes and Tony Wilding, the Australian Championships were slow in taking a firm foothold. Indeed, it was not until 1922 that the next step forward was made; women were at last able to compete in singles, doubles and mixed doubles.

It was also in 1922 that New Zealand withdrew to mount its own Davis Cup challenge. Gradually, Perth and Brisbane were dropped from the cities staging the tournament and efforts were concentrated on staging it in rotation in Sydney, Melbourne and Adelaide. The change of name to just the Australian Championships was made in 1926, when the tournament was also held for the first time on new courts at Kooyong and changed to its now customary date at the end of January, encompassing the Australia Day weekend holiday.

Over the next 30 years, despite the extended travelling time needed for international competitors to reach Australia, the tournament thrived. As Joseph Johnson wrote in *Grand Slam Australia*, the winners in that period indicated the consistently high quality of the fields – Jean Borotra, Fred Perry, Don Budge, Maureen Connolly, Louise Brough and Dorothy Round were all triumphant in addition to Australia's own great champions.

The 1939–45 war over, the Australian Championships continued to attract many of the best in the world but what delighted the crowds even more in the 1950s and 60s was the way the development programmes organized by Sir Norman Brookes and coach Harry Hopman meant that home heroes became dominant. Adrian Quist and Frank Sedgman set the example and were then followed in quick and lasting succession by Ken McGregor, Ken Rosewall, Mervyn Rose, Neale Fraser, Lew Hoad, Ashley Cooper, Roy Emerson, Rod Laver, Fred Stolle and John Newcombe, not to mention those such as Tony Roche, one of the finest doubles players the game has seen.

The successes those players enjoyed all round the world, at a time when Australia also won the Davis Cup 16 times in 19 years, meant it really was a golden age for Australian tennis. On the other hand the world was changing and the hypocritical stance of international officials – in refusing to recognize the commercial climate developing in sport by acknowledging professionals, but at the same time condoning under-the-counter payments – was doomed to fail. What became the annual departure of the world's best players in one year, to join professional groups in the United States the next, hit Australian tennis hardest of all. For not only did it end their Davis Cup supremacy, but the entry for the Australian Championships also suffered, with consequent loss of public support.

During the first 20 years of Open tennis, problems remained. The Australian Open, like Wimbledon and the other Grand Slams, was weakened, particularly in 1972 and 1973, by political absences. In 1972 it was also decided to change the date of the event from the end of January to coincide with the Christmas–New Year holiday. This pleased the public, because many of them were on holiday at the time and it pleased the tournament's first title sponsor, Marlboro, because it guaranteed extended television time. But it did not please many of the players, especially those with families who did not want to be away at that time. Over the next 10 years the quality of entry dropped and there were some years when none of the world's top 10 men or women, other than Australians, were prepared to take part.

Various counter-measures were adopted, including the introduction of a separate women's tournament in November, beginning in 1980. It was brilliantly successful in its first two years but the whole essence of the Grand Slams is that they should bring all the world's finest players – men, women and to some extent the next generation as well – together in a showpiece festival four times a year in different parts of the world. Happily the lessons were learned in time. Far from being the poor relation, in terms of presentation and facilities for the public and the players especially, the Australian Open has set new standards in recent years, which have

inspired the constant upgrading plans of others.

Great matches have abounded. One of the most memorable was the semi-final between Laver and Roche in the 1969 inaugural Open. Laver was back as top seed after his years in the professional wilderness. Roche was seeded fourth and had justified being one place above his doubles partner Newcombe by beating him over five sets in the quarter-finals.

Recalling the occasion, Allan Stone, doubles runner-up at Wimbledon with Colin Dowdeswell in 1975, said: "The heat in Brisbane that day was incredible, but although there were probably only around 200 spectators in the crowd itself, all the other players came to watch. And when something like that happens, you know it's something special. What I remember most of all was the breathtaking shot-making. It was a classic."

The sizzling pace was sustained for 4 hours 35 minutes and spanned 90 games, with the second set alone lasting more than two hours. Laver eventually won 7–5, 22–20, 9–11, 1–6, 6–3 but in the second set, well before the introduction of tie-breaks, Roche had three set points at 7–6 and Laver two at 12–11. In the first set Roche had three times broken back immediately after losing his own serve and his courageous defiance was redoubled in the third when he broke back at 2–3 and 7–8.

Serving at 3–4, 15–30 on the fifth, a shot from Laver was given in when Roche and many in the crowd were convinced his shot was well out. The point stood but although the craggy left-hander fought back again to deuce, he still lost the game and Laver then served out for the match.

The 1975 final between John Newcombe and Jimmy Connors was

another classic, not least because both players, in their differing ways, had given the impression that it was a "grudge match". Connors had won 99 out of 103 matches during the previous year, winning the Australian, Wimbledon and US titles. Not surprisingly, he felt that, but for being banned from the French because of his participation in World Team Tennis, he would have joined Budge and Laver as a Grand Slam champion.

Newcombe and Connors had not met since 1973 when "Newk" won both times and the Australian's declaration that "a match with Connors is something I've wanted for a long time" was countered by Connors with "He should do more talking with his racket than his mouth. Every time I reach a final, Newcombe is missing."

When Newcombe won the first set, a voice from the crowd called to Connors "What happened, mouth?"

PETE SAMPRAS *unable to hold back the tears (in the 1995 Australian Open) on the day that he learned his coach, Tim Gullikson, was terminally ill*

The American promptly won the second set. Then, when Connors was serving for 3–3 in the third set, the American for the first and only time, at least in professional tennis, knowingly gave away a point. Having reached 40–15 with not one but three questionable calls, Connors then deliberately double-faulted. Newcombe broke back and took the set 6–4.

One theory was that Connors chose that moment to try and win back the support of a hostile crowd. Interestingly Newcombe, who held match point when serving for victory at 5–3 in the fourth set but twice had to save set points before taking the tie-break 9–7, said: "I wouldn't have thrown it away as he did" – to which Connors added, "There's no way I'll ever give away a point like that again." Despite the aggravation beforehand, the crowd rose as one after the 174-minute battle to give both players a standing ovation, and Newcombe said: "Today Jimmy Connors proved to me that a champion has to know how to win – and lose. He's proved to me that he's a true champion."

More recently, Mats Wilander's 8–6 win in the fifth over Pat Cash in the 1988 first final at Melbourne Park was another of epic proportions. Among the women, nothing yet quite surpasses the quality and drama of the 1981 final between Martina Navratilova and Chris Evert. Despite the wind swirling round the centre court at Kooyong, which meant there were more unforced errors than usual when these two megastars of women's tennis met, the mental battle which ensued gripped everyone who saw it. Navratilova had slipped from first to third in the world rankings and, when she lost the first-set tie-break, the signs were ominous. Thereafter, however, her only problem was closing out what became a 6–7, 6–4, 7–5 victory. She had six game points to lead 3–0 in the final set, but lost them all. She then led 5–1 only for Evert, in typical fighting spirit, to make it 5–5 whereupon Navratilova produced the final surge that was needed.

As for matches at what is now Melbourne Park, the disqualification of John McEnroe in 1990 for his offen-

JAROSLAV DROBNY, *whose persistence was rewarded on clay and grass*

sive remarks to and about officials, making him the first player in Open tennis to be dismissed from a Grand Slam; Pete Sampras shedding tears in a staggering recovery to beat Jim Courier in 1995; and the 1996 women's quarter-final in which Chanda Rubin beat Arantxa Sanchez Vicario 6–4, 2–6, 16–14 in 3 hours 33 minutes, with the final set alone lasting a record 2 hours 22 minutes, are only a few among the magnificent stories which will be passed on to future generations.

FRENCH OPEN

Ironically, although it was the impact of Suzanne Lenglen which made it imperative for Wimbledon to find larger premises to cope with the crowds she attracted to The Champi-

onships, it was further success in the Davis Cup which prompted the French Championships to follow suit. Not that Lenglen was any less a star in Paris than she was in England. They adored her.

Yet in those days, indeed until Chris Evert and Martina Navratilova came along in the 1970s, there was a general antipathy towards women's tennis in so many European countries, other than Britain. In such circumstances, until Lenglen and Helen Wills met for the one and only time in Cannes in 1926, when the whole sporting world took notice, there was not the same opportunity for spectators to fully appreciate Lenglen's standing in the tennis world. Even in the first two years of international French Championships, just before she retired, Lenglen dropped only three games in the 1925 final and just one a year later. In addition, Lenglen had greater

publicity than was the case when she played in Britain, for instance, for she reigned at very much the same time as the Musketeers, Borotra, Lacoste, Cochet and Brugnon.

It was not until 1925 that the French allowed any "outsider" from another country to take part. Until then, the French tournament, which had started in 1891 (14 years after Wimbledon, 10 years after the US Championships and 14 years before there was a similar event in Australia), was rigidly restricted to players who had French nationality or who were members of French clubs.

Another reason for the French Championships being relatively late in welcoming players from other countries was that from 1912, until they were abolished by the International Lawn Tennis Association in 1924, the world clay court championships took place in Paris at the Faisanderie in the St Cloud Park. Their demise was the final impetus for the national French Championships to go international.

In those early days the French Championships were played alternately at the Racing Club at Croix-Catelan and the Stade Français at the Faisanderie but, as reports at the time indicate, those two Parisian clubs were soon "caving in" under the weight of spectators eager to see matches between "Big" Bill Tilden and any of the Musketeers or the exploits of the one they called the "Divine" Suzanne.

Matters came to a head in 1927 when, after they had twice finished runners-up to the United States, France won the Davis Cup for the first time in 1927, beating the Americans 3–2 in the Challenge Round in Philadelphia. The question then was where could they stage the Challenge Round in Paris the following year, for such was the excitement over the 1927 victory that thousands queued for hours to get a glimpse of the trophy when it first arrived in France.

Officials of the two clubs which had been staging the French Championships and Albert Canet from the

YEVGENY KAFELNIKOV, *the first Russian singles champion at a Grand Slam*

BJORN BORG *on the way to the first of his six French Open titles in 1974*

Tennis Club de Paris, who was about to become president of the French Tennis Federation, successfully sought help from the city of Paris. An area of land near the Porte d'Auteil, belonging to the Stade Français, was made available and within a year the new stadium, named after French aviator Roland Garros, was ready for use. A challenge match between the women's teams of France and Britain, who won 8–4, was the first event to take place on the famous red clay, followed two days later by the French Championships, won by Henri Cochet and Helen Wills.

As for the Davis Cup, France won the 1928 Challenge Round in their new art deco-style home and kept the cup there until Britain took it from them in 1933.

It is no wonder that the magnificent second court for the tournament, first brought into use in 1995, is named after Suzanne Lenglen or that statues of her and the Musketeers adorn the marble patio, for they represented a golden age for French tennis. From 1925 until 1932, either Lacoste, Cochet or Borotra were triumphant in the French Championships in addition

to their joint achievements in the Davis Cup. Thereafter France had to wait until Marcel Bernard in 1946.

Honours from the mid-1930s to the outbreak of the 1939–45 war were shared principally between an Australian, Jack Crawford, with his long flannels and long-sleeved shirt; the dashing Englishman with the pounding forehand, Fred Perry; and a flame-haired American, Donald Budge. Yet there were occasional interlopers such as Baron Gottfried von Cramm, a young German aristocrat who took the title in 1934 and 1936.

Among the women, it was the era belonging essentially to Helen Wills and then Britain's Margaret Scriven and Germany's Hilde Sperling, before Simone Mathieu restored French prestige in the women's singles with her victories in 1938 and 1939.

Marcel Bernard was 32 when he won the first post-war tournament in 1946 and his success – which included victories over the new generation of champions, Pancho Segura, Budge Patty, Jaroslav Drobny and the French favourite, Yvon Petra, who was to win the first post-war Wimbledon

– was all the more remarkable for he only entered the singles because his partner for the mixed doubles decided not to play.

Drobny's subtle skills were ideally suited to the surface at Roland Garros, but it was not until he had been runner-up twice that he eventually won the title two years in succession. Although Frank Parker was triumphant in 1948 and 1949 and Tony Trabert then won in successive years, 1954–55, American men, either then, or since, have never been as successful at Roland Garros as their female compatriots. The immediate post-war years were dominated by Americans Margaret Osborne, later Margaret Dupont, Doris Hart, Shirley Fry and, of course, Maureen Connolly before Britain's Angela Mortimer interrupted the success of the Stars and Stripes.

Over the next decade men's tennis produced a succession of huge new talents which were often lost just as quickly to the professional ranks. Ken Rosewall, Lew Hoad and Rod Laver were among those who came, triumphed and went, although the stylish Europeans, Nicola Pietrangeli and Manuel Santana, both two-time winners, became favourites at the tournament. It was Santana's first victory in 1961, after he had twice been a set down, which prevented the Italian from achieving a third consecutive victory but at the end it was the toothy Spaniard who burst into tears and Pietrangeli who consoled him. Laver's victory the following year was also a thriller for he came from two sets down and saved a match point to beat fellow Australian Roy Emerson 3–6, 2–6, 6–3, 9–7, 6–2.

For his part, Emerson, who won the last amateur French Championships in 1967, also won the doubles a record six times in this spell of Australian dominance, during which time Fred Stolle and Tony Roche also won the singles title. By now too, Australian women were also much in the ascendancy. Although three more British champions, Shirley Bloomer (Brasher), Christine Truman and Ann Haydon (Jones) followed Mor-

Belgian Justine Henin-Hardenne delivers one of her trademark backhands during the French Open

timer as women's singles champion in alternate years until 1961, Margaret Smith and Lesley Turner then shared the honours over the next four years.

Although the first international Open tournament had been staged in Bournemouth a few weeks earlier, the first Open Grand Slam event was in Paris in May 1968. It coincided with student unrest, but despite a general strike affecting public transport a capacity crowd was enthralled by a men's final in which Rosewall won the title for a second time, 15 years after his first, beating Laver who 12 months later used victory at Roland Garros as his springboard to becoming the first man to complete the Grand Slam twice.

Nancy Richey from the United States was the first women's singles champion in the Open era, followed by a succession of giant names such as Margaret Smith, Evonne Goolagong, Billie Jean King and the teenage Chris Evert, while on the men's side another period of European dominance was led first by Jan Kodes, Andre Gimeno and Ilie Nastase before Bjorn Borg exploded on the scene, an 18-year-old Viking with long blond hair. That was in 1974. In eight astonishing years he played seven times, won six and was beaten only once, by Adriano Panatta in the 1976 quarter-finals.

Little more than a month after Borg, still only 26, retired, 17-year-old Mats Wilander, who had won the junior title a year earlier, became the youngest winner at 17 years 9 months with victory against the vastly more experienced Guillermo Vilas. Wilander was to win again in 1985 and 1988. His defeat in the 1983 final was by Yannick Noah, with a wonderful, swashbuckling performance. Philippe Chatrier had captured Noah for the French from the Cameroons, on the advice of Arthur Ashe, and he became the first French men's singles winner at Roland Garros for 37 years.

These were epic years for French finals. In 1984, just when everyone was wondering if Ivan Lendl would ever win a Grand Slam title after losing in five finals, John McEnroe, of all people, let him off the hook with his dramatic loss of form after he had been leading by two sets to love and a break at 4–3 in a final he was to lose 3–6, 2–6, 6–4, 7–5, 7–5. It transformed the career of the tall, stern Czechoslovakian, who was eventually to become a United States citizen. He triumphed in Paris twice more before also figuring in one of the greatest upsets in the history of the tournament, in 1989. It all looked plain sailing for Lendl when, in the fourth round, he led newcomer Michael Chang, who was only three months past his 17th birthday – especially as the diminutive Californian was starting to cramp so badly that one wondered how much longer he could last. But last he did!

During an astonishing comeback – in what his coach Jose Higueras called "the most incredible match I've ever seen" – Chang had the audacity to slip in an underarm serve at the height of his problems with cramp in the fifth set, which not only won the point but added to Lendl's disbelief and agitation at what was happening. This startling demonstration of brilliant footwork and extraordinary hand-eye co-ordination earned him not just victory over the top seed but swept him on to become the youngest champion when he beat Stefan Edberg from two sets to one down in the final.

All this time on the women's front, after three years in which Sue Barker, Mima Jausovec and Virginia Ruzici took full advantage of much absenteeism among top 10 players, Hana Mandlikova, the 1981 champion, quickly found herself overshadowed by the increasing rivalry between Chris Evert and Martina Navratilova and then Steffi Graf. Between them in the 1980s they won 33 of the 40 Grand Slam tournaments. Yet in 1989, while Chang was leading the youthful fling in the men's singles, another 17-year-old, Arantxa Sanchez Vicario, took the women's singles, defeating the defending champion Steffi Graf after the world champion had served for the title again at 5–3 in the final set.

Thereafter in the women's singles Monica Seles became the queen of clay, at least in Paris, and who knows how many times she would have taken the title but for the intervention of the German maniac who stabbed her on court in Hamburg in 1993. Graf took over once more as champion that year and repeated her success in 1995 and 1996, though never with the same conviction and authority which marked her earlier successes. That was especially so in 1996 when Graf had to save two points to avoid going 2–5 down in the final set of a classic, titanic final.

One of the great joys of Roland Garros, particularly in recent years when the combination of modern rackets and a firmer base to the courts has speeded up the surface, is that artistry, not always evident on some surfaces, not only continues to thrive but has been given a sharper edge. While the finest clay courters should still prevail, certainly the finest all-rounders now have more incentive to shine, as demonstrated in 1996, when after dual successes for Jim Courier and Sergi Bruguera and a reward for Thomas Muster's persistence and fitness, Yevgeny Kafelnikov produced a performance of truly brilliant all-round quality to become the first Russian winner of a Grand Slam title, with a straight-sets win over Michael Stich.

Andre Agassi finally collected the title on his third final appearance following a five set thriller against Andrei Medvedev. Another colourful character, the effervescent Gustavo Kuerten took over at the turn of the century before the title was annexed by Spain barring one year when Argentina claimed it, the year before the flamboyant piratical Rafael Nadal burst on the scene in 2005.

Mary Pierce became the first home winner since Francoise Durr in 1967 when she overcame Conchita Martinez, a more experienced clay-courter 6-2, 7-5, in 2000. She was to make the final again five years later only to be humiliated by Justine Henin-Hardenne, the diminutive Belgian with a glorious backhand as she secured her second French title, a title she retained 12 months later.

WIMBLEDON

Wimbledon! Nowhere else in the world is there one place so synonymous with one very special sporting event. It is the oldest, the most famous and certainly the most prestigious tennis tournament in the world, held for two weeks at the height of the British summer on the perfectly manicured lawns of the All England Club. "That little bit of tennis heaven in London's SW19", was how "Teach" Tennant, then coach to the first women's Grand Slam champion, Maureen Connolly, once described it. And nearly 60 years on – despite extensions to stands and the site itself; a handsome new, purpose-built Court No. 1, plus the fact that demand for tickets continues to outstrip availability – the club is determined that the tournament should retain the ambience of tennis in an English country garden.

The story of how The Championships began is now part of sporting legend. Founded in 1868, the All England Croquet Club discovered in 1875 after one lawn had been set aside for the game of lawn tennis that, by the time the increasing rent for their four acres of land between Worple Road and the old London and South Western Railway had been paid, there would not be sufficient to pay for the repair of the pony roller.

"Why not hold a lawn tennis tournament?" it was suggested. It was agreed that this new game, which was increasingly popular among the country set of England, might be their salvation. It was through an announcement in *The Field* publication on June 9, 1877, that Wimbledon was officially born.

The announcement read:

"The All England Croquet and Lawn Tennis Club, Wimbledon, propose to hold a lawn tennis meeting open to all amateurs on Monday July 9 and the following days; entrance £1 1s [£1.05 in today's money]. Names and addresses of competitors to be forwarded to the Hon Sec before that day or on that day before 2.15 p.m. at the club ground. Two prizes will be given – one gold champion prize to the winner, one silver to the second player. The value of the prizes will depend on the number of entries and will be declared before the draw; but in no case will they be less than the amount of the entrance money or less than £10 10s and £5 5s."

As it happened 22 men entered and the winner, watched by 200 spectators paying 1s (5p), was Spencer Gore, a former captain of cricket at Harrow, who beat W.C. Marshall in the first final. The tournament was not completed until Thursday July 19 because no matches were possible on July 13 and July 14 as they would have clashed with the Eton vs. Harrow cricket match at Lords, which in those days was one of the major social occasions of the English summer calendar.

Incidentally, that roller now stands by Court19 on the walkway surrounding No1 Court, having been moved in 2006 from the old entrance to the Wimbledon Tennis Museum which has become not only an increasingly popular stop for tennis fans on the London tourist trail, but an evocative link between the past and the present. Until 1884, the men's singles was the only event. Then came the introduction of the women's singles, won from among 13 entrants in the first year by Maud Watson, and the introduction of the men's doubles which between 1879 and 1883 had been staged by the Oxford University Lawn Tennis Club.

The popularity of Wimbledon grew so swiftly that by the mid-1880s – when the prowess of the Renshaw twins was so evident and Lottie Dod became the youngest champion, at the age of 15, in 1887 – permanent stands began to replace the initial temporary accomodation. Even then there followed a period of such decline, until the Doherty brothers Laurie and Reggie re-awakened enthusiasm with their 10-year reign covering the turn of the century, that in 1895 The Championships actually lost money – £33.

Contrast that with 1997 when there was a record crowd of 405,327, so that the surplus – which since the mid-1930s has had to be handed over to the Lawn Tennis Association for the development of tennis in Britain – exceeded £31m, also a record. These days, the surplus has slipped to around the 27 million mark

What is it that makes players such as Federer, Venus Williams and countless other great champions before them so unequivocal in naming Wimbledon when asked which tournament they would choose if there was only one they could win in their life? What is it that makes hun-

dreds, sometimes thousands of people of all ages queue overnight for the daily quota of seats which have not been sold in advance, or simply soak up the special atmosphere by watching matches on the outside courts?

Tradition is obviously one factor. The grass is another. From time to time there are cries for it to be dug up and replaced by something less testing. Yet as Mats Wilander, who has won everything else on the Slams except Wimbledon, said, "They should never change it. They could destroy the tournament if they did so."

In fact, the All England Club constantly makes changes and improvements which blend in so well with what went before that they brilliantly give the impression that everything remains the same. But some things don't. Since 1900 The Championships have always started on the sixth Monday before the first of August, although the club has expressed a willingness to look seriously at the possibility of staging it a week later, to provide a third week between Wimbledon and the French Open if there is unanimous support from players and others involved. The winner of the men's singles always knows that he will be asked to open play on the Centre Court the following year at 2 p.m. precisely (except in 1997 when it was delayed to allow a full-scale opening ceremony of the new No 1 Court). And, of course, there is the predominantly white clothing rule.

In other respects, Wimbledon has been in the forefront of change. The men's singles entry, which had been growing annually, was fixed at 128 in 1924; seedings, which have varied in number from 8 to 10 to 12 to 16, were introduced to the men's singles in 1924, and qualifying began in 1925. Most significantly, though, it was Wimbledon, in conjunction with the LTA, which forced the rest of the world to end the hypocrisy of "shamateurism" by allowing Open tennis to begin in 1968. Records show that as far back as the mid-1930s, The All England Club was pressing the ILTF to accept Open tennis, but it was not until 1967, when Wimbledon stunned the rest of the tennis world by allowing a professional tournament to be

LOTTIE DOD, *Wimbledon's youngest champion at 15 years 285 days*

staged over three days on the Centre Court, that Wimbledon made it clear that, whatever anyone else did, they would accept professionals to compete against amateurs the following year.

The service line monitor was also a Wimbledon innovation which

the rest of the world adopted, together with increasingly sophisticated marketing techniques. As Wimbledon and the other Grand Slam tournaments have grown, physically as well as commercially, so too, thanks most of all to television, has its popu-

JIMMY CONNORS AND CHRIS EVERT *were engaged when they both won Wimbledon in 1974*

larity. *Breakfast at Wimbledon* has become a firmly established feature of NBC's summer in the United States even if, for Californians, it means rising by 6 a.m. to watch the first balls being hit in the finals.

In Australia such is Wimbledon's impact that there are regularly all-night vigils around television sets, especially in 1987 when Pat Cash became their first Wimbledon men's singles champion since John Newcombe in 1971.

It is impossible in the space provided to mention more than a representative sample of Wimbledon's greatest champions, matches and special occasions. The most outstanding individual achievements are recorded in other chapters of this book. Some, though, demand special respect.

To look at women first, throughout the generations there have been champions and personalities whose performances and exploits are engraved in Wimbledon history: Lottie Dod, of course, Dorothea Lambert Chambers, Suzanne Lenglen, Kitty Godfree, who actually became better known and loved when she was playing in her 80s than when she was Wimbledon champion in 1924, Helen Wills, Maureen Connolly, Margaret Court, Billie Jean King, Chris Evert, Martina Navratilova, Steffi Graf and now Venus Williams and Maria Sharapova.

On the men's side the selection of outstanding names from the past is tougher. No disrespect to the champions of yesteryear, particularly before the abolition of the Challenge

Round. Many would doubtless have been just as successful today, but the first man to make the same sort of impact as Lenglen was surely Britain's own outstandingly charismatic Fred Perry. The fact that his statue, situated on the left as you enter the grounds through Gate 5, on the side of the Tabernacle facing the front of the club house, underlines just how much he meant to Wimbledon and to British tennis. It is worth remembering, as Tim Henman, Greg Rusedski and now Andy Murray vie to become Britain's first Wimbledon champion since Perry in 1936, that Perry was the first British champion since Arthur Gore in 1909.

Nowadays, of course, the media pay far more attention to the personalities

and private lives of champions and considerably less to the strength and subtlety of their forehands and backhands, which is why modern champions such as Ilie Nastase, Bjorn Borg, Jimmy Connors, John McEnroe, Boris Becker, Andre Agassi and Pete Sampras make even more impact on the news than equally gifted post-war champions such as Rod Laver, Lew Hoad and the gentleman among all gentlemen, Stefan Edberg.

One of Wimbledon's greatest matches was undoubtedly the first women's singles final after the First World War, between Mrs Lambert

BORIS BECKER *in typically energetic and audacious form at Wimbledon in 1991*

Chambers, the defending champion from 1914, who still in those days did not have to play before the Challenge Round, and a 20-year-old French newcomer playing for the first time on grass, Suzanne Lenglen. Despite being weighed down by her years – she was nearly 41 at the time – and her starched petticoats against an audacious challenger whose one-piece dress ended daringly just below the knee, Mrs Lambert Chambers rallied from 1–4 in the final set to hold two match points at 6–5 but, as she recalled later, "My arm suddenly felt like cotton wool." Lenglen saved the first

match point by returning a lob with a shot off the frame which then even hit the net before dropping as a winner. At 40–30, it was Lambert Chambers' own shot which hit the net but bounced back on her side. She was to lose 10–8, 4–6, 9–7.

For brilliant comebacks, there have been few to match the extraordinary efforts by Henri Cochet in 1927 – the first year, incidentally, in which seeding was used in all five events for the first time, matches were broadcast from Centre Court for the first time and all eight players in the quarter-finals of the men's singles

were from overseas. Playing Bill Tilden, the towering American, in the semi-finals, Cochet was two sets and 5–1 down, but suddenly he went into overdrive. He hit 17 consecutive aces and dropped only two points over the next five games. It was suggested that Tilden, who eventually lost 6–3 in the fifth, had been hypnotized by a group of Hindus. In the final Cochet, who had also recovered from two sets down in the quarter-finals, did so yet again to beat fellow countryman Jean Borotra 4–6, 4–6, 6–3, 6–4, 7–5, after escaping a third match point at 3–5 in the final set with a backhand winner during a lightning volleying duel which many thought was a double hit.

Jack Crawford's 4–6, 11–9, 6–2, 2–6, 6–4 defeat of Ellsworth Vines in 1933 was another which fitted into the epic category, as indeed were Jaroslav Drobny's triumph against Ken Rosewall in 1953 and Stan Smith's defeat of Ilie Nastase in 1972. Among the women, the stuff of legends includes the combination of power and deft accuracy which Maureen Connolly deployed to win the second of her three successive titles in 1953, plus Steffi Graf's narrow escapes before beating Gabriela Sabatini in 1991 and Jana Novotna two years later. The magic memories, like Wimbledon itself, are never-ending with the most recent being Goran Ivanisevic, as a wild card entry, securing an incredible but popular five set victory over the favourite and equally popular Pat Rafter in 2001, and Roger Federer's remarkable four successive titles, plus the Williams sisters claiming between them, five of the six Championships between 2000 and 2005.

US OPEN

The first recorded tournament in the United States appears to have taken place in Nahant, Massachusetts, in August 1876, in which games spanning 15 points – as in rackets – were played. It was only after what was originally called the United States National

Lawn Tennis Association – the 'National' was dropped in 1920 and the "Lawn" in 1975 – was formed at a meeting of 34 clubs at the Fifth Avenue Hotel in Manhattan, New York, in 1881 that the first US national singles Championships were organized. They were staged at the Newport Casino under rules adopted from Wimbledon, using balls imported from Britain and even some British competitors. Indeed one of them, William E. Glyn, reached the final but was beaten by his Harvard opponent, Richard Sears, 6–0, 6–3, 6–2.

Sears, with the advantage of the Challenge Round, which was started in 1884 and abolished for the men in 1912 and the women in 1919, went on to win for another six years as the popularity of the game began to grow faster than the threat to his supremacy. His partner, with whom he won the doubles five times in six years, was James Dwight, one of the principal pioneers of American tennis.

The women's championships, singles and doubles, began in 1887 at the Philadelphia Cricket Club, although the doubles was not recognized as a championship event until 1889. It was not until 1935 that the men and women were united in one event at Forest Hills. The men had moved in 1915 from Newport to Forest Hills, where the event remained until 1977, except for a three-year stay at the Germantown Cricket Club between 1921 and 1923 while the new West Side Stadium was being built. The women had also moved to Forest Hills in 1921, but as a separate event. The first women's singles champion was Ellen "Nellie" Hanswell who, like all her rivals, according to reports at the time, "employed sidearm serves, sliced ground strokes and never, but never went to the net."

The launching of the Davis Cup was said to have been a major factor in the rapid increase of affiliated clubs in the United States, at a time when golf was also beginning to take hold, from 44 in 1900 to well over 100 eight years later, mainly concentrated on the east and west coasts. From California were to emerge May Sutton and Hazel Hotchkiss. May, later Mrs Thomas Bundy, won the US Championships in

PAT CASH joined Australia's list of Wimbledon champions in 1987

54

1904 at the age of 16. A year later on a return visit to England, where she had been born, she became the first American to win a Wimbledon title.

In essence, though, it was the events of the years immediately after the 1914–18 war – when Bill Tilden proved insuperable for six years among the men, Molla Mallory and Helen Wills dominated among the women and the new stadium at Forest Hills, at the time second only to Wimbledon in size, was built – which firmly established the competition. Despite the depression in the 1920s, there was no lessening of interest or support for the US Championships which by now were regularly attracting the support of the leading players from all over the world. Indeed from 1925, when Tilden's run of six consecutive victories ended, René Lacoste, Henri Cochet and Fred Perry won the title in five of the next nine years.

Cochet's defeat of Tilden in a 1926 quarter-final is generally regarded as one of the finest contests, at least during the first 50 years of the tournament. Cochet, such a shrewd tactician, somehow absorbed the speed of the American's serve and used it to his own advantage, storming the net at every opportunity and then volleying magnificently. Tilden, worried by a knee injury he had suffered a few days earlier, rallied from 1–4 to 4–4 in the fifth set with his own spectacular winners at the net, but Cochet again outwitted him with what Allison Danzig described in the *New York Times* as "counter strokes of craft".

During the 1939–45 war, tennis was only slightly restricted in the United States so that unlike Wimbledon, which was used as a military centre during the war leaving bomb damage to be repaired, the US Open swung straight back into full-scale action. In 1946, the gates at Forest Hills frequently had to be closed on capacity crowds – the first sign of a dilemma which all the Grand Slams suddenly faced with a vengeance after Open tennis arrived in 1968. A new name, Tom Brown, sped to the fore, beating Frank Parker and Gardner Malloy before losing in the final to Jack Kramer, who is also famous as the first to win Wimbledon wearing shorts.

BILL TILDEN, *whose cannonball serving won Wimbledon three times*

After Kramer in 1946–47, Pancho Gonzales was champion for the following two years although in 1949, after he had suffered several losses against reputedly lesser opponents, Ted Schroeder, fresh from victory at Wimbledon, was expected to snatch the title from him. The first set went to 18–16 and ended controversially with Gonzales suffering what was generally thought to be a bad call in the 33rd game. He lost the second as well but, as at Wimbledon an amazing 20 years later, Gonzales, feeling hard done by, roared back like a wounded tiger to win the last three sets 6–1, 6–2, 6–4.

Gonzales, of course, like a host of other Americans and Australians in particular who followed him, was an ideal candidate for the growing professional tours. So throughout the 1950s and 60s, until the game went Open, domestic triumphs at the US championships came principally from a generation of women players: Pauline Betz, Louise Brough, Margaret du Pont, Maureen Connolly, Doris Hart, Shirley Fry, and Althea Gibson.

Although they eventually came round to the idea and then gave Wimbledon and the British LTA influential support, it was no secret at the time that the USLTA fought long and hard for the game to remain amateur. Indeed during the first two years after amateurs and professionals were allowed to compete together, they continued to stage international US amateur championships at Longwood, Boston. On the other hand for the Open, at Forest Hills, they provided $100,000 prize money, making it the richest event in the world. Against most expectations, the professionals struggled and the final went to Arthur Ashe, still an amateur, who also won the US amateur title that year, beating the Netherlands' Tom Okker, a "registered" rather than full-blooded professional, inasmuch as he accepted prize money but remained under the jurisdiction of his national association. Virginia Wade, who fell into the same category, collected $6,000 as the first Open winner of the women's singles.

The following year was one of the most important in the life of Rod Laver for, by beating compatriot Tony Roche 7–9, 6–1, 6–3, 6–2, he became the only man to achieve the Grand Slam for a second time, in the same arena where Don Budge had made history as the first Grand Slam champion in 1938. Yet rain meant the final had to be held over until a third Monday when a further 95 minutes' delay was necessary while a helicopter hovered over the Stadium Court as part of a spectacular drying process. In the circumstances Laver's triumph, during which he switched to spikes to help his footing on the still-slippery grass, was witnessed by only 3,708 spectators, with none of the mass coverage it would warrant today.

Margaret Court, who won the women's singles, had her moment of Grand Slam glory the following year, when tie-breaks were introduced for the first time, while Rosewall became men's singles champion, despite playing for much of the match with a crack in the wooden frame of his favourite racket.

Thereafter the tournament continued to grow in popularity. Equal prize money was introduced in 1973, to the women's delight, with John Newcombe and Margaret Court both earning $25,000 by winning the singles. One year later it was goodbye

FLUSHING MEADOW, *the impressive new site of the US Open since 1978*

to grass, making it possible to unveil not only new green clay courts, much to the liking of Chris Evert, but also night matches under floodlights. However, not even two daily sessions could cope with the numbers thronging the West Side Club. The 1977 tournament, when Tracy Austin, 14, and John McEnroe, 17, made their first appearances, and trans-sexual Renée Richards, 42, lost in the first round to Wade but reached the doubles final with Bettyann Stuart, was the last to be played there.

Finding a new site within easy reach of Manhattan and with sufficient room for everything necessary to stage a Grand Slam tournament was not simple. There was an additional hazard, probably not fully appreciated at the time, in that the old Louis Armstrong Stadium, the chosen site, was directly under one of the flightpaths

MARIA SHARAPOVA *celebrates match point against Elena Likhovtseva during the U.S. Open*

in and out of La Guardia Airport. It was certainly a memorable first year. Pam Shriver, 16, armed with a Prince jumbo racket, reached the final before losing to Evert, and Connors, the only player to take the title on three different surfaces, defeated Bjorn Borg, who was destined to be no more successful at Flushing Meadows than at Forest Hills.

Others, though, have thrived at the new venue. In 1979 Tracy Austin, at the age of 16 years and 28 days, became the youngest winner of the women's singles, and Roscoe Tanner's bullet-serving broke not only the centre court net but also Borg's chances again before McEnroe claimed the title for the first time, beating Vitas Gerulaitis in the final.

There was the Borg-McEnroe classic final in 1980, the second of McEnroe's four wins. Connors went one better by winning five times and then there were three wins in a row for Ivan Lendl. Among the women, Evert, the six-times winner, Martina

Navratilova and later Steffi Graf and Monica Seles all produced great performances there.

In 1990, Pete Sampras made his mark for the first time, becoming the youngest champion ever at 19 years and 28 days. Some of his most thrilling and emotional matches have taken place there, not least his extraordinary quarter-final against the luckless Alex Corretja, who double-faulted on match point, in 1996. The fact that Sampras, who had been physically ill on court, went on to win his first Grand Slam title since Tim Gullikson, his coach, had died of cancer made it all the more poignant.

For many years the demands of TV decreed that on the second Saturday both the men's semi-finals would sandwich the women's final on 'Super Saturday'. This unfair practice was amended in 2004 to a more favourable programme scheduling the women's final to a fixed time in the evening. In 2006 both Andre Agassi and Martina Navratilova brought

the curtain down on their respective careers, unlike Pete Sampras who, having won his 14th Grand Slam title in 2002, simply faded from the scene.

THE WTA TOUR

Although 39 years after the advent of Open tennis women have not quite achieved parity with men in terms of prize money, there is little argument over how much the current superstars owe to those who fought – and mainly won – the battles to give the WTA Tour, and women's tennis in general, the recognition it has today.

In 2006, by means of 65 tournaments in 34 countries from January to November, players could compete for prize money totalling over $40m. Even allowing for the enormous inflation there has been in the meantime, such a jackpot is worth remembering when one recalls the struggle necessary to get the bandwagon rolling. One thinks particularly of Billie Jean King and Gladys Heldman, then publisher of the American magazine *World Tennis*. They were the tennis suffragettes of their day back in 1970.

While they did not exactly chain themselves to the railings of tournaments to underline the inequity between how much they and the men were being paid, their militancy was unmistakeable and justified. Matters came to a head when Jack Kramer, the 1947 Wimbledon champion who had become probably the leading tennis promoter in the United States, refused to improve the prize money structure for the Pacific South West Championships in Los Angeles.

He was offering a total of $12,500 to the men's singles winner and a meagre $1,500 to the winner of the women's singles. Billie Jean and her equally incensed, long-time doubles partner, Rosie Casals, decided it was time to act. They contacted Mrs Heldman, whose fighting spirit was inspired rather than doused when Kramer's response to being told there was a chance of the women boycotting his event was, "That's fine with me. I'll take the money set aside for the girls and add it to the pot for the men."

Things then moved quickly. Within days Mrs Heldman had used her contacts in Houston to organize an eight-woman event, offering $5,000 prize money, at the Houston Racquet Club. She also contacted her friend Joseph Culman III, then chief executive of Philip Morris Inc, who contributed a further $2,500 provided that they named the event after the new Virginia Slims cigarette being launched at the time.

On September 23, 1970, only a couple of weeks after Margaret Court had earned barely one-third of the amount collected by the men's champion for winning the women's singles at the US Open, Mrs Heldman gathered together nine players in her Houston home where they signed symbolic one-dollar contracts with World Tennis to

become contract professionals. It was the only way they could be reasonably sure of overcoming regular threats from the United States Tennis Association, which had refused to sanction the Houston event, that the players who took part would be banned.

The players who took that stance were Peaches Bartkowic, Rosie Casals, Julie M. Heldman, Billie Jean King, Kristy Pigeon, Nancy Richey and Val Ziegenfuss plus two doughty Australians, Judy Dalton and Kerry Melville.

A day later the USLTA sent telegrams to all the Americans involved, telling them that their membership had been suspended and they were therefore ineligible to play in the Grand Slams, the Federation Cup or the Wightman Cup. But the rebels refused to give in. The Houston tournament went ahead, as did two others, and by 1971 there was a genuine circuit in operation, involving tournaments in 19 cities.

By 1972, the "Original Nine" had attracted almost 50 others, but the biggest breakthrough came in 1973 when the USLTA sponsored a rival tour, featuring Chris Evert and Evonne Goolagong, whose fresh and exhilarating talents were now beginning to dominate the scene, but offering less money than the 22 events on the Virginia Slims Tour. Then on Sep-

PAM SHRIVER, *one of the feistiest competitors in modern women's tennis*

tember 20, 1973, Billie Jean King beat Bobby Riggs in the second of his "Battle of the Sexes" matches. A record crowd of 30,472, plus an estimated 50 million on television, watched this historic occasion when tennis first crossed the border between sport and showbusiness. The USLTA realized it could no longer curb, let alone control, the commercial progress of the game. Not only did they step aside and allow the Virginia Slims Tour to expand without hindrance but they agreed to give equal prize money to the men and the women at the next US Open – a situation which remains the same today with the Australian Open joining them in 2001 and Roland Garros in 2005, though the French limited the parity to just the Championship match. However, statistics still show that, given the choice, more people want to watch men's matches than women's matches. At the same time, women-only events, with the right field and especially in countries with their own top women players, generally thrive.

Ironically the current trend is for a return to closer harmony between the men's and women's circuits and not just at the Grand Slams. Since the success of the Nasdaq-100 Championships, the German, Italian and Indian Wells tournaments are now also combined events – if not wholly merged, then at least in successive weeks.

Nowadays the WTA Tour caters for more than 1,000 players representing some 76 nations and continues to embrace wider geographical representation.

It would be wrong to suggest that women's tennis has enjoyed nothing but success. There have been lean years when top-quality players with box-office appeal have been difficult to find. For too many years from the mid-1980s to the early 1990s, there was certainly a feeling that serious competition in the women's singles at the Grand Slams rarely began before the quarter-finals.

Apart from the rich crop of young and exciting new faces which have burst upon the scene in the last two or three years such as the Russians led by Maria

BILLIE JEAN KING, *carried off court in triumph after winning her "Battle of the Sexes" challenge against Bobby Riggs in 1973*

Sharapova, Ana Ivanovic, Tatiana Golovi and Sania Mirza , there is little doubt that the refreshingly positive style much more evident today has stemmed from the advances in racket technology. While it may have had an adverse impact on the men's game, it has made women's tennis more exciting.

Perhaps one of the most challenging tasks the WTA, together with the International Tennis Federation, has had to face has been the issue of age eligibility. Although Lottie Dod won Wimbledon when she was 15, making her the youngest player to win a Grand Slam singles title, it was decreed many years later that a girl had to be 16 before she could compete in the women's singles. It hardly seemed to be a problem until, in 1974,

a tall, slim, highly gifted Russian junior, Natasha Chymreva, was discovered to be 15 after she had won her first-round qualifying match for The Championships at Roehampton. She had to withdraw.

Subsequently the age barrier was dropped and, from 1976 until new age restrictions allowing youngsters to compete in a steadily growing number of tournaments between the ages of 14 and 17 were introduced in 1995, all sorts of age records were broken. Players such as Tracy Austin, who won her first title on the Avon Futures Tour in Portland, Oregon at the age of 14 years 28 days, and Steffi Graf were playing in Slams when they were still only 13. Andrea Jaeger, Pam Shriver, runner-up at the US Open when still 15 in 1978, Kathy Rinaldi and Jennifer

Capriati were among the more prominent teenage prodigies who followed. Yet it was not long, either, before it started to become obvious, not just among under-16s playing on the tour, but even more so among many more still trying to get their first foot on the ladder, that there could be serious problems for young girls playing too much tennis too soon.

Most were physical problems, resulting in ice packs being attached to knees, elbows, shoulders and almost anywhere else they could be perched on youngsters of school age. Of even more concern in many instances, and not only the highly publicized ones, was the psychological harm young girls could suffer when, instead of being able to grow up mentally and physically within their own

age groups, they were suddenly expected to cope with all the pressures of living in an exclusively adult world. For those who rapidly became dollar millionaires, the potential for disaster was all the greater.

In the early 1990s, even before Jennifer Capriati's world began to collapse, research into the problem was well underway. After at least two years of extensive discussions with players, parents, coaches, doctors, trainers and psychologists, in 1995 age eligibility rules, effectively limiting the number of adult tournaments girls can play between the ages of 14 and 18, were introduced.

Allowances were made for players such as Martina Hingis, who made her debut on the tour before the rules came into effect, and Anna

Kournikova, who had already given notice that she intended to play professional events when she was 14. The one codicil added to the rules has been that once a player is 15 she is allowed to play in one or more of the four Grand Slams, provided her world ranking gives her direct entry.

Perhaps the other most significant innovation by the women's tour was the decision in 1984 to have a best-of-five-sets final at the end-of-the-year Championships, the first in women's tennis since the US Open women's singles five-set final was abolished in 1902. Even so it was not until 1990, when Monica Seles just outlasted Gabriela Sabatini, that it became necessary for five sets to be played. It only happened twice before it was discontinued in 1999, most spectacularly in 1996 when Steffi Graf had been pushed to the brink by Hingis, then just 16, who made it two sets all but was so mentally and physically drained that she had nothing left to give in the 6–0 decider.

The honours list at the Championships, dating back to 1972, underlines the credibility of the Tour for there have been only 15 different winners in 35 years – Chris Evert, Evonne Goolagong, Martina Navratilova, Tracy Austin, Sylvia Hanika, Steffi Graf, Gabriela Sabatini, Monica Seles, Jana Novotna Martina Hingis, Lindsay Davenport, Serena Williams, Kim Clijsters and Amelie Mauresmo – and all bar Hanika have either been on top or in second place in the world rankings.

Margaret Court holds the record for the most titles won in a season on the Tour, 18 in 1973, followed by Billie Jean King with 17 in 1971 and Evert and Navratilova who in their most successful year each won 16 titles. The longest winning streak was achieved by Navratilova who, after losing to Hana Mandlikova in the Virginia Slims at Oakland in January 1984, won 74 consecutive matches before losing to Helena Sukova at the semi-finals of the Australian Open on December 6 that year. She had won 13 titles in the

VENUS WILLIAMS, *one of the new generation of exciting players bringing fresh magic to the women's game*

meantime. Evert won a staggering 125 consecutive matches on clay between August 12, 1973 until May 12, 1979 when Austin beat her, though only by 6–4, 2–6, 7–6, in the semi-finals of the Italian Open in Rome.

THE ATP TOUR

Strictly speaking, the history of the ATP Tour only dates back to 1990. That was the first year in which the players, through the delegates they elect and the officials they appoint, broke away from the combination of players, tour directors and International Tennis Federation representatives which used to administer the circuit under the banner of the Men's Grand Prix.

Curiously enough, by 1998, clear signs were emerging that the ATP Tour, despite several considerable achievements in the meantime, was coming back round to the idea that a united tennis family, with all the various members playing their part, might not be such a bad thing after all.

The Grand Prix circuit, forerunner of the ATP Tour, was the brainchild of Jack Kramer, the former Wimbledon champion and successful tournament entrepreneur, who in the early days of the old Association of Tennis Professionals was their president. It began in 1970, sponsored by the ILTF, as it was in those days, and Pepsi-Cola, bringing together 20 of the traditional tournaments in three different categories. It was a radical attempt to provide an orderly organization for the tournament calendar, with players earning points according to the category of the event which then qualified them for a top bonus prize of $25,000 at the end of the year.

The Grand Prix at that stage began in Bournemouth in April and ended with the Swedish Indoor Championships in Stockholm in November. It included Wimbledon, the French Open and US Open, but not the Australian. The initial year-ending winner was the American Cliff Richey, followed by Arthur Ashe, Ken Rosewall, Rod Laver and Stan Smith. The top six also qualified for the inaugural Grand Prix Masters,

staged in Tokyo and played at that time as a round-robin, offering a further $15,000 to the winner. Richey had to drop out because of illness and victory went to Smith, who was about to be conscripted into the US forces.

By 1974, with Commercial Union now providing the overall sponsorship, there were 48 tournaments, including the Australian Open, but most of them were crammed into the second half of the year after the World Championship Tour had completed its worldwide circuit of 26 tournaments. This often provided different tournaments in the same week, one in Europe, the other in the Americas. In what became known as "the race to Dallas", the top eight competed not merely for a top singles prize of $100,000 but for various other baubles, such as a solid gold tennis ball and one year even a share in an oil well.

With the WCT Tour being held for the last time in 1977, the Grand Prix became a monolithic 95-tournament marathon the following year. After a worldwide tour from Tokyo, to Paris, Barcelona, Boston, Melbourne, Stockholm and Houston in the meantime, the Masters was given a permanent home in New York's Madison Square Garden, where it stayed until the players went their own way.

Those early Masters had produced their fair share of excitement and controversy. The manner in which Guillermo Vilas beat John Newcombe, Bjorn Borg and Ilie Nastase on grass at Kooyong in 1974 was a breathtaking achievement for a player brought up entirely on clay. A year later in Stockholm there was the extraordinary spectacle of first Arthur Ashe and then Ilie Nastase being disqualified in the same match

JACK KRAMER, *who supported the men's boycott of Wimbledon in 1973*

ARTHUR ASHE, *a fine player and a great ambassador for the sport*

minated." Ramirez was disqualified.

Yet 40 minutes later, while Stahr was telling his side of the incident to journalists, a head popped round the press room door to announce, "Hey, they're playing again." Tournament officials had decided that Ramirez should be re-instated and the match resumed with a different umpire, though the Mexican did not win another game.

Arguments continue to rage over the legitimacy of a round-robin format before the semi-finals. Traditionalists certainly find it hard to accept a structure which allows a player to lose but remain in the tournament and, fairly frequently, go on to finish as champion. Indeed, on only five occasions since the Masters became the ATP Tour Championships in 1990 has the champion finished with a 5-0 record. They were Michael Stich in 1993, Lleyton Hewitt in 2001 and 2002 and Roger Federer in 2003 and 2004. In the other 15 years the Champions – Sampras five times, Becker twice and Alex Corretja, Gustavo Kuerten, Federer and David Nalbandian – have all lost one of their round-robin group matches.

For three years, starting in 1982, a 12-man knockout format was introduced. This was partly to prevent the abuse which seemed apparent on some occasions when, because the winner of one group automatically played the runner-up from the other

STEFAN EDBERG, *one of the modern game's most stylish serve and volleyers*

group in the semi-finals, it suited some not to finish as group winner. This way the public were assured of seeing every player in at least three matches, and this prompted a return to round-robin preliminaries in 1986.

Since 1990, the Grand Slam tournaments, though independent of the Tour, continue to count as far as world rankings are concerned. Indeed they rightly offer more round-by-round and bonus points than any of the other tournaments which fall into three categories, the Masters Tennis Series, such as Miami, Indian Wells, Monte Carlo, the German Open and Italian Open; the International Series Gold; and the International Series. Below that there is an ever-growing circuit of challenge events and satellite circuits, the latter financed largely through national associations or the ITF.

There are close to 2,000 players with world rankings, while the 68 principal events in 2005 were spread among 31 countries and there were 30 different winners from 15 countries. The most significant change during the 25 years since ATP itself was formed has been the decline in American dominance and the progress of the game in Europe, thanks to such champions as Borg setting the example in Sweden, Yannick Noah in

– and then being reinstated. It happened on the opening night. Ashe was leading 1–6, 7–5, 4–1 when the American, exasperated by the constant time-wasting, protesting and general antics of his opponent, could take no more and walked off, just as German referee Horst Klosterkemper, who had already warned the Romanian, was about to intervene. "I was about to disqualify him for refusing to continue the match," Klosterkemper explained. "But then Ashe left and wouldn't return so I had no alternative but to disqualify them both."

That posed a dilemma for it would have taken two players out of a four-man group in the round-robin section of the tournament. The next day, on the intervention of new ILTF president, Derek Hardwick, it was decided that the match should be awarded to Ashe, as his offence was regarded as the less serious, but that Nastase should be allowed to play his remaining matches. He did so with such awesome ability that he still qualified for the semi-finals where he beat Vilas and then defeated Bjorn Borg

for the loss of only five games in three sets in the final.

One year later, there was more drama on court and behind the scenes. Raul Ramirez, the Mexican, seemed to be drifting between interest and boredom in his error-strewn match with Brian Gottfried in Houston. Having made no attempt to return a serve when the American led 2–0, 30–15 in the third set, Ramirez said he thought he had seen the linesman raise his arm to indicate a fault and asked Jack Stahr, one of the most respected umpires in the United States, for a let. Stahr, for some inexplicable reason, asked Gottfried if he was prepared to give one. The linesman said he had neither called nor signalled – the outstretched arm, it transpired, belonged to a courtside photographer. Gottfried passed it back to Stahr. Ramirez persisted in his claim for a let and by now the crowd was starting to take sides. Stahr ordered him to play on, eventually telling him he had only 10 more seconds to comply. The Mexican, almost mockingly, raced to his position, but Stahr counted him out and announced, "This match is ter-

Rosie Casals (left), Julie Heldman, Billie Jean King and Ann Jones

France, Boris Becker in Germany and a host of talented players in Spain.

Over those 35 years, by the start of 2006, 23 different players had held the number one ranking, starting with Ilie Nastase, who stayed there for 40 weeks in 1973 and followed by John Newcombe (eight weeks), Jimmy Connors (268), Ivan Lendl (270), Mats Wilander (20), Stefan Edberg (72), Boris Becker (12), Jim Courier (58), Pete Sampras (286), Andre Agassi (32), Thomas Muster (6), Marcelo Rios (6), Carlos Moya (2), Yevgeny Kafelnikov (6), Patrick Rafter (1), Marat Safin (9), Gustavo Kuerten (43), Lleyton Hewitt (80), Juan Carlos Ferrero (8), Andy Roddick (13) and Roger Federer (100).

Prize money for the men has soared from around $1.3m in 1969, just before the Grand Prix began, to more than $75m today, with more than 330 players having become at least dollar millionaires. Sampras outstrips them all. His prize money alone totalled $43m, followed by Agassi with $30m, Becker with $25m, and Kafelnikov, $23m.

DAVIS CUP

There are few team events in any sport, not just tennis, which have stood the passage of time so well as the Davis Cup. It is a competition which remains as relevant today as it was when it was first devised with the dawning of the twentieth century, in 1900. Indeed, with the structural changes to the format of the competition in recent years, the Davis Cup probably does more now to spread the tennis gospel than at any other time in its history, even though still further ways of adapting the format to meet the growing commercial and social needs of the time are under discussion. Certainly the name Davis Cup is synonymous with the sport of tennis the world over and it provides a magnificent flagship for the International Tennis Federation, whose former president Philippe Chatrier used to call it "the blue riband of the sport".

As with so many other things in the history of tennis, the Davis Cup has a strong Anglo-American background. In 1900, Dwight Filley Davis

NICOLA PIETRANGELI *holds the record for playing the most consecutive Davis Cup rubbers and ties*

from St Louis, Missouri, then a 21-year-old leading American player who had just graduated from Harvard, donated a trophy for international competition. Such an idea had been talked about for years, but when eventually it came to fruition only two nations, Britain and the United States, were able and willing to take part.

The trophy was a massive solid silver punchbowl, lined with gold and valued at that time at $1,000. Today,

even without the extra bases which have been added to accommodate the names of the players in nearly 100 winning teams, it is priceless – if not in monetary terms, then certainly in a historical sense. The first three times the Davis Cup was staged – there was no event in 1901 when Britain could not provide a team to travel – Britain and the United States were the only countries which took part so only one match was needed. In 1904, though,

when the United States temporarily dropped out, Belgium and France accepted invitations to play a preliminary match to determine which of them would challenge Britain for the trophy. Belgium won but then lost to Britain, or the British Isles as it was then called, 5–0.

Nowadays, it enjoys the support of a record 134 nations, a staggering figure which itself has more than doubled in the last 20 years. Yet only 12 countries have so far won it – United States, Australia, Britain, France, South Africa, Sweden, Italy, Czechoslovakia, Germany, Spain, Russia and Croatia.

Over the years, as the appeal of tennis has expanded to all parts of the world, a growing number of countries have wanted to feel part of the big time by entering the Davis Cup – and the structure of the competition has had to change. The first major development came in 1923, by which time there were 16 entries and it was found necessary to introduce two zonal competitions, one based in America, the other in Europe, with the matches in Europe beginning in mid-May. Countries from outside these two continents were allowed to enter the zone of their choice, but their matches still had to be staged in that geographical area. The winners of the two zones would then play each other to decide which of them would go on to compete against the previous year's winners in the Challenge Round.

It was in that inaugural year of zone matches that a 17-year-old prodigy by the name of René Lacoste, who was to become the fourth of the French "Musketeers", made his first appearance in the Davis Cup for France against Denmark in Bordeaux – and lost his opening match. Two other developments of note in that year were that the British Isles became Britain for the first time and that Ireland, North and South, competed together as they still do today in both tennis and rugby union, though not in soccer.

By the time Britain, inspired by Fred Perry, was enjoying its Davis Cup golden years in the mid-1930s, there were 24 teams regularly competing in Europe. Separate North and South American zones had their own play-off before the inter-zone final. Then in later years, when the American zones combined again, an Eastern zone was started. Even with the advent of a second European zone, though, the competition was starting to become enormously unwieldy and that, combined with the arrival of Open tennis, meant several years of crisis for the competition.

For the first three years after amateurs and professionals were allowed to play in the same tournaments, the Davis Cup was restricted to those listed as "registered players" – those who could take prize money in open tournaments but still accepted the authority of their national association and were therefore also eligible for so-called amateur competition. The problem with that was that major nations, such as the United States and, in particular, Australia – who had been assuming that once again they would be able to call upon their full complement of talent after a decade in which almost everyone winning Wimbledon or the US Championship had turned professional – found that was not so.

If that was not enough, political problems over South Africa's participation led to some teams defaulting rather than play against them – including India in the 1974 final – and demonstrations at some games, such as the 1969 European zone final when bags of flour were thrown on to the court during South Africa's 3–2 defeat by Britain in Bristol. The apartheid issue first came to a head when the South African government refused a visa for Arthur Ashe to play in a tournament in Johannesburg. Following months of impassioned debate, it was agreed that, while the South African tennis officials themselves could not be blamed, their Davis Cup membership, stretching back to 1913, should be suspended from the 1970 competition. They were reinstated two years later, but placed in the American zone south,

THE DAVIS CUP, *which has grown from two teams in 1900 to a record 131 entries in 1998, is about to celebrate a centenary*

where it was hoped there would be less likelihood of teams refusing to admit them. The following year, though, Argentina withdrew rather than play South Africa in a zonal match and India defaulted the final for the same reason. In 1975, Mexico and Colombia followed suit and claimed that defaulting them was unfair because they were merely following United Nations policy and that of the International Olympic Committee.

The frequent impasses as countries refused to play South Africa continued until South Africa voluntarily withdrew, ostensibly "to prevent further damage to the competition" – a situation which remained until they were welcomed back following the official ending of apartheid in 1992.

During these years, there seemed to be one problem after another. In 1973, although the barring of contracted professionals was lifted, the boycott of Wimbledon by 93 of the leading men players stemmed from a Davis Cup controversy. Niki Pilic, who had turned professional in 1967 and joined World Championship Tennis, refused to play for Yugoslavia in a tie they would then have been expected to win against New Zealand. The Yugoslav Federation suspended him for nine months. On appeal to an emergency committee of the ITF, this was reduced to one month but was still too long to allow him to compete at Wimbledon. Hence 92 other players withdrew to support him.

There were also other political hot potatoes. In 1976 the Irish government would not allow its team to play Rhodesia, who, realizing that Egypt, their next opponents, would follow the same line, withdrew. There were attempts, strongly supported by the United States, Britain and France, to suspend any nation which withdrew for political reasons. The move was defeated, leading to threats from the three prime movers of the motion to quit. No sooner had this crisis been averted than Russia refused to play Chile that year on the grounds that human rights were not being observed by the Chilean junta. Just to add to the confusion for the game's administrators, Russia, Czechoslovakia and Hungary withdrew from the Federation Cup

NIKI PILIC. *His suspension led to the Wimbledon boycott*

about to be held in Philadelphia, in protest against the inclusion of South Africa and Rhodesia.

Meantime other momentous decisions had been taken. In 1971, recommendations from a working party that it was time to axe the Challenge Round, which by then was giving too great an advantage to the defending champions each year, were accepted. The United States, the 1971 winners, therefore had to play through to the final in 1972. Although they then won a classic 3–2 victory in Bucharest against Romania – when Stan Smith smiled away his inner anger at blatantly bad calls by Romanian linesmen to beat Ion Tiriac and give the Americans a winning 3–1 lead – the abolition of the Challenge Round was still a symbolic moment in Davis Cup history.

Until then only four countries had won the Davis Cup. During the next nine years, when the structure was changed again with a World

Group and a steadily growing number of lower-ranked groups being introduced, there were five different winners, three of them (Sweden, Italy and South Africa) for the first time. Since then, Germany has been added to the honours board, while the introduction of promotion and relegation has led to a healthy interchange of nations in the top division, including some new stars such as Zimbabwe (Rhodesia), Switzerland and Denmark.

By the start of the 2006 Davis Cup, the records showed that 149 different countries had taken part at some time since 1900. The United States continued to boast the most wins, with 31, followed by Australia with 28, Britain 9 (though all of them before the abolition of the Challenge Round), France 9, Sweden 7 (all since Bjorn Borg's arrival made tennis such a major sport in that country), Germany 3, Spain 2, Czechoslovakia, Italy, South Africa (on a walkover) Russia and Croatia one

each. A further 8 countries have played in finals.

A succession of great American players – most notably Bill Tilden, who played in a record 11 Challenge Rounds with a 17–5 singles and 4–2 doubles record, followed in the Open era by Arthur Ashe, Stan Smith, John McEnroe and Pete Sampras, to name just a selection – have helped emphasize the American domination. Two of them, McEnroe and Sampras, actually made their debut in World Group finals. McEnroe did so in 1978 when Britain, having unexpectedly trounced Australia in the semi-finals, faced the Americans in a December final in Palm Springs, where the temperature fluctuated from a balmy 70 degrees as McEnroe beat John Lloyd in the opening rubber, 6–1, 6–2, 6–2, to below freezing, with icicles hanging off the lemon trees by the time Buster Mottram pulled Britain level with a five-set defeat of Brian Gottfried.

That was the only British success. The United States won 4–1, but in 1991, when Sampras made his debut in one of the most emotional finals most can remember at the Palais des Sports in Lyon, he effectively froze under the pressure of such a high-powered occasion and lost a vital first-day singles to Henri Leconte 6–4, 7–5, 6–4. Worse still for Sampras was that he also lost to Guy Forget, 7–6, 3–6, 6–3, 6–4, in the rubber that made France, exuberantly coached by Yannick Noah, champions for the first time in 57 years. Jean Borotra, one of their 1932 heroes, was among the first to congratulate them in the locker room.

Since then, Sampras has more than restored his Davis Cup big-match image – never more so than at the Olympic stadium in Moscow in 1995 when he first beat Andrei Chesnokov over five sets in the opening rubber, was called up unexpectedly to partner Todd Martin for a match-turning victory in the doubles and then fought off exhaustion for a 6–2, 6–4, 7–6 victory over Yevgeny Kafelnikov to give the United States a winning 3–1 lead. It was a weekend of epic commitment at the highest level.

Even so it is an Italian, Nicola Pietrangeli, rather than an American who holds the record for playing both the most Davis Cup rubbers and the most ties. He represented Italy 66 times and played in 164 rubbers. His singles record was 78–32 and his doubles record 42–12. In contrast, Roger Federer the World No1 from Switzerland, is selective with his appearances. At the start of 2006 he had played in 13 ties and achieved a 19-6 record in singles.

A Davis Cup match is decided over five rubbers, with two singles on the first day, the doubles on day two and the reverse singles on day three. In recent years the rules have been relaxed so that, in the case of a confirmed injury, a player can be replaced. This was not always the case. Choice of venue, once the draw has been made depends on where those countries met the last time they were in Davis Cup competition since 1970. The team which had to travel on the previous occasion has home advantage the next time. Only if the teams have never met before, or at least not since 1970, is there then a draw to see which of them will be at home.

In recent years, as the depth of competition has increased and neutral umpires as well as neutral referees have been introduced, some officials have been concerned about the time many rubbers take to be played. Despite the introduction of tie-breaks in all but the fifth sets in 1989 and the reduction of dead rubbers, once one team has a winning margin, to best-of-three-set contests, there has been a growing tendency for first-day matches, especially, to take seven hours or more to be completed. Thus the whole structure of the competition is regularly reviewed. One change frequently mooted by one or two leading players, including Pete Sampras, is that the Davis Cup should only be staged every other year – and never in Olympic years – because of the added pressures it places on players.

FED CUP

The Fed Cup began life as the Federation Cup in 1963, celebrating the 50th anniversary of the Internation-

al Tennis Federation – more than 40 years after the idea had first been mooted. It was in 1919 that Mrs Hazel Hotchkiss Wightman, impressed by the success of the Davis Cup, suggested that a similar international team competition should be introduced for women. The problem was that, with the exception of the United States and Britain, there was insufficient support for the idea among ITF member nations, whose own organizations in those days were almost exclusively male-orientated.

Undaunted, Mrs Wightman launched what became an annual USA vs. Britain women's competition, bearing her name and played in alternate years in the two countries. She continued to hope that one day her original dream would be realized, but it was not until 1962 that Mary Hardwick Hare, the former British Wightman Cup player who was living in Chicago at the time, rallied enough support to present a dossier to the ITF which demonstrated the clear need for such a worldwide competition. Approval was given for a team competition to begin the following year, staged over one week on a knockout basis at a different venue each year.

The first Fed Cup was staged at Queen's Club in London. There were 16 entries, with each team comprising two singles players and a doubles team. The countries who took part in the inaugural event were Britain, United States, Australia, France, West Germany, Italy, South Africa, the Netherlands, Canada, Belgium, Switzerland, Czechoslovakia, Hungary, Denmark, Austria and Norway. The matches were scheduled to be played on grass, but heavy rain made all the outside courts unplayable so they had to be switched to the indoor courts on wood – a new experience for many of the players.

The United States were the first champions, but only after a thrilling final before a capacity indoor crowd, during which Australia's Margaret Court lost only three games to Darlene Hard with an awesome effort in the opening rubber. Billie Jean Moffitt, as she was then, levelled the match by recovering from 5–7 in the first set

to win the next two 6–0, 6–0. Then, in the decisive doubles, the Americans made a last-minute change of nomination, choosing Hard and Moffitt in preference to Hard and Carole Graebner. Three times they broke back when the Australians were serving, to win 3–6, 11–9, 6–3.

Over the next eight years, the Australians and Americans continued to dominate as the event toured Philadelphia, Melbourne, Turin, Berlin, Paris, Athens, Freiburg and Perth before South Africa, with home advantage in Johannesburg, joined the list of winners. Between then and 1997, they were joined on the honours list by Czechoslovakia, Spain and France, while the number of venues visited – until there was a complete change of format, along Davis Cup lines, in 1995 – took in Bad Homburg, Naples, Aix-en-

Provence, Eastbourne, Madrid, Tokyo, Santa Clara, Zurich, Sao Paulo, Nagoya, Prague, Vancouver, Atlanta, Nottingham and Frankfurt (where it remained for three years, 1992–94).

In the early days before prize money was introduced, many nations did not have the funds to send teams and often players met their own travelling and accommodation charges. Things began to change with the advent of sponsorship.

Before sponsorship there was also a considerable social as well as competitive element to the event, with one day kept completely free in the middle of the week for everyone involved – players, officials and the media – to be taken out together by the host nation. Each Fed Cup week provided its own special memories, but perhaps none more special than

MARY HARDWICK HARE *masterminded the founding of the Fed Cup*

THE ITALIAN TEAM *celebrates after winning the Federation Cup final against Belgium in 2006*

in 1986 when Martina Navratilova, by then a US citizen, returned to her native city of Prague to play for the Americans. Her reception from the crowds was tumultuous, and clearly of some embarrassment to officials of a communist country who for so long had banned more than token mentions of her successes, since her defection, in Czechoslovakian newspapers.

Fittingly, the final was between the United States and the hosts. Chris Evert gave the Americans the lead by beating Helena Sukova, 7–5, 7–6. Then, in the match every tennis fan was waiting to see, Navratilova, who had been in the first Czechoslovakian team to win the trophy with a 3–0 defeat of Australia in Melbourne in

MARTINA NAVRATILOVA *remained philosophical when a 10th Wimbledon title eluded her*

1975, faced Hana Mandlikova, who in the three previous years had led Czechoslovakia to victory. There were no doubts who most of the capacity crowd wanted to win. It must have been demoralizing for Mandlikova to listen to the roars of approval for each Navratilova winner in a 7–5, 6–1 victory, but it was the only way the public could respond to the political shackles which allowed them so little freedom of expression.

As the number of teams taking part grew, the competition was becoming too unwieldy to be staged in one place in its original form. So in 1992 regional qualifying rounds were played to produce 32 teams for the final stages. Now the format has settled with 16 nations contesting a World Group played over three weekends, with four teams progressing to the Group Finals played at one venue. All other countries compete in

Regional Qualifying events, a necessity considering over 100 nations enter nowadays.

WIGHTMAN CUP

This women's competition began in 1923, and was exclusively between the United States and Britain. It was a best-of-seven rubbers match, comprising five singles and two doubles. Mrs Hazel Hotchkiss Wightman, winner of a record 45 US national singles and doubles titles, who donated the trophy, also played in the American team which won the first match 7–0.

Over the years every leading American and British woman player took part. The matches were staged alternately in the United States and Britain (usually at Wimbledon until it

switched from the summer to late autumn and followed the American example of visiting different parts of the country). America's dominance, which made sponsorship and credibility increasingly difficult to attract, led to the event being dropped after 1989 when the Americans were leading 51–10. A 21-and-under version continues with USA and Great Britain teams competing for the Maureen Connolly trophy.

LEGENDS OF THE COURT

It may be a cliché to say that great champions in the majority of sports are born not made, but it is certainly true and cannot be stressed too often. In tennis this is certainly the case.

Of all the qualities which go into the make-up of a champion, natural flair and ability are obviously two of the essential characteristics. Yet another which provides a common thread among the 14 stars of the game featured here, is a special form of stubbornness – a determination not so much to be awkward in a negative way but to succeed against all odds and obstacles, real or imaginary, which they felt at the time were stacked against them and, more often than not, to come out on top.

On many occasions it has been demonstrated not so much in an act of bravado – although there have also been plenty of them – but as a clear act of defiance … a sort of "I'll show you!" response to any person or incident which is seen to be provocative or deliberately intimidating by opponents, officials or even spectators.

One glorious example involved Bjorn Borg at the Italian Open in 1978. He was playing the Italian favourite, Adriano Panatta, and before the match had started Italian officials had made a special appeal urging spectators to be fair to the Swede, bearing in mind the outrageous manner in which the crowd had baited the Spaniard, José Higueras, in the match in the previous round, doing everything they could to unsettle him as Panatta clawed his way back to victory from 0–6, 1–5.

The appeal fell on deaf ears and Borg was clearly furious, protesting to the umpire when coins started to be thrown at him when the match went into a fifth set. Yet he regained his composure and found the perfect way to halt the attacks by calmly going round, picking up the coins and then putting them in his pocket! It was game, set, match and even more lira to him.

A constant driving force for Fred Perry, was to cock a snoot at every opportunity against the game's establishment, especially The All England Club and the Lawn Tennis Association, which in the strictly amateur, upper-class attitudes in tennis in the 1930s really did not know how to deal with this upstart son of a Labour MP. He eventually forced them to realize that success in tennis went far beyond the bounds of wearing an old school tie after the game had finished.

Similarly, in more recent times, Jimmy Connors and John McEnroe epitomised the rebellious, cavalier attitutude of young men in a hurry to reach the top which, thanks probably to the Beatles as much as anyone, was starting to become what we now regard as the norm today – when respect for others is minimal and every rule is made, if not to be broken, then at least to be stretched, and whereby every possible loophole is a loophole that needs to be explored.

Others, such as Steffi Graf, show stubbornness through their extraordinary brave battle to overcome career-threatening injuries. Others with less pride in their performance and less determination to stay at the top, would no doubt have lost a similar fight.

SWEDISH *tennis star Bjorn Borg being congratulated by tennis legend from the past, Fred Perry after winning the 1978 Wimbledon final*

AGASSI

REBEL WITH A CAUSE

An icon of the modern game, Andre Agassi became an inspiration to players in a career spanning over two decades. Acclaimed the savior of American tennis when that country's dominance in the sport was on the wane, he became the rebel who embraced the establishment having helped establish the sport as a major global attraction.

Andre Agassi

Born: *April 29, 1970*
Las Vegas NV, USA

At 36 years of age, Andre Agassi brought his career to an end at Flushing Meadows following his third round loss at the 2006 US Open. Ordinarily a retirement wouldn't cause much more than a ripple in the self centered bowl of professional tennis but in this instance, the 23,000 people packed into the Arthur Ashe stadium, rose as one to acclaim a living tennis legend.

They gave him a five minute standing ovation and he responded tearfully, acknowledging their warmth. "The scoreboard says I lost but what it doesn't say what I have found," he said in a voice cracking with emotion and tears filling his eyes. "Over the last 21 years, I have found loyalty, you have pulled me up on the court and also in life. In my last 21 years I have found you and will take the memory of you with me, for the rest of my life."

That will also be the case as far as millions of tennis fans are concerned, especially those who had the fortune to watch him at any stage of his remarkable career.

Andre Kirk Agassi was born and raised in Las Vegas. He was always a showman and first burst onto the tennis scene from the Nick Bollettieri hothouse in Florida as a long-haired 16 year-old tennis prodigy with a flair for outlandish tennis clothing.

In his formative years on the tour he was perceived a rebel, even going as far as snubbing Wimbledon by refusing to compete between 1988 and 1990.

However his relationship with Wimbledon changed dramatically over the years as he admitted that his love affair with tennis really blossomed within the walls of the AELTC.

It all started in 1992 when the mild-mannered, soft spoken American unleashed his blistering returns to beat former champions Boris Becker and John McEnroe on the way to defeating Goran Ivanisevic over five sets for the Wimbledon title. That year he also helped the USA regain the Davis Cup, a trophy he first helped them win two years earlier.

Since then he has amassed a total of eight Grand Slam titles including four Australian and two US Opens and is only one of five men to have won all four Grand Slams during his career.

In those far-off days, Agassi admitted he "hated" just about everything about Wimbledon, in particular their insistence on making him play in whites when he was renowned for his colourful outfits. All that though, changed as he matured both as a player and individual, a feat he attributes to Wimbledon: "This is where it all started for me. It's 14 years ago but it feels like yesterday. This Championship has allowed me to grow into the player and person I am today and I have so many people to thank for that."

His fighting ability, his spirit, his service returns, his ability to turn defence into attack where the main features of an aggressive base line game which accrued him 60 titles. But more importantly, he inspired other players and became a legend amongst them. Lleyton Hewitt, for instance, declared "He'll go down as one of the

guys that changed our sport in many ways. Not only by the way he played the game but the way he conducted himself both on and off court, the kind of character he was."

Hewitt, himself a former Wimbledon champion who beat Agassi in the semi-finals en route to his first title in Adelaide 1998, added "For me growing up, he was an idol. Especially on grass, I drew a lot of confidence from watching him win Wimbledon."

The extrovert double French Open champion Rafael Nadal picked up on his place in history. "He's a legend. It is very difficult to win on all the surfaces. You need to have a very complete game and that's very, very difficult. Only special players can do that."

Pat Cash, another former Wimbledon champ, recalled: "After McEnroe and Connors retired, Andre was the savior of men's tennis. He was tremendous for the game by capturing the imagination of youngsters the world over. The world owes him a huge vote of thanks."

He was introduced to tennis by his father Mike who boxed for Iran in the 1952 Olympics but no one could have guessed at what a roller-coaster of a career he would have whilst remaining so firmly in the public eye, despite prolonged periods when he effectively opted out of the tennis scene. Fewer had the chance at the age of four to be filmed hitting with great champions such as Bjorn Borg, Ilie Nastase and Harold Solomon. Fewer still, even before Agassi's marriage to the American stage actress Brooke Shields – whose grandfather, Frank, had to concede the 1931 Wimbledon

final through injury – could boast such a galaxy of the leading players in Hollywood among their friends.

Agassi, who is also renowned for his charity work, especially helping underprivileged children, lost his desire for the game after winning Olympic gold in Atlanta in 1996 and in less than a year slipped from eighth in the world rankings to below 140 before deciding he would attempt to start from scratch again.

Then he roared back to the fore collecting the French Open and US Open crowns in 1999 plus two more Australian Open titles. He also reached the final at Flushing Meadows on two other occasions. He was voted the ATP Player of the Year in 1999 and married Steffi Graf, herself the holder of 22 Grand Slam singles titles, in October 2001 with whom he has two children, Jason Gil and Jaz Elle.

Five-times women's Grand Slam champion Martina Hingis provides the best epitaph when she commented: "He's an inspiration in many ways. I don't think there will ever be another Andre Agassi and I am sure tennis will miss him."

CAREER MILESTONES	
1990	Won inaugural ATP World Championships in Frankfurt; helped USA to Davis Cup title
1992	Won his first grand slam title at Wimbledon
1994	Defeated five seeded players to win US Open title to become first unseeded champion since 1966
1996	First American to win Olympic singles gold since 1924.
1999	Won the French Open for first time and his second US Open.
2000	Became first player to reach four consecutive Grand Slam finals since Rod Laver's winning Grand Slam year of 1969.

BORG

THE ICE MAN

The Swede with the long, blond locks was the first professional tennis player to receive pop star adulation at Wimbledon where he was invincible for five years.

Bjorn Borg

Born: *June 6, 1956*
Sodertaljie, Sweden

During the US Open in 1980, an enterprising travel agent delivered a letter to every desk in the Press Box at Flushing Meadow, detailing cheap flights he could arrange from anywhere in the world for tennis writers to cover the Australian Open. He, like many others, was convinced that Bjorn Borg, who had already won the French Open and Wimbledon for a third successive year, was bound at last to break his duck in New York and become only the third man to win the Grand Slam in Melbourne three months later.

The fact that, despite losing a remarkable 18–16 tie-break in the fourth set of the Wimbledon final, Borg had gone on to beat John McEnroe in the fifth set to keep his title at the All England Club strongly reinforced the view that this really would be his year. But it was not to be. Borg was on record after that most dramatic of his five Wimbledon successes as saying, "I want to be the best ever."

His preparations were not ideal. A knee injury forced him to retire during his Canadian Open final against Ivan Lendl, and the US Open draw told him that if he reached the last eight he would again face Roscoe Tanner, the thunderbolt server from Lookout Mountain, Tennessee, who had served him off the court at the same stage of the tournament a year earlier.

Tanner boomed down the aces – 19 of them – to lead by two sets to one and a break. For once that stubborn streak for which Borg was famous came to the rescue, just as it had done against McEnroe at Wimbledon two months earlier. The "Slam" was still on and he was living so dangerously, even having to come back from two

sets down against Johan Kriek in the semi-finals, that it appeared that fate was taking a hand. He had lost in 1976 and 1978 to Jimmy Connors, and now it was McEnroe standing between him and glory.

While lacking the artistry of their Wimbledon final, the New York final was almost as thrilling, if only at times because both players made so many unexpected unforced errors. With Borg's serve deserting him frequently, McEnroe won the first two sets 7–6, 6–1, but Borg took the next two 7–6, 7–5, at which point the American said, "I thought my body was going to fall off." But it held together well enough – or rather, Borg's serve faltered again and then his dreams fell apart, for two more double-faults cost him the break in the seventh game and McEnroe won it 6–4. So Borg, who was to lose to McEnroe in four sets in the 1981 final, two months after the American had ended his five-year reign as Wimbledon champion, was left without either a Slam or the US Open title to his name, and there is little doubt that it was his realization that he would never achieve them which prompted his premature retirement from the game at the age of 27.

Bjorn Rune Borg burst on the scene with what became his trademark, shoulder-length fair hair, controlled by a headband, at Wimbledon in 1973. The slim youngster, who much preferred to rally persistently from the back rather than venture beyond the service line, had fallen in love with Wimbledon when he won the junior boys' title a year earlier and he often spoke of "that magical feeling I have every time I pass through the Church Road gates".

So often success in all walks of life can depend on being in the right place

at the right time. That was certainly so in Borg's case in the summer of 1973, for the strike by 93 members of the ATP Tour, after Wimbledon upheld a suspension imposed on Niki Pilic by the International Tennis Federation for a Davis Cup dispute with his native Yugoslav association, meant the tournament was crying out for a new, glamorous and talented personality. Borg, thanks to his age, appearance and talent, answered the call. He may not have boasted the most athletic appearance, with his round shoulders and his quick-stepping gait, but by the end of the first week he was the player all the girls especially wanted to see and special arrangements had to be made to prevent him being mobbed every time he walked from the locker room to the players' restaurant.

Borg's initial talent – and his double-handed backhand – was encouraged by Percy Rosberg – the same coach who realized when Stefan Edberg was in his early teens that his more aggressive style made it essential for him to change from a two-handed to single-handed backhand. It was during his 12 years with Lennart Bergelin, though, that Borg's skills began to blossom. He was still a few days short of his 18th birthday when he won his first major title at the Italian Open in 1974. With his immaculate topspin and quick court coverage, in addition to a more than worthy serve and a commanding authority from the back of the court, he was almost invincible on European clay for the next seven years. As time went on, he also registered significant triumphs indoors and, most of all, on grass.

Two weeks after his first triumph in Rome, he became the youngest champion at the French, a record since lowered by Michael Chang, while in 1975 his performances made Sweden the Davis Cup champions for the first time. He did so with his 19th consecutive victory in a Davis Cup rubber, a record he extended to 33.

Yet it was at Wimbledon that

Borg's star shone brightest of all. Idolized by young followers, especially in his native Sweden, where the constant flow of champions in his wake is testimony to his impact, he reached the quarter-finals in that first year before losing to Britain's Roger Taylor. There were blips in the next two years and suggestions that perhaps the strain of his success made the expectations on him too heavy a burden. In 1974 he lost tamely to the Egyptian, Ismail El Shafei, and in 1975 to Arthur Ashe, the eventual champion, but from then until McEnroe ended his ruthless dominance in the 1981 final, Borg won a record 41 consecutive rubbers. In two of the years in which he won both the French and Wimbledon crowns, there was only one week in between for him to recover both mentally and physically to go from clay to grass.

Although he made two unsuccessful attempts to return to the circuit, in 1984 and then seven years later when he lost somewhat ignominiously to Jordi Arrese in his first match, Borg says he has no regrets. "People say I could probably have won more Grand Slams and it's probably true, but the decision was mine and I'm glad I made it."

CONNOLLY

THE STUNNING BUT ALL-TOO-BRIEF CAREER

Just when it looked as if "Little Mo" was on course to become the most successful post-war champion, a horse riding accident when she had still not reached her 20th birthday, forced the retirement of a player who had already won nine Grand Slam titles.

CAREER MILESTONES		
1951	Won French and US Championships at age of 16.
1952	Won first of three consecutive Wimbledon titles.
1953	First woman to achieve the Grand Slam.
1954	Won Australian singles and doubles titles but also broke her leg in riding accident and retired.
1969	Died from cancer.

Maureen Connolly

Born: *September 17, 1934*
Died: June 21, 1969
San Diego, CA, USA

The most remarkable of many outstanding features about Maureen Connolly was that although she was naturally left-handed, she became one of the great players of all time playing right-handed.

She wrote with her left hand and used her knife at a dinner table in the left hand. But Wilbur Folson, a tennis coach in San Diego, who spotted enormous natural talent in the youngster who first came to him to earn pocket money as a ball girl, informed her that no one had reached the top in tennis as a left-hander, so she would have to learn to play right-handed instead.

One would never have guessed from watching the delightful tennis Maureen was to produce in her momentous, though tragically brief, international career. Maureen's mother wanted her daughter to become a prima ballerina and the way she moved about a tennis court was poetry in motion.

Maureen was much happier riding horses, a love she was to maintain later with her husband, Norman Brinker, but she realized that there would not be enough money for her to pursue horse-riding as a career and gradually her interest in tennis grew. It was at the instigation of a member in the first club she joined that she met the top woman's coach in those days, Eleanor "Teach" Tennant. It was a fateful move.

In 1951, aged 16, Maureen beat Shirley Fry 6–3, 1–6, 6–4 to win the US Championships at Forest Hills and for the next two years she had an astonishing unbroken run of success at the highest level. On her first visit to Wimbledon as a 17-year-old in 1952, Maureen, who had already won Surbiton and Manchester and helped the Americans win the Wightman Cup again, developed a shoulder injury in practice during the London Grass Court Championships (now the Stella Artois tournament for men only) at Queen's Club. Tennant, who had worked with Alice Marble and Bobby Riggs, told Maureen that she should withdraw from Wimbledon rather than risk further damage which might have very serious long-term consequences. The advice was not appreciated.

Maureen called a press conference to announce not only that she would compete at The Championships but that she had sacked Miss Tennant as her coach. At the time it seemed a hasty, precocious act. Three weeks later, however, "Little Mo" was Wimbledon champion for the first time, although the British player, Susan Partridge pressed her so severely that in the third set the American was 4–5, 15–30 with only a second serve to come before the killer instinct returned, just in time. She was to win the ladies' singles three times before she was 20, conceding only that set and another to Thelma Long, also in 1952. She also won the US Championships in three successive years, the French Championship twice and the Australian in 1953 when she became the first woman to win the Grand Slam.

What needs to be remembered is that her dominance came during what was generally regarded as one of the most formidable periods in the history of women's tennis in the United States, for others champions such as Doris Hart, Louise Brough, Margaret du Pont and Shirley Fry were all her contemporaries.

By any yardstick, then, Connolly will always be affectionately and admiringly remembered as an outstanding champion, who was not just invincible in her own time but easily worthy of being listed as one of the best of all time. In 1953 when, as top seed, she dropped only eight games in five matches before beating Doris Hart 8–6, 7–5 to complete her successful defence of the title at Wimbledon, J.L.Manning, one of Fleet Street's finest sports columnists wrote in the long-since defunct *Sunday Dispatch*, "There will never be perfection in sport but I was near to seeing it at Wimbledon yesterday."

In that same year, Connolly also figures in the most one-sided doubles final in Wimbledon's history – though on the wrong side. Partnered by Julie Sampson, a Californian whose principal role was as chaperone for the 18-year-old, they reached the final but were then routed 6–0, 6–0 by Hart and Fry. It was the only serious blot on her record in that Grand Slam year. Just three weeks after winning the US title in 1954, Maureen, not yet quite 20, was out riding on her favourite horse, Colonel Merryboy, when a cement lorry ran out of control round a blind corner. As the startled horse shied, Maureen was thrown and the animal crashed down on top of her twisted leg.

This champion – who was such a perfectionist that when she was once asked what her funniest experience had been in tennis replied, "I have never had one, my tennis was always a very serious business" – was never to play tennis again, although she was determined to continue living as rich a life as ever. She married Norman Brinker, who had been a US Olympic rider, and had two daughters, Cindy and Brenda, who have also played their part, with their mother's great friend and former tennis partner, Nancy Jeffett, in spreading the "Little Mo" gospel of tennis through the Maureen Connolly Tennis Foundation, established in Dallas not long before she died of cancer aged just 34.

Maureen once wrote on the subject of Wimbledon: "Here was the realm of my hopes, my fears, my dreams and, as long as I live, I shall be there in spirit, savouring the glory, tasting the heartbreak." The glorious memories of everything she achieved live on.

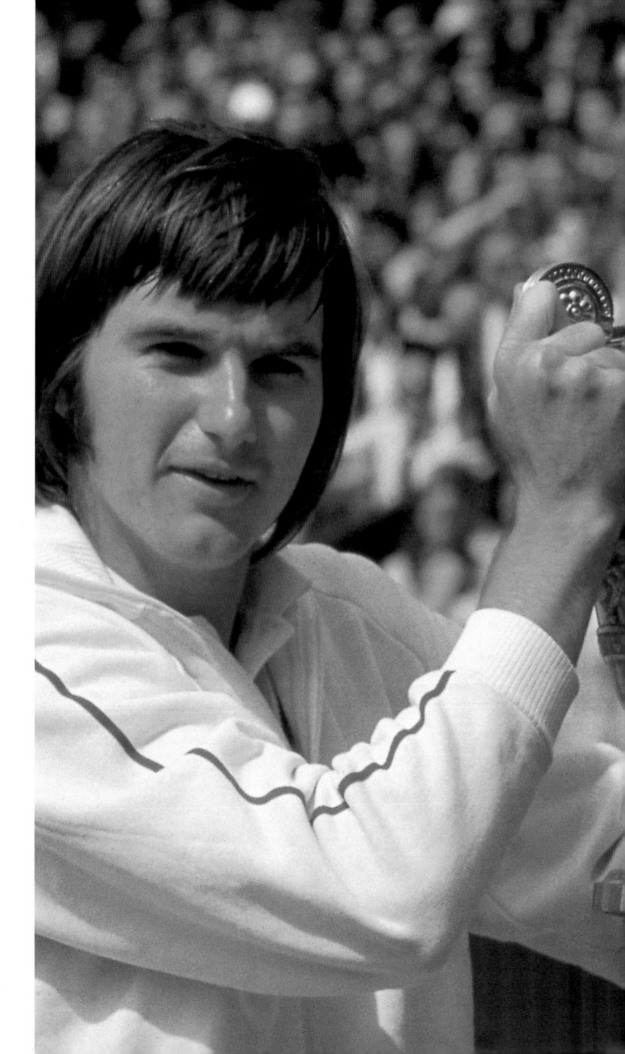

CONNORS

SWASHBUCKLER SUPREME

To him almost every night was like the opening night of a new production with him determined to steal the show by fighting until his opponent buckled.

Jimmy Connors

Born: *September 2, 1952*
Belleville, IL, USA

A poll among readers of *Tennis Magazine* in the United States in 1995 voted James Scott Connors the most exciting player of the past 30 years. To that might also have been added, the greatest showman and the most intense fighter. These traits, which were to help the 5ft-10in left-hander win what is still a record 109 singles titles in the Open era and hold first place in the world rankings for 268 weeks, as he became one of the most durable champions in the history of the sport, were inherited from his mother, Gloria, herself a fine player.

Having moved to California when still a teenager, Connors came under the influence of the two Panchos, Gonzales and Segura, and some of their attitude to life and other people also rubbed off on him. Indeed Segura, himself once the finest entertainer on the court, described Connors as "a real killer with the heart of a lion" after he had watched him produce "unbelievable tennis" to overwhelm Ken Rosewall for the loss of only six games for his first Wimbledon crown in 1974.

"The first thing I noticed when he first came to me for coaching when he was 15 was his mental approach and pride in his own performance. Even when he lost to me while still a kid, he was steaming." That never changed. Not only major defeats such as the enormous blow to his pride when he was outsmarted by Arthur Ashe in the 1975 Wimbledon final, but losses later in life, when the body was no longer able to react quickly and powerfully enough to the instructions the brain was giving it, left him seething with discontent.

Connors, also shrewdly managed in the early years of his career by Bill Riordan, won his first professional title in Jacksonville in 1972. His last came 18 years later in Tel Aviv. In between he was to become the only player to win the US Open on three different surfaces, grass (1974), clay (1976) and hard (1978, 1982–83), Wimbledon for a second time no less than eight years after his first triumph there (1982) and the Australian, still then on grass, in 1974.

There was a ruthless streak of independence about him which meant he had little time for established practices or even traditions. His deliberate failure to participate in the parade of former champions on Centre Court when Wimbledon celebrated its centenary in 1977 led to him being booed the following day when he walked out to play. For years he steadfastly refused to become a member of the Association of Tennis Professionals. And in 1974, after he had been banned from the French Open for signing a contract to play in World Team Tennis, he began lawsuits eventually amounting to $10m against ATP and its president, Arthur Ashe – with whom he also crossed swords severely when Ashe became the US Davis Cup captain. Connors is convinced that the issue also cost him the Grand Slam, for he would certainly have been favourite to win the French, as well as the other three majors in that year and had a win-loss match record of 99–4. The dispute and the involvement of Ashe certainly added spice to their Wimbledon final in 1975, when Connors was so completely outwitted.

He was happiest playing in the United States, especially after the US Open moved from the private club atmosphere of Forest Hills to the noisy, brash surroundings of Flushing Meadow. That was where his swashbuckling approach came into its own. In 16 of the 19 years he played at the Open, he reached at least the quarter-finals. His most dramatic year there was not one which ended with him as champion but 1991, when most regarded him as a spent force.

In 1990, having been troubled by an elbow injury for many months, Connors had played only three matches and lost them all; his ranking dropped to 939. Following surgery, however, he was, as he put it "smoking again". He still needed a wild card to play in the Open, but his wily experience, together with his still extraordinary skill and willpower, carried him through to the semi-finals in a series of matches full of heroics.

His first victim was Patrick McEnroe, who could do nothing, once the crowd helped the Connors bandwagon to start rolling, to turn his two-set lead into victory. Next it was the turn of Michiel Schapers and 10th-seeded Karel Novack to be swept on one side. Then up stepped fellow American Aaron Krickstein, but it was Connors' 39th birthday and absolutely nothing, not even a 5–2 deficit in the fifth set, was going to be allowed to spoil the party.

In the quarter-finals Dutchman Paul Haarhuis won the first set, but became so nervous when confronted by what he felt was the intimidatory nature of the crowd, that he lost the next three. It was left to Jim Courier to douse the Connors flames, which he did most effectively 6–3, 6–3, 6–2, but

the former champion will certainly have plenty to tell his grandchildren when he recalls the time he became the oldest semi-finalist in New York since Ken Rosewall reached the final in 1974. And the player who beat Rosewall then? Jimmy Connors.

Even then Connors was not done. The next year he was back again, celebrating his 40th birthday by beating Jaime Oncins of Brazil. It was his 98th win at the tournament – also a record.

Apart from the titles he won, Connors reached 54 other finals, playing and winning more tournaments than any other male professional before or since. His comeback adventures against his main rivals were monstrous. He saved four set points to win a vital third-set tie-break 11–9 on his way to beat Bjorn Borg in the 1976 US Open final and was three points from defeat before beating John McEnroe over five sets in the 1982 Wimbledon final. The heart continues to beat as strongly as ever and the fists to punch with that same demonstration of intent and bravado in the Seniors' Tour – which the champion, who told us never to expect him near a tennis court again once he retired from the main circuit, did so much to launch and develop.

COURT

CHAMPION SUPREME

No man or woman has matched the amazing record in Grand Slam tournaments of a girl who learned to play tennis by sneaking through a fence to watch others on courts near her home. And no other player can pass her achievement of winning the Grand Slam as both a singles and doubles player.

Margaret Court
Born: *July 16, 1942*
Albury, NSW, Australia

The first thought which came into Margaret Court's mind after she won the US Open in 1970, to become the first woman to achieve the Grand Slam in the Open tennis era, was not one of instant joy but, quite simply, "Thank God that's over." In fact it wasn't. The Australian, popularly known as "Big Marge", was to continue adding to her still-unchallenged record of Grand Slam tournament titles for another three years, although she now says with hindsight, "I probably shouldn't have played much more after that."

From 1960 when, as a 17-year-old, she beat Maria Bueno to win the Australian singles title for the first of 11 times, she won virtually every event that was worth winning, many of them several times, to set records which one doubts will ever be broken. Her Grand Slam titles alone add up to 62 – 24 in singles, six more than Martina Navratilova, 19 in doubles (compared with 31 by Navratilova) and 19 in mixed doubles, four more than Doris Hart, who is next in this category with 15. Add to that major titles at the Italian, the German and South African Championships, all held in great esteem at the time, and the total soars to 92. Her last significant triumph, 15 years after her first, came at Forest Hills in 1975 when she and Virginia Wade defeated Billie Jean King (who had become her chief rival for singles honours and Rosie Casals in the doubles final).

Her most memorable year, of course, was 1970 when she became only the second woman after Maureen Connolly to complete the Grand Slam

although, as she was to recall many years later, it did not have the same cachet which it does today. There was hardly any mention of it at the time, especially in Australia. "I saw Rod win both his Grand Slams and really nothing much was made of them at the time. You have to remember that there was no TV or the money which there is today to make such a big thing of it and it wasn't until I came back to the circuit after getting married that the idea of me going for a Grand Slam started to become a major goal."

Indeed when seven years earlier, she and fellow Australian, Ken Fletcher, had become the only partnership so far to have achieved the Grand Slam in mixed doubles, it passed by with hardly a mention and certainly not the recognition there would be in similar circumstances today. Margaret Court, whose fierce serve and sharp volleys made her such an attacking force in women's tennis, was also an all-court competitor in every sense of the word. She was one of the few top singles players who also enjoyed consistent success in mixed doubles. Indeed, she is the only player who has won the singles, doubles and mixed titles at all four of the Grand Slams and been triple champion at all of them bar Wimbledon – two more records which surely will never be broken.

Now the Reverend Margaret Court, this devout Christian began life as Margaret Smith in fairly humble circumstances in the River Murray border town of Albury, in New South Wales. The young Margaret used to sneak on to local courts through a hole in the netting to play until Wal Rutter, who was club groundsman as well as professional, chased her and her friends away. It was not long,

though, before he sensed the enthusiasm and determination of this skinny youngster and he encouraged her to make tennis her primary recreational activity.

Progress was swift. Junior titles were soon being achieved. Her first trophy, won in a local 12-and-under tournament when she was still only 10, was a Buddha statuette. "It brought me luck and stands in a special place among the many trophies I won later," she says. Rutter asked Frank Sedgman to cast an eye over his protégée. The 1952 Wimbledon champion was immediately so impressed that he not only decided to coach her, but arranged for the then 15-year-old to be given a job by a Melbourne sporting goods company. The first priority was to impress upon her the need for physical fitness. She needed little encouragement.

It was not only because of her height and weight that Margaret Court was to become the fittest and strongest player in women's tennis until Martina Navratilova showed the benefit of such training to a whole new generation of players. Many years later Margaret told the renowned Australian journalist Murray Hedgecock: "I sometimes enjoyed the training and fitness side more than the tennis. It was a joy for me to do, but for many people it isn't. At that time I was looked down on. No woman ever did that sort of training, but fitness was what Martina Navratilova had over other players and it was probably the same with me."

Never was that more evident and decisive than in 1970 when Margaret outlasted Billie Jean King, 14–12, 11–9, the longest Wimbledon women's singles final on record, lasting 148 minutes. What made this epic

victory even more remarkable was that it came four years after she had initially retired, saying she was "tired of the rat race of international tennis". Yet little more than 12 months later she returned, after her marriage to Barry Court, an international yachtsman whose father was the prime minister of Western Australia.

In 1971, Margaret reached the final of all three Wimbledon events, but suffered three defeats. From then until her real retirement when she was 33, in 1977, she returned to Wimbledon, between the births of a son and a daughter in 1973 and 1975, when, although beaten by Evonne Cawley in the semi-finals, she made it a triumphant swan-song by winning the mixed with Marty Riessen. Religion was now becoming an increasingly important part of her life and when finally her rackets were put away, she said: "I shall not play any more tournament tennis. If I had been meant to play tennis again God would have led me to it, but it is no good playing if my heart is not in it. There might be a lot of money involved, but that does not matter. Wimbledon and Forest Hills mean nothing beside my beliefs." She was ordained the Reverend Court in 1991.

CAREER MILESTONES

1960	Won Australian title. Remained champion for seven years.
1962	Won Australian, French and US titles.
1963	First Wimbledon title.
1965	Again won three Slams – runner-up at the French.
1969	Three Grand Slam wins, Australian, French and US.
1970	First woman in open era to achieve Grand Slam.
1973	Won Australian, French and US titles.
1975	US Open doubles champion, last of her 62 Grand Slam titles.
1991	Ordained the Rev. Court.

FEDERER

THE SWISS MASTER

Roger Federer is setting new standards which his successors will find hard to beat once he decides to lay down his racket. With nine Grand Slam titles already to his name the 25 year-old sits fifth on the all-time major winners list and is being acknowledged by many former stars as the best ever.

ROGER FEDERER

Born: *August 8, 1981*
Basel, Switzerland

No one thought in that summer of 2001 that within just a few years, Roger Federer would be hailed as possibly the greatest tennis player ever. The occasion was Federer's fourth round victory over his idol Pete Sampras when he ended the Wimbledon champion's 31 match-winning streak on the lawns of the All England Club 7-5 in the fifth set and, in the process, prevented the American from possibly equaling Bjorn Borg's run of five consecutive titles.

At the time Federer described it as "the biggest win of my life", adding appropriately, "Obviously its something special for me." What no one realized is how special that moment was to prove for five years later, he was in turn dominating the game, raising standards to new levels having collected nine grand slam titles to be well on course to overtake Sampras' record of 14 and equal the Swede's five consecutive Championship wins achieved back in the late seventies.

Federer was always considered to have an exceptional talent. He won Junior Wimbledon in 1998 and broke into the top 100 the following year, aged 18 years and 4 months but, despite that victory over Sampras, it wasn't until 2003 that he made his mark at the top levels when he captured his first Grand Slam title at Wimbledon to become the fourth player behind Borg, Pat Cash and Stefan Edberg to win both the senior and junior titles at The Championships.

That victory became the real turning point in the Swiss star's career, for, from that moment, he virtually became unbeatable. At Grand Slam level he won eight of the 13 majors that followed, the only one to elude him being the French Open. He also collected 7 titles from 9 finals in 2003, and in each of the two following years won 11 ATP titles, plus 3 Masters Series in 2004 and 4 in 2005 having claimed back to back Master Cup victories (2003–04)

His dominance is best illustrated by the fact that in 2004 he became the first player since Mats Wilander in 1988 to win three Grand Slam championships in a calendar year and only the fourth to have achieved that in the Open era (Jimmy Connors in 1974 and Rod Laver in his Grand Slam year of 1969) – a feat he was to repeat in 2006 to become the first player to do it twice. In the process he defeated every other player in the top ten and established a new Open era record of winning 13 consecutive finals.

The following year, 2005, he again dominated the rankings and became only the fifth player to be ranked at No1 throughout the year, a feat he again repeated in 2006. His streak of winning consecutive finals was finally broken at 24 when he lost to David Nalbandian in the Masters Cup final at Shanghai. However, he remains unbeaten on grass since 2003 establishing a successive 48-match winning streak (overtaking Borg's 41) to increase, by the end of 2006 (having added a further 4 Masters Series titles and 6 from the ATP Tour to his tally) his bank balance to over $27million from prize money

alone. That year, his eighth as a professional, the Swiss Master also became the first player to win three consecutive Wimbledons and three consecutive US Opens in the same three years!

His fluid and effortless game is a delight to watch, in great contrast to his main rival, the muscular Spaniard, Rafael Nadal, the player who not only prevented him winning the French for a first time, but also took a set off him in the 2006 Wimbledon final, his fourth back-to-back.

He has great court coverage and is always able to raise his game at the vital and critical moments of a match. Pressure rarely gets to him as the majority of his opponents seemingly find themselves at a disadvantage before they step on court, such is his stature within the locker room. He is the master on court, controlling points in much the same manner as a conductor would his orchestra, with spin and slice, change of pace and angles, all suitably backed up with a solid, commanding and accurate serving.

John McEnroe, a tennis legend himself, believes Federer could well be the most talented player to have ever graced the sport and as a result, has won numerous awards, including the prestigious Laureus World Sportsman of the Year and the ATP Player of the Year, both in 2004.

His demeanor – soft spoken, polite and self assured – hides a steely determination on court which is not necessarily mirrored off court where he has pursued charity work with great purpose, becoming a UNICEF Goodwill Ambassador

and forming his own Roger Federer Foundation to help South African children. He was also quick to support the Tsunami and Hurricane Katrina appeals following those disasters.

His relationship with fans is also strong. He rarely misses an opportunity to sign autographs and is always available to speak to the media, fully accepting the responsibilities which come with being the World No1 and the need to promote the sport at all levels.

A remarkable person and player who fully deserves all the accolades which have been showered on him in recognition of his achievements. The next few years should see this personable former ball boy from Switzerland, who speaks six languages and was chosen to be his country's flag bearer at the opening ceremony for the 2004 Olympics in Athens, go on to even greater heights.

CAREER MILESTONES

1998	Won Junior Wimbledon title and ended year as Junior World No1.
2001	Defeats defending champion Pete Sampras in Wimbledon quarter-final.
2003	At Wimbledon wins his first Grand Slam.
2004	Won Australian Open, Wimbledon and US Open. Ends year as World No.1.
2006	Becomes only second player in modern era to reach the finals of all four Grand Slams in the same year losing just the French. Victories at Wimbledon and US Open make him the first player to successfully defend his titles over the same three successive years.

GRAF

THE GOLDEN GIRL

Not only has she won more major titles than her contempories but has done so against the background of considerable strain and stress both on and off court.

Steffi Graf

Born: *June 14, 1969*
Bruhl, Germany

Until 1997, when her year was ruined by injuries, Steffi Graf had won at least one Grand Slam title in each of the previous 10 years, an achievement surpassed only by Chris Evert who, despite winning three fewer Grand Slam titles (18) than the German, spread her successes over an even more astonishing 14 years. Yet in terms of success in the Open era, Stephanie Marie Graf has a record which surpasses all others, including Martina Navratilova.

Between August 1987, when she first assumed leadership of the women's world rankings, until March 1997, by which time the injuries were taking their toll and she was overtaken by Martina Hingis, Graf had spent 374 weeks as number 1, well ahead of the previous record of 331 held by Navratilova and more than a 100 weeks more than the best so far on the men's circuit, 270, held by Ivan Lendl.

By the summer of 1997, when she needed surgery on her left knee after it had let her down in the quarter-finals of the French Open, she had 103 titles to her name, a total beaten in modern times only by Navratilova and Evert. When she won the US Open in 1995 she became the only player ever to win each of the four Grand Slam tournaments at least four times.

These are just some of the achievements in the career of this fair-haired, powerfully athletic figure who, had she not been a tennis player, might well have excelled as a 400-metre runner. Indeed in 1988 it was found that her time over the distance would have placed her third among German woman athletes hoping to

win selection for the Olympic Games in Seoul.

Graf's first major success was beating Evert, eight times the champion, at Hilton Head in 1986. The following year, a few days before her 18th birthday, came the first of her Grand Slam victories, when she beat Navratilova 6–4, 4–6, 8–6. It was 1988, though, that was the big year when she not only became the first woman in Open tennis history to complete the Grand Slam but also made it a golden slam by winning gold in Seoul, when tennis returned to the Olympic Games for the first time since 1924. She won eight other titles and finished with a match record of 71–3, losing only to Gabriela Sabatini (twice) and Pam Shriver – and that was at the Virginia Slims Championships when she was suffering from flu, ending a run of 46 consecutive victories.

Until 1988 Graf had not carried the happiest memories of the Australian Open. Indeed on her first visit in 1983 she slipped on the wet grass at Kooyong and snapped a tendon in her right thumb. However, on the pristine hard courts in the brand-new stadium just across from the River Yarra, all went well for the top seed who reached the final against Evert, for the loss of only 22 games in 12 sets. With Graf leading in the final 2–1, the grey skies gave way to such heavy rain that, although the roof was closed, making it the first indoor Grand Slam tournament final, there was a delay of 89 minutes before it could resume. "For two weeks I've seen a blue sky and all of a sudden I see a black roof," said Evert, who was the one more disorientated by the changed conditions. It was only after Graf had sped to 6–1, 5–1 and served for the match at 5–2 that Evert's old fighting instinct surfaced and, although the more

experienced American forced a second-set tie-break, her young opponent's flowing serves and superb forehands turned the screw again to win it 7–3.

Next stop on the Grand Slam trail was Paris, where Graf was the defending champion. This time such was her dominance that she retained the title in less than five-and-a-half hours' playing time. With Evert losing to Arantxa Sanchez Vicario in the third round and Navratilova to Natasha Zvereva in the fourth, only Sabatini, who was beaten 6–3, 7–6 in the semi-finals, provided the champion with more than token resistance. Poor Zvereva was so nervous in the final that she did not even do that. Graf won 6–0, 6–0 in 32 minutes. It was the first whitewash in a women's Grand Slam final since Wimbledon 1911 when Dorothea Lambert Chambers trounced Dora Boothby.

At Wimbledon, where Graf began with a 6–0, 6–0 victory, she dropped a mere 17 games en route to the final, but there things were different and at 5–7, 0–2 it looked as if she would again fall prey to Navratilova's more rounded attacking game. Suddenly, with a dramatic change of gear, Graf's sledgehammer forehand took charge and, from losing six consecutive games, she won the next nine to win 5–7, 6–2, 6–1.

So it was on to Flushing Meadow, where illness forced Evert to default the semi-final. Sabatini, the only player to have beaten her all year at that stage, tried pluckily to repeat the winning formula, but Graf's stronger nerve, as well as that forehand, gave her a 6–3, 3–6, 6–1 win – and the Grand Slam. Graf and Sabatini were also to meet in the gold medal match in Seoul, but again the German, despite wavering in the quarter-finals against Larisa Savchenko, hit not just a flood but a torrent of forehand winners before modestly saying of the glorious peak in her historic year, "I'm amazed. I came here really tired after New York, not expecting too much from myself. I think this is something

that not many people after me will achieve."

In the decade which followed, Graf's joy on court was interspersed with personal and physical pressures. Four times she needed surgery, once on each knee, once on each foot, quite apart from a chronic, inherited back problem. All the while, too, there was the controversial lifestyle of her father, which regularly filled more column inches than her matches and culminated in his being sent to prison for tax fraud, costing her $20m in reparation. The fact that she continued to achieve so much with such determination and dignity adds to her status as an all-time great.

The esteem with which she was held was fully demonstrated in Hanover one evening in February 1998. When at last, after two false dawns when comeback dates had to be cancelled at short notice, Graf played competitively for the first time in eight months, and no less than 3,500 were present to welcome her back.

KING

THE FEARSOME FIGHTER BOTH ON AND OFF THE COURT

Billie Jean King was a champion ready and eager to take on anyone, anywhere about almost anything. By doing so she achieved just as much success for her efforts in winning proper respect for women's tennis as she did as a player.

CAREER MILESTONES

1961	Won doubles at Wimbledon at first attempt.
1966	First of six singles wins at Wimbledon.
1967	Won US singles for first time.
1968	Winner of Australian championships.
1970	Led prize money revolt by women players which led to formation of their own circuit.
1973	Record crowd (30,492) watched her beat Bobby Riggs in Battle of the Sexes.
1973	Last player to achieve triple crown at Wimbledon.
1979	Won her 20th singles and doubles Wimbledon title – a record.
1983	Reached her 29th final in 265 Wimbledon matches.

Billie Jean King

Born: *November 22, 1943*
Long Beach, CA, USA

Few people have had a greater impact on the progress of women's tennis than Billie Jean King. After nearly 20 years as one of the finest players, both in singles and doubles, she has been equally influential within the political and commercial boundaries of the game, working tirelessly to gain respect and recognition for successive generations of women players.

An indefatigable competitor on court, full of natural exuberance, she delivers her outspoken views on all aspects of the modern game in the same forthright manner that she used to display in her groundstrokes and volleys, as she won 39 singles, doubles and mixed doubles titles in Grand Slam tournaments. That places her in third position on the all-time list just behind two other giants of the game, who were also contemporaries for much of her career, Margaret Court and Martina Navratilova.

Despite the thinly veiled threat she made about trying to organize a women's event in competition with The Championships the following year unless the women were granted equal prize money as a reward for their loyalty in 1973, when Wimbledon was boycotted by 93 of the leading male players, this was the tournament which meant most to her. After she was presented with one of the original 1922 benches from the Centre Court by the president of Home Box Office Television, the cable network for which she has been a resident commentator at Wimbledon for 20 years, she described it as "the best present anyone could have given me".

As a player Billie Jean, whose earliest triumphs came while she was still Billie Jean Moffitt, competed 22 times at Wimbledon in 23 years. She missed only in 1981, although in 1976 she surprised many by deciding not to defend the singles crown she had won for a sixth time the previous year and played only in doubles. Overall she played a record 265 matches in the three main events at The Championships, winning all but 41 of them. Her win-loss statistics in singles alone were 95–15.

Not only did she play more matches than any other player, male or female – 41 more than Jean Borotra, who competed in 224 matches in a remarkably enduring career from 1922 to 1964 – but she also won 20 titles, which itself is a record. They comprised six singles, 10 doubles and four in mixed doubles, although the day she finally clinched the record, July 7, 1979, was also tinged with sadness. On the eve of Billie Jean and Martina Navratilova winning the women's doubles title, Elizabeth "Bunny" Ryan, who had won 19 titles in doubles and mixed, though none in singles, was taken ill at the All England Club and died, aged 87, that evening from a heart attack, with her record still intact.

The following day King recalled how Ryan had watched her play in junior tournaments at the Los Angeles Tennis Club. "In a way I grew up with her," she said. "When I heard that she had passed away, my whole life passed in front of me too." She told of how she had been influenced by a chapter about Ryan in a book written by Ted Tinling called *Love and Faults*. It revealed some of Ryan's own philosophies about tennis and what she thought were the reasons for her success.

"I made a point of reading that," said King. "People who make records push everything to a different level and even though you know deep down that sometime later someone will come along and break the record, the important thing is to make sure you keep pushing and stretching the standard as much and as often as you can."

Billie Jean, who was also the last player to win the triple crown at Wimbledon when she and Owen Davidson won the mixed in 1973, won 12 titles at the US Championships, four each in all three events; one singles, one doubles and two mixed at the French; and one singles and one mixed at the Australian. Despite knees which had been operated upon so often that she used to joke that you could play noughts and crosses between the scars, she was still a singles semi-finalist and mixed doubles runner-up with Steve Denton at Wimbledon in 1983.

Yet for all that, this bespectacled, irrepressible net-rusher, who oozed confidence, probably earned most attention from winning a match which is missing from all the official records. It was before a world-record tennis crowd of 30,492, at the Astrodome in Houston when, aged 29, she beat 55-year-old Bobby Riggs 6–4, 6–3, 6–3 in a Battle of the Sexes challenge for a purse of $100,000. Whatever doubt there might have been before, that was the night on which tennis made the transition from sport to show business. And Billie Jean King, appropriately enough, was in the vanguard of the new development.

LAVER

THE RED-HEADED ROCKET FROM ROEHAMPTON

Rod Laver was the first tennis player to earn $1m in prize money but that was during the relatively modest early developments in the Open era. The mind boggles as to how much the only player, man or woman, to have achieved the Grand Slam twice, might have won had he been born 20 years later. For almost 20 years he built up a record and reputation which persuades many to rate him as the best of all time.

<table>
<tr><td rowspan="11">CAREER MILESTONES</td><td>1959</td><td>Made Davis Cup debut.</td></tr>
<tr><td>1960</td><td>First Grand Slam singles title in Australia.</td></tr>
<tr><td>1961</td><td>Won Wimbledon for first time.</td></tr>
<tr><td>1962</td><td>Winner of the Grand Slam.</td></tr>
<tr><td>1963</td><td>Turned professional.</td></tr>
<tr><td>1968</td><td>Won first Open Wimbledon.</td></tr>
<tr><td>1969</td><td>Only man to achieve Grand Slam in Open tennis.</td></tr>
<tr><td>1973</td><td>Led Australia to 5-0 defeat of USA in Davis Cup final.</td></tr>
<tr><td>1977</td><td>Retired from competitive tennis aged 39.</td></tr>
</table>

Rod Laver

Born: *August 9, 1938*
Rockhampton, Queensland, Australia

No one meeting Rod Laver today would guess from his modest, unassuming manner and style that they were in the company of one of the most accomplished champions in any sport. The impression was the same when he was still playing – until, that is, he walked on to the court and started to wield his racket with a combination of power, skill, control and intuitive magic that no one, many believe, has yet equalled. John McEnroe, it could be argued, reached even greater heights of perfection on select occasions, such as his 1984 Wimbledon final against Jimmy Connors, but his overall record does not stand up alongside that of the only man to complete the Grand Slam not just once but twice, the second time in 1969 making him the sole achiever in that context since the advent of Open tennis 30 years ago.

Laver first began hitting those stunning topspin groundstrokes on an antbed court, crushed fine and rolled flat so that it played very similarly to clay, at his parents' home near Rockhampton in north Queensland. As a boy his forehand was always more impressive than his backhand until Charlie Hollis, his first coach, helped him become one of the first left-handers to come over the ball with a rolled backhand on that side.

One day Laver's father drove him to Brisbane to attend a tennis clinic being given by the late Harry Hopman, arguably the finest coach in the history of the game, who eyed the skinny lad up and down for a moment and then said, "OK Rocket, let's see what you can do." The name stuck for evermore. So did that rolled backhand.

Laver was still just 17 when he first appeared at Wimbledon, to be beaten by the giant Italian Orlando Sirola in the first round of the men's singles and by Ron Holmberg in the final of the juniors. Three years later he reached the final for the first time, losing to Alex Olmedo, and in 1960 his fellow Australian, Neale Fraser, also beat him in one of those rare Wimbledon finals between two left-handers.

Everyone sensed it would be only a matter of time before this red-headed tennis genius would take the title. In 1961 he beat Chuck McKinley in the final. The following year success came against Martin Mulligan and, by the end of the year, after Laver had also won in Paris, New York and back home in Australia, Don Budge was no longer the only Grand Slam champion.

Like most other Wimbledon champions in those days, Laver then turned professional and was absent for five years before the international game was at last liberated, and this most admired Australian celebrated his return by picking up where he had left off – as champion. Indeed, in the five years he was able to compete, between losing to Fraser in the 1960 final and being beaten in such dramatic fashion by Britain's Roger Taylor in the fourth round in 1970, he was unbeaten at The Championships in 31 matches, a record which lasted until Bjorn Borg extended it to 41 as champion from 1976 to 1980 and by reaching the final in 1981.

Take away the years between 1962 and 1967 when he was barred from playing and the records show that Laver, who is married with a son, played in six consecutive Wimbledon finals, 1959-62 and then again in 1968-69, an achievement matched only by Borg, who appeared in six in succession, since the abolition of The Challenge Round in 1922.

In the professional ranks before Open tennis arrived, he continued to dominate, despite being at 5ft 8in, one of the shortest players in modern times to have won a major title – one inch shorter even that Marcelo Rios, the much-lauded Chilean who won the Lipton Championships in 1998.

Laver, who now lives in California, and who was often introduced at events on the WCT Tour in the late 1960s as "the man with the copper hair but a golden touch", became the first prize-money millionaire in tennis.

Laver's intensely competitive nature on court helped him win many matches from two sets to love or two sets to one down, in both major championships and Davis Cup contests. When he beat Fraser 8–6 in the fifth to win the first of his three singles titles at the Australian Championships, it was from match point down. He also rescued a match point in the fourth set of his 6–4, 3–6, 2–6, 10–8, 6–2 defeat of fellow Australian Mulligan in the quarter-finals on the way to winning his first French title in 1962.

In addition to taking the Big Four titles in 1962, Laver also collected the Italian and German titles. He was a member of the Australian Davis Cup team from 1959 to 62 and then again in 1973, winning 20 of his 24 rubbers, while his overall singles record at Wimbledon was played 50, won 43.

The statistics are impressive, but just as impressive was the way they were accumulated by a player always regarded by his peers as the consummate professional, an absolute sportsman who on court let his racket do the talking in the most eloquent, entertaining and often awesome way.

LENGLEN

DIVINE SUZANNE

Such was the fame of Suzanne Lenglen that more than once, King Gustav of Sweden, a useful player in his own right, asked her to be his partner in mixed doubles.

Suzanne Lenglen
Born: *May 25, 1899*
Died: *July 4, 1938*
Paris, France

Until Martina Navratilova won a record six consecutive Grand Slam tournaments during 1983–84 and also went on to win Wimbledon more times than any other woman, Suzanne Lenglen undoubtedly led the field among immortals in women's tennis. Born in Paris, the daughter of a pharmacist who had been a professional cyclist, she began a brilliant career just before the First World War and established a degree of dominance from 1919 to 1926 which was regarded as unassailable for more than half a century.

Her impact began in earnest in 1914 when she won the World Championship in Paris, so that by the time she first came to Wimbledon four years later, she was already regarded with awe.

In her first Wimbledon challenge, playing on grass for the first time, she dismissed most of those who tried to resist her. The semi-final for Lenglen was much tougher. She was taken to 6–4, 7–5 by her doubles partner Bunny Ryan before reaching the Challenge Round where she beat another prodigiously successful player, Dorothea Lambert Chambers, seven times champion between 1903 and 1914.

Their match stands in the annals of lawn tennis as one of the most spectacular of all time. With her father, who was also her coach, throwing her sugar lumps soaked in brandy, Lenglen saved two match points in the third set of a 10–8, 4–6, 9–7 triumph watched by King George V and Queen Mary. They, like everyone else, were impressed by Lenglen's ambitious, often extravagant, shot-making. What they thought of her dress was

another matter. Wimbledon crowds, used to seeing women players in tight-fitting corsets, blouses and layers of petticoats, gasped when Lenglen arrived on Centre Court in a revealing one-piece dress with sleeves actually above the elbow and a hemline only just below the knee.

Lenglen had led 4–1 in the final set before Lambert Chambers, then aged 40, fought back to hold two match points at 6–5. Lenglen saved the first with a lucky winner off the frame, the second with a backhand, and went on to take the title.

This, of course, was when Wimbledon was still being staged at its original home in Worple Road. But Lenglen's arrival on the international scene, with her magnetic presence, acrobatic style and extraordinary ball control and concentration, soon lifted the appeal of tennis to an altogether higher level. By 1920 the crowds flocking to see her were so great that Worple Road could no longer cope, prompting the All England Club, as a matter of urgency, to move to the new, larger headquarters it had found in Church Road.

Between 1914 and 1926, Lenglen won 81 singles titles, 73 in doubles and 87 in mixed. On eight occasions she won matches 6–0, 6–0. Her doubles partner was the Californian, Bunny Ryan, winner of 19 Wimbledon doubles and mixed doubles titles. She and Lenglen were not merely unbeaten in six attempts at winning the doubles there. They lost only one set.

Three times Lenglen won the triple crown at The Championships, in 1920, 1922 and 1925, and in that last year, after missing Wimbledon in 1924 through illness, she won her five matches in the singles for the loss of just five games. At the French she played six times and was unbeaten in singles, doubles and mixed.

In 1921 Lenglen went to the Unit-

ed States for the first time. The Americans, eager to see how she would perform against their own Norwegian-born champion Molla Mallory, waited in a state of high excitement for her arrival. A difficult sea crossing meant she arrived in New York only two days before the US Nationals were due to begin. It was by no means ideal preparation and to her despair she found that because there was no seeding her very first opponent, after she had received a walkover in the first round, would be Mallory.

Without practice and feeling unwell, Lenglen was in trouble. Coughing and appearing weak, in front of what was then a record 8,000 crowd for a women's match in the United States, she lost the first set 6–2 and after losing the first game of the second set to love and the first point of the next game and double-faulting to 0–30, she began to weep. She went to the umpire's chair and told the official that she was too ill to go on.

She was severely criticized in the American press, especially when over the following days she did not allow her illness to restrict her social engagements. The American tour was abandoned.

Less than 12 months later Lenglen and Mallory met again in the 1922 Wimbledon final. The American was routed 6–2, 6–0 in 25 minutes. No journalist ever again dared hint that La Lenglen was not supreme. Four years later another American star was rising: Helen Wills Moody, whose classic 1926 confrontation with Lenglen in Cannes is fully documented in the Great Matches section of this book.

It was to be Lenglen's final year on the tour and no one could have dreamed that it would also end in tears and controversy on Wimbledon's Centre Court. Lenglen was defending all three titles but, despite the ease with which she had won them in the

previous year, she was not in the best mood. The French Federation had ruled that instead of continuing to play in the doubles with Bunny Ryan she must have a French partner, Didi Vlasto, instead.

All this blew up after she had reached the third round of the singles. As it happened, Wimbledon referee Frank Barlow, who had always been meticulous in telling Lenglen as soon as possible exactly when she would be playing her next match, forgot to send the messenger to her hotel on this occasion. So she was unaware that she was due on the Centre Court the next day at 2 p.m., or that Queen Mary was to be in the Royal Box at that time.

She arrived late to find that the order of play had had to be altered and retired to the dressing room in tears. When she eventually appeared to partner Jean Borotra in mixed doubles, the crowd, under the impression that she had insulted Queen Mary, booed her. Although she went on to win Wimbledon for a sixth time, taking her overall match record in singles and doubles there to 91–3, a few weeks later she departed the traditional lawn tennis stage and turned professional. It was very much the ending of an era.

CAREER MILESTONES		
	1914	World hard court champion in Paris, aged 15.
	1919	Won Wimbledon singles and doubles.
	1920	Olympic gold in singles.
	1920	Triple crown winner at Wimbledon .
	1921	Retired ill on only visit to US championships.
	1922	Won singles, doubles and mixed at Wimbledon.
	1925	Wimbledon triple crown for third time. Lost only 5 games in 5 singles matches.
	1926	Retired following Wimbledon to turn professional.
	1938	Died aged 39 in Paris.

McENROE

JECKYLL AND HYDE

The lad who messed about when no one was looking, when he was supposed to be practising, grew up to be a tennis genius, as well as the scourge of officials on the courts.

John McEnroe

Born: *February 16, 1959*
Wiesbaden, Germany

No player attracted such universal attention or provoked such contrasting emotions – from admiration to hatred – as American lawyer's son John Patrick McEnroe, who now, at least partially mellowed, has become the most wanted tennis commentator for television companies all round the world.

As a player he was certainly an enigma, there being no easy explanation for the switchback moods this brilliantly gifted New Yorker so frequently demonstrated in both his tennis and his disposition. Certainly it is difficult to recall any other tennis player who at one minute in a match could be boiling with fury over a decision or some issue of principle and then in the next play a point overflowing with exquisite skill, control and concentrated perfection.

This Jekyll and Hyde quality was a trait which merely added to the attraction of a sporting genius, who contributed so many of the best and worst things which happened to the sport during the years spanning his playing career. On the one hand, there is an honours list which records, among other things, no fewer than 77 titles in singles and an equal number in doubles, including three singles and five doubles titles at Wimbledon, his participation in the most memorable tie-break ever witnessed at The Championships, plus four singles titles at the US Open and four more in doubles. On the other, there is a list of disciplinary matters which put McEnroe in the Hall of Shame long before he began to build a record worthy of the Hall of Fame.

For four consecutive years, 1981–84, McEnroe finished as number one in the world rankings, while he achieved a 59–10 record in the Davis Cup from 30 ties, including a 41–8 record in singles. All this for someone who, despite a superb natural sense of timing and ball control, whether kicking a football around near his Douglaston home or when he started to wield a tennis racket, never won a junior singles title.

The world's first introduction to John McEnroe as a player was when he was just 14 and competing as a junior at the Port Washington Tennis Academy. Harry Hopman, the legendary Australian coach and Davis Cup captain, who played such a vital role in the development of such champions as Lew Hoad, Rod Laver, Ken Rosewall and John Newcombe, was in charge of operations there at the time. Pointing to this short, skinny lad messing about in the corner of a court, he said: "Take a good look at that boy over there … He could be a world champion." At the time John had an impressive serve and splendid groundstrokes, though not yet that fantastic ability to play the first volley with finer timing, sharper angles and more astute variety than any other player before or since. In a way everything started to take off for the tousle-haired youngster with the headband, who had once ball-boyed at the US Open for Bjorn Borg in his match against Niki Pilic.

At the French Open in 1977, while most people were concentrating on Borg and Co., hardly anyone noticed the intruder who defeated Australian Alvin Gardiner in the first round before losing to Phil Dent in the second. On the other hand, a few did begin to be interested when, from an admittedly modest field, McEnroe and Mary Carillo, now also a successful sports commentator in the United States, won the mixed doubles.

McEnroe's plans for Wimbledon that year were to try to qualify for the tournament he had heard so much about and also to try to win the junior title. That idea went out of the window when McEnroe not only won his way into the main draw but became the first qualifier to reach the semi-finals before losing to Jimmy Connors.

Ironically Connors was the "bad boy" at Wimbledon that year. He was roundly booed for snubbing the Centre Court centenary parade on the first day. Behind the scenes, though, McEnroe was already starting to collect black marks. In Paris he had escaped punishment for screaming abuse at a linesman in the mixed doubles final. At Wimbledon he was also the subject of a formal complaint to referee Fred Hoyles from those who umpired his matches while he was on the way to becoming the first 18-year-old to reach the last four.

Thereafter, however much his career may have been paved with good intentions, the glory of his performances was too often scarred by loss of self-control. His game, like his personality, was a contradiction in terms, blissfully attractive one minute, inexcusably intolerant the next. In July 1981 he was fined $6,000, a record at that time, after coining the phrases "Pits of the world" and "You cannot be serious". But he went on to end Borg's modern record run of victories by beating him in four sets in the final.

His outbursts were not confined to officials. In 1983 he was fined for calling his Czech opponent, Tomas Smid, a "communist bastard". A year later his "outrageous behaviour" led to the United States Tennis Association refusing to retain him in the Davis Cup team. And so it went on, interspersed all the time with performances which others could only dream of matching.

It culminated in his becoming the first player to be disqualified from a Grand Slam tournament in the Open era for repeated foul language in January 1990. He admitted that, had he known that the rule had just been changed so that players were then allowed only three misdemeanours instead of four before being thrown out, he would not have gone that far – which made one question whether his outbursts, which on one occasion he said sickened even him, were instinctive as some insisted rather than premeditated.

His peak as a player was in 1984. His match record was 82–3 and after losing to Ivan Lendl, despite being two sets up, in the French Open final, he trounced Connors in the Wimbledon final and then Lendl, also in straight sets, at Flushing Meadow. "It was an unbelievable feeling. I said to myself, 'God, you really are a level above other people right now'." McEnroe once reflected, "My mistake was that I sort of sat back and waited to see what they did instead of pushing on." He did not win a Grand Slam singles title after that.

Years later he said: "I'm not at all concerned about my place in the history of tennis. OK, I didn't win as many tournaments as Connors or Lendl in singles, but I still will put my record up against anybody's. It comes down to this: do they consider the tennis I played or the number of times I told an umpire to screw himself?"

NAVRATILOVA

RECORD-BREAKER

July 7, 1990 will forever be inscribed in Martina Navratilova's memory as well as the history books of tennis. It was on that day that she won Wimbledon for a record ninth time.

Martina Navratilova

Born: *October 18, 1956*
Prague, Czechoslovakia

Arrayed along one of the shelves in Martina Navratilova's home in Colorado are nine replicas of the gilt silver salver which champions have proudly held aloft since the All England Club first presented this trophy for the winner of the women's singles in 1886.

They are a permanent testimony, not only to the record-breaking achievements of one of the most accomplished modern gladiators in any sport, but also to her love affair with Wimbledon. For three years, from the time she won the game's most significant singles title for an eighth time in 1987, equalling the record held since 1938 by Helen Wills Moody, until she broke that record in 1990, she often seemed to feel as if she was in some kind of career vacuum.

When, on July 7, 1990, Navratilova, then 33, overwhelmed an overawed Zina Garrison 6–4, 6–1 in just 75 minutes, she declared: "This tops it all. I've worked so long and so hard for it." Having shaken hands with her opponent and the umpire, she dropped to her knees, as if about to kiss the turf. She eventually contented herself with enthusiastic waves to the crowd and a small clump of grass to put with the piece of rockery from the All England Club grounds, which she had been carrying round the world in her racket bag for some years, for luck.

Navratilova, whose determination to take the Wimbledon record had become even more of an obsession with her than Ivan Lendl's yearning to win the men's singles title, said: "Wimbledon is like a drug. Once you win it for a first time you feel you've just got to do it again and again and again." She said the memory of how Chris Evert, her great friend and rival, had won the French Open for a record

seventh time in 1986 had been a constant spur. "They say good things are worth waiting for", said the fully Americanized Czech exile who had bypassed not only the French Open in 1990 but also the Australian Open a few months earlier, just to keep her mind focused on the work necessary to achieve the only title which could bring her peace of mind.

Her memories of Wimbledon dated back to her childhood when, although Czechoslovakians were not able to watch The Championships on television, at least there were results for her to follow in the newspapers. When eventually the authorities in Czechoslovakia did allow the Wimbledon finals to be shown on television, albeit in black and white, Navratilova, who had never seen a grass court, desperately tried to imagine what it would be like: "How much grass could there be? I thought it would be about two inches high, like it is for other sports." She remem-bers peering at the tiny screen for evidence.

It was not until a week before her first Wimbledon appearance, that her questions were answered. Like generations of players before her, she went to Queen's Club to practise. "The first thing I did was to kneel down and touch it," she recalls. "I was amazed at how tight and firm it was. I just had no idea."

When Navratilova looks back upon her sometimes troubled but mostly illustrious life in tennis, it will not be difficult for her to select both the highest and lowest points. Her parents had divorced when she was three and she hardly knew her natural father. He died when she was nine, and it was some years before she discovered that he had committed suicide. She was 11 when Soviet tanks rolled into Prague and the true meaning of the Iron Curtain was brought home to her.

She loved her mother and father dearly so one can imagine her heartache when, because of commercial as much as sporting pressures, she decided to defect to the United States during the 1975 US Open, at the age of 19. It was perhaps to ease the loneliness she often endured in the first year that she was permanently away from her family and mother country that she took to a diet mainly comprising "junk food", ballooning from 135 lbs to 167 lbs. One year after her defection, Navratilova left the court at Forest Hills sobbing uncontrollably. As third seed she had slumped out in the first round of the US Open against Janet Newberry, an American who had virtually retired from the tennis scene.

Yet it was not until the summer of 1981, by which time she had won Wimbledon twice but then started to slump again, that it dawned on her that she was "going nowhere. I realized it was time to give it my best shot or forget it." Adopting new dietary and training regimes, she made becoming a champion a science and it was not long before her production line of victories began to roll.

The US Open that year was something of a watershed. Life in general was looking good for her again by then; not only was she immensely wealthy and well settled in her relationship with Renée Richards as coach and Nancy Lieberman as confidante and trainer, but she had just learned that her application to become a US citizen had been accepted. When she recovered from a break down in her semi-final against Evert it looked odds-on that she would win this title for the first time. It was not to be. She let slip enough chances to have beaten Tracy Austin and lost 1–6, 7–6, 7–6. "I froze up," Navratilova confessed. It was by no means for the first or last

time. All the while, though, she was patiently and shrewdly working on becoming the most aggressive woman player the game had ever seen.

Her game, which hinged upon her serve-and-volley approach working to perfection, reached its peak on a warm, sunny afternoon in Paris in 1984 when she became the first player since Margaret Court, in 1970, to hold all four Grand Slam titles at the same time, although not won in the same tennis year.

Navratilova won the US Open four times, the Australian three times, and the French twice. Within that record of nine wins at Wimbledon, were six triumphs in succession – a feat unrivalled in the history of The Championships. The players she beat in those finals were Chris Evert three times, Andrea Jaeger, Hana Mandlikova and Steffi Graf. "If I ever reached the stage where winning Wimbledon was no big deal I'd know it was time for me to get out of the game", said the left-hander, who played there for 22 consecutive years. She played 279 matches there, also a record, and 14 more than Billie Jean King.

Aged 49, Martina continues to play at the highest levels, albeit mainly doubles.

CAREER MILESTONES

1975	Defected to USA.
1978	First of record nine wins at Wimbledon.
1981	Won Australian Open first of three times.
1982	First French Open title.
1983	Won three Grand Slam singles, inc. US Open.
1984	Modern Grand Slam. Won six consecutive Slam titles.
1986	Returned to Prague in winning US Fed Cup team.
1990	Won Wimbledon ninth time.
1991	Broke Chris Evert's record (1,309) of most matches won. Ended with 1,442.

PERRY

THE LEGEND THAT WAS FRED

The teenager who first conquered the world of table tennis, then took up tennis as a healthy, outdoor occupation and became the greatest British player of all time.

Fred Perry

Born: *May 18, 1909*
Died: *February 2, 1995*
Stockport, UK

Fred Perry was the last British player to win the men's singles title at Wimbledon, a triumph he achieved three times in succession, 1934–36. He was also the first player to win all four of the Grand Slam tournaments, though without ever holding all four at the same time, while his contribution to Britain's Davis Cup supremacy in 1933–36 was immense.

Especially memorable was the decisive final rubber he played against France in Paris in 1933. Perry, who had taken five sets to beat Henri Cochet on the opening day, recovered from losing the first set and from being two set points down in the second to beat André Merlin 4–6, 8–6, 6–2, 7–5.

During his career Perry competed in 20 Davis Cup matches, winning 34 of his 38 rubbers in singles and 11 out of 14 in doubles. Since then Britain has reached the final (other than The Challenge Round as champions in 1937) only once, when they were beaten by the United States.

Perry first made his name as the world table tennis champion and he brought to the tennis court the same speed of reaction and some of the shots that he had developed on the table. One of his specialities was the running forehand, taken early and often with great risk. Above all Perry had a wonderful eye and a strong wrist. He favoured the continental grip with no change of hand position between backhand and forehand.

Fred never understood why so few modern players watch other competitors, leaving it instead to their coaches to assess future opposition. "I always liked to see and learn for myself," he once said, adding how much he learnt from rivals such as Henri Cochet and Bill Tilden. He told how he modelled his game a great deal on Cochet, "because he was the one in those days who hit the ball early. Because I was bigger, stronger and faster, I hit that forehand of his, delivered with a short swing, so that less could go wrong. It stood me in good stead many times."

Perry's brilliant shot-making was matched by his competitive steel. He trained far more zealously than most of his rivals. Twice on his way to becoming Wimbledon champion for the first time he was stretched to five sets. He was under far less pressure in the following two years, dropping only three sets in 1935 and just one in 1936 when, in the final, he beat an injured Gottfried von Cramm 6–1, 6–1, 6–0. And in 1935 and 1936 he also won the mixed doubles with Worcestershire Sunday School teacher Dorothy Round.

Frederick John Perry was born in Stockport, the son of a cotton spinner who became secretary of the Co-operative Party and later Labour MP for Kettering. Towards the end of the First World War the family moved to Ealing, near London, and it was then that his sporting talents began to blossom. His father was so concerned at the amount of time his son spent in what he called "smoke-filled rooms" playing table tennis that he told him on one occasion, "You look like death warmed up. Why don't you concentrate on your tennis instead?"

Probably for the only time in his life Fred complied. He had played in the Junior Championships at Wimbledon, but lost in the fourth round after breaking the only racket he possessed. In senior tennis, though, his progress was so rapid that in 1930 he was chosen to join a four-man LTA team to tour the United States.

That tour introduced him to a new way of life. In Hollywood he was to meet and make friends with Mary Pickford, Marlene Dietrich, Douglas Fairbanks, David Niven, Errol Flynn and Bebe Daniels. To Perry such company was irresistible. His tennis thrived too. He won the US National Championships, now the US Open, in 1933, 1934 and 1936, the Australian singles and doubles in 1934 and the French singles in 1935.

It is now part of tennis legend that, although Perry had what he called "my lifelong love affair with Wimbledon" since the first time he saw the Centre Court as a paying customer in 1928, his early relations with the All England Club were prickly, to say the least. In 1984, by which time his statue within the grounds and the dedication of the Perry Gates underlined how much the club had since embraced him, he wrote: "Both of us have mellowed from the days when some elements in the Club and the LTA looked down on me as a hot-headed, outspoken tearaway rebel, not quite the class of chap they really wanted to see winning Wimbledon, even if he was English."

Not until after the Second World War were there any on-court presentation ceremonies at Wimbledon. The chairman would seek out the champion, congratulate him and present him with the club tie as confirmation of his then being an honorary member. Perry often told how, taking a long soak in the bath after beating defending champion Jack Crawford in the 1934 Wimbledon final, he overheard a member of the All England Club tell the Australian, "Congratulations. This was one day when the best man didn't win." Crawford was then handed a bottle of champagne. All Perry received was the club tie draped over his chair and a £25 voucher redeemable at Mappin & Webb. No congratulations were offered. "Instead of Fred J Perry the champ I felt like Fred J Perry the chump," he recalled.

The situation was not improved when, having turned professional in 1935, his membership was rescinded. Any mention of the word professional remained an anathema until Perry and several others were welcomed back after Open tennis began in 1968.

A knee injury forced Perry to retire from active competition in 1946, but in 1950 he founded the sportswear company which bears his name and also set about developing a much-respected media career spanning newspapers, radio and television. A lovable rogue and charmer rolled into one, who set high standards and expected the same from others, Fred Perry was unique.

SAMPRAS

"PISTOL" PETE — THE BEST

In a recent poll by players past and present and the world's leading tennis writers, Pete Sampras, who has his heart set on winning more Grand Slam titles than anyone, was voted the best player in the 25-year history of the ATP Tour.

Pete Sampras

Born: *August 12, 1971*
Potomac, MD, USA

In 1990, on the eve of Pete Sampras, a 6ft-1in son of Greek immigrants, winning the first of what by the start of 1998 was more than 50 titles on the ATP Tour, two of the legendary champions in the game, Fred Perry and Don Budge, were musing in the lounge of a hotel in Philadelphia. "This lad's for real. He'll be a Wimbledon champion one day."

Considering that on his first visit to The Championships in 1989 seven months earlier, the swarthy lad with a loopy grin had been beaten in the first round, and that he suffered the same fate again five months after such a fearless forecast was a bit puzzling. Sampras, then 19, upset Ivan Lendl, John McEnroe and Andre Agassi from the quarter-finals onwards to become the youngest US Open champion of the century.

Although, as it proved, Sampras was not mature enough either physically or mentally for his game to take off, the wise commentators, like Perry and Budge, knew from the sustained skill, determination and concentration that Sampras had displayed over those last three matches at Flushing Meadow that it would only be a matter of time before he would be winning every trophy the game has to offer.

That never quite happened. After 13 attempts, the French Open always eluded him. Sampras always had three principal yearnings. One was to finish on top of the year-end rankings as often as possible, despite his protestations that he cared more for Grand Slam titles than being world number one. The second was to win the French and the third to overtake Roy Emerson's record of 12 Grand Slam singles titles.

He realised two of them. He finished the year as the top player for six consecutive years (1993–1999) and won 14 Grand Slam singles titles, his last secured aptly at Flushing Meadows in 2002, the venue where he first sprang to prominence some 13 years earlier.

In terms of success exclusively within the Open era, Sampras, with seven titles at Wimbledon, five at US Open plus two at the Australian, also had an excellent Davis Cup record appearing in two victorious US teams (1992 and 1995).

As a youngster, especially after one of his earliest coaches, Dr Pete Fischer, persuaded him to change from a two-handed to a single-handed backhand, he once declared that he wanted to become a right-handed version of Rod Laver. It is a quote which has haunted him to some extent, although from mid-1993 onwards, when he won Wimbledon for the first of seven times over eight years, that dream has come true.

There is a lengthy list of epic performances by Sampras, none more epic than in the 1995 Davis Cup final in Moscow when he was supreme in both his singles rubbers and also in the match-turning doubles as the United States beat Russia 3–2. An even more significant match, during which Sampras won over many of the disbelievers, was his 1994 Wimbledon quarter-final against Michael Chang. On grass one would have expected Sampras to win, of course. But the way he did so, 6–4, 6–1, 6–3, was most impressive, for he was awesome on that day in every aspect of his game except the serve. Chang, who until then had won more matches than he had lost against Sampras, simply had no adequate response to Sampras' range, quality and consistency of winners.

Sampras was just seven when two lawyer friends of the family saw him play on public courts near his home and told his father, "Forget about sending him to college, just make sure someone looks after his tennis."

His first coaches were Dr Fischer, Jo Brandi, then the late Tim Gullikson and finally Paul Annacone, who was brought in by "Gully" after it was discovered during the Australian Open of 1995 that, at the age of 43, he was suffering from four brain tumours. The diagnosis was made on the day that Sampras had to play Jim Courier in the quarter-finals in Melbourne; Gullikson had collapsed in the locker room after conducting Sampras's practice session that morning. A few hours later Sampras, who twice broke down in tears, recovered from two sets down to beat Courier in probably the most emotional match in the history of any of the Grand Slams.

Sampras demonstrated a courage and willpower then matched only by his performance in the 1996 US Open quarter-final against Alex Corretja. Struggling grimly against severe dehydration, even to the extent of being sick on court and frequently leaning on his racket between points, as if unable to continue, he saved a match point at 6–7 in the fifth-set tie-break, an ace to lead 8–7 and then won on his opponent's heart-breaking double fault.

CAREER MILESTONES

1990	Youngest US Open champion.
1993	Won Wimbledon and US Open.
1993	Began five year reign as world no 1.
1994	Winner at Australian Open and Wimbledon.
1995	Completed hat-trick of Wimbledon wins and regained US title.
1995	Led USA to Davis Cup final win in Moscow.
1995	First player to win more than $5m in a year.
1997	Won Australian Open, Wimbledon and Grand Slam Cup. Retained ATP championships title.
2000	Won Wimbledon for a fourth consecutive year
2002	Won US Open for a fifth time to set a new record of 14 Grand Slam singles titles.

Gullikson died on May 3, 1996, since when Sampras has been an active member of the American Cancer Society's Public Awareness Council. In 1997 he started his "Aces for Charity" campaign, to which he donated $100 for every ace he himself served. That alone raised $62,700 in the first year.

There are some who describe Sampras as boring, both as a person and as a player. That is because they do not really know him and while it is sometimes true that he won matches with almost mechanical ease, it is hard to blame him for the fact that opponents neither had the tactical imagination or the range of strokes to divert him from a winning path.

Pete Sampras slipped quietly into retirement after his 2002 US Open victory and has resolutely stayed out of the limelight though in 2006, he picked up a racket to compete in the World Team Tennis series for the first time.

He married the actress Bridgette Wilson with whom he has a son, Christian Charles, born in 2002.

THE GREAT PLAYERS

The history of tennis overflows with great champions from all parts of the world. The potted biographies which follow, underline the rich breadth of fine players, from one generation to the next, from all round the world, who have contributed immensely to the appeal of a sport no longer restricted by social barriers.

Andre Agassi
Born: *April 29, 1970*
Las Vegas, NV, USA
(See Legends pp72–73)

Vijay Amritraj
Born: *December 14, 1953*
Madras, India

Vijay Amritraj won 16 singles titles on the ATP Tour, at least one every year between 1973 and 1980, the last of them at Bristol in 1986, when he beat Henri Leconte. Like most other Indian players, he often produced his best tennis on grass and competed for 16 consecutive years at Wimbledon (1972–87). Although he never went beyond the quarter-finals, which he reached twice, he figured in some memorable matches there, not least when he took the first two sets from Jimmy Connors in 1981.

A delightfully skilful, versatile player, whose brothers Anand and Ashok also played on the Tour, he was the backbone of the Indian Davis Cup team for 20 years and led them to the final twice, first in 1974, when they defaulted rather than play South Africa in the days of apartheid, and then in 1987 when they lost in Sweden. He was twice a quarter-finalist at the US Open and starred as an Indian agent with Roger Moore in the James Bond film *Octopussy*.

Arthur Ashe
Born: *July 10, 1943*
Richmond, VA, USA

Few players have left a deeper mark on the sport than Arthur Ashe, after whom the main stadium for the US Open at New York's Flushing Meadows is now named. Despite the many offensive racial obstacles he had to overcome as a black youngster when segregation was still the law in Virginia, he grew up to become not only one of the great players in a white-dominated game but one of the most admired and respected sportsmen in the world.

Because Davis Cup rules at the time demanded it, Ashe, then a first lieutenant in the US Army, was still an amateur when, in 1968, he won not only the US Amateur Championships but also the US Open, which was being staged for the first time. Of the many tournament and Davis Cup successes which followed – he spent 12 years among the top 10, reaching a peak of number two in May 1976 – one of the most memorable was in the 1975 Wimbledon final when he spectacularly outwitted top-seeded defending champion Jimmy Connors, regarded as almost invincible at the time, in four sets. He won 27 singles rubbers in the Davis Cup, second only to John McEnroe, before captaining the team in 1981–85. Three years later, during major heart surgery, he contracted AIDS through a blood transfusion and died on February 6, 1993.

Cilly Aussem
Born: *January 4, 1909*
Cologne, Germany

Between 1927, when she first became the German champion, and a fever which severely damaged her sight less than 10 years later, when she had become the Contessa della Corta Brae, Cilly Aussem's agility and

VIJAY AMRITRAI *competed in 16 consecutive Wimbledon Championships*

cherubic appearance made her one of the most charismatic players of her time. Although only 5ft tall, Aussem seemed to believe that defeat was a disgrace and this inspired a fighting spirit which led to several remarkable comebacks, not least when she reeled off 11 consecutive games in recovering from 2–6, 2–5 to beat Mrs Holcroft-Watson at the French Championships in 1928.

Bill Tilden not only helped her develop a reliable serve, but won the mixed doubles title with her at the French in 1930. At Wimbledon that year Aussem beat Helen Jacobs but, with the score at 4–4 in the final set of her semi-final against Elizabeth Ryan, she fell, sprained her ankle and had to be carried off court on a stretcher. Compensation followed a year later when, in the absence of Helen Wills Moody, Aussem not only won at Roland Garros but went on to win the first all-German final against Hilde Krahwinkel.

Tracy Austin

Born: *December 12, 1962*
Rolling Hills, CA, USA

The best-known member of a family which produced three other professional players, Pam, Jeff and John, Tracy Austin set various age records during a career in which for years her pigtails and pink gingham dresses emphasized the growing impact of youth on the women's game. In 1979, after an outstanding junior career in which she won a record 25 US national titles, she became the youngest winner of the US Open, and in August the following year she became the first athlete, male or female, to reach a career total of $1m prize money. In 1980, she and John became the first, and so far only, brother and sister team to win the mixed doubles title at Wimbledon.

Renowned for her relentless double-handed backhand driving from the baseline, which was even more effective than her impressive forehand, Austin won her first major title in Rome when she beat Chris Evert for the Italian Open title, ending her fellow American's 125 clay-court match-winning streak. She won the US Open for a second time

CILLY AUSSEM *in Cannes, France, 1933*

in 1981, but a succession of elbow and neck injuries – which despite her denials suggested burnout from having played too much too soon – forced her to retire. Her attempted comeback in 1989 ended after she broke a leg in a motor accident. Now Mrs Scott Holt, she is a frequent tennis commentator for American television stations.

Wilfred Baddeley

Born: *January 11, 1872*
Bromley, Kent, UK

Until Boris Becker won the title for the first time at the age of 17 in 1985, Wilfred Baddeley was the youngest

men's singles winner at The Championships. He was 19 years, 5 months and 23 days when he beat Joshua Pim in the 1891 final – a year when there was no Challenge Round, because the defending champion, who in those days did not have to play again until the winner of the All-Comers event the following year came through to meet him, did not defend the title.

He and his twin brother Herbert, while not regarded by contemporaries as being as talented as the Renshaw twins who preceded them or the Doherty brothers who came later, nevertheless dominated the scene in the early 1890s. Wilfred retained the title in 1892, when Pim won the All-Comers to reach the Challenge Round, and won it again three years later, while he and Herbert were doubles champions on four occasions, 1891 and 1894–96. His successes, which included becoming Irish champion in 1896,

were somewhat downgraded at the time because lawn tennis, even Wimbledon, was in decline and in the year that Wilfred won his third and last title, The Championships lost £33. There was even talk that the All England Club might be taken over by the Queen's Club!

Mansour Bahrami

Born: *April 26, 1956*
Arak, Iran

While not a great player according to the normal definition, this remarkable self-taught right hander, who learned how to play from watching others as a ballboy in a club in Teheran, is capable of providing more skilful trick shot entertainment on a tennis court than most.

Despite his obvious potential, serious hope of his establishing a formidable career on the Tour was effectively destroyed when tennis was banned in Iran in the late 1970s. All tennis courts were closed and for three years – until he was able to move to Paris in 1981, though still severely hampered by travel restrictions for anyone with an Iranian passport – he did not play at all. Yet he and Eric Winogradsky still reached the doubles final at the 1989 French Open. Now, with his clowning but brilliantly timed and executed style, he is an enormous attraction on the Seniors' Tour.

Sue Barker

Born: *April 19, 1956*
Paignton, Devon, UK

The first time Dan Maskell, the legendary voice of tennis on British television for 40 years, watched Sue Barker play, in the British covered-court Championships when she was 13, he said "She has the sort of talent, especially in her forehand, that the Gods rarely provide." That talent, exemplified by a natural all-round athletic ability, was to reach its peak in 1976 when, admittedly in a year when several of the highest-ranked players were missing, she won the French Open.

Barker reached the semi-finals of the Australian Open in 1975 and the semi-finals at Wimbledon in 1977, before losing unexpectedly to Betty

Stove, who then lost to Virginia Wade in the final. Leg injuries hampered the later stages of her career, although in 1978 she won a critical singles against Tracy Austin to help Britain to rare triumph in the Wightman Cup. Barker was known as one of the most personable players on the Tour, and it was no surprise to those who knew her when she began to carve out a broadcasting career, which has led to her becoming one of the leading sports presenters for BBC Television.

Boris Becker
Born: *November 22, 1967*
Leimen, Germany

Boris Becker, a promising junior who dropped out of school to become a professional at the age of 16, burst on to the tennis scene in the summer of 1985, winning the Stella Artois tournament, the first of 49 titles during his illustrious career. Three weeks later he beat Kevin Curren to become not only the first and youngest German to win the men's singles crown at Wimbledon but also the first unseeded champion since seeding began in 1922.

With his booming serve, heavy forehand and fearless, diving volleys, the red-headed Becker immediately became a hero for youth all round the world. His impact in Germany was phenomenal. Girls camped all night outside hotels where he was staying just to catch a glimpse of the teenager who did so much to transform the style of the game – and opened up so many commercial possibilities which are now commonplace.

From 1985 until late in 1993 he was never out of the top 10. He successfully defended his Wimbledon title in 1986, won it again in 1989 and was runner-up for a fourth and last time in 1995. He won the US Open in 1989 and the Australian Open both in 1991, when he also became number one in the world rankings, and in 1996. A member of Germany's Davis Cup-

winning team in 1988–89, by the end of 1997 his Davis Cup singles record was an astonishing 38–3.

Pauline Betz
Born: *August 6, 1919*
Dayton, OH, USA

Now Mrs Addie, Pauline Betz was a very intelligent, fast-moving player whose baseline game proved too much for most of her contemporaries. Her brilliantly elegant backhand was only one reason why some called her the American Lenglen and, but for the interruption of the 1939–45 war, she would most probably have earned many more international successes. She was the most successful American player throughout that time, particularly on the grass courts at Forest Hills where her fine strokes helped her beat Louise Brough twice and Margaret Osborne to win three successive American titles in 1942–44.

When at last, aged 26 in 1946, she was able to play at Wimbledon, this dashing, all-court player was at her outstanding best. She dropped only 20 games in her six matches, beating Brough 6–2, 6–4 in the final and, by

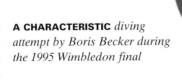

A CHARACTERISTIC *diving attempt by Boris Becker during the 1995 Wimbledon final*

turning professional after beating Doris Hart to win the US Championships three months later, remains one of only four women champions who never lost a singles at Wimbledon. The others are Lottie Dod, Suzanne Lenglen and Maureen Connolly.

Blanche Bingley Hillyard
Born: *November 3, 1863*
Greenford, Middlesex, UK

Blanche Bingley, as she was when she competed in the inaugural women's singles event at Wimbledon in 1884, went on to become one of the leading pioneers of women's tennis. Apart from winning the singles title six times, there was an amazing 14-year span, a record, between her winning for the first time in 1886 and the last in 1900. Indeed, as late as 1912, at the age of 48, when she competed for the 23rd and penultimate time, she still reached the semi-finals before losing to the champion, Ethel Larcombe.

In 1887 Blanche, who was noted for her sportsmanship, especially when playing someone less gifted than herself, married George Hillyard, an equally enthusiastic player who, after retiring as a Commander in the Royal Navy, was secretary of the All England Club from 1907 to 1924. Their tennis house parties at Thorpe-Satchville in Leicestershire were, as Alan Little, the librarian to the All England Club, has discovered in his meticulous research, "notable lawn tennis events in themselves".

Bjorn Borg,

Born: *June 6, 1956*
Sodertaljie, Sweden
(See Legends pp74–75)

Jean Borotra

Born: *August 13, 1898*
Arbonne, Basses-Pyrénées, France

Despite his flamboyant style, emphasized by the way he would suddenly don his black beret at a crucial stage in a match to denote that he was about to redouble his challenge, few can ever have taken tennis, or life for that matter, so seriously as Jean Borotra, who was 95 when he died. Until a couple of years before that, "The Bounding Basque", as this player seemingly made of india rubber was known, still played tennis once or twice a week, with his competitive instinct as strong as ever.

Borotra's game consisted of fearless attacking at the net and there are many who say that his backhand volley and smash were the best the game has ever seen. The best-known of France's "Musketeers", who dominated the Davis Cup and men's tennis generally in the second half of the 1920s and early 1930s, Borotra won Wimbledon in 1924 and 1926, the Australian in 1928 and the French title in 1931, in addition to doubles or mixed titles at all four of the Grand Slam tournaments. He was also a member of the French Davis Cup team in 1922–37 and again in 1947.

A passionate supporter of ICs, the International Clubs around the world, he still competed in veterans' tournaments, including Wimbledon, until 1977. And that made him unique for it meant he had taken part in the celebrations for the 50th, 75th and 100th anniversary of The Championships.

John Bromwich

Born: *November 14, 1918*
Sydney, NSW, Australia

This master of spin and strategy is regarded as one of the finest doubles players in the game's history and another whose successes were probably limited because he was just beginning to reach his peak when the Second World War prevented inter-

national competition for six years. Bromwich was an unorthodox player, ambidextrous – although he used both hands on the forehand – both for the drive and his volleys. His major singles triumphs were recorded at the Australian Championships in 1939 and again in 1946, when he beat fellow Australian Adrian Quist, with whom he won the US doubles title just before the outbreak of war. This famous partnership was to win the Australian doubles title eight times, 1938–40 and 1946–50.

After the war he reached the Wimbledon final in 1948 but, despite

JEAN BOROTRA, *the Bounding Basque, complete with black beret*

holding three match points when leading 5–3 in the fifth set, he decided to play safely and paid a heavy price. He allowed Bob Falkenburg to escape and beat him 7–5, 0–6, 6–2, 3–6, 7–5.

Sir Norman Brookes

Born: *November 14, 1877*
Melbourne, Victoria, Australia

A left-hander with a fine volley, he won the All-Comers' singles on his first visit to Wimbledon in 1905 but was so exhausted that he had insufficient energy left when he met Laurie Doherty in the Challenge Round. Two

years later, though, aged 29, he was in devastating form and became the first overseas player to win the men's singles at The Championships, repeating his success seven years later in 1914 when his volleying and smashing denied victory to New Zealander Tony Wilding, who partnered him to success in the doubles in both his years of singles triumph.

Returning to Wimbledon as defending champion after the war, he lost the Challenge Round to Gerald Patterson. He competed for the last time in 1924, aged 47 and thrilled the crowds by volleying his way to the fourth round, especially in one match which lasted an exhausting five sets. Seven times a member of winning Australian teams in the Davis Cup, he was also a first-class golfer and cricketer and was awarded a knighthood in 1939.

Louise Brough

Born: *March 11, 1923*
Oklahoma City, OK, USA

For three years, 1948–50, Louise Brough dominated Wimbledon more completely than any other player before or since those days, by reaching nine finals and winning eight of them. In addition to winning the singles and doubles crowns three years in succession, this aggressive volleyer won the mixed doubles with John Bromwich in 1948 and with South African Eric Sturgess in 1950. She had played in 51 matches over those three years and won 50, the one defeat coming in the mixed doubles final of 1949, when she played all three finals on one day.

She had walked on to Centre Court at 2 p.m. precisely and beaten Margaret du Pont 10–8, 1–6, 10–8. Together they beat Gussie Moran and Pat Todd 8–6, 7–5 in the doubles. Then, almost seven hours after she had started playing, she and Bromwich were beaten by Sturgess and Sheila Summers in the mixed final. Brough had played 117 games in eight sets.

Between 1946 and 1957, Brough who became Mrs Clapp in 1958, never failed to reach at least the quarter-finals at Wimbledon and won Wimbledon for a fourth time in 1955. In addition, apart from winning the US singles in 1947, the Australian in 1950

LOUISE BROUGH *in the 1950 Wimbledon final against Darlene Hard*

and building a 12–0 singles record in the Wightman Cup, she and Margaret du Pont were almost unbeatable in doubles. They won Wimbledon together five times and the US title 12, while in mixed doubles she won Wimbledon four times with three different partners.

Jacques Brugnon

Born: *May 11, 1895*
Paris, France

Brugnon was the doubles specialist among the French "Musketeers". Although a sometimes brittle temperament limited his achievements in singles – he five times missed match points which would have taken him into the 1926 Wimbledon final – he had the skill and ability to blend with almost any confident partner in doubles and Bill Tilden is on record as saying "What 'Toto' (as he was called) doesn't know about doubles isn't worth knowing."

He won the doubles at Wimbledon and the French twice each with Jean Borotra and three times at the French and twice at Wimbledon, with Cochet. Brugnon also won the French mixed five times with Suzanne Lenglen. He won the Australian title with Borotra in 1928 and succeeded in 22 of his 31 Davis Cup rubbers. Brugnon was made a Chevalier of the Legion of Honour and later became Davis Cup captain. He and Borotra were still one of the finest teams when both were into their 40s, coming within a point of reaching the French final in 1939. They made their Grand Slam farewell performance, aged 53 and 51 respectively, at Wimbledon in 1948, where crowds thronged to cheer their progress to the third round.

Sergi Bruguera

Born: *January 16, 1971*
Barcelona, Spain

Coached by his father, Luis, this 6ft-2in right-hander made fine progress during 1997 towards restoring his ranking and reputation after a prolonged foot injury had prevented him building on consecutive successes at the French Open in 1993–94. Having sustained a fourth-place world ranking in those two years, he slipped to 81 by the end of 1996, but over the following 12 months soared once more to finish in eighth place. Even so he was the first since Jimmy Connors in 1987 to qualify for the end-of-the-year Championships without winning a tournament in the previous 12 months.

Having demonstrated his clay-court prowess so effectively, Bruguera has since been determined, like a growing band of Spaniards, to broaden his game, and in Key Biscayne in March 1997 his new-found attacking tennis surprisingly upset Pete Sampras, among others, on his way to the final where he lost to another traditional clay-courter, Thomas Muster. In early summer of 1997 looked set to claim a third triumph at Roland Garros, but was well beaten by the hungry newcomer Gustavo Kuerten.

Don Budge

Born: *June 13, 1915*
Oakland, CA, USA

Don Budge will always be remembered as the first player to win the Grand Slam. When he won the French singles title in 1938 he became the reigning champion of the four major tournaments – Wimbledon, US, French and Australian – at the same time. And he went on to maintain that unique status by winning the Wimbledon and American titles for a second time, so that he had also then won all four of them in the same calendar year.

Budge, a dynamic player with a volley to match, is also in the Wimbledon record-books as the only player to complete a hat-trick of all three titles at The Championships in consecutive years, 1937–38. A great favourite with crowds all round the world, who admired his famous grin and fiery red hair almost as much as his brilliant backhand and wonderful temperament, Budge played his most famous match at Wimbledon in the Davis Cup. It was against Gottfried von Cramm on the Centre Court in the Inter-Zone final in 1937. Budge recovered from 2–5 in the fifth set of the deciding fifth rubber to take the Americans into the final where they regained the trophy for the first time since 1926 by beating the holders, Britain (Fred Perry had by then turned professional), in the Challenge Round. A peerless competitor, he won 25 of his 29 Davis Cup rubbers before he turned professional in 1939.

Maria Bueno

Born: *October 11, 1939*
São Paulo, Brazil

A player of rare grace and artistry, Maria Bueno is one of the few players whose success provoked her compatriots to issue a postage stamp bearing her portrait, and her statue still stands in one of the main parks. Her rivalry with Margaret Court (Smith) was a major feature of women's tennis in the 1960s. In style

SERGI BRUGERA, *twice French Open champion*

MARIA BUENO *on her toes in the 1959 Wimbledon final*

they were so different – Bueno so artistic and with such economy of effort, Court with such impressive power – but in the end the Brazilian's efforts were weakened by poor health and arm injuries which meant a premature end to her career.

Maria first made her mark internationally when, aged 18, she won the Italian Championship in Rome after saving match points against the holder, Shirley Brasher (Bloomer) in the quarter-finals. Between 1958 and 1967 she won 115 matches at Wimbledon, including 49 in singles, taking the title three times – in 1959, 1960 and, after building up her game following an attack of jaundice which prevented her playing in 1961, again in 1964. She was also four times winner of the US singles and 1960 champion in Australia. The most dramatic of her many clashes with Margaret Court was in the final of the Italian in 1962 when the Australian's greater athleticism and stamina pulled her through 8–6, 5–7, 6–4.

Jennifer Capriati

Born: *March 29, 1976*
New York, NY, USA

Although Jennifer Capriati has never gone beyond the semi-final at any of the four Grand Slam tournaments, she has still had a wide-ranging and lasting effect on the game. Her problems off the court, largely stemming from the mounting pressures she faced on it, undoubtedly contributed to the decision to re-introduce a minimum age limit of 14 for competitors in international tournaments.

Capriati was first in the spotlight when, aged 13, she played for the United States in the Wightman Cup

and beat Britain's Clare Wood 6–0, 6–0, prompting Billie Jean King, who had been watching, to predict that she would be world champion by the time she was 18. For a time that looked possible. Aged 14, she was the youngest to be ranked in the women's top 10. Aged 15, she became Wimbledon's youngest semi-finalist in 1991 after beating Martina Navratilova and in the same year finished among the top 40 highest-paid athletes in the world.

Success, though, was becoming increasingly difficult for her to live with and, despite winning the gold medal by beating Steffi Graf from a set down in the Olympic final in Barcelona in 1992, most of her efforts were limited to a series of short-lived comebacks, as she has tried to put allegations of drug-taking and shoplifting behind her. She finally overcame such problems to regularly make the latter stages of the majors with back-to-back Australian Open titles (2001–02) and the French Open (2001) when she also ended the year ranked No2.

Rosie Casals

Born: *September 16, 1948*
San Francisco, CA, USA

Her ebullient personality and ability to retrieve from all parts of the court, rather in the style that Arantxa Sanchez Vicario copied a couple of decades later, made Rosie Casals a welcome arrival to the international tennis scene in 1966. Yet her lack of stature, just 5ft, coupled with a relatively humble background, meant that for most of her career she was more often one of the supporting acts, rather than the star.

She reached a career-best sixth in what were then unofficial world rankings provided by the *New York Times* and the *Daily Telegraph* in 1967, but enjoyed her greatest successes in doubles with Billie Jean King. They won Wimbledon five times between 1967 and 1973. She also won the US doubles four times, twice with Mrs King and then with Judy Dalton in 1971 and Wendy Turnbull in 1982.

Toward the end of her lengthy career, in which she lived through the transformation from non-prize-

money to fortune-making days, she also made headlines at a time when tennis was just about getting used to pastel colours, by appearing in a shimmering Stars and Stripes outfit made for her by Ted Tinling. It was the talk of the Tour!

Pat Cash

Born: *May 27, 1965*
Melbourne, Victoria, Australia

In recent years Cash has been fighting a frustrating, increasingly fruitless battle against injuries, but no one will ever be able to take away from him that memorable Sunday afternoon in July 1987 when this classic hard-fighting server and volleyer won the title he wanted more than any other – Wimbledon. To do so, he beat Jimmy Connors in the semi-finals and Ivan Lendl in the final, both in straight sets. It was an astonishing achievement after the events of the previous year when a back injury and then an emergency appendectomy saw his world ranking slump to 413, but he defiantly went ahead and played at Wimbledon three weeks after the surgery – and reached the quarter-finals.

By May 1988 he had reached the semi-finals at the Australian Open for a second time and climbed to a career-best fourth in the world list. He looked ready to challenge seriously for all the major honours, just as he had first done when he held two match points for a place in the US Open final against Lendl, when still a teenager, in 1984. But in April 1989, while playing in Tokyo, he ruptured the Achilles tendon in his right ankle and, despite occasional triumphs since then, the last of the six singles titles won by this London-based, guitar-playing music fan was in Hong Kong in 1990. He now plays in Seniors events.

Michael Chang

Born: *February 22, 1972*
Hoboken, NJ, USA

A devout Christian, who never misses an opportunity to stress the fact, Michael Chang was introduced to tennis by his father, Joe, who like his mother, Betty, is a research chemist. Michael's career became very much a family enterprise for, since 1991, he

PAT CASH'S *athleticism helped him become Wimbledon champion in 1987*

José-Luis Clerc

Born: *August 16, 1958*
Buenos Aires, Argentina

In 1981 this lean six-footer, who had already attracted attention as an outstanding junior on clay courts, dominated the American summer circuit by winning four consecutive Grand Prix tournaments and, together with Davis Cup performances, enjoying a 28-match winning run before losing in the last 16 of the US Open. He had captured his first major title by winning the Italian Open, and for the first time had overtaken Guillermo Vilas as the highest-ranked player in Argentina. In addition he also contributed immensely to Argentina's achievement in reaching the final of the Davis Cup for the only time.

For all his elegant skills, though, Clerc's temperament was brittle – he too easily allowed himself to become disheartened, despite the encouragement he should have derived from twice reaching the semi-finals at the French, losing over five sets to Ivan Lendl in 1981 and then over four sets to Mats Wilander a year later.

Kim Clijsters

Born: *June 8, 1983*
Bilzen, Belgium

One of the most popular players on the circuit, Kim Clijsters overcame serious injuries to re-establish herself on the circuit in 2005. Prior to that, she reached four Grand Slam finals but failed to claim any of them. However she did win the end of season WTA Championships in 2003, the year she first topped the rankings in August.

A serious injury to her wrist collected in March 2004 sidelined the Belgian, preventing her from challenging for any honors for a year. But when she finally returned in 2005 having rehabilitated from surgery, it was dramatic. She won nine titles including her first at Grand Slam level, the US Open, with wins over Wimbledon champion Venus Williams, the top seeded Maria Sharapova and in the final, Mary Pierce who was also rediscovering lost form. Her victory netted her $2.2 million in prize money, the largest purse ever won by

was coached by brother Carl, with whom he occasionally used to compete in doubles.

He made his mark early. In 1987 he became the youngest player, at 15 years 6 months, to win a main draw-match at the US Open and one month later became the youngest to reach the semi-final of an ATP Tour event in Scottsdale. It was at the French Open in 1989, though, when still only 17 years 3

months, that he struck the jackpot. He became the youngest winner of the French Open and the youngest male winner of a Grand Slam title, plus the first American to win at Roland Garros since Tony Trabert in 1955.

Total focus, consistency, concentration and commitment have been the match-winning characteristics of a game which has worn down so many of his most gifted opponents, most

notably his epic fourth-round defeat of Ivan Lendl on his way to the French title, when he suffered so badly from cramp that he even served underarm at one point, rather than submit as he recovered from two sets down to a win after 4 hours 37 minutes. He was runner-up in three other Grand Slam finals and until 1997 was never ranked lower than 6th, peaking at 2 in 1996.

HENRI COCHET *on No. 1 Court at Wimbledon, 1929*

a woman player in the history of sport.

As one of the new breed of power players, she is exciting to watch, especially when deploying her trademark sliding splits while retrieving wide shots.

With 30 titles to her name at the end of the 2005 season, she has already indicated that she intends retiring in 2007 but having reclaimed the world number one slot, she may well reconsider if she remains healthy and is still challenging at the highest levels.

Henri Cochet

Born: *December 14, 1901*
Villeurbanne, Lyons, France

Henri Cochet, who died in April 1987, was described by contemporaries as "one of the greatest geniuses tennis has even seen". There was certainly a wonderfully extravagant artistry to his volleying, a ruthless authority to his smash, and his ability to counter the most feared servers of his time became legendary. The third of the French "Musketeers" to win Wimbledon, not just once but twice, his triumphs came in 1927 and 1929. His initial success was achieved in a manner fit for a fairytale. He won his quarter-final against the American Frank Hunter from two sets down, the semi-final from Bill Tilden not just from two sets down but also from 1–5 in the third set, and the final, also from two sets down, against fellow Frenchman Jean Borotra, who had six match points.

His overall singles record at Wimbledon was 43–8, while he also won the doubles twice. At the French Championships he won the singles every other year during 1926–32, the men's doubles three times and won 44 of his 58 Davis Cup singles rubbers. With the other three Musketeers, he six times helped France win the Davis Cup Challenge Round, but it was his defeat by Fred Perry in 1933 which proved the key rubber, when Britain snatched the trophy from them in such dramatic fashion.

Maureen Connolly,

Born: *September 17, 1934*
San Diego, CA, USA
(See Legends pp74–75)

Jimmy Connors,

Born: September 2, 1952
Belleville, IL, USA
(See Legends pp76–77)

Ashley Cooper

Born: *September 15, 1936*
Melbourne, Victoria, Australia

At a time when Ken Rosewall and Lew Hoad had turned professional and were banned from traditional tournaments in which only amateurs were permitted, this determined, hard-hitting competitor was more than capable of helping to maintain Australian dominance. He was only 17 the first time he played at Wimbledon in 1954, losing in the fourth round to Rosewall. He returned to Europe two years later when he reached the semi-finals in singles and the final of the doubles with Hoad, so he had served a solid apprenticeship by the time it was his turn to take full responsibility.

His first Grand Slam title came in Australia in 1957 and, although there was a setback to his confidence when he was outplayed by Hoad, winning only five games in that year's Wimbledon final, he really came into his own in 1958. Apart from winning both singles and doubles in Australia, he won the French doubles (with Neale Fraser) for a second time, the singles at Wimbledon and the singles and doubles in the US Championships. He was also in the Australian Davis Cup teams which won 1957 and finished runners-up in 1958.

Charlotte Cooper

Born: *September 22, 1870*
Ealing, Middlesex, UK

One of the first women to demonstrate an impressive volley at Wimbledon, Charlotte Cooper won the women's singles title five times, in 1895, 1896, 1898, 1901 and 1908. She competed in the singles event 18 times between 1893 and 1908, initially when she was living with her parents in Surbiton.

She used to cycle to and from The Championships, which were then staged in Worple Road, with her racket clipped on to a bracket on the fork. It is said that one evening when she returned her father was by the front gate, clipping the hedge. "Where have you been dear?" he inquired. "To Wimbledon, of course, father", she replied. "Ah yes, I remember now, you mentioned it. You were playing in the final, weren't you? How did you get on?" "I won", she said quite simply. "I'm so glad", said her father ... who then continued to cut the hedge.

In 1902 Charlotte, by then Mrs Sterry, defended her title in the Challenge Round against Muriel Robb. Weather conditions were so bad that the match was halted at one set all. But next day, instead of continuing from that point, officials decided that the match should begin all over again. Miss Robb, who had been 4–6, 13–11 overnight, won 7–5, 6–1 so mathematically, at least, the women's final lasted a record 53 games.

Jim Courier

Born: *August 17, 1970*
Sanford, FL, USA

A prominent junior who twice won the Orange Bowl, 1986 and 1987, Jim Courier began 1998 as one of only six players in the Open era who had reached the singles final of all four Grand Slam tournaments. He had won two of them: Australia twice (1992 and 1993), after both of which he celebrated by taking a dip, still in his tennis kit, in the nearby Yarra river in Melbourne; and twice at the French, 1991 and 1992.

Following an injury during 1996, which ended his run of playing in 30 consecutive Grand Slam tournaments and led to him dropping out of the top 10 for only the second time in six years, he has struggled to find the penetrative power needed in a game based more on energy and effort than artistry.

JIM COURIER, *a tenacious fighter*

During 1992 Courier, also famous for his white baseball cap, briefly moved to the top of the world rankings but stayed there for only six weeks. He was more successful a year later, which was also the only year in which he has gone beyond the quarter-finals at Wimbledon, by staying at number one for 17 weeks.

Margaret Court,
Born: July 16, 1942
Albury, New South Wales, Australia
(See Legends pp78–79)

Thelma Coyne Long
Born: *October 14, 1918*
Sydney, NSW, Australia

Her beautiful strokes and often delicate, but no less decisive, volleying made Thelma Long almost invincible in tournaments in Australia. The former Miss T.D. Coyne won the singles title at the Australian Championships in 1952 and 1954, but the doubles title no less than 12 times, 10 with Nancy Wynne Bolton and later twice with Mary Hawton.

In 1952 she was triple Australian champion and at Wimbledon took a set from Maureen Connolly, something only one other player achieved in the American's three glorious years at The Championships. For good measure, she also reached the final of the mixed doubles with Enrique Morea.

Jack Crawford
Born: *March 22, 1908*
Albury, NSW, Australia

A stylish, classical player who impressed everyone with his craftsmanship and elegance. Bill Tilden rated him second only to Henri Cochet as an artist. Fred Perry, who was only just beginning to make his move at the top of the game when Crawford won the Australian title in 1931, was always equally lavish in his praise of an opponent he was to come to know so well.

Tall and heavily built, Crawford usually played in a long-sleeved cricket shirt, without even rolling up the sleeve of his playing arm as he wielded a square-headed racket, generally from the baseline and always with accurate pace. That was

LINDSAY DAVENPORT, *one of the new wave Americans*

never better demonstrated than in the 1933 Wimbledon final when he beat Ellsworth Vines. The score, 4–6, 11–9, 6–2, 2–6, 6–4, reflected the changing flow of a final which was hailed at the time as the best there had been.

Crawford went on to Forest Hills, the outstanding favourite to complete the Grand Slam, but by then he was overplayed and Perry, maintaining unrelenting pressure from the net, beat him in five sets. He was never the same again.

Lindsay Davenport
Born: *June 8, 1976*
Palos Verdes, CA, USA

Although the tall, sturdily built right-hander made a strong early impression by reaching the quarter-finals of both the Australian Open and Wimbledon when she was 18, her progress then shuddered to a halt for a while before starting to take off

again in 1996. Psychologically she received a tremendous boost when she beat four higher-ranked players to win the gold medal at the Olympic Games in Atlanta, while in doubles she and Mary Joe Fernandez won five titles, including the French Open.

By the start of 1998 Davenport was third in the women's world rankings, after briefly flirting with second place at the end of 1997, during which she had reached her first Grand Slam tournament semi-final at the US Open. She went on to reach five Grand Slam finals, winning the US Open title and Wimbledon. In addition to 10 major semi-final appearances, she also won the WTA Championships in 1999, finishing the year at the top of the rankings on four occasions.

Owen Davidson
Born: *October 4, 1943*
Melbourne, Victoria, Australia

During an eventful and varied career, which included being professional to the All England Club and coach to Britain's Davis Cup team 1967–70, the bulk of Owen Davidson's significant victories came in doubles, not least at Wimbledon in 1973 when it was with

his support in the final of the mixed doubles that Billie Jean King became the last triple champion at SW19.

It was their fourth triumph at The Championships and in 1966 they had also won the mixed in South Africa, France and the US, while the same year Davidson won at the Australian Open with Lesley Turner. In men's doubles he won the Australian with Ken Rosewall in 1972 and the US Open with John Newcombe in 1973. His best Grand Slam performance in singles was in reaching the Wimbledon semi-finals in 1966, losing to eventual champion Manuel Santana.

Sven Davidson
Born: *July 13, 1928*
Boras, Sweden

One of the outstanding Swedish players before the advent of Bjorn Borg, Sven Davidson was ranked three in the unofficial world list in 1957 after his determination had been rewarded, when he beat Ashley Cooper and then Herbie Flam in the final, by winning the French title after being runner-up in the two previous years to Flam and Lew Hoad. It was Hoad who again thwarted him in the

Wimbledon semi-finals, also in 1957.

At a time when regular international competition was still restricted to a very few, he progressed rapidly from dominating tennis at home. He was one point away from beating Ken Rosewall in the quarter-finals of the US Championships in 1953. He won the doubles at Wimbledon in 1958 with Ulf Schmidt and won 61 of 84 Davis Cup rubbers during 1950–60. He now lives in America.

Dwight F. Davis

Born: *July 5, 1879*
St Louis, MO, USA

Famous as the donor of the Davis Cup, he played in the opening match in 1900, winning in both singles and doubles. His intention was that the trophy should be called the International Lawn Tennis Challenge Trophy, but it was originally referred to by members of the Longwood Cricket Club where the Davis Cup was launched as "Dwight's Pot".

He became US Secretary of War in 1925, then Governor of the Philippines, and died in November 1945. As a player, this aggressive, big-serving, left-handed Harvard graduate, who won the NCAA title in 1899, developed a notable partnership with fellow American Holcombe Ward. They won the US doubles in 1899–1901 when they were also runners-up to the Dohertys at Wimbledon in the All-Comers' final.

Eddie Dibbs

Born: *February 23, 1951*
Brooklyn, NY, USA

The story may be apocryphal, but it is said that someone once left an Eddie Dibbs match in the middle of a point to buy a hot dog and a drink from a nearby concession stand, and when he returned the same point was still being played. Whatever the truth of that story, the diminutive American who was the highest prize-money-earner on the circuit in 1984 when he won 84 of 111 matches, was certainly one of the toughest opponents to break down and one of the greatest retrievers.

He turned professional in 1972 and was particularly effective on clay courts, reaching the semi-finals of the

French in 1975–76, although his best performance at the US Open was in three times reaching the last eight. He won 22 singles titles and was four times in the top 10 in end-of-year rankings. His best was 5th in July 1978.

Lottie Dod

Born: *September 24, 1871*
Bebington, Cheshire, UK

In recent years, especially before a minimum 16 age limit was introduced, more and more girls of school age have made a considerable impact at Wimbledon. None, though, has yet beaten Charlotte (Lottie) Dod's record as the youngest singles champion of any sex. She was 15 years 285 days old when she won the title for the first of five times in 1887. Indeed, she was never beaten there. Her tremendous forehand and fiery attacking at the net, impressively backing up her canny underarm serving, were already well known. She had won her first tournament, in which adults were also eligible to compete, when she was 11, albeit in doubles. In those days, the number of entries varied considerably. In 1887 she had to play three matches to become champion. It was the same in 1891, when she won after not having played for two years. Otherwise her only matches were in the Challenge Round.

Frustrated that she was not suffi-

LOTTIE DOD – *a legend*

ciently tested, she succeeded, too, in other sports. She won the British Women's Golf Championships at Troon in 1904 and was twice capped for England at hockey, in 1899 and 1900. An archery silver medallist at the 1908 Olympic Games in London, she was an outstanding skater, did the Cresta Run, rowed and was an accomplished musician. Not surprisingly she was nicknamed the "Little Wonder".

Laurence Doherty

Born: *October 8, 1875*
Wimbledon, London, UK

Like his brother, Laurence Doherty suffered a premature death. He was

only 43 when he died in 1919, 17 years after he had won the Wimbledon singles titles for the first time. In many ways he and Reggie were the game's first major heroes, for both were renowned almost as much for their impeccable sportsmanship as for their successes. His second Wimbledon singles victory came in 1906, but by then there were many other triumphs listed against their names. At the 1900 Olympic Games they won two gold medals each, while both were members of the British Davis Cup team in 1902–06 when Laurie was unbeaten in singles and doubles with his brother.

They also became the first overseas pair to win the US doubles title, in 1902, and the following year not only repeated the achievement but were instrumental in beating the Americans in the Davis Cup final – the first time the British Isles team, as it was called then, had been successful.

Reginald Doherty.

Born: *October 14, 1872*
Wimbledon, London, UK

The Doherty brothers, Reggie and Laurence, known to their contemporaries as "Big Do" and "Little Do", monopolized the singles and doubles at Wimbledon between 1897 when Reggie won the singles for the first of

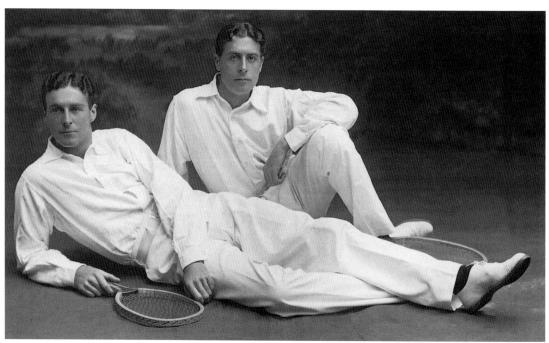

THE DOHERTY BROTHERS, *Laurence in the forefront and Reggie*

four consecutive occasions and 1906, the last of their 10 successive appearances in the final of the doubles which they won eight times.

Reggie, whose backhand was the envy of his contemporaries, was renowned for his magnificent all-court tennis, something he had honed first at Westminster School and then at Cambridge, a path his brother was to follow three years after him.

Despite frequent bouts of poor health – he died at the age of 36 – Reggie beat former champion Wilfred Baddeley on his way to winning Wimbledon for the first time in 1897, without losing a set, and successfully retained the trophy for another three years. He was also a formidable golfer.

Dorothea Douglass Chambers

Born: *September 3, 1878*
Ealing, Middlesex, UK

As Dorothea Douglass, she won the first of her remarkable seven Wimbledon singles championships in 1903, but her extraordinary impact on women's tennis spanned two decades and, in many ways, two completely different eras. During most of the early years of the twentieth century, leading into the 1914–18 War, this outstanding sportswoman, who was also the All England women's badminton champion in 1903, dominated women's tennis with her tenacity and wide variety of teasing and thrusting shots.

When she won Wimbledon for a fifth time in 1911, by which time she had become Mrs Lambert Chambers and started a family, she won the Challenge Round against Dora Boothby without dropping a game. After missing the 1912 tournament, she returned to win again in 1913 and 1914, but perhaps her most memorable match was in the first post-war final in 1919, the first visit by the legendary Suzanne Lenglen. In one of the most dramatic contests imaginable, one era came to an end and another, even richer, started, as Lenglen won 10–8, 4–6, 9–7, but Dorothea, then 40, held two match points before being forced to surrender her title. She went on to become a coach in 1928 and died in 1960.

Jaroslav Drobny

Born: *October 12, 1921*
Prague, Czechoslovakia

Jaroslav Drobny, who first played at Wimbledon as a Czechoslovakian, played in the 1952 final as an Egyptian and was living in London by the time he won the title two years later, will always be remembered as the man who, probably more than any other, prevented Ken Rosewall winning the one major title to elude him.

For their final in 1954 Rosewall, then 19, was the favourite, not least because there were question marks about Drobny's ability to win big matches under the pressure of being expected to win. These, though, were to be swept away in magnificent style. Drobny, a left-hander with a glorious touch, who had already won the French title twice and the Italian three times, beat second-seeded Lew Hoad in the quarter-finals and Budge Patty to reach the final.

It was Drobny's third appearance in the final and one of the most emotional in the history of The Championships as the bespectacled, burly "Drob" displayed his superb forehand, dynamic overheads, a serve which even by modern standards would be regarded as fast and supreme volleying to the full for a 13–11, 4–6, 6–2, 9–7 triumph. He went on to compete four more times after that storybook occasion, before retiring in 1960, 22 years after his first Wimbledon as a 16-year-old.

Françoise Durr

Born: *December 25, 1942*
Béziers, France

This likeable, devoted tennis enthusiast, who in recent years has played a leading role in helping to guide new generations of women players in France, enjoyed considerable success for someone who was self-taught and therefore developed an unorthodox style, which eventually became her trademark. Despite being ungainly, her backhand was hugely effective, while her serve, which at times looked to be little more than a pat into the court to get the play started, was clearly more than that judging by how often it led to her winning service

points. Although most of her principal successes came in doubles – she was runner-up at Wimbledon no less than six times, with five different partners – she was the first French national to win the French singles championship for 19 years when she took the title in 1967.

In that same year she also began a run of five consecutive doubles victories at Roland Garros. "Frankie", as she is popularly known, was one of the first women players to turn professional once the Open era began in 1968 and she was ranked in the world's top 10 consistently from 1965 to 1975.

Stefan Edberg

Born: *January 19, 1966*
Vastervik, Sweden

When the illustrious career of this elegant craftsman ended with his retirement in 1996, the Swedish Tennis Association presented him with a telescope. "You've been a star all your life so now you can look at the stars," they told him.

At a time when men's tennis was moving ever faster into the age of power and pace, Edberg, a long-time London resident, was a joyful reminder of times past, as well as the present, with his subtle mix of speed, skill and style. The first winner of a junior Grand Slam in 1983, he went on to collect six Grand Slam titles (two each at Wimbledon, Flushing Meadows and the Australian Open), while making a record 54 consecutive appearances in Grand Slam tournaments from Wimbledon 1983 to the US Open of 1996.

He won 41 singles titles plus 18 doubles titles and was twice a member of winning Swedish Davis Cup teams. In the increasingly harsh commercial world of professional sport, he remained the consummate sportsman, winning the ATP Tour's Sportsmanship Award so many times that now the award is named after him.

Roy Emerson

Born: *November 3, 1936*
Blackbutt, Queensland, Australia

Going into 2000, Roy Emerson still had his eminent place in the game's history, as the winner of more Grand Slam singles titles (12) than any other. They include the Australian five years in succession, 1963–67, admittedly when many of his contemporaries were turning professional, the French, Wimbledon and US Championships twice. He was, in fact, unlucky not to have won Wimbledon for a third consecutive year since, having won in 1964 and 1965, he was the strong favourite to win again when he was injured in the quarter-finals and beaten by compatriot Owen Davidson.

His injury was the outcome of chasing a drop shot at high speed and colliding with the net post. Such dashing pace was typical of the world number one in 1964 and 1965, who had, as a boy, run 100 yards in 10.6 seconds. In 1964 he beat fellow countryman Fred Stolle in the finals of the Australian, Wimbledon and the US, but a semi-final defeat by Nicola Pietrangeli at the French denied him a Slam. Emerson, who won the French doubles title for six consecutive years, 1960–65, with five different partners and won 34 out of his 38 rubbers for Australia in 18 Davis Cup ties, including nine successive Challenge Rounds, was in the vanguard of players who proved by example that it was possible to serve and volley throughout for five sets.

Thomas Enqvist

Born: *March 13, 1974*
Stockholm, Sweden

An early beginner – he started playing at the age of five – Enqvist, who won the junior titles in Australia and Wimbledon in 1991, has since pressed hard to try and emulate such success at the senior level, although injuries and illness in 1997 meant him slipping out of the top 10 to 23rd in the world rankings.

Enqvist, a solid, all-round player, particularly strong off the ground, looked all set to make the big breakthrough in 1996. In the previous year, after reaching six finals on the ATP Tour and winning five of them, he was

STEFAN EDBERG, *a master of perfection*

voted the Tour's Most Improved Player and, on his debut at the year-ending Championships, reached the semi-finals where only his lack of experience in such surroundings denied him the chance to beat Boris Becker.

It wasn't until 1999 that he made his only Grand Slam final appearance, losing to the Russian Yevgeny Kafelnikov in four sets. One of the highlights of his career was his contribution in 1996 towards Sweden's brave bid, after Stefan Edberg had been injured, to win an epic Davis Cup final. Having beaten Arnaud Boetsch on the first day, he recovered from two sets to love down to beat Cedric Pioline at the start of the third day to level the scores at 2–2. His effort was in vain – but heroic nonetheless.

Chris Evert Lloyd

Born: *December 21, 1954*
Fort Lauderdale, FL, USA

Mention the name Chris Evert in tennis circles and three qualities in particular immediately come to mind: concentration, determination and sophistication. In a career spanning 19 years, Christine Marie Evert set a whole series of records which only an even more exceptional champion, Martina Navratilova, has broken.

Long before Chris began drilling those double-handed backhands with an accuracy and consistency which almost every other woman player in the world wanted to copy, the name Evert was already one of the most respected in tennis circles in Florida. The persistent and, above all, patient ability of her father Jimmy, winner of the Canadian men's singles title in 1947, to draw the best out of countless youngsters who were first coached by him in Fort Lauderdale was well known. Yet neither he, Chris nor anyone else could have sensed the full extent of what was to follow when, as a 15-year-old schoolgirl and already one of the most promising of her age anyone in the United States could remember, she competed in a relatively insignificant tournament in North Carolina in the autumn of 1970 and beat Margaret

Chris Evert, *the perfect ambassador*

Court, who was not only the best player in the world at the time but had only recently become the first woman, since the arrival of Open tennis two years earlier, to win the Grand Slam.

Evert had been raised on clay courts and had had instilled into her the need to make sure she rallied from the baseline longer than the girl on the other side of the net, so it was no surprise that the majority of her major successes came on clay, including a record seven at the French Open.

Evert's remorselessly efficient double-handed backhand, developed more by accident than design, was to be her most significant weapon on the way to winning 157 singles titles, second only to Navratilova, and $8.8m in prize money. Having retained her amateur status until 1972, she was to become the first woman to reach career prize money of $1m, three years later. Her record on clay was phenomenal and included a winning streak of 125 matches from August 1973 to May 1979, when Tracy Austin defeated her 6–4, 2–6, 7–6 in the 1979 Italian Open, a figure not beaten on a single surface by any other player, man or woman.

In the early years her romance with Jimmy Connors added to the fascination surrounding this petite, pony-tailed youngster. Throughout her career she had two great playing rivalries. The first was with Evonne Goolagong and ended with Evert holding a 21–12 advantage. The other, which is now part of tennis legend, was with Navratilova.

Familiarity, they say, breeds contempt, but where these two great champions were concerned it created not just huge respect but inspiration

and a constant challenge to both in terms of personal pride.

They were to meet a total of 80 times. Evert, more experienced and more mature, won 11 of the first 12 contests, but Navratilova eventually overtook her and finished 43–37 ahead, winning nine of the 13 major finals in which they faced each other.

Evert, who went on to become president of the Women's Tennis Association, was a model ambassador for the sport. Her behaviour was impeccable, with seldom more than pursed lips or a lifting of an eyebrow, no matter how obvious an error a line call may have been. She was number one in the rankings from 1975 to 1982, and never lower than fourth until announcing her retirement at the 1989 US Open.

Mary Joe Fernandez

Born: *August 19, 1971*
Dominican Republic

Although injuries and ill health dogged much of her career since she first came to prominence in 1985 as the youngest player (14 years 8 days) to win a match at the US Open, this slim, always polite and friendly Floridian maintained a record of impressive consistency. Six times in the period 1990–97 she completed her programme with a place in the top 10.

Her physical limitations were more than compensated for by her dedication and court craft, especially her returns and passing shots off the backhand. The nearest she came to winning a Grand Slam singles title was finishing as runner-up to Steffi Graf in Australia in 1990 and the French in 1993, and to Monica Seles at the Australian in 1992. Yet there have been Grand Slam successes in doubles, at the Australian with Patty Fendick in 1991 and at the French with Lindsay Davenport in 1996, when she was also given special permission to partner Gigi Fernandez (no relation) in Atlanta in defence of their Olympic gold doubles

title from Barcelona in 1992. They repeated their original triumph.

Roger Federer

Born: *June 14, 1969*
Bruhl, Germany
(See Legends pp82–83)

Wayne Ferreira

Born: *September 15, 1971*
Johannesburg, South Africa

Playing in his very first Grand Slam singles match in 1990, this tall, ginger-haired right-hander upset Yannick Noah, who was seeded 16 at the time. Since then the world number one in junior doubles 1989 has gone on to be one of very few modern players who have won titles on all four principal surfaces, grass, hard, clay and carpet. Until 1997, when he lost ground, this versatile, all-court player had hovered round the world's top 10, the first South African to reach that status since official rankings began in 1973. A strong server, with a reliable service return, he has played an important role in lifting South African tennis since the ending of apartheid made it possible for their players to resume travelling freely and their teams to enter international competitions once more. A former schoolboy cricketer, soccer and badminton player, he reached the quarter-finals in singles and doubles at the Atlanta Olympics.

Ken Fletcher

Born: *June 15, 1940*
Queensland, Australia

One of the finest doubles players of his time, this erratic but often quite brilliant player, whose disputes with the Australian tennis authorities led to him becoming domiciled in Hong Kong, will best be remembered for his outstanding partnership in mixed doubles with Margaret Court at Wimbledon. They won the title four times, 1963–68, and in that first year they became the first team to complete the "Grand Slam" in that event. In addition Fletcher won the French doubles in 1964 with Roy Emerson and the Wimbledon doubles two years later with John Newcombe.

Fletcher had fallen foul of the Australian authorities in 1964, when, together with Emerson, Fred Stolle, Marty Mulligan and Bob Hewitt, he was suspended for leaving for the overseas tournament circuit before they said he should. Such things happened in those days. Emerson and Stolle were reinstated after reaching the Wimbledon final. Fletcher emigrated.

Guy Forget

Born: *January 4, 1965*
Casablanca, Morocco

This slim, elegant left-hander, one of the finest counter-hitters of his time, especially on service returns, is one of the few players at any level of the game to have won the same title as his father and grandfather. It happened in Toulouse in 1986 and was his first major success in a career which was to span 16 years. Among the peaks was his match-winning singles victory over Pete Sampras when France won back the Davis Cup for the first time since 1932 in a thrilling final against the United States in 1991.

He needed to undergo knee surgery twice, the second time in 1994 when, having slipped to 1175 during his time recuperating, he returned to the Tour in April but was still only ranked 1130 at the start of Wimbledon, where he took full advantage of a protected pre-injury ranking to be a direct entry. He reached the quarter-finals, beating Jim Courier on the way and ended the fortnight at 213 in the world list. It was the biggest one-tournament rise since official rankings began only eight years after he was born.

Forget's other main successes came in doubles – 28 titles and twice runner-up at Roland Garros, with Jakob Hlasek in 1986 and Yannick Noah in 1987.

Neale Fraser

Born: *October 3, 1933*
Melbourne, Victoria, Australia

From the moment he first picked up a racket as a schoolboy, Neale Fraser's life has been tennis, first as a player, where this powerful left-hander was to become Wimbledon champion in 1960; then, for 20 years, as captain of

the Australian Davis Cup team, winning 18 of the 21 rubbers he played (1958–63) and now as a member of the International Tennis Federation's Davis Cup committee.

In 1962 he and his brother, Dr John Fraser, established a record, at least in this century, as the first brothers to reach the semi-finals at Wimbledon in the same year. His contemporaries remember him most for his cunningly varied serve, which sometimes prompted opponents, finding it impossible to fathom, to liken it to a googly in cricket.

Fraser had lost to another Australian, Ashley Cooper, in the 1958 Wimbledon final, but eventually won the title at his sixth attempt, after saving six match points in the

quarter-finals against Butch Buchholz, who collapsed with cramp at 15–15 in the fourth set and had to retire. Fraser, who also won the US title for the second time that year, enjoyed frequent major successes in doubles.

Shirley Fry

Born: *June 30, 1927*
Akron, OH, USA

For much of her career, this determined player was overshadowed by her American rivals, such as Margaret

GUY FORGET, *a Frenchman at home on any surface*

du Pont, Louise Brough, Doris Hart and Maureen Connolly, so it was a measure of her persistence, as well as her skill, that she eventually became Wimbledon champion when she was already 29, in 1956, eight years after her first attempt.

Shirley Fry, now Mrs K.E. Irvin, achieved her target during a remarkable fortnight. She was seeded five, but to reach the final upset first Althea Gibson in the quarter-finals and then the fading Brough in the semis. Beverley Fleitz, the former Beverley Baker, as second seed, should have come through from the other half but during The Championships discovered she was pregnant and immediately scratched before her quarter-final with Britain's Angela Buxton, who then beat Pat Ward to become the first British finalist since Kay Stammers in 1939.

The final itself was not too much of a test for Fry. She won 6–3, 6–1 and went on to win the singles at the US Championships and the Australian title a few months later, to add to her singles crown in Paris in 1951. She also won doubles titles at all four of the Grand Slams and topped the unofficial world rankings in 1956.

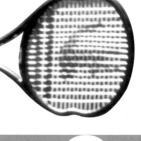

Zina Garrison

Born: November 16, 1963
Houston, TX, USA

Zina, who began playing at the age of 10, owed much to the tuition and above all the opportunities she was offered as a product of John Wilkerson's public parks programme in Houston. She first came to wider attention in 1978 when she reached the final of the US national 14-and-under Championship. From then on her game, and her horizons, broadened and flourished.

Her peak, during a career which saw her reach fourth in the world rankings in November 1989, undoubtedly came during Wimbledon 1990 when she beat Monica Seles and Steffi Graf in successive matches, both over three sets, to become the first black woman to reach the final since Althea Gibson in 1957.

When tennis returned as a full medal sport in the 1988 Olympic Games in Seoul, Zina, who became Mrs Garrison Jackson, partnered Pam Shriver to gold in the women's doubles and won bronze in the singles. While her ability was not always supported well enough by consistency, this quick-moving, aggressive volleyer was always one of the more adventurous players in an era of baseline dominance in the women's game.

Vitas Gerulaitis

Born: *July 26, 1954*
New York, NY, USA

For many the Wimbledon men's singles semi-final in 1977 in which Gerulaitis was beaten 6–4, 3–6, 6–3, 3–6, 8–6 by Bjorn Borg, on the way to successfully defending the title, was *the* finest match they ever saw. From start to finish it was an enthralling contest, played at lightning pace, with the competitive atmosphere supreme. The final set was tremendous. Gerulaitis, a speedy, lean six-footer, with his long, often unruly blond locks blowing in the wind, broke to love to lead 3–2, but Borg broke back immediately and the captivating stalemate remained until he broke again for the match in the 14th game.

Gerulaitis' fighting spirit and tenacious approach were always evident. He recovered from losing a two-set lead to beat Britain's John Lloyd for the Australian Open title in 1977; made a stunning comeback to beat Roscoe Tanner from two sets and a break down to reach the US Open final in 1979; and in that year also won five of his six Davis Cup singles, including a semi-final recovery from triple match point down in the third set against Australian Mark Edmondson, to help the Americans retain the trophy.

ZINA GARRISON – *from public park to Wimbledon final*

He died accidentally, from a leaking gas heater in the poolhouse at a friend's home, at the age of 40, just when he was developing a successful broadcasting career.

Althea Gibson

Born: *August 25, 1927*
Silver, SC, USA

Tall, powerful and wonderfully athletic, she was the first black woman to achieve major success in lawn tennis, although partly because of the racial hurdles she had to overcome she reached the top of the tree comparatively late. She was already 28 before it was possible for her compete regularly outside the United States, making the triumphs which followed all the more remarkable.

Once given the chance, she wasted no time. On her first visit to Roland Garros in 1956, she won the French singles and doubles title (with Britain's Angela Buxton, who became a loyal friend). Four weeks later the Wimbledon doubles title followed and was to be retained by them for another two years. In 1957 the American's power on Wimbledon's

grass courts was irrepressible and she took the title without losing a set and went on to become the US champion as well. Having underlined her prowess by again winning at Wimbledon, which meant she had won five out of six titles there in three years, and having also retained her title at Forest Hills in 1958, the undoubted world number one of her years turned professional.

Andres Gimeno

Born: *August 3, 1937*
Barcelona, Spain

The son of a former professional tennis player, this tall and graceful clay-courter, with typically solid groundstrokes, also turned professional in 1960 before his talents as an amateur were fulfilled and at a time when the professional opportunities were still heavily restricted. Even so, before leaving the amateur ranks, he played in the Davis Cup for Spain consistently, 1958–60, and won 14 out of 22 rubbers.

When the game went Open in 1968, he returned to the full international scene and on three occasions

between 1969 and 1972, reached the top 10, climaxing his career at the age of 34 by being the oldest winner in the Open era at the French in 1972 where he had been a semi-finalist in 1968. He was also runner-up to Rod Laver at the Australian Open in 1969. He remains a familiar figure at most major tournaments, as a commentator for Spanish television.

Andres Gomez

Born: *February 27, 1960*
Guayaquil, Ecuador

Gomez achieved a lifelong dream at Roland Garros in 1990 when he stunned the tennis world by beating Andre Agassi to become the first Ecuadorian to win a Grand Slam title at the relatively advanced age of 30 years, 3 months. After achieving other clay-court successes in Barcelona and Madrid, he climbed that year to a career-best fourth place in the world rankings.

Although mainly regarded as a clay-court specialist, he was an extremely gifted left-hander who could play well on most surfaces, and was a quarter-finalist at Wimbledon and the US Open. He also excelled in doubles, winning the French in 1988 with Emilio Sanchez and the US Open in 1986 with Slobodan Zivojinovic. He won 21 singles titles and for 12 years was in Ecuador's Davis Cup team.

Pancho Gonzales

Born: *May 9, 1928*
Los Angeles, CA, USA

Few players can have had their list of potential achievements so curtailed by the years of procrastination before Open tennis was finally permitted as did Ricardo Alonso Gonżales, a big Californian-Mexican by race, who is regarded by many as the best player never to have won Wimbledon. Those who marvelled at the way he delivered touch shots of exquisite beauty during performances based on a thunderous serve and all-court strength, when at last he was allowed to display his talent to worldwide attention from 1968 onwards, could only mourn how much the whole game had missed by what amounted to his 20-year suspension.

Gonzales, a loner who became famous for his rages against opponents, officials and occasionally even spectators, was doubles champion at the French Open and Wimbledon in 1949. But three months later, after winning the US singles title for a second time, he became a contracted professional and, apart from occasional tours by the pro circus, that was the last most of the tennis world saw of this magnificent athlete until 1968. By then he was 41 and already a grandfather, but the magic was still there in abundance and his electrifying 1969 first-round comeback from 22–24, 1–6, 16–14, 6–3, 11–9 over two days against Charlie Pasarell, which lasted 5 hours 12 minutes and involved 112 games, set a Wimbledon record for the longest singles match. He was supreme both as a player and as a showman. He died, during The Championships, in 1995. His only Davis Cup appearance had been in the 1949 Challenge Round against Australia when he beat both Frank Sedgman and William Siddwell.

EVONNE GOOLAGONG *enchanted crowds wherever she played*

Evonne Goolagong Cawley

Born: *July 31, 1951*
Barellan, NSW, Australia

For sheer joy and enchantment, few have graced the world of women's tennis more delightfully than this part-aborigine daughter of an itinerant sheep-shearer, whose talent as a budding champion long preceded her first trip to Europe under the guidance of her long-term coach and mentor, Vic Edwards. Here was a happy-go-lucky girl, who radiated fun wherever and whenever she played, and the enormous popularity she earned at Wimbledon on her first visit in 1970 quickly spread to the rest of the world.

Despite an occasionally suspect forehand – and an equally frustrating tendency to "go walkabout" for periods of her matches – Goolagong won the French Open on her first visit in 1971 and then moved gaily on to Wimbledon where she romped past one great former champion, Billie Jean King, in the semi-finals and then another, her compatriot Margaret Court, in the final, both in straight sets. Her second Wimbledon singles triumph came in 1980 after a nine-year gap, three losing performances in finals, four singles and doubles triumphs in the Australian Open and the birth of her two children. She was the first mother to win the title for 66 years and she had lost none of her free-flowing skills and carefree temperament.

Brian Gottfried

Born: *January 27, 1952*
Baltimore, MD, USA

Brian Gottfried won 25 singles and 54 doubles titles during his professional career, but never quite managed to attract the same degree of attention at that level as he had done as an outstanding junior. Then, he had won 14 national junior titles and finished runner-up in both singles and doubles at the 1972 NCAA Championships.

A hard-working right-hander, he enjoyed his finest year in 1977 when he reached the finals of 15 tournaments in what was then the Grand Prix, won five and built up a record of 109–23 (132 total) which no top 10 player, barring possibly Yevgeny Kafelnikov, would even contemplate today. He was runner-up at the French Open in 1977 and a semi-finalist at Wimbledon in 1980, but his biggest titles came principally in doubles, especially when partnered by the Mexican, Raul Ramirez. They won 39 titles including Wimbledon, the French and the Italian.

Arthur Gore

Born: *January 2, 1868*
Lyndhurst, Hampshire, UK

Arthur Gore's record as the oldest Wimbledon champion is unlikely to be broken. He was 41 years, 182 days when he won the title, which he had already held in 1901 and 1908, for a third time in 1909. No player in the history of the game has competed in singles at The Championships over a longer period of time. His first appearance was in 1888, his last, when he was 54, in 1922 and for many years, until Jimmy Connors overtook him, his total of 64 singles matches won at Wimbledon was also a record.

Even after he stopped entering the singles, Gore continued to play in the doubles, which he won in 1909, for another three years, extending his overall Wimbledon record to 156 games in 35 years. He was also in the very first British Isles team to challenge, albeit fruitlessly, for the Davis Cup when the competition began in 1900. In his penultimate year at Wimbledon, as part of the Golden Jubilee of The Championships, he and Roper Barrett beat the Duke of York, who was to become King George VI, and Louis Greig in the first round of the doubles.

Spencer Gore

Born: *March 10, 1850*
Wimbledon, London, UK

This bearded Old Harrovian became the first Wimbledon champion, records at the All England Club show, at "some time after half past four" on Thursday July 19, 1877 – three days later than planned, because of the weather. He was a 27-year-old surveyor at the time and had cycled from his home on nearby Wimbledon Common to play the five matches necessary, including his 6–1, 6–2, 6–4 defeat of William Marshall in a final watched by 200 spectators paying one shilling (5p) for the privilege.

It was a rather different game from the one we know today. The net was 5ft high at the posts and 3ft 3in high in the middle. Some felt it was unsportsmanlike of Gore, (no relation to Spencer) a cricketer and rackets player, to volley, while his underarm serve with a double dose of cut also raised eyebrows in that inaugural year. His penchant for volleying may have worked brilliantly in 1877, but in the Challenge Round a year later Frank Hadow was waiting with lobs which ruthlessly undermined the tactic. Gore went back to rackets and cricket.

Steffi Graf

Born: *June 14, 1969*
Bruhl, Germany
(See Legends pp82–83)

Frank Hadow

Born: *January 24, 1855*
London, UK

History says that Frank P. Hadow was even less enamoured with the game of tennis than his predecessor as champion, Spencer Gore. It was while on leave from Ceylon, where he was a tea planter, that he was encouraged by friends to try what was still a new sporting adventure. He took to it so quickly that he won his five matches in the All-Comers and then another in the Challenge Round against Gore, without losing a set, but then returned to Ceylon, reputedly saying he could see no future for the game. As a result, he remains the only player never to have lost a set in The Championships.

Darlene Hard

Born: *January 6, 1936*
Los Angeles, CA, USA

Although she won several major singles titles, including the US Championship in 1960 and 1961, the French in 1960 and the South African in 1964, this formidable Californian volleyer, who became a coaching professional in 1963, is best remembered for her doubles triumphs with Maria Bueno.

She won the Wimbledon doubles four times, twice with Bueno after earlier successes with Althea Gibson and Jeanne Arth, while she won the French doubles three times (with different partners) and the US five consecutive years (1958–62, with three partners), and a sixth, in 1969, long after she had retired from regular competition, when she and Françoise Durr overcame a 0–6 first set to upset Margaret Court and Virginia Wade in the final.

She was twice runner-up in the singles at Wimbledon, losing to Gibson in 1957 and to Bueno three years later.

Doris Hart

Born: *June 20, 1925*
St Louis, MO, USA

The tall brave lady with the limp. Doris Hart first took up tennis at the age of six as a remedial exercise for an illness which threatened to cripple her and went on to become one of the finest champions. She not only won the Wimbledon singles at her fifth attempt in 1951, but lost only one set in becoming the triple champion that year, winning the doubles with Shirley Fry, whom she had trounced 6–1, 6–0 in the singles final, and the mixed with the Australian, Frank Sedgman.

She never won Wimbledon again, finishing runner-up for a third time in 1953, when she was beaten by Maureen Connolly, but she was to win 35 singles, doubles and mixed doubles titles at the four Grand Slam tournaments – a record surpassed by only three other women, Margaret Court (62), Martina Navratilova (54) and Billie Jean King (39). Her five consecutive victories in the Wimbledon mixed doubles, 1951–55, the first two with Sedgman, the others with Vic Seixas, remains a tournament record. In the Wightman Cup, where she was to become team captain in 1970, she remained unbeaten in 14 singles matches over seven years and won eight of her nine doubles rubbers.

Justine Henin-Hardenne

Born: *June 1, 1982*
Liege, Belgium

Justine Henin-Hardenne is the diminutive Belgian with the exquisite backhand who loves a challenge, and, as her hobby of sky-diving well illustrates, fears nothing. As a player she launched her senior career in 1999 and at the time, as a wild card entry, became the fifth woman to win her debut event. Injuries to her wrists were to provide an insight into her future problems but in the interim, her

DARLENE HARD – *a stalwart of American tennis.*

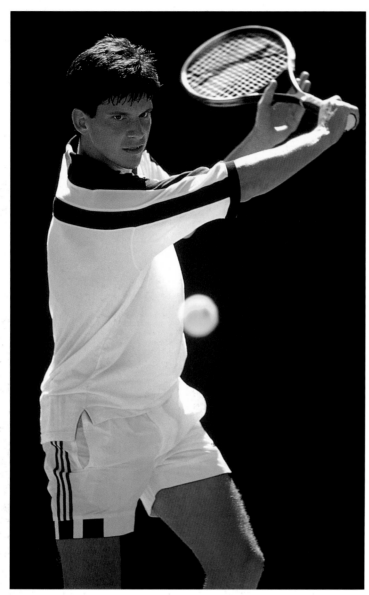

TIM HENMAN – *a key role in rejuvinating British tennis*

improving overall form and determination saw her collect the French and US Open titles in 2003, as well as make the semis of the Australian and Wimbledon, all helping to lift her to the top of the rankings in October.

She began the following season as World No1 and added the Australian Open to her now growing list of titles but was forced to withdraw from Antwerp with a respiratory illness. She returned and picked up her winning form, only to be struck down a few months later with a debilitating viral illness. A second round loss as defending champion at Roland Garros followed as she went down with glandular fever only returning to the fray for the Olympics where she struck gold with some vintage tennis only to succumb

again to her illness after losing her US title in round four.

It wasn't until the spring of 2005 that she finally shook off her health problems to regain her French Open title, which successfully defended the following year. Some hamstring problems were then to mar the rest of her season but she still ended the year well ensconced in the top ten, with a reputation of being hard to beat, as evidenced by her reaching all four Grand Slam finals in 2006.

Tim Henman

Born: *September 6, 1974*
Weston-on-the-Green, Oxford, UK

At 17 the general belief was that this handsome, talented but slightly built

player would achieve more in doubles than singles. Then suddenly, two years later, his singles game began to take off and, despite breaking his leg in three places just above the ankle in September 1994, his progress has been as exciting as it has been rapid.

He reached the top 100 (99) in 1995 and became one of the most consistent players on the Tour reaching a career high of 4 in July 2002.

Carrying the full weight of British expectation he made the last four at Wimbledon on four occasions, only failing to make at least the quarter-finals once between 1996 and 2004. With semi-final appearances also at the French and US Opens, both in 2004, Henman has established himself for the present, as the best Briton since Fred Perry, despite never making a Grand Slam final.

However the Oxford player did leave a mark at Wimbledon when he became the first player to be disqualified from The Championships whilst playing doubles following an unfortunate incident in 1995 when he struck a ball in frustration which unluckily hit a ballgirl.

A recurring back injury in 2005 has resulted in a recent loss of form.

Bob Hewitt

Born: *January 12, 1940*
Dubbo, NSW, Australia

Bob Hewitt first came to prominence when he won the doubles with compatriot Fred Stolle at Wimbledon in 1962 and 1964, but at that time he was not alone among top players in finding it hard to live with the restrictions imposed on players by the Australian tennis authorities, so he moved to his wife's home in Johannesburg. Never having represented Australia in the Davis Cup, he became eligible, as a resident, to play for South Africa instead and there began one of the most unorthodox but successful doubles partnerships in the game's history. Bob Hewitt and Frew McMillan became synonymous with doubles perfection. Somehow Hewitt's fiery temperament, accentuated by his baldness and a beard, and McMillan's always calm exterior gelled perfectly and for the next 15 years they collected major titles all round the world,

including three at Wimbledon, two in Australia and one each at the French and the US.

In singles Hewitt had an impressive 22–3 record, while he was twice a quarter-finalist at Wimbledon, US clay-court champion in 1972 and ranked six in the world in 1967, the last year before those who had turned professional came back into the reckoning.

Lleyton Hewitt

Born: *February 24, 1981*
Adelaide, Australia

A player who epitomizes the sporting spirit of Australia choosing, at the age of 13, to pursue a tennis playing career rather than one in Aussie Rule football where he also excelled. With a never-say-die attitude, reversed baseball cap, long hair and oversized shirt, the 5'11" pint-sized (in relation to other players) Aussie made his mark as a pugnacious teenager. He captured his first senior title, in his home town of Adelaide, at the age 16 years and 10 months having the previous year, became the youngest player to ever qualify for the Australian Open.

In 1999 he appeared in four finals, capturing his first clay court title in Delray Beach. However, the highlight of his year was helping his country become Davis Cup champions, a feat he was to repeat in 2003. In the interim he won four titles in 2000 and became the first teenager to make the end of season Masters Cup. The following year he became the first Aussie to end the year at World No1 and win the Masters Cup having collected his first Grand Slam title at Flushing Meadows.

He maintained his position at the top of the rankings throughout 2002, collecting five ATP titles and his second Grand Slam title, this time on the grass of Wimbledon.

His mobility and speed, as well as his retrieving and overall aggressive baseline game, is exciting to watch. Injuries and illness have hampered him over the last few years during which time he also married the Australian actress Bec Cartwright with whom he has a daughter Mia Rebecca.

MARTINA HINGIS, *unbridled joy as Wimbledon champion, 1997*

He has yet to fulfill his one ambition, winning his home Grand Slam but did make the final at Melbourne in 2005 where he lost to the Russian Marat Safin.

Martina Hingis

Born: *September 30, 1980*
Kosice, Slovakia

With a victory in Key Biscayne in March 1997 – already her fifth title of the year – Martina Hingis soared above the absent and injured Steffi Graf to become the youngest world number one. By the end of a year in which she had also become the youngest player to win a Grand Slam singles title at the Australian Open in January and then won Wimbledon and the US Open for the first time to finish the year with a 78–5 record, it was difficult to foresee anyone rapidly displacing her. Indeed, but for an accident in April – while horse-riding, her other great passion – she might well have become the youngest to win the Grand Slam. Although she recovered in time to compete at the French Open, her lack of match preparation and general fitness showed as she was beaten in the final by Iva Majoli.

There is a delightful freshness about Hingis's approach to tennis. Between matches at the 1997 Australian Open, which she successfully-defended in 1998 and 1999, despite the significance of the event, she was to be found roller-blading in the car park at Melbourne Park. Coached by her mother, Melanie Molitor, with whom she moved to Switzerland when she was seven, she had the talent to become as gifted an all-court player as the other Martina (Navratilova) – after whom she was named.

Hingis retired in 2002 with ankle problems having won 40 singles and 36 doubles titles, including a Grand Slam of doubles in 1998, but at the age of 25, decided to reverse her decision and marked her return with a semi-final appearance at Melbourne in 2006.

Lew Hoad

Born: *November 23, 1934*
Glebe, NSW, Australia

Anyone who had the pleasure of meeting Lew and shaking him by the hand could testify to the enormous strength in that wrist which gave him the ability to generate ferocious power with such apparent ease. At his best, few, if any, could stand against this "boy wonder" as coach Harry Hopman called him after he had been instrumental in Australia's Davis Cup defeat of the United States in 1953.

Hoad was a big man in every sense of the word, with a personality to match. And that at times was a problem, for he much preferred to go for a blistering winner at the earliest opportunity rather than become embroiled in lengthy rallies. Nevertheless, he could do so when he was inclined, as he proved when he won the French title on slow red clay in 1956. Hoad was the first player in the post-war era to win Wimbledon two years in succession, 1956–57, and the power with which he demolished Ashley Cooper in the 1957 final, the last he was to play in The Championships, was devastating.

Soon afterwards Hoad, who had also won the Australian title in 1956, turned professional, but his impact there was soon restricted by a chronic back injury so that he was semi-retired by the time Open tennis allowed him to return to the main circuit in 1968.

Harry Hopman

Born: *December 8, 1906*
Melbourne, Victoria Australia

Arguably the finest coach the game has ever known. The conveyor-belt of Australian talent in the 1950s and 60s which benefited from his guidance, such as Frank Sedgman, Lew Hoad, Ken Rosewall, Ashley Cooper, Neale Fraser, Roy Emerson, Rod Laver, John Newcombe and many more, tends to overshadow his own success as a fine doubles player. He won seven major titles, starting with the Australian doubles with Jack Crawford in 1929–30, and four mixed titles with his first wife, Nell – a record for a married couple.

Under his direction, Australian Davis Cup teams compiled a 38–6 record and won the trophy 16 times. After returning from the captaincy in 1969, he emigrated to the United States where he continued coaching and eventually established his own Tennis Academy in Florida. While he was teaching at Port Washington, John McEnroe and Vitas Gerulaitis were among those he helped. There in 1972, he pointed out a scraggy, shy-looking 13-year-old in the corner of one of the courts and said: "See that little fellow over there, he'll be world champion one day." He was right. The little fellow was John McEnroe.

Hazel Hotchkiss Wightman

Born: *December 20, 1886*
Healdsburg, CA, USA

This shy college girl, who had never played on a grass court until she entered the US Championships when they were staged in Philadelphia in 1909, is best remembered for the Wightman Cup, the now-defunct annual competition between the United States and Britain, for which she donated the trophy in 1923. Yet she was a notable player in her own right and a formidable influence on women's tennis, in the United States, for more than half a century.

Quick about the court, fiercely and enthusiastically competitive, she was unique in winning a national title (the women's indoor doubles) in 1943, no less than 34 years after her first in 1909 – the first of three consecutive US Championships titles, to which she added another in 1919. She won the indoor doubles crown for a record 10th time. One of her many protégées was Helen Wills, with whom she won Wimbledon, US and Olympic doubles titles in 1924, while she also won gold in the mixed doubles with Dick Williams.

Anke Huber

Born: *December 4, 1974*
Bruchsal, Germany

Consistently in the world's top 15 since 1991 and reaching a career-best, fourth-placed ranking in October 1996, this lively but not quite consistent enough competitor has undoubtedly suffered from being hailed for so long in Germany as "the next Steffi Graf". That began when she turned professional as a 14-year-old in 1989, climbed 370 places in the rankings in her first year and began challenging for a place in the top 10.

By the end of 1997, though, the closest she had come to winning a major title had been at the Australian Open in 1996, where she reached the final but was then overpowered, as well as outclassed, by Monica Seles. However, in 1995 she reached the last 16 of all four Grand Slam events and only lost to either the winner or the runner-up in all of them. She is happier to try and rally from the baseline, waiting for her opponent to make the error, rather than creating opportunities to dictate from the net because her volleying confidence is not great, which tends to detract from her having one of the stronger serves in the women's game.

Goran Ivanisevic

Born: *September 13, 1971*
Split, Croatia

Just as the powerful serving by this 6ft-4in left-hander has been the key to much of his success, so it has been his Achilles' heel under pressure when facing some of his most important challenges. So it was in the 1992 Wimbledon final when, despite serving 37 aces, he was beaten by Andre Agassi. Serving to stay in the match, Ivanisevic, who had struck at least one ace in all but four of his service games and four more to make it 2–2 in the fifth set, began with two double faults. Then at 30–40 he came in behind a second serve and completely mistimed what should have been an easy put-away volley. Things were different in 1994. Pete Sampras, having countered what was then the most menacing serve in the game to win two tie-breaks, romped past the increasingly dispirited Croatian in the third. Then in 1998, for a third time, the big serving Croat completed his Wimbledon challenge as runner-up, again to Sampras over another tense five-setter.

On a good day Ivanisevic can play the most excitingly aggressive and even controlled tennis. Yet he can, as he puts it, just as easily "go mad" in the mind and blast the ball everywhere except where it needs to be. In 1996 he served more than 1,500 aces and as early as 1990 reached the final of the French doubles with Petr Korda but, despite reaching a career-best second in the world rankings in July 1994, he remained a victim of his own wildly erratic temperament until 2001, when as a wild card entry, he conquered the Wimbledon field including the local favourite Tim Henman in a three-day rain-affected semi-final and subsequently the title favourite Pat Rafter, on the third Monday, 9-7 in the fifth set, to claim the title he coveted most.

With that victory, his only one at Grand Slam level, Ivanisevic succumbed to the strains imposed by a problem shoulder and quietly slipped into retirement.

ANN JONES *at the moment of victory in the 1969 Wimbledon final*

Helen Jacobs

Born: *August 6, 1908*
Globe, AZ, USA

Women's tennis in the 1930s was dominated by the two Helens. Unfortunately for Helen Jacobs, she almost always finished second best, when they met, to Helen Wills Moody. Indeed in their first seven meetings she did not even win a set. Then, in the final of the US Championships in 1933, her victory was soured to some extent by the way Wills, trailing 0–3 in the final set, told the umpire that her legs felt so weak that she would have to retire. Jacobs won at Forest Hills for four consecutive years, 1932–35, but only that once when Moody was also taking part.

When Jacobs, seeded two, eventually won Wimbledon at her ninth attempt by beating Hilde Sperling in 1936, it was again an occasion when Moody was not among the entries. They met four times in the Wimbledon final, but the nearest Jacobs, full of courage though lacking her principal rival's power, came to winning one of

those clashes was in 1935. She led 5–3 in the final set and even reached match point but, as she advanced to the net to put away what should have been the match-winning smash, a strong gust of wind deflected the ball just enough to make her miss. It broke her nerve, as well as her heart.

Anders Jarryd

Born: *July 13, 1961*
Lidkoping, Sweden

At his peak, this tenacious, sometimes fiery, quick-stepping Swede reached fifth in the world rankings in 1985 and, despite not winning a major singles title, was a proven player on all surfaces. He reached the last 16 or better in all four of the Grand Slams and won every Grand Slam tournament doubles title at least once. In 1991, partnered by Australian John Fitzgerald, he won the doubles in Paris, Wimbledon and Flushing Meadows. Indeed he won the French three times – on the other two occasions with Robert Seguso (1987) and Hans Simonsson

(1983) and also the US Open three times, twice with Stefan Edberg, with whom he also won the Australian Open in 1987. Overall he won 47 doubles titles with 15 different partners.

In singles his best year was 1985, when he reached the semi-finals before losing a semi-final against Boris Becker, which was interrupted overnight by rain, in four sets. He took his revenge the following year when he beat Becker, again over four sets, in the final of the prestigious WCT Finals in Dallas.

Bill Johnston

Born: *November 2, 1894*
San Francisco, CA, USA

Regarded for many years as the world number two, "Little Bill" as this frail stockbroker was called, was fated to compete more often than not at the same time as "Big Bill", his great friend, Bill Tilden. Although Johnston won the US Championships twice, in 1915 and 1919 – the latter one of the rare occasions he beat Tilden, for five

of the next six years it was "Big Bill" who carried off the title beating Johnston each time.

A right-hander, who developed his game on public courts, he was renowned just as much for his fighting spirit as for his terrific western grip forehand and impressive volleys. He competed only twice at Wimbledon, winning in 1923 when he dropped only one set against the Hon. Cecil Campdell, an Irishman, in the quarter-finals. Johnston, whose health was never robust after he served with the US Navy during the 1914–18 war, also established an outstanding Davis Cup record, winning 18 of the 21 singles and doubles rubbers he played in 10 ties. Apart from tennis, his other passion was bridge.

Ann Jones

Born: *October 17, 1938*
Birmingham, UK

Like Fred Perry, this shrewd, consistent left-hander excelled in table tennis before transferring her attention to lawn tennis and in various table tennis events reached five finals in the World Championships. On the tennis court she quickly graduated from being British junior champion in 1954–55 to make her mark in senior tournaments and she reached the semi-finals at Wimbledon seven times before winning the title at last in 1969.

In a rousing climax to the fortnight, she upset top seed Margaret Court 10–12, 6–3, 6–2. Then in the final she beat second-seeded Billie Jean King, who had beaten her four times before at The Championships, 3–6, 6–3, 6–2. A model of patience and persistence, Mrs Jones, then 30 years and 270 days, was the first left-hander to win the women's title and she crowned a marvellous performance by also winning the mixed doubles the next day with Fred Stolle.

She was a member of the British Wightman team for 13 years between 1957 and 1975 and also played 34 rubbers in 18 Fed Cup matches. In recent years, she has continued to serve the game by captaining British teams at junior and senior level and as referee at British events on the WTA Tour.

Yevgeny Kafelnikov

Born: *February 18, 1974*
Sochi, Russia

In 1996 Yevgeny Kafelnikov became the first player since John McEnroe to finish in the top five of the rankings in both singles and doubles. It was the reward for a year in which he won his first Grand Slam tournament titles, singles and doubles, at the French Open – the first to do so since Ken Rosewall in 1968 – and won three other singles and four other doubles titles. His breakthrough at Roland Garros also made him the first Russian to win a Grand Slam title and his success in the final followed even more impressive victories in earlier rounds against Richard Krajicek and Pete Sampras.

PETR KORDA *celebrates winning his first Grand Slam title at the 1998 Australian Open at the age of 30*

Kafelnikov began playing when he was six and, because of his love of playing both singles and doubles, competes in many more matches than anyone else in the top 10. In 1994 and 1996 he competed in 171 matches, but in future years is expected to reduce his doubles commitment in a bid to win more major singles titles. He suffered a freak accident when he broke his hand on a punchbag in the gym while training for the Australian Open in January 1997 and this effectively prevented him playing for the first four months of the year, but he still managed to finish the year ranked four, one below his career best. He retained the French title in 1999.

Billie Jean King,

Born: *November 22, 1943*
Long Beach, CA, USA
(See Legends pp84–85)

Bill Knight

Born: *November 12, 1935*
Northampton, UK

This tenacious British left-hander moved on from being an outstanding junior, both in England and abroad, to earn the respect of most world-class players with his form on clay courts in particular. He first came to international prominence in the mid-1950s and three times won the British hard-court Championships, which traditionally launched the European clay-court season (1958, 1963–64).

A rugged competitor, his biggest success came when he won singles and mixed titles at the German Championships in 1959, while he was also mixed doubles champion at the French in 1959. After a lengthy spell away from mainstream tennis, while running the family furniture business, he returned in the late 1980s, eventually becoming manager of British men's tennis, and he is credited with playing a major role in the successful transition by Tim Henman from junior to senior tennis. In 1958 he was a regular member of the British team which reached the Inter-Zonal final of the Davis Cup. He did so with other prominent players of that era, Mike Davies, who went on to become a top administrator for the WCT, the ATP and the ITF, and Bobby Wilson.

Jan Kodes

Born: *March 1, 1946*
Prague, Czechoslovakia

Because he won Wimbledon in 1973, the year when 93 players obeyed a call by the Association of Tennis Professionals to boycott the event as part of the developing power struggle between players and national associations, this dogged, hard-working rather than spectacular player has never been given full recognition for his achievement. Nor did he help matters by insisting so often beforehand, as a player brought up on clay, that "grass is only for the cows".

Yet it should not be overlooked that he had already won the French Open singles in 1970 and 1971 the second time by beating the more talented but less consistent Ilie Nastase in the final. As if to prove that his Wimbledon triumph had been no fluke, he also reached the final of the US Open for the second time three months later. His brilliant returning was often the key, not least against Stan Smith in the semi-finals, when he had to save a match point, but in an exciting final the rugged John Newcombe had just too

ANNA KOURNIKOVA, *whose photographic appeal spread way beyond the quality of her tennis*

much power as he took revenge for his first-round defeat by Kodes at Forest Hills two years earlier. Kodes took Czechoslovakia to the Davis Cup final for the first time in 1975, was a member of the winning team five years later and won 39 of his 59 singles rubbers.

Petr Korda

Born: *January 23, 1968*
Prague, Czechoslovakia

Despite his wafer-like frame, this former ballboy for Ivan Lendl in Davis Cup matches in Prague has proved himself one of the most resilient players on the circuit. A reasonable, rather than especially prominent, junior, except in doubles, it was not until his fifth full year on the Tour that he won his first singles title, beating Goran Ivanisevic in New Haven in 1991. That year he also reached the final of the French Open, where he lost to Jim Courier, but – partly due to injuries, including two groin operations in 1996, and partly through an occasional loss of confidence – he did not wholly fulfil expectations.

In 1997, things started to flow sweetly again for the 6ft-3in left-hander. He played brilliantly to upset Pete Sampras at the US Open and, despite retiring with a fever in his next match against Jonas Bjorkman, qualified for the Compaq Grand Slam Cup, which he had won in 1993, and took part in one of the best matches of the year before losing an epic semifinal against Pat Rafter. Korda finally won a Grand Slam event in 1998, crushing Marcello Rios in the final at the Australian. He is one of the few players married to a former player on the WTA Tour, Regina Rajchrtova. and is the first player to have received a ban for producing a positive drugs test in 1998,

Anna Kournikova

Born: *June 7, 1981*
Moscow, Russia

Anna Kournikova started playing when she was five and was already obviously full of precocious talent when she and her mother moved to Bradenton, Florida, and the Nick Bollettieri Tennis Academy in February 1992. As a junior she won the Orange

RICHARD KRAJICEK'S *finest moment – becoming the first Dutchman to win Wimbledon in 1996*

Richard Krajicek
Born: *December 6, 1971*
Rotterdam, Netherlands

A succession of shoulder and knee injuries has prevented this 6ft-5in right-hander from taking full advantage of a serve which provides the backbone to his game. He was obviously thrilled in 1996 when he made history as the first Dutchman to win Wimbledon. Unseeded when the draw was made, he was only given a seeding position after Thomas Muster withdrew, but he proceeded to defeat two former champions – Michael Stich and the previous year's champion, Pete Sampras – with brilliantly sustained performances before being too strong for the unseeded MaliVai Washington in the final. He lost only one set in the fortnight – against New Zealander Brett Steven, in the third round, but it was still the only tournament he won during another year which began and ended with injuries.

The son of Czech immigrants, he started to make a major impact after he switched from playing two-handed on both flanks to one-handed at the age of 12. Following his Wimbledon triumph, he established the Richard Krajicek Foundation in the Netherlands to assist promising young players who might otherwise not be able to pursue their tennis development through lack of funds.

Jack Kramer
Born: *August 1, 1921*
Las Vegas, NV, USA

When Kramer was chosen to play doubles alongside Joe Hunt in the United States Davis Cup team for the 1939 final against Australia, aged 18, he was the youngest to compete in the Challenge Round. Yet that, and his being the first man to win the singles at Wimbledon wearing shorts instead of long trousers, are probably the least significant of his considerable contributions to all aspects of international tennis as a player, promoter, politician and television commentator.

He was reaching his prime when international tennis resumed after the war in 1946. That year he won the US Championships but lost to Jaroslav

Bowl and European 18-and-under Championships and became the International Tennis Federation 18-and-under world junior champion while still only 14, when she also became the youngest player to compete in and win a Fed Cup match as Russia beat Sweden.

She has matured swiftly and considerably during her first three years in senior events, and, with long blond hair tied into a ponytail, she took over from the retired Gabriela Sabatini as the favourite target for photographers. During 1997 she climbed from 56 to 32 in the world rankings with a 17–10 match record, which included a first Grand Slam semi-final appearance at Wimbledon, where her all-court style helped her to overcome a host of more experienced opponents including Anke Huber, Helena Sukova and the French Open champion, Iva Majoli. She says that, if she had not decided to become a tennis player, she would love to have been an actress. However, she virtually retired in 2004 without winning a singles title on Tour, albeit she twice won the Australian Open doubles in partnership with Martina Hingis.

Drobny in the third round at Wimbledon, where a badly blistered hand added to his problems. The next year, though, he was supreme. Although dropping a set to Dinny Pails in the semi-finals, he overwhelmed Tom Brown so ruthlessly in a 48-minute final, 6–1, 6–3, 6–2, that he lost only 37 games in seven matches, a figure which has never been bettered since the Challenge Round was abolished in 1922.

A few weeks later he retained the US title, but then turned professional and enjoyed continuing success as both a player and promoter of professional tours until the advent of Open tennis, when he devised the Grand Prix, which initially pulled all the tournaments together. His popularity in Britain dipped sharply in 1973 when he led the ATP player boycott of Wimbledon.

Johan Kriek
Born: *April 5, 1958*
Pongola, South Africa

Johan Kriek reached the quarter-finals of the US Open in his first full year on the Tour in 1979 and the semi-finals a year later, but he was never quite consistent enough to sustain a top 10 ranking. Twice a semi-finalist at the French Open, he illustrated his ability on all surfaces by winning the Australian Open in 1981 and retaining the trophy the next year, beating Steve Denton in both finals, although at the time the event was the poor relation of the Grand Slams, with few leading players taking part.

Kriek won 14 singles and eight doubles titles during his career. He took American citizenship and moved to Naples, Florida, when many countries refused to admit holders of South African passports, and is now a regular competitor on the Seniors' Tour.

Ramanathan Krishman
Born: *April 11, 1937*
Madras, India

This sturdy Indian, whose son Ramesh was to become world junior champion and then enjoy a lengthy distinguished career of his own, was India's most powerful and fluent player before Vijay Amritraj reached even greater heights. The flow of talent from one generation to another was underlined in 1979 when Ramesh won the Wimbledon junior boys' singles, exactly 25 years after his father had done the same.

Ramanathan, who caused one of the major upsets of the 1956 Championships by beating Jaroslav Drobny, reached the semi-finals twice, first in 1960 when he lost to Neale Fraser and then a year later when he was beaten by Rod Laver. He played in the Davis Cup for India, 1953–68, and achieved a best world ranking of six in 1961.

Gustavo Kuerten
Born: *September 10, 1976*
Florianopolis, Brazil

One of the most treasured memories for this engaging Brazilian is the good-luck call he took from legendary soccer star Pele on the eve of his French Open final in 1997. Kuerten, who was 20 at the time and, with his long floppy hair not entirely curbed by a headband, soccer-style shirt and colourful sneakers, looked as if he had just stepped off a beach near his home, did not let Pele or their country down.

With his own brand of sustained, uninhibited attacking tennis, he overwhelmed former champion Sergi Bruguera 6–3, 6–4, 6–2 in 110 minutes to become the first Brazilian man to win a Grand Slam singles title. He was ranked 63 at the time, but this astonishing triumph – which included victories in earlier rounds against two other previous champions, Thomas Muster and Yevgeny Kafelnikov – sent him soaring to 12th and a seeding position for his first appearance at Wimbledon. And he proved it wasn't a flash-in-the-pan returning to reclaim the title in 2000 and successfully defending it the following year.

Unfortunately back injuries have subsequently hampered his career and whilst he hasn't retired, the signs are that he will in the next few years.

René Lacoste
Born: *July 2, 1904*
Paris, France

When he died in October 1996, aged 92, it meant the final passing of the "Four Musketeers", that extraordinary group of Frenchmen who had dominated international tennis for much of the 1920s. By the end of that decade Lacoste, whose name will live on through the sportswear company he founded which bears the famous crocodile logo, was reckoned by some to have been the best player in the world. He won Wimbledon in 1925 and 1928, the US in 1926 and 1927 and the French in 1925, 1927 and 1929. In 1927 he also helped France to win the Davis Cup by beating both Bill Tilden and Bill Johnston, triumphs made all the more remarkable by his indifferent health.

Lacoste was always regarded as the thinker. He studied his opponents and planned tactics in a way which might seem commonplace today (when coaches do that job), but was almost unheard of in those times. Pale and delicate in appearance, he hardly looked like a champion but he practised assiduously and, while never possessing the panache of Jean Borotra or Henri Cochet, developed immaculate length and control from the back. Few players could equal the accuracy and telling quality of his lobs. He epitomised style and great artistry.

RENE LACOSTE, *a baseliner who likened tennis to a game of chess*

Bill Larned

Born: *December 30, 1872*
Summit, NJ, USA

One of only three players to win the US Championship seven times – the others being Dick Sears and Bill Tilden – he first competed in 1891 and over the next 19 years only failed to reach at least the semi-finals twice, establishing a match record of 61–12. He won his first title when he was 28 and his last 10 years later, which made him the oldest US singles male champion.

A powerful ground-stroke player, he played in five Davis Cup teams but never competed internationally. He committed suicide in New York in 1926.

Art Larsen

Born: *April 6, 1925*
San Leandro, CA, USA

Often described as a lawn-tennis genius, his touch on the volley and astute rallying made him one of the most attractive players to watch. Known universally as "Tappy", because of his unorthodox style, he became the first left-handed US champion when he outlasted Herbie Flam over five sets in 1950. The last shot was a perfect lob that fell on the baseline.

His best efforts at Wimbledon were three quarter-final appearances. The first, in 1950, saw him beaten by Frank Sedgman in an epic struggle in which the Australian recovered from two sets down. Although he only played for the United States in the Davis Cup in 1951 and 1952, he had a 4–0 winning record.

Rod Laver,

Born: August 9, 1938
Rockhampton, Queensland, Australia
(See Legends pp86-87)

Henri Leconte

Born: *July 4, 1963*
Lillers, France

A gifted, often unpredictable player with great shot-making skills, this fine left-hander's time on the circuit was often interrupted by serious back problems which twice led to his undergoing surgery. He was renowned for demonstrating his emotions with typical Gallic flair and humour, which delighted crowds everywhere. He was runner-up

HENRI LECONTE, very much a flamboyant modern Musketeer

at the French Open in 1988 and a member of the Davis Cup team for more than a decade from 1982. One of the main highlights of his career was the Davis Cup final in 1991 when he beat Pete Sampras in straight sets in singles and then teamed with Guy Forget to win the doubles as France regained the trophy for the first time since 1932. He beat Bjorn Borg in what was originally going to be the Swede's final Tour appearance at Monte Carlo in 1983, and again when Borg attempted a comeback at Stuttgart in 1984. The winner of eight titles, his most consistently successful year in singles was 1986 when he was a semi-finalist at both the French Open, where he lost to Mikael Pernfors, and at Wimbledon, where he was beaten by Boris Becker.

Ivan Lendl

Born: *March 7, 1960*
Ostrava, Czechoslovakia

Perhaps the most hard-working and dedicated professional the game has known, Ivan Lendl has an encyclopaedic memory which enables him to recall in amazing detail key points in his most important matches. Such was his high-level consistency that for 13 consecutive years, 1980–92, he finished in the top 10 of the world rankings.

His career was suddenly transformed in 1984 when, having finished runner-up in three of the four Grand Slam tournaments, he won the first of his eight Grand Slam titles as John McEnroe

IVAN LENDL

let him off the hook after winning the first two sets of the French. Thereafter Lendl became renowned for maintaining a relentless pressure on opponents which almost always forced them to submit, except at Wimbledon, where he was twice runner-up and a semi-finalist on five other occasions. He never truly believed that he could conquer the vagaries of playing on grass.

He reached number one in the world rankings for the first time in February 1983 and four times ended a year as number one. Two of the game's longest winning streaks – 44 matches starting on October 18, 1981 and a 66-match indoor winning streak from the same time to January 1983 – belong to him. He is the winner of 94 singles titles and runner-up in a further 52.

Suzanne Lenglen,

Born: *May 25, 1899. Paris, France*
(See Legends pp88–89)

John Lloyd

Born: *August 27, 1954*
Leigh-on-Sea, Essex UK

One of the most gifted British players of recent times who, by his own admission, did not always demonstrate the dedication and determination required to fulfil his potential. Yet he reached the final of the Australian Open in 1977, losing to Vitas Gerulaitis, to become the first British man to reach a Grand Slam singles final since Fred Perry in 1936. The following year he and his older brother David were both members of the British team which reached the final of the Davis Cup for the first time since 1937. They lost to the United States in Palm Springs. The second of three brothers who all played in professional events, John, apart from playing regularly on the ATP Seniors' Tour, is also coach to the British Davis Cup team, captained by David. He also works for the HBO television network as a tennis analyst.

Formerly married to Chris Evert and now living with his wife Deborah and their two children in Pacific Palisades, California, he achieved his career-best world ranking of 21 in July 1978. He won three Grand Slam mixed doubles titles, all with Wendy Turnbull, including successive Wimbledon victories, 1983–84.

Bob Lutz
Born: *August 29, 1947*
Lancaster, PA, USA

Although he won nine singles titles, it is for his exceptional doubles record, generally partnered by Stan Smith, that this sturdily built player earned most fame. No other team has won US titles on four different surfaces, grass, clay, hard and indoor, while they also had a 13–1 record in the Davis Cup. Their four victories in the US Open doubles spanned 13 years, the first being in 1968, the last in 1980 against Peter Fleming and John McEnroe, who beat them twice in Wimbledon finals. In Grand Slam singles Bob Lutz reached the semi-finals of the Australian in 1969.

John McEnroe,
Born: *February 16, 1959*
Wiesbaden, Germany
(See Legends pp90–91)

Ken McGregor
Born: *June 2, 1929*
Adelaide, South Australia

Although a finalist in singles at Wimbledon in 1951 and Australian singles champion the following year, Ken McGregor was principally a doubles specialist and his partnership with Frank Sedgman was one of the most feared of its time. In 1951 they completed the doubles Grand Slam and a year later retained all but the US title.

Their quarter-final defeat at Wimbledon in 1950, 6–4, 31–29, 7–9, 6–2 (64 games), lasting 4 hours, 5 minutes, was a record, although it is now held by Gene Scott and Niki Pilic who beat Cliff Richey and Torben Ulrich in a 1966 first-round match over five sets, spanning 96 games.

He was an unexpected singles choice for the Australian Davis Cup team in 1950, but stunned the Americans by beating former Wimbledon champion Ted Schroeder in straight sets to help his team capture the trophy. A successful former soccer player, he also beat Tony Trabert in the Davis Cup Challenge Round in 1952, just before turning professional.

Kathleen McKane
Born: *May 7, 1896*
Bayswater, London, UK

Kitty Godfree, as she became known and loved after her marriage to Leslie Godfree, was unmistakably a legendary figure in British tennis, for her many triumphs, her longevity as a player and above all her charm. Clearly the finest British woman player before the First World War, she won Wimbledon singles and mixed in both 1924 and 1926, and in both years set records of special significance.

In the 1924 singles final, though trailing by a set and 1–4, she recovered to become the only player ever to beat Helen Wills (4–6, 6–4, 6–4) at The Championships. In 1926, by which time she was married, her second mixed doubles victory with Leslie made them the only married couple who have won the title. Among other successes, she won the doubles (twice) and the mixed doubles (once) at the US Championships, the singles bronze medal in both the 1920 and 1924 Olympic Games, the doubles gold in 1920 and silver in 1924, the mixed silver in 1920 and bronze in 1924.

All England badminton singles champion four times, 1920–22 and 1924, she continued to drive herself to play tennis at the All England Club – and to cycle to do her shopping in Sheen – until well into her 80s. At the Seoul Olympics in 1988, aged 92, she was asked to give a press conference and fluently held international journalists spellbound with her reminiscences and thoughts on modern tennis for over an hour.

Charles "Chuck" McKinley
Born: *January 5, 1941*
St Louis, MO, USA

Runner-up to Rod Laver in 1961, this chunky and sturdily energetic player won Wimbledon two years later in a year of extraordinary upsets after needing special permission to take part from Trinity College, San Antonio, where he was studying. Not only did McKinley never have to play another seeded player, not even in the final, when he inflicted the first of three consecutive defeats on Fred Stolle, but neither was there any men's singles match that year involving two seeded players.

McKinley, who was US doubles champion three times – 1961, 1963 and 1964 – represented the United States in the Davis Cup regularly

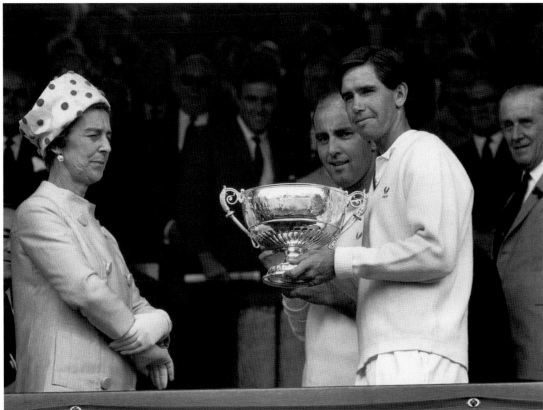

FREW McMILLAN *(right) and Bob Hewitt hold the Wimbledon men's doubles trophy, in 1967*

between 1960 and 1965, winning 29 of his 38 rubbers, and rounded off his most memorable year in 1963 by leading the US to a 3–2 victory in the Challenge Round against Australia. Long before Boris Becker made it part of his trademark, McKinley delighted crowds with his fearless diving and leaping to put away overheads.

Frew McMillan
Born: *May 20, 1942*
Springs, South Africa

Listening these days to his analysis of players and matches on radio and television, it is easy to understand why this consummately efficient player always seemed to be one stroke ahead of most of his rivals, especially on the doubles court, where thinking needs to be so much more instinctive. The combination of his unorthodox style – he held the racket with two hands on both sides – with the thrustful aggression of Bob Hewitt made them a brilliantly entertaining, as well as successful, doubles partnership.

Brought together by fate, after Australian-born Hewitt emigrated to South Africa in the early 1960s, they won the South African title four times, Wimbledon three times and once each at the French and the US, with an 11-year gap between the first and third victories at Wimbledon. And in 1978 they not only beat John Newcombe and Tony Roche in the quarter-finals, but Peter Fleming and John McEnroe in the final.

"We were touch and thrust", says McMillan, who invariably wore a white cricket cap when he played. "The secret was that we always knew what the other would be doing." His individual total of 74 doubles titles places him third on the all-time list behind Tom Okker (78) and McEnroe (75). He also won five mixed titles, including two Wimbledon and two US Opens with Betty Stove.

Peter McNamara
Born: *July 5, 1955*
Melbourne, Victoria, Australia

For several years resident in Hertfordshire, England, because it was a more suitable base for his extensive travelling in Europe and the United States, this richly gifted right-hander saw his career ruined by a freak accident when he was playing on a carpet court in Rotterdam in March 1983. A few days earlier he had consolidated his status in the top 10 by beating Ivan Lendl in the final in Brussels. Although he attempted a comeback after knee surgery later in the year, he eventually decided to concentrate on coaching – and now the less strenuous seniors' tennis instead. Together with fellow Australian Paul McNamee he won the doubles at Wimbledon in 1980 and 1982 after they had teamed up to win the Australian doubles in 1979.

One of the first players to adopt an oversize racket, McNamara figured in one of the longest matches in ATP Tour singles history when he lost a marathon Hamburg final to Jose Higueras in 1982, which lasted 5 hours and 6 minutes.

Iva Majoli
Born: *August 12, 1977*
Zagreb, Croatia

Iva Majoli started playing at the age of seven and had consistently been in the top 10 for the previous two years without quite fulfilling her full potential. Suddenly she came to the fore with a series of brilliant performances which made her the first Croatian to win a Grand Slam tournament at the French Open, in June 1997. Ranked nine at the time, she had beaten Jana Novotna to win Hanover and then Ruxandra Dragomir for the Hamburg title. She had to battle through four consecutive three-setters at Roland Garros, one against Lindsay Davenport and another against Steffi Graf's conqueror, Amanda Coetzer, to reach the final where she gave Martina Hingis her first defeat of the year in a 79-minute contest during which she did not have to fend off a single break point. Unfortunately the adrenalin, ecstasy and reassurance were not sustained during the second half of the year. Although she reached the last eight at Wimbledon before losing to Anna Kournikova, the conviction

MANUELA MALEEVE-FRAGNIERE, *oldest of three sisters on the tour*

faded quite seriously and from a peak of fourth place in the rankings, which she held from July to October, she had slipped to sixth by the end of 1997.

Manuela Maleeva-Fragnière
Born: *February 14, 1967*
Sofia, Bulgaria

The eldest and so far the most successful of the three sisters Manuela, Katerina and Magdalena. Coached by their mother, nine times Bulgarian champion Yulia Berberian, all were introduced to tennis while still at kindergarten and all broke into the top 10. When they played in the French Open in 1990 it was the first time that three sisters had all played in the main draw of the same Grand Slam event. They made more history in 1993 when all three were seeded at the Australian Open. Manuela, though now retired, could still boast the highest career-best ranking among them by the end of 1997. In 1985, when she reached the quarter-finals of two Grand Slams and the last 16 of the other two, she briefly held third place, one higher than Magdalena achieved, just as briefly, in 1996.

Manuela, a bronze medal winner at the Seoul Olympics in 1988, reached the semi-finals of the US Open in 1992 and 1993 and 11 other Grand Slam quarter-finals – four at both the French and Flushing Meadows, two in Australia and one at Wimbledon.

Molla Mallory-Bjurstedt

Born: *March 6, 1884*
Mosvik, Norway

Molla Mallory-Bjurstedt inflicted the only defeat Suzanne Lenglen suffered as an amateur in international competition. It was in the second round of the US Championships in 1921 when Mallory, who had started playing in Norway but emigrated to the United States in 1914, caught the French heroine off guard by setting and maintaining a furious pace and wearing her opponent down in long rallies, while waiting for the chance to put away a magnificent topspin forehand down the line. She stormed into a 6–2, 2–0 lead when Lenglen, coughing and weeping, told the umpire she was too ill to continue.

It was the sixth of Mallory's record eight US Championships triumphs, the last of them in 1926, by which time she was 42, and the limitless endurance of this sturdy daughter of an army officer was the key to so many of her successes, which included the US doubles title in 1916 and the mixed in 1922 and 1923.

Hana Mandlikova

Born: *February 19, 1962*
Prague, Czechoslovakia

A superb athlete, overflowing with natural talent, Mandlikova was coached by one Wimbledon runner-up, Betty Stove, and now coaches another, Jana Novotna. She won 23 titles during her 13-year career, but would probably have amassed many more had it not coincided with two of those even more gifted champions, Chris Evert and Martina Navratilova. The 1978 world junior champion, Mandlikova broke into the top 10 in 1980 and for six of the next seven years never finished below fifth place.

She won the Australian Open in 1980 and 1987, the French in 1981 and the US Open in 1985 but victory at Wimbledon, where her graceful skills and mixture of touch and power should have been rewarded, always eluded her. She was runner-up twice, first in 1981 when she was ranked five and, much to the annoyance of the WTA, the seeding committee made her second seed. The way she dismissed

Navratilova in the semi-finals justified their decision, but she was then outplayed in the final by Evert, then Mrs John Lloyd. In her second semi-final five years later she defeated Evert, but then could not prevent Navratilova from exacting revenge.

Alice Marble

Born: *September 28, 1913*
Plumeo County, CA, USA

To look at her trim, athletic figure, few would have believed that Alice Marble was one of the most aggressive

TODD MARTIN, *so close but never victorious at Wimbledon*

American players before the 1939–45 war, as she took serve-and-volley-tennis to new heights. It was all the more remarkable because, just when she seemed set to challenge for major honours, she went down with tuberculosis and was told she would never be able to play again.

Yet after two years away from competition, she fought back, winning the US Championship in 1936 when she beat the reigning Wimbledon champion, Helen Jacobs. The following year, wearing the shortest shorts yet seen on the Centre Court, she made her first Wimbledon bid, only to lose to the Polish player Jadwiga Jedrzejowska in the semi-finals. In 1938 Jacobs beat her, again in the semi-finals, but after recapturing the US title that year, which she then retained for two more years, Marble felt considerably greater confidence about her Wimbledon prospects in 1939.

Her dream was fulfilled. She reached the final, dropping only 19 games in 10 sets, and then crushed the British player Kay Menzies (Stammers) 6–2, 6–0 to complete the triple crown, for she had already retained the mixed doubles with Don Budge and the women's doubles with Sarah Fabyan.

Todd Martin

Born: *July 8, 1970*
Hinsdale, IL, USA

Although he is never likely to challenge for the top 10 most extrovert players, this 6ft-6in right-hander, who spent most of 1997 trying to restore his form to the peak it had reached before first a groin injury and then major elbow problems developed in the summer of 1996, is one of the most astutely intelligent players on the main Tour.

In many ways this former top-ranked NCAA player and indoor intercollegiate champion is the archetypal modern player, attempting to take full advantage of his height and power in the most aggressive fashion on serve and off the ground. He was runner-up at the Australian Open in 1994, when he also reached the semi-finals at Wimbledon and the US Open, gaining a career-best fifth in the world rankings.

With one or two exceptions, his performances are generally as solid

"GENTLEMAN TIM" MAYOTTE *never gave the crowds less than 100 per cent*

and dependable as the mood he exudes, though he admits that he "froze up" when leading 5–1 in the final set of his 1996 Wimbledon semi-final. He lost against MaliVai Washington, double-faulting three times when he first served for the match.

Conchita Martinez
Born: *April 16, 1972*
Monzon, Spain

Conchita Martinez has never hit her double-handed backhand, a principal strength of her game, better than in the 1994 Wimbledon final when she denied Martina Navratilova a 10th singles title in her farewell singles appearance and also became the first Spanish player to win this event. Two years later she became the first woman to win the Italian Open in four consecutive years and also won a bronze medal in doubles, with Arantxa Sanchez Vicario, at the Olympic Games.

Overall, though, she has suffered from a lack of consistent self-confidence and, in particular, her reluctance to go to the net at a time when an all-court game is increasingly necessary for success. She reached a career-best world ranking of two in October 1995 and was unbeaten as she led Spain to a third consecutive Fed Cup triumph.

In the same year she was a semi-finalist at all four Grand Slams but in 1996–97 titles became harder to come by, particularly in 1997 when her ranking dropped to 12, her lowest since her first full year on the circuit in 1988.

Amelie Mauresmo
Born: *July 5, 1979*
St Germaine en Laye, France

The powerfully built French woman was fast becoming known as the player with a major nerve problem, for despite winning 19 titles, she would regularly fall during the latter stages of any of the majors. However, at the age of 26, she finally made her mental breakthrough by winning the Australian Open in 2006.

With that victory she gained the confidence which swept her back to the top of the rankings - a feat she had achieved briefly the previous September - to establish herself early in the season as a stronger favorite for her home Grand Slam.

It was also ironic that her only previous appearance in a Grand Slam final was Australia back in 1999 when she was outplayed by Martina Hingis. It took her two years before she again started to feature in the latter stages of the majors with two semi-final appearances in 2002, followed by two quarter-finals the following year when she was also hampered by back problems. However, in 2004 she showed great form by never losing before the last eight and reaching the semis at Wimbledon for the second time, a feat she was to repeat in 2005.

As a former Junior champion of both the French and Wimbledon, with her powerful and elegant game and only once ending a season outside the top 10 since 1999, she shows great consistency and has always been ranked amongst the contenders for every event she enters, despite her brittle reputation. However, having also won the WTA Tour Championships at the end of 2005, it would seem she has finally matured into the player many had forecast she would be, claiming her second Grand Slam title at Wimbledon.

Gene Mayer
Born: *April 11, 1956*
Flushing, NY, USA

This eloquent All-American at Stamford, who gained his political science degree in three years, finished in the top 10 for four consecutive years (1980–83), reaching a best fourth place in 1980 when he collected five singles titles and reached the semi-finals of the Masters, with first-ever wins over John McEnroe and Bjorn Borg.

Intermittent injury problems impeded further progress. In 1981 a serious wrist problem forced him to default in the French and miss Wimbledon. Then, two points from a straight sets victory over Ramesh Krishnan in the fourth round of the US Open, he was so severely stricken with cramp that he could not continue.

Despite further injuries and a sight problem, Mayer, who was happiest on clay courts, reached the last eight of the US Open for a second time in 1984 and also won three Grand Slam doubles titles, twice at the French, with Hank Pfister and then with his brother Sandy, who also partnered him to success at Wimbledon in 1980.

Tim Mayotte
Born: *August 3, 1960*
Springfield, MA, USA

One of eight children, who studied history at Stamford, where he was NCAA champion in 1981 and reached the final in Bristol in his first tournament as a professional, Tim Mayotte was one of the most whole-hearted competitors of his time. With his powerful serve-and-volley game, he was always regarded as a threat to almost anyone at Wimbledon, especially when he reached the quarter-finals on his first appearance and the semis before losing to John McEnroe, at the top of his form, in 1982.

Curiously that was Mayotte's only semi-final appearance at The Championships, although his success in reaching at least the last 16 nine times in 10 years was testimony to his sustained ability. He was runner-up in the 1988 Olympic singles final. Mayotte, who was also a semi-finalist in Australia in 1983, was known as "Gentleman Tim" – and with good reason. His sportsmanship was never more significantly demonstrated than in Wimbledon's fourth round of 1985. Leading Boris Becker by two sets to one, he made no complaint then, or since, that a misunderstanding between the umpire and referee allowed the German, then 17, double the normal time to recover from a fall. It was a gesture which may have changed the course of both their careers.

Miloslav Mecir
Born: *May 19, 1964*
Bojnice, Czechoslovakia

For the connoisseur of skills, demonstrated in the most seemingly effortless manner, watching this lean and laid-back 6ft-3in right-hander was pure joy. He was nick-named "The Big

Cat" and, observing his stealthy movement about the court, coupled with an elongated stride and even longer reach, it was easy to see why. He did not always look it, but he was one of the quickest players in the game at the time.

Sadly, a serious back problem, which had been a near-constant handicap and ended his career after he had to undergo surgery to repair a herniated disc in 1990, limited his time on the Tour. Even so he still became one of the few to win titles on four different surfaces. He made his first big move in 1985, winning Rotterdam and Hamburg, and went on to win eight more Tour events plus, much more significantly for a country where Olympic achievements are so important, gold in Seoul in 1988. In 1989 he lost the Australian Open final, played in extreme heat, to Ivan Lendl.

His last major match, in the second round of Wimbledon 1990, was like one of the finest he played – but also lost – at Wimbledon against Stefan Edberg. Their 1988 semifinal, when he was already a victim of back problems and nearly had to pull out on the eve of the tournament, was a classic.

Andrei Medvedev

Born: *August 31, 1974*
Kiev, Ukraine

This fine athlete, with an infectious smile and ready wit, made such a huge impression when he first appeared on the Tour as a 16-year-old that his failure to justify such exciting potential and early promise has disappointed many, not least his various coaches. He began playing at the age of 8 with the help of his mother, Svetlana, who coaches his sister, Natalia Medvedeva on the women's Tour.

Although happiest on clay, his game, based on powerful groundstrokes, is well able to bring reward on all surfaces, and between 1993 and 1995 he successively reached the last eight at Flushing Meadows, Roland Garros and the Australian Open. Even more impressively, in 1993 he reached the semi-finals of the French Open, but was then trounced by Sergi Bruguera, the eventual champion, who

ANDREI MEDVEDEV, *a mercurial talent from the Ukraine*

allowed him only six games.

By the end of 1997 he was ranked 27, an improvement on the previous year but well below his best of fourth in May 1994, and had won 11 ATP Tour tournaments including the German Open, three years in succession (1995–97). Like a growing number of players, he had been hampered by injuries to his back and shoulder.

Kerry Melville

Born: *August 7, 1947*
Sydney, NSW, Australia

Although seldom a headline-hitter, this efficient Australian produced consistently solid form throughout a career which spanned both the amateur and Open eras. She never won a Grand Slam singles but was runner-up in Australia in 1966 and a semi-finalist at the other three – French,

United States and Wimbledon.

Married to former Australian player Raz Reid, she maintained the reputation throughout her career of seldom losing matches she was expected to win. In 1974, as her touring was coming to a close, she still reached semi-finals in Australia and Wimbledon, beating former champion Evonne Goolagong along the way, was runner-up in four Virginia Slims tournaments, reached the last eight at Forest Hills and won the South African Open.

A particularly fine doubles player, she won the Australian title in 1968 with the late Karen Krantzcke and was runner-up in three of the next five years, while she was also a member of Australia's Fed Cup team in 1974. She was one of the pioneering players when World Team Tennis began in the United States in the mid-1970s.

Born: *March 5, 1876*
Brooklyn, NY, USA

The final of the WTA Tour Championships at Madison Square Garden is now the only occasion when women players compete in a best-of-five sets match. Yet there was an 11-year spell between 1891 and 1901 when it was commonplace in the US Championships. It was the experiences of Bessie Moore, especially in 1901, which made officials decide that henceforth women should only play the best of three sets.

In that year Moore, who had first reached the final as a 16-year-old in 1892 – the youngest until Pam Shriver in 1978 – and lost to Ireland's Mabel Cahill in what was the first women's match to last the full five sets, won the title for the second time. In the All-Comers final she beat Marion Jones 4–6, 1–6, 9–7, 9–7, 6–3, a total of 58 games. The next day, in the Challenge Round, she beat the defending champion, Myrtle McAteer, 6–4, 3–6, 7–5, 2–6, 6–2 – another 47 games – to become the only woman to play, let alone win, two matches over five sets on successive days.

Women players of the day were not pleased when the rule was changed. They felt they were being "patronized" by the men. Moore especially, who went on to win again in 1903 and 1905, felt that limiting them, at least in the final, to the best of three sets was wrong.

Olga Morozova

Born: *February 22, 1949*
Moscow, Russia

Now living in the UK and coaching for the Lawn Tennis Association, she had the greatest moment of her tennis life in 1974 by becoming the first Soviet woman to reach the Wimbledon singles final. Although overwhelmed 6–1, 6–2 by top seed Chris Evert, thirdseeded Morozova had played solidly throughout the fortnight and taken full advantage, in a year when there were only eight seeds, of not having to meet another of them before the final.

A qualified physical education teacher, she had already set new standards for Soviet women by becoming the first to reach any Wimbledon final in 1968 when she and Alex Metrevelli were runners-up in the mixed. She was also the first Russian to reach the singles final of any major international tournament when she was runner-up at the Italian Open in 1972, where a year later she won the doubles with Virginia Wade.

Although there were no longer any barriers between amateur and professional in tournaments, prize money won by Soviet players at that time went to the Russian Federation, rather than to them, and in 1977 Morozova and other fellow countrymen were frozen out of international events when the Russian authorities ordered them not to play. They knew moves were afoot to bring tennis back into the Olympics and did not want to jeopardize the amateur status of any of their players in the meantime. It was a wasted ploy. When tennis returned the Olympic Games had also dropped the ban on professionals.

Angela Mortimer

Born: *April 21, 1932*
Plymouth, Devon, UK

The most modest and underrated of all Britain's post-war Wimbledon champions. Six years before her triumph at Wimbledon in 1961, she had won the French title in 1955 – the first British player to do so since Peggy Scrivens in 1934 – and the doubles at Wimbledon with Anne Shilcock. She was also runner-up at Wimbledon to Althea Gibson in 1958 and six months earlier had won the Australian title.

Such a fine record reached its peak when she outlasted Christine Truman 4–6, 6–4, 7–5 in the first all-British final at Wimbledon for 47 years and was all the more remarkable because she overcame a physical impairment throughout her career. Angela, married to former British Davis Cup player and captain John Barrett, now senior tennis commentator for BBC Television, is partially deaf. But she insists that instead of being an insuperable handicap, it was an advantage inasmuch as it helped her to shut out all other distractions.

A relatively late recruit to the game, she did not start playing tennis until she was 15 but coached, like Mike Sangster and Sue Barker, by Arthur Roberts at Torquay, she developed a forthright game, based on well-controlled groundstrokes, a formidable forehand and a resolve and speed around the court which were often decisive.

Carlos Moya

Born: *August 27, 1976*
Palma de Mallorca, Spain

Before the arrival of his Mallorcan countryman, Rafael Nadal, Carlos Moya was the original pin-up boy of Spanish tennis, the first player from that country to reach the top of the world rankings, albeit briefly, in March 1999 but then suffered back problems which curtailed the latter part of his season.

Moya's sole success at Grand Slam level was at Roland Garros in 1998 having made the final of the 1997 Australian Open and the semi-finals of the 1998 US Open. Since those heady days, no doubt as a result of his back problems, his best performances have been quarter-final appearances on three occasions, twice at the French and once in Melbourne.

However he has been a consistent player, using his top spin game to great effect winning three Masters Series events, and appearing in three other finals, as well as the Tennis Masters Cup in 1998. In total he has collected 18 titles and been a stalwart of his country's Davis Cup team, helping them to the finals in 2003 and overall victory the following year.

Gardnar Mulloy

Born: *November 22, 1914*
Miami, FL, USA

An outstanding doubles player, Gardnar Mulloy's experience and enduring love of the game were evident throughout a career which spanned more than 20 years. He was first given a US national ranking in 1936 and was still competing in the Davis Cup in 1957, when he and Budge Patty recorded an astonishing triumph in the doubles at Wimbledon. At the ages of 43 and 33 respectively, they became the oldest post-war champions by upsetting Lew Hoad, 22, and Neale Fraser, 23, in the final.

Earlier his dipping serve returns and decisive volleys had made him an ideal partner for Bill Talbert and they won the US title four times between 1942 and 1948, also winning the decisive rubber in the 1948 Davis Cup victory over Australia at Forest Hills. A lawyer by profession, with an apparently nonchalant air which belied his commitment, he also became the oldest runner-up in the US singles in 1953 when, aged 38, he beat Ken Rosewall and Ham Richardson before losing to Sedgman, 14 years his junior.

Andy Murray

Born: *May 15, 1987*
Dunblane, Scotland

In British terms the most exciting youngster to have emerged from these shores in recent years. Already being acclaimed, at 18 years of age, as a world beater having taken over from Tim Henman, early in 2006, at the top of the national rankings.

Whilst still inexperienced, the young Scot has picked up his first ATP Tour title (San Jose in 2006) and become a major attraction with tournament directors, all keen to include him in their draws.

He made a remarkable entrance into the senior game when he reached the third round at Queen's, losing to Thomas Johansson and a fortnight later, was the last Briton left standing at Wimbledon, again reaching round three where he lost a tight five-setter to David Nalbandian.

The youngster, the first Briton to win the Junior US Open (2003) lived up to his growing reputation when he reached the final in Bangkok where he gave Roger Federer a close match.

His success during the year led to him rising 449 ranking places to finish 65 and, in the process, became the first teenager since Buster Mottram in 1974, to finish the year in the top 100.

The son of a former Scottish National Coach, Judy Murray, the youngster – who is proud to be a Scot – showed his gutsy potential earlier in the year when, as the youngest player to represent Britain in Davis Cup competition, he destroyed, in partnership with David Sherwood, the world recognized Israeli doubles pairing of Jonathan Erlich and Andy Ram. Now coached by Brad Gilbert, Murray has risen even further up the rankings.

Thomas Muster

Born: *October 2, 1967*
Leibnitz, Austria

"The Iron Man" or "The King of Clay". Call him what you will, but this dour, unforgiving left-hander impressed everyone with his strength of will, as well as his astonishing fitness on court. In the 10 years after winning his first title in Hilversum in 1986, he won 42 titles, all but two of them on clay, where in 1995 especially he reigned supreme for a second successive year. He won no less than 12 ATP Tour events, including six when he was defending the title from the previous year. The two which meant most to him were the French Open which highlighted his clay-court record spanning 1994–95 of 111–5 and Essen, for that was the breakthrough he achieved in 1997 on hard courts.

Some of his contemporaries, most notably Andre Agassi, questioned the legitimacy of his status, because it was based so heavily on one-surface performances, when he became the first left-hander since John McEnroe to become (albeit briefly) world number one in February 1996. Yet the way he had battled back from major knee surgery which could have ended his career, after a road accident a few hours after he reached the 1989 final in Key Biscayne, won universal admiration. Even this hard man of tennis buckled under the emotion when, eight years on, he won the title at Key Biscayne.

Rafael Nadal

Born: *June 3, 1986*
Manacor, Mallorca

Rafael Nadal, better known as 'Rafa' to his friends and fans, is one of the most exciting players to have emerged in recent years. The young Spaniard, who hails from the island of

Mallorca, is a clay court exponent but also likes the American hardcourts, and perhaps even more surprisingly, has set his sights on Wimbledon. In addition to his on court success, he has become the main exponent of the pirate look with his three-quarter length trousers, sleeveless shirts and tightly-tied bandana. However, whilst the trousers haven't as yet caught on with any of his playing contemporaries, the shirt certainly has.

As a player he is powerful, fast with an excellent defense and a quick brain which can turn defensive play into an all-out attack. His heavy topspin off the ground and his acute angles on court mesmerizes opponents and delights spectators.

Still a teenager, he became the first Spaniard to end 2005 ranked world No2 having virtually matched Roger Federer title for title during the year. The big difference was that the Swiss collected all the majors bar the French which fell to Nadal who became the first player since Mats Wilander in 1982, to win the French on his debut, and the first teenager to win a Grand Slam since Pete Sampras (US Open 1990).

In fact 2005 was a remarkable year for the Spanish Teenage Sensation. Like Federer he won 11 titles and 4 Masters Series events, breaking another Wilander teenage record of 9 titles in a year. His resilience on court was well illustrated by his

incredible 5-hour and 12-minute marathon final to win the Rome Masters Series title.

His tenacity was first witnessed the previous year when he helped Spain win the Davis Cup, defeating Andy Roddick in the final, a feat which again established another record as he became the youngest player, at 18 years, 6 months, to register a victory for the winning team at that stage of the prestigious competition.

Nadal, whose full name is Nadal Parera, won his first ATP title in 2004 at Sopot, and now, with 17 ATP titles to his credit, including back-to-back titles at Roland Garros, he becomes the most successful teenager in the Open era, overtaking Borg's mark of 16. Nadal also set another remarkable record winning 60 consecutive clay court matches and in the process surpassed Guillermo Vilas' record of 53 set in 1977.

Definitely a youngster to watch for he is the player who, providing he can remain healthy, everyone expects will give the incomparable Federer a run for his money.

David Nalbandian

Born: *January 1, 1982*
Cordoba, Argentina

Of all the players to emerge from South America, David Nalbandian has come closest to winning Wimbledon when he surprised everyone by

reaching the final in 2002 only to lose to the then dominant Lleyton Hewitt.

That run effectively put Nalbandian on the map and despite injuries, thanks to his tenacious and muscular baseline play, has retained a place in the top ten for the past three years, winning the season ending Masters Cup in Shanghai in 2005 when he beat Roger Federer in the final.

And whilst he has yet to emulate or improve on his 2002 Wimbledon run the 24-year-old has featured consistently in the latter stages of Grand Slams, with five quarter-final appearances, three in Melbourne plus Wimbledon and New York, as well as semis at the French and US Opens.

Ilie Nastase

Born: *July 19, 1946*
Bucharest, Romania

One of the most gifted and flamboyant players the game has known, this champion who was loved one minute and loathed the next won 57 titles during his career, including Grand Slam titles at the US Open in 1972 and the French a year later. Yet he should have won many more, especially Wimbledon, where he was runner-up in 1972 and 1976.

He was an entertainer second to none. The racket in his hand did not just talk but teased and tormented. The trouble was that he too often got carried away by a volatile personali-

JOHN NEWCOMBE – *Wimbledon 1971*

ty which meant he never realized when he was overstepping that narrow border between creating laughter and causing offence.

He first came to prominence when he played a leading role in the 1969 Zone final defeat of Britain at Wimbledon as Romania qualified for the final – a feat repeated in 1971 and 1972.

They lost each time to the United States, most notably after his nervousness led to a straight sets defeat for him in the 1972 opening rubber against Stan Smith, three months after the cool American had beaten him over five sets in a match which, because of the weather, had been the first men's singles final staged at Wimbledon on a Sunday. In between, though, he beat Arthur Ashe from 2–4 down in the fourth and a service break down in the fifth in the US Open final. Nastase, who established a close friendship and winning doubles partnership with Ion Tiriac, won 109 out of 146 Davis Cup singles and doubles rubbers and went on to become Davis Cup captain and then president of the Romanian Tennis Federation.

Martina Navratilova,

Born: *October 18, 1956*
Prague, Czechoslovakia
(See Legends pp92–93)

John Newcombe

Born: *May 23, 1944*
Sydney, NSW, Australia

One of the game's most charismatic figures, who did not concentrate his

ILIE NASTASE, *the champion who also loved to be the clown*

wide-ranging sporting prowess on tennis until he was 17 – and before growing the moustache which has become his trademark – this powerful Australian shares with fellow countryman Rod Laver the distinction of winning the Wimbledon men's singles title as both an amateur and a professional. Indeed he won the last amateur event there in 1967, was runner-up to Laver in 1969 and champion in the two following years. He would have been well in contention for a third consecutive triumph had his entry not been barred by the International Tennis Federation, which would not accept professionals contracted to World Championship Tennis, the American organization whose own Tour clashed with several traditional international tournaments.

In his Davis Cup debut, as a 19-year-old in 1963, he was given the daunting task of playing singles in the Challenge Round against the United States. He lost both rubbers and was not picked for singles again until 1967, by which time he was recognized as one of the sturdiest, most competitive serve-and-volleyers in the game both in singles and doubles, where his partnership with Tony Roche was outstanding. Five of his six Wimbledon doubles titles were with the left-hander, as were four of his five Australian titles. In 1967 he won the US singles and also the first of three doubles titles with Britain's Roger Taylor in a bizarre final. With darkness falling when Newcombe and Taylor were leading two sets to one, it was decided that rather than postpone it overnight, they would play the sudden-death nine-point tie-break then in experimental use. Newcombe and Taylor won it 5–3.

Kurt Nielsen

Born: *November 19, 1930*
Copenhagen, Denmark

This exciting Dane, with a menacing

YANNICK NOAH, *a supreme athlete, living life to the full*

serve, twice reached the Wimbledon final unseeded in 1953 and 1955, losing first to the superior volleying of Vic Seixas and then to the super-efficient Tony Trabert. In 1951 he had pushed the champion, Dick Savitt, harder than anyone to five sets in the third round. Nielsen based his game on power and this was particularly successful at Wimbledon in 1955 when he upset Abe Segal, Nicky Pietrangeli and Ken Rosewall on his way to the final.

In Scandinavia he was supreme, especially on wood, and he won their indoor Championships five times and the doubles four times. He also won the US and French indoor titles and

was British hard-court doubles champion at Bournemouth in 1954. A fun-loving competitor, who turned professional in 1960 and later moved into tournament administration as a referee and supervisor, he played 96 Davis Cup rubbers for Denmark between 1948 and 1960 and had an unofficial ranking of seven in 1953.

Yannick Noah

Born: *May 16, 1960*
Sedan, France

Although born in France, he was discovered as a 10-year-old by Arthur Ashe during a goodwill visit to Cameroon, where Noah and his family were then living. Ashe contacted Philippe Chatrier, president of the French Tennis Federation, who arranged for the youngster to be sent to their training school in Nice. The rest, as they say, is history.

A strapping fellow, he loved to play aggressively from the baseline but had a wondrous touch when it was needed. He won the first of 23 Tour titles in Nancy in 1979 and four years later became the first Frenchman since Marcel Bernard in 1946 to win the French Open when he beat defending champion Mats Wilander. It was a highly emotional occasion, surpassed only when, as Davis Cup captain, he masterminded France's first Davis Cup success for 59 years as they beat the United States in Grenoble in 1991. He captained them again to the trophy in Sweden in 1996.

He finished in the top 10 in singles consistently in 1982–87 and in 1984 partnered fellow Frenchman Henri Leconte to win the French Open doubles title. A pop star in his "spare time", he was co-founder, with his mother, of a charity which helps impoverished children.

Jana Novotna

Born: *October 2, 1968*
Brno, Czechoslovakia

After several disappointments, she finally won her first major title by taking the Chase Championships, the women's end-of-the-year showpiece in New York's Madison Square Garden, in November 1997, beating

Mary Pierce in three straight sets and therefore going into 1998 with a career-best second-place world ranking.

For so long Novotna, one of the most skilfully gifted players of her generation, has been called "the nearly woman". One of the last natural serve-and-volleyers, she has a game perfectly suited to grass courts, and although she twice reached the Wimbledon final, her nerve deserted her the first time in 1991 and injury cruelly thwarted her in 1997. However, little did she realize that the best was still to come.

Novotna, coached by Hana Mandlikova, will forever deny that mental frailty struck when she was leading Steffi Graf 4–1 in the final set of the 1993 final, but she double-faulted on the point for 5–1, never won another game and so the everlasting memory is that of the Duchess of Kent sympathetically cradling the sobbing runner-up against her shoulder during the presentation ceremony. 1997 was so near yet so far, as Martina Hingis came back from one set down to win, but it was third time lucky for Jana in 1998 as she beat Nathalie Tauziat to win her first Grand Slam title.

Tom Okker

Born: February 22, 1944
Haarlem, Netherlands

Known as "The Flying Dutchman" because of his speed about the court, Tom Okker belongs to that growing, though still exclusive, club whose members have won more than 100 singles and doubles professional titles. But some of his earliest successes, such as winning the Italian, German, and South African Championships in 1968, when he was also runner-up to Arthur Ashe in the first US Open, were achieved while he was still "a registered player" – able to accept prize money, but also able to play as an amateur in the Davis Cup because he

remained under the jurisdiction of his national association.

A regular in the top 10 between 1968 and 1973, he went on to reach the semi-finals in singles of the three other Grand Slam tournaments and the doubles final in all of them, either partnered by John Newcombe, in 1973, or more often with Marty Riessen, with whom he won the US Open in 1976. He also played in the Davis Cup for 11 years between 1964 and 1981.

Alex Olmedo

Born: *March 24, 1936*
Arequipa, Peru

Like many others from his part of the world, Alex Olmedo refined his tennis in the United States. Eventually, indeed, he opted to play for them in the Davis Cup at a time when Peru did not field a team, although his decision, encouraged by Davis Cup captain

MANUEL ORANTES, *a Spanish master with much-admired skills*

Perry Jones, led to howls of protest that as a resident, rather than a citizen, he should not be chosen. An aggressive volleyer who always felt his place should be at the net, he reached his peak in a short but hugely successful major career before turning professional in 1959, when he won both the Australian and Wimbledon titles, but lost in the US final to Neale Fraser.

Seeded one at Wimbledon, he beat Roy Emerson in the semi-finals and then the still up-and-coming Rod Laver in the final. He repeated that success in the Davis Cup a month later, but it was not enough to prevent Australia taking the trophy home from Forest Hills. In 1958 he was the first player to win three live rubbers – two singles and one doubles – in a Challenge or final round of the Davis Cup, for the United States, a feat since equalled by Stan Smith against Romania in Bucharest in 1972, John

McEnroe at home to Argentina in 1981 and Pete Sampras against Russia in Moscow in 1995.

Manuel Orantes

Born: *February 6, 1949*
Granada, Spain

His success at the US Open in 1975, only 10 years after Manuel Santana had been the first Spanish winner at Forest Hills, was one of the most astonishing. Having beaten Ilie Nastase in the quarter-finals, he won a marathon late-night, five-set semifinal against Guillermo Vilas with a remarkable recovery from 0–5 and three match points down and then 1–5 and two more match points down in the fourth set. Exhausted when he returned to his hotel after midnight, he got his big toe stuck in the tap as he lay back trying to relax in the bath.

Despite such adventures, this most affable and courteous competitor returned to the court 15 hours later and produced the most immaculate display of impeccable clay-court wizardry, as well as potent aggression from the baseline, to thrash defending champion Jimmy Connors in straight sets. A stocky left-hander, who made his mark early on the junior international scene, he was German and Italian champion in 1972 and repeated that Hamburg triumph in 1975, which was to be his best, lifting him into the top 10 for the first time. Winner of 32 singles and 24 doubles titles on the Tour, including the Masters in 1976, he reached his highest world ranking (4) in 1976.

Margaret Osborne du Pont

Born: *March 4, 1918*
Joseph, OR, USA

Second only (probably) to Elizabeth Ryan as an amateur in doubles, she was a key member of that powerful group of players who made the United States so dominant in women's tennis in the first decade after the 1939–45 war. Her partnership with Louise Brough broke all records and yet, although they had already won the first of their five doubles titles at The Championships at their first attempt in 1946, it was in singles a year later that she first caught the public imagination when she became champion without losing a set.

She was an aggressive server, both agile and punishing at the net, and further successes came thick and fast. Although she did not win the Wimbledon singles again, finishing runner-up to Brough in 1949–50, she won the US singles three years in succession, 1948–50, the French twice, 1946 and 1949, and developed an unblemished Wightman Cup record in 18 rubbers, the first in 1946, the last in 1962, when she won the mixed at Wimbledon with Neale Fraser. In addition to their Wimbledon triumphs, she and Brough won 12 US titles and three French. In all she won 37 Grand Slam tournament titles in singles, doubles and mixed. Only Margaret Court, Martina Navratilova and Billie Jean King have won more.

Rafael Osuna

Born: *September 15, 1938*
Mexico City, Mexico

This lithe, exceptionally speedy player about the court was rated the best player in the world in 1963, after his subtle mix of chips and lobs had helped unsettle Frank Froehling III in straight sets in the final of the US Championships. In the same year he had won the doubles at Wimbledon for a second time – the only Wimbledon titles so far won by a Mexican – more than fulfilling the exceptional promise he had shown in collegiate tennis in the United States.

His first Wimbledon doubles triumph was in 1960 with Dennis Ralston, then only 17, with whom he had never played before. Unseeded, they were taken to a fifth set by British qualifiers Gerald Oakley and Humphrey Truman before winning it 16–14 on their way to the final where they beat another British pair, Mike Davies and Bobby Wilson. Osuna loved playing in the Davis Cup and, tragically, it was only a few days after he had led Mexico to an unexpected 3–2 defeat of Australia in 1969, with him beating Bill Bowrey in the match-winning fifth rubber, that he was killed in an air crash when a private plane, carrying him on a business trip, crashed near Monterrey.

Adriano Panatta

Born: *July 9, 1950*
Rome, Italy

More than 20 years on from his flamboyant successes, especially at Rome's Foro Italico, this handsome, dark-haired right-hander remains one of the heroic figures of Italian tennis. The most spectacular successes for this dashing player, with classic Latin looks, who loved living dangerously in matches, especially with his defiant volleying at the net, came in 1976. With the beseeching cries of "Ahhd-dree-an-no" more fervent than ever from the crowds packed on the marble steps which provided the seating at the Foro Italico in those days, he became the first Italian to win in Rome for 15 years, but only after incredibly saving no less than 11 match points against Australian Kim Warwick in the first round.

Moving on to Paris, he also had to save a first-round match point against Pavel Hutka before going on to beat Bjorn Borg, the defending champion, in the quarter-finals and then two Americans, Eddie Dibbs and Harold Solomon, for his only Grand Slam title. Four months later he led Italy to their only success in the Davis Cup, winning two singles and also the doubles as they beat Chile 4–1 in the final in Santiago. A gloriously stylish player to watch, he continued playing regularly until 1983, with a best end-of-year ranking of seven in 1976.

Frank Parker

Born: *January 31, 1916*
Milwaukee, WI, USA

Though sometimes limited by a lack of authority on the forehand, this steadfast groundstroker formed a successful and durable partnership with Don Budge and together they were largely responsible for the United States beating a rebuilt post-Perry British team in the Davis Cup Challenge Round in 1937. He won 12

of his 14 Davis Cup rubbers, including both singles in 1938 when the Americans successfully defended the trophy against Australia.

Twice winner of the French, his consistency within American tennis was considerable. He was ranked among their own top 10 for 17 years, 1933–49, a record which lasted until Jimmy Connors bettered it in 1988. He was also the oldest player to compete in the US Championships when he was 52 in 1968, 36 years after competing in the event for the first time. He had turned professional in 1949, to tour with Jack Kramer, Pancho Gonzales and Pancho Segura. This was his first chance since then to compete and he decided to enter so that he could feel that he was part of the Open era. He lost in the first round – but only to the eventual champion, Arthur Ashe. He was ranked number one in the world in 1948.

Gerald Patterson

Born: *December 17, 1895*
Melbourne, Victoria, Australia

A strapping Australian, with a cannonball serve which was his launching pad to a daring game, and a second serve which was almost as effective, he won the Military Cross during the 1914–18 War before making his Wimbledon debut in 1919. He became the first man to have to play eight matches to win – seven in the All-Comers and then the Challenge Round, where he beat fellow countryman Norman Brookes, who because of the war had had to wait five years to defend his triumph of 1914.

He was a worthy, impressive winner although a year later Bill Tilden also won seven matches to reach the Challenge Round, where he had the all-round court craft to tame Patterson's pace. Curiously enough, when Patterson returned to Wimbledon again in 1922, with the Challenge Round abolished and the tournament being staged for the first time at Church Road, he received a first-round walkover and had to win only six matches to become champion for a second time.

Patterson's powerful, though sometimes wildly erratic, serving was seldom better demonstrated than when he won the Australian title in 1927, for he hit 29 aces and an equal number of double faults. He also won five Australian doubles titles plus the mixed at Wimbledon in 1920, and won 32 of his 46 Davis Cup rubbers.

Budge Patty

Born: *February 11, 1924*
Fort Smith, ARK, USA

One of the most elegant players of his time, with a forehand volley which was the envy of most, he created the first of many major upsets during his career at the US Championships in 1946 by dismissing the new Wimbledon champion, Yvon Petra, in straight sets. It was in 1950, though, that his skill and strength were best appreciated when

BUDGE PATTY *in classic attacking style in Berlin*

he achieved the remarkable double, especially for an American, of winning the French and Wimbledon titles in the same year. Only two other Americans, Don Budge and Tony Trabert, boast such a record and in Open tennis it has been achieved only twice, by Rod Laver and Bjorn Borg.

A handsome champion in every respect, with beautiful touch, he dropped only four sets on the way to his Wimbledon success, beating Frank Sedgman in the final. Three years later he figured in one of Wimbledon's epic contests, a third-round match with Jaroslav Drobny, which began around 5 p.m. and lasted nearly four-and-a-half hours before the exiled Czech won 8–6, 16–18, 3–6, 8–6, 12–10 (93 games) in fast fading light. In 1957 Patty, then 33, joined with Gardnar Mulloy (43), unseeded, to beat two Australians at the peak of their careers, Neale Fraser and Lew Hoad, and became the oldest post-war doubles champions.

Fred Perry,

Born: *May 18, 1909*
Stockport, UK
(See Legends pp94–95)

Yvon Petra

Born: *March 8, 1916*
Cholun, Indo-China

At 6ft 5in, this towering French-Colonial right-hander remains one of the tallest winners of a Grand Slam singles title. Yvon Petra learned his tennis playing in Indo-China in bare feet and used his serve and forcefulness at the net to mask what was generally regarded as a weaker backhand. A surprise Wimbledon champion in the first post-war Championships in 1946, especially as it was uncertain how well he would play after undergoing a delicate knee operation while a prisoner of war, he was also the last to win the title still wearing long flannels.

Having astonished everyone by beating Dinny Pails in the quarter-final, he then upset Tom Brown, from two sets down in the semi-finals and Geoff Brown, after losing a two-set lead, in the final. Twice winner of the French doubles and an automatic choice for Davis Cup selection, he saw his game suffer following a foot

operation early in 1947 and in January of the next year he gave up playing to become a coach. He had been runner-up in the mixed doubles at Wimbledon and the US Championships in 1937.

Mary Pierce

Born: *January 15, 1975*
Montreal, Canada

Mary Pierce became eligible to compete for France during her early teens when, unhappy with what her family thought was a lack of support from the USTA, she persuaded the French Federation to take advantage of the French citizenship she held through her mother. Her early days as a professional, highlighted by a semi-final defeat of Steffi Graf at the French Open in 1994, were punctuated by problems involving her father, whose fiery abuse of not only her but also other players, coaches and even spectators led to him being banned from all venues on the WTA Tour. Mary returned to form in 1997, when she finished the year at seventh in the world rankings after a frustrating time the previous year when she damaged a shoulder, missed much of the last three months of the Tour and dropped to 20th. Two years earlier, ranked five, she had won her first Grand Slam title, the Australian, with a surprise defeat of Arantxa Sanchez Vicario in the final.

She was the first French winner in Melbourne and the first to win any Grand Slam singles

MARY PIERCE *hungry for success?*

title since Françoise Durr won at Roland Garros in 1967. In January 1997 she again reached the Australian Open final, but was beaten in the final by Martina Hingis but three years later she won her home Grand Slam at Roland Garros defeating Monica Seles, Martina Hingis and finally Conchita Martinez. That run of success lifted her to 3 in the world rankings.

At 31 she remains one of the top players on the circuit ending 2005 ranked 5.

Nicola Pietrangeli

Born: *September 11, 1933*
Tunis, Tunisia

Although he reached the final just four times and won the title only twice, from the mid-1950s until well into the late 1960s, Nicky Pietrangeli *was* the Italian Open. Except for some unforeseen complication, he seldom played anywhere other than on the centre court of the Foro Italico and rarely, it seemed, before 5 p.m., so that there would be a full complement of enthusiastic Italian supporters to cheer him and bay their fury at any linesman or umpire who ruled a close point against him.

That was even more noticeable in the Davis Cup where in successive years, 1960–61, he led Italy to the Challenge Round, the first time after beating a powerful United States team from 0–2 in the semi-final. On grass, though, he and the giant Orlando Sirola were no match for the Australians in Perth. He played in 163 Davis Cup rubbers and won 120 of them – a record in both cases – in a career which ran from 1954 to 1972 and involved 66 ties. At least when Italy won the Davis Cup for the first and so far only time in 1976, he was still there – as captain.

Other highlights include consecutive victories at the French, against Ian Vermaak in 1959 and Luis Ayala a year later, while he was also runner-up in 1961 and 1964. A fifth-seeded semi-finalist at Wimbledon in 1960, he lost only 6–4 to Rod Laver in the fifth.

CEDRIC PIOLINE, a player overflowing with Gallic flair

Niki Pilic

Born: *August 27, 1939*
Split, Yugoslavia

The first professional athlete in the then Yugoslavia when he joined the Dallas-based "Handsome Eight", run by World Championship Tennis, this 6ft-3in left-hander had a distinguished playing and coaching record, not least as captain of Germany's Davis Cup team, but he will best be remembered as the player who, however unwittingly on his part, caused the Wimbledon boycott by 93 of the professional men players in 1973. The other players rallied to his support when Wimbledon, under pressure from the International Tennis Federation, agreed to respect the suspension imposed on him by the Yugoslav Federation for not fulfilling a Davis Cup commitment he denied ever making. Ironically, two decades later, he was given a special award by the ITF for services to the Davis Cup.

Away from the politics, his fine serving and heavy forehand made him the second-oldest runner-up at the French in 1973, a semi-finalist at Wimbledon in 1967, runner-up with Boro Jovanovic in the Wimbledon doubles in 1962 and British covered-court champion in 1963. As a professional from 1968, he won four singles and seven doubles titles.

Cedric Pioline

Born: *June 15, 1969*
Neuilly/Seine, France

His first sporting interest was volleyball. Hardly surprising, since his mother was a member of the Romanian World Championships team and his father played for Le Racing Club de France. But the craggy, 6ft-2in Pioline took up tennis after a painful leg operation, needed because one leg was fractionally longer than the other and had to be shortened.

He reached his first Grand Slam final at the US Open in 1993, but was trounced by Pete Sampras. He did not win his first title on the Tour until 1996, in Copenhagen. It was his 10th final and, once he had broken the hoodoo, his confidence soared. He played inspired tennis to help France win the Davis Cup final in Gothenburg a few months later and in 1997 won in Prague before enjoying the finest moment of his career at Wimbledon. By beating British hero Greg Rusedski in the last eight, and then former champion Michael Stich by serving and volleying magnificently in five spectacular sets, he became the first French finalist there since Yvon Petra won the title in 1946. Although he again lost to Sampras in straight sets, it helped him finish the year 20th in the world list.

Adrian Quist

Born: *August 4, 1913*
Medindia, South Australia

A doughty competitor, best appreciated for his doubles skill, Adrian Karl Quist was the only man to win a Grand Slam singles title before and after the 1939–45 War. He won the Australian in 1939 and 1940, then again in 1948, but he also won a record 10 doubles titles, including eight with John Bromwich, the most recorded at the tournament by any team.

One of his two Wimbledon doubles victories was also with Bromwich. That was in 1950, barely a month before his 37th birthday and a staggering 15 years after his first victory there, with Jack Crawford, who had been his partner in triumph in the French doubles a few weeks earlier. Quist, the left-court half of the team, won 42 of his 55 Davis Cup rubbers in 28 ties. Few were more exciting than two in 1939 when, having lost his opening singles the first day to Frank Parker, he and Bromwich began the only successful comeback there has been in a final from 0–2, by beating Jack Kramer and Joe Hunt in the doubles. On the third day Quist found fresh energy and adrenalin after losing a two-set lead to beat Bobby Riggs before Bromwich beat Parker to win the rubber, the match and the trophy.

Patrick Rafter

Born: *December 28, 1972*
Mount Isa, Queensland, Australia

This highly personable Australian, who had been struggling to return to form after a wrist operation in October 1995, suddenly and dramatically made the biggest breakthrough of anyone in 1997. The impressive serve-and-volleyer crowned an increasingly successful year by winning his first Grand Slam title at the US Open where he dismissed, among others, Andre Agassi and Michael Chang, before proving too good for Greg Rusedski in the final.

The first major indication that Rafter's game was coming together in exciting fashion had emerged during the French Open where he reached the semi-finals before losing to former champion Sergi Bruguera. His triumph at Flushing Meadows made him the first Australian to win the US Open since Mark Edmondson in 1976,

PATRICK RAFTER *emerged from the shadows to become US Open champion in 1997*

when the event was played on clay at Forest Hills. Despite twice losing to Pete Sampras at the end of the year, in the Grand Slam Cup and then at the ATP Tour Championships in Hanover, where he was the first Australian qualifier since Pat Cash in 1987, Rafter, the third youngest of nine children, soared from 62 in the rankings at the start of 1997, after two years of various injuries, to a career-best placing of second by the end of the year. That made him the most successful Australian in an end-of-year list since John Newcombe was also second in 1974.

Dennis Ralston
Born: *July 27, 1942*
Bakersfield, CA, USA

Ralston made a striking Wimbledon debut in 1960 when, aged 17, he paired with the Mexican, Rafael Osuna, for the first time and, after almost losing in the first round, won the title. The following year he was in the news again when he had the unique experience of losing the chance of winning the mixed doubles at the US with Darlene Hard. He was suspended, between reaching the final and the match being played, for alleged misconduct in a Davis Cup match against Mexico a few weeks earlier. The pair had to concede to Bob Mark and Margaret Smith.

Yet it was Ralston, so aggressive in his personality as well as his game as a youngster, whose coolness as captain on the side of the court, in the face of enormous crowd intimidation in Bucharest, helped calm his players as the United States won an explosive Davis Cup final in 1972. He is one of the elite band who have also won the Davis Cup as a player (1963), with a 14–5 record in singles. He won the US doubles title three times with Chuck McKinley, with whom he also had an 8–2 record in Davis Cup doubles. Apart from his coaching successes with the US Davis Cup team, he also coached Chris Evert.

Raul Ramirez
Born: *June 20, 1953*
Ensenada, Mexico

One of the best all-round players and certainly the finest Mexican in the for-

Mexican **RAUL RAMIREZ**, *a regular winner in singles and doubles*

mative years of Open tennis. He enjoyed consistent, rather than spectacular, success in Davis Cup matches and on the Tour 1971–83, winning 17 singles and 62 doubles titles. Many of his doubles victories were achieved with Brian Gottfried and included the French Open twice, 1975–1977, and Wimbledon, 1976. At the Italian Open, where he had his greatest triumph in 1975 by beating reigning champion Bjorn Borg for the title, this tall, nimble player – who learned his tennis, like so many, at the University of Southern California and was runner-up at the NCAA Championships in 1973 – won the doubles four years in succession, 1974–77, with Gottfried. The generally impressive quality of his play, which made him a

French and Wimbledon semi-finalist and earned him a 22–8 singles record in the Davis Cup, was underlined by his qualification for the end-of-year Masters consistently in 1974–78.

Willie & Ernest Renshaw
Born: *January 3, 1861*
Leamington, Warwickshire, UK

The twins are credited by most historians as the architects of modern tennis. Certainly they were among the first to take it seriously throughout the year, competing on the French Riviera when winter weather drove them off the courts in England and Ireland. Taught at Cheltenham School and both right-handers, they dominated the game, especially Wimbledon in

the 1880s, with a fluency, power and audacity which put them well ahead of their time.

Ernest had the touch but William the power, especially overhead and at the net. Three times they met in the Wimbledon final, but Ernest triumphed only once, in 1888, by which time William had won the first six of his titles (1881–86) before being forced to default the Challenge Round in 1887 with an elbow injury. A seventh title followed, when he took revenge on his older brother by 15 minutes, in 1889. It was touch and go. In the All-Comers final he not only escaped six match points in the fourth set in recovering from 2–5, but also trailed 0–5 in the fifth. He eventually won 8–6. Seven men's singles titles remains a Wimbledon record, as does the seven doubles championships they won together in 1880–89. They missed out only in 1883–84.

Renée Richards
Born: *August 19, 1934*
New York, NY, USA

Born Richard Raskind, this ophthalmologist wrote his way into tennis history after he underwent surgery in 1975 which changed him from being a man into a woman. Two years later, despite considerable opposition – and an International Olympic Committee ruling which largely prevented competition outside America – the New York Supreme Court made it possible for Richards to enter tournaments in the United States. Less than a month later 6ft-1in Richards, a Yale graduate who had competed at Wimbledon in the Oxford & Cambridge v Harvard & Yale match as a student in the mid-1950s, created history by competing in the women's singles of a tournament in which she had been a men's singles competitor more than 20 years earlier. Richards, who first played in the US Championships in 1955, was 43 when beaten by reigning Wimbledon champion Virginia Wade, on the centre court at Forest Hills in the first round of the 1977 event. Two years later she reached the third round and was beaten by Chris Evert. She returned to medicine in 1982, having reached a peak world ranking of 22.

Cliff Richey

Born: *December 31, 1946*
San Angelo, TX, USA

A determined, often fiery son of a professional tennis player, whose career was inevitably interlinked with that of his older sister, Nancy. They made history in 1965 by becoming the first brother and sister to be ranked in the world top 10 in the same year. A doughty fighter, prepared to run until he dropped, Cliff won the US clay-court title in 1966 and the indoor title two years later, but his most important victories came in 1970 when he had a 93–19 record, won eight titles, including the US clay-courts, reached the semi-finals of the French before losing a gruelling five-setter to Zeljko Franulovic and also led the United States to Davis Cup victory against Germany.

Nancy Richey

Born: *August 23, 1942*
San Angelo, TX, USA

One of the most successful United States clay-court players and the only one to win the clay-court championships six times. Like her brother she was more a determined, functional player than an instinctive one during a career which spanned both the amateur and professional years of the game. As an amateur, famous for wearing shorts and a peaked cap, she won the 1966 doubles in Australia with Carole Graebner and at Wimbledon with Maria Bueno, the US doubles (1965–66) with both of them and the Australian singles in 1967, when the tournament was still played at Kooyong on grass.

In singles she was also twice runner-up at Forest Hills, the first time as an amateur, but her most notable victory came when, in 1968, she won the first open French Championships, beating Ann Jones in the final and going on to end the year with a career-best third place in the world rankings. She regularly represented the United States in the annual Wightman Cup competition against Britain and was also a member of their winning Federation Cup (now Fed Cup) team in 1969.

Marty Riessen

Born: *December 4, 1941*
Hinsdale, IL, USA

A tall, rangy, always dependable right-hander whose easy style was as pleasing as his personality. He was one of those solid competitors whose game progressed at a commendable and even pace rather than fluctuating between exciting highs and despairing lows, seldom failing to make his seeding but seldom, either, exceeding expectations. In singles he was a quarter-finalist at Wimbledon, the US Open (twice), the Italian and the German, and a runner-up in South Africa.

It was in doubles that he was mostly prominent both before and after turning professional with Lamar Hunt's World Championship Tennis. His regular partner was Dutchman Tom Okker. They won the US title in 1976, the Italian in 1968, the German in 1968 and were runners-up in the world doubles in 1973. Riessen also won the French Open with Arthur Ashe in 1971. He excelled, too, in mixed doubles, especially in partnership with Margaret Court. They won the French in 1969, the US title in 1969, 1970 and 1972, and were runners-up at Wimbledon, in 1971.

Bobby Riggs

Born: *February 25, 1918*
Los Angeles, CA, USA

Robert Lorimer Riggs, who died on October 26, 1995 after a long fight against cancer, was the only man to achieve the triple crown at Wimbledon, winning the singles, doubles and mixed on his first and only visit to The Championships in 1939, a few weeks before the outbreak of the Second World War. He will be best remembered, though, for what happened 34 years later in 1973.

Always known as "The Hustler" because of his passion for gambling, and always eager to find new sources of finance, he devised what was called "The Battle of the Sexes", challenge matches between himself and the best women players in the modern game at the time. The self-proclaimed "king of male chauvinist pigs" had described feminism, which was then beginning to be a prominent issue, as ridiculous and had thrown down the gauntlet with his proclamation that "the best of today's female professionals would not be able to beat even an old man with one foot in the grave, like me". He first challenged Margaret Court in a winner-take-all contest at a Californian resort he was helping to promote and beat her 6–2, 6–1. Then, after an enormous build-up, he played Billie Jean King, the most outspoken leader in tennis of the feminist cause. The world's media gathered at the Houston Astrodome in September 1973 and a crowd of close to 30,500, the largest ever at a tennis match, saw King win easily – but Riggs reputedly earned $500,000 for his humiliation. Yet he was far more than just a showman. He twice won the US title, twice helped the US win the Davis Cup and, but for the war, would surely have been recognized as a great champion.

Marcelo Rios

Born: *December 26, 1975*
Santiago, Chile

A mercurial player who never realized the potential of his talent first displayed as a youngster when he dominated the world game at junior level. Certainly the best player ever to emerge from Chile but his dour personality and a 'couldn't care less' attitude con-

MARTY RIESSEN, *one of the best doubles competitors of his day*

tributed to his lack of general appeal. However, when his game was on song, he was one of the most exciting players to watch as he moved the ball around, and pulled his opponents about with consummate ease.

Unfortunately a back problem brought his career to an early end but in the three years between 1997 and 1999, he made the final of the Australian Open, won five Master Series events, was runner-up at two others and made the top of the rankings in March of 1998.

Tony Roche
Born: *May 17, 1945*
Tarcutta, NSW, Australia

Shoulder trouble, which became so severe that at one stage he even consulted a faith healer, restricted to some extent what was still an outstanding career for this sturdy left-hander, who went on to become just as successful at the highest level as a coach, principally with Ivan Lendl and the Australian Davis Cup team. Unusually for an Australian, his earliest successes came on clay when he won the French title in 1966 and the doubles a year later, when he was also runner-up in singles, but he went on to prove himself on all surfaces. He was runner-up at Wimbledon against Rod Laver in 1968 and was beaten at the same stage of the US Open the following two years, first by Laver and then by Rosewall.

Yet he benefited, as well as suffered, from being one of a large pack of Australian contemporaries, for his enduring partnership with John Newcombe was one of the finest. His menacing left-handed serves and sharp volleying, coupled with Newcombe's all-round confidence, earned them 11 Grand Slam titles together, including five at Wimbledon, the best this century until 1997 when another Australian pair, Mark Woodforde and Todd Woodbridge, won for the fifth successive year. His Davis Cup career ran from 1964 to 1978, with a 7–3 record in singles and 7–2 in doubles.

TONY ROCHE, *respected champion and coach*

Andy Roddick

Born: *August 30, 1982*
Omaha, Nebraska

As a former World Junior No1 with two Junior Grand Slam titles to his credit, Andy Roddick became American's big hope for the future. Under the coaching eye of Brad Gilbert, he did go on win his only Grand Slam title to date, the 2003 US Open, but has yet to produce the success which his obvious talent would expect though he has made back-to-back finals at Wimbledon losing, on both occasions, to Roger Federer.

With his big serve - he holds the world record for delivering the fastest serve at 155mph, struck during a 2004 Davis Cup semi-final - he is an imposing player, albeit by current standards, seemingly one-dimensional on court. However, when his game is on song, he has proven to be difficult to beat, especially on grass where he has won the Stella Artois Championships at Queen's Club for the three consecutive years.

With 20 titles to his credit at the end of 2005, and a brief stint as World No1 in November 2003, 'A-Rod' as he is affectionately known, remains the best hope America has of a player ever filling the shoes of Pete Sampras.

Mervyn Rose

Born: *January 20, 1930*
Coffs Harbour, NSW, Australia

Fred Perry once described this sturdy left-hander who volleyed so magnificently, as possessing "the most rhythmic game in tennis". A great individualist, with a profound knowledge of tactics, he was at his best on clay courts and won the French title in 1958, after several years in which he had been a quarter- or semi-finalist, and then turned professional. A few weeks earlier he had also won the Italian title at the Foro Italico, performances which earned a world ranking of three in his final year on the regular Tour.

He won the Australian singles in 1954, at a time when he looked in danger of being overshadowed by the exciting youngsters Lew Hoad and Ken Rosewall, and the German in 1957, when he also won the doubles

and mixed, but the majority of the other most important titles had been won in doubles. These included the US in 1952–53, first with Vic Seixas and then with Rex Hartwig, his partner when he also won the Australian and Wimbledon titles in 1954. When he returned to Europe in 1957, after a three-year absence, he was the only man to take a set off Hoad in the quarter-finals and he won the mixed doubles title with Darlene Hard. In recent years Arantxa Sanchez Vicario has frequently called upon him to help her improve her net game.

Ken Rosewall,

Born: November 2, 1934
Sydney, NSW, Australia

There have been many superb players who have never won Wimbledon, but probably none more graceful and talented than Kenneth Rosewall.

Despite his lack of a powerful serve, Rosewall has long since written himself into lawn tennis history on two counts. The first was the beauty of his style, distinctive in particular for the superb quality of his groundstrokes, especially his backhand, which must rank as one of the finest of all time.

The other was his unique longevity as a player of the highest class, spanning three decades from 1953, when he won his first major titles at the Australian and the French, to 1978 when, aged 43, he won the last of his 32 international singles and 18 doubles titles.

His consistency of success, all the more remarkable because of those years between 1957 and 1968 when, as a professional, he was not permitted to compete in any of the game's most prestigious events, is quite phenomenal. There was a gap of 19 years between his first and last triumphs at the Australian Open, 14 years between his first and last success at Forest Hills and 20 years between his first Wimbledon final against Jaroslav Drobny in 1954 and his second and last, 20 years later, against a vibrant young Jimmy Connors in 1974.

Born in Sydney, he won eight Grand Slam singles titles, as well as nine in doubles, though never at Wimbledon, where his style, skill and manner were especially appreciated.

Marc Rosset

Born: *November 7, 1970*
Geneva, Switzerland

At 6ft 7in Marc Rosset is one of the tallest players in the game's history, but his mood does not always quite reach for the sky in the same way. There have been brilliant successes, most noticeably at Barcelona in 1992, when he won the gold medal at the Olympic Games and also, together with Jakob Hlasek, led Switzerland to their first appearance in the Davis Cup final, losing 3–1 to the United States at Fort Worth. But there have also been too many disappointments, especially in Grand Slam tournaments, with one semi-final appearance in the French his best going into 1998. In 1995, after breaking into the top 10 for the first time, he broke a bone in his right foot in a Davis Cup match in February, but returned three months later to win his first comeback tournament in Nice, beating Yevgeny Kafelnikov in the final. He also added a grass-court win to his growing collection of titles in Halle in 1995 but, despite wonderful touch and power off the ground to support a fearsome serve, the erratic nature of his form also led to him dropping to 31 in the rankings in 1997. He is among that select band who have reached the top 10 in both singles and doubles.

Dorothy Round

Born: *July 13, 1909*
Dudley, Worcestershire, UK

Apart from Kitty Godfree, this reserved Worcestershire Sunday-school teacher, famous for her sweeping groundstrokes and testing drop shots, as well as for her much-publicized refusal to play on Sundays, is the only British woman to have won Wimbledon twice since the abolition of the Challenge Round after the 1921 tournament. A distinguished junior, her first important Wimbledon success came in 1931 when she upset the favoured Spanish player Lily d'Alvarez, but she took the title three years later by raising her game just when it was most needed to beat Helen Jacobs in the final.

In the same year she began the first of three consecutive victories in

the mixed doubles, first with the Japanese player, Ryuki Miki, the other two with Fred Perry. The following year the pace of her groundstrokes coupled with the instinctive potency of her volleys brought her back to peak form in singles and, although only seeded seventh, she again beat d'Alvarez and Jacobs, the holder, on the way to the final where this time she defeated Poland's Jadwiga Jedrzejowska, 6–2, 2–6, 7–5. Internationally her greatest success came when she went to Australia as the only overseas player and won the title in 1935. Mrs Little, as she became, went on to write for the *Sunday Express* for many years. She died in 1982.

Greg Rusedski

Born: *September 6, 1973*
Montreal, Canada

In 1997, awards were showered on this 6ft 3in left-hander who adopted the British nationality of his Yorkshire mother in May 1995. He climbed in the world rankings from 48 to sixth – a record for any British player since official rankings began in 1973 – having touched a career-best fourth place in the autumn after reaching the finals of the US Open and Vienna, winning in Basel, for his second title of the year and qualifying for the ATP Tour Championships in Hanover. All this, on top of being a quarter-finalist at Wimbledon for the first time and regaining the record as the fastest server of the ATP Tour (143mph), led to a social whirl at the end of the year when he became the first British tennis player to win the prestigious BBC Television Sports Personality of the Year award and won the top awards from ITV, the sportswriters and the LTA as well as the Services to Tennis award from the Lawn Tennis Writers' Association.

The ever-smiling Rusedski (except on court, of course) accepted the plaudits gracefully, but insisted that it was only the start. There is much more he wants to achieve. During 1997, when he unexpectedly switched coaches from Brian Teacher to Stefan Edberg's former guru, Tony Pickard, his vastly improved backhand and sterner volleying proved beyond doubt that his game does not only work well when his serve is on full power and working accurately.

To date he has accumulated 15 titles and successfully staved of a positive drug test which threatened to end his career prematurely in 2004.

Elizabeth Ryan

Born: *February 5, 1892*
Anaheim, CA, USA

Regarded by many of her contemporaries as the best player of her time never to win the singles at Wimbledon, her record in doubles, 19 titles including seven in mixed, stood supreme until Billie Jean King took her 20th overall Wimbledon title when she and Martina Navratilova won the doubles in 1979. Curiously, Miss Ryan, who won more than 650 singles and doubles tournaments in a career running from 1912 to 1934, was at Wimbledon that year and collapsed and died at the All England Club, with her record intact, the night before it was broken.

She twice won the All-Comers' singles at The Championships, 1914 and 1920, only for this noted volleyer and exponent of a wonderful chopped forehand to lose both times in the Challenge Round. Her 12 doubles titles and 13 finals remain Championship records, as does her seven in the mixed, which she won with five different partners. In the doubles she was triumphant with four different partners, but most regularly with Suzanne Lenglen. They won five years in succession, 1919–23, and again in 1925. Elsewhere she won the French doubles four times and the US just once. Her insatiable love of tennis was best reflected in 1924 when she won 75 titles: 27 singles, 27 doubles and 21 mixed.

Gabriela Sabatini

Born: *May 16, 1970*
Buenos Aires, Argentina

After months of trying to recover from a serious stomach muscle injury,

MANUEL SANTANA, *a dominant figure for more than 30 years*

Sabatini retired in October 1996. Yet although she earned more than $8.7m prize money, making her fifth on the all-time women's list, hers was still a career of lost opportunities and unfulfilled potential. In many ways her face and figure were a bigger fortune than her tennis. Her various endorsements and sponsorships are said to have been worth five times her prize money. She was one of the most marketed and photographed female athletes in the world. Yet when one considers her talent, she was also one of the great under-achievers, especially from 1992 when she won only two titles in her last four years on the circuit.

Sabatini produced spectacularly exciting tennis to upset reigning champion Steffi Graf and become US Open champion in 1990. It was expected to be the moment when the player whose skills had been admired since she was the youngest world junior champion at the age of 13, and Olympic silver medalist in Seoul when she was 18, would blossom substantially. Alas for tennis, as much for her, it did not. Several times she climbed to third in the world rankings but was never able to take those extra two steps. She went so close at Wimbledon in 1991. Twice in a thrilling final set she served for the title against Graf, but each time the girl with a rose and

two perfumes named after her wilted under the pressure.

Pete Sampras

Born: *August 12, 1971*
Potomac, MD, USA
(See Legends pp98–99)

Manuel Santana

Born: *May 10, 1938*
Madrid, Spain

The first Spaniard to reach the heights of the men's game, "Manolo", was the first European to achieve worldwide recognition for his all-round skill after the 1939–45 war. A player of rare virtuosity and style, he not only won the French, played on the surface on which he first learned the game as a ballboy, in 1961 and 1964, but the US Championship in 1965, when it was played on grass and, even more signficantly, Wimbledon, in 1966. His forehand was a gem, his touch majestic. Add to that a defiance which frequently enabled him to claw his way back to win matches and an unusually warm personality and you have the ingredients for a truly gifted champion.

Still the most successful player in Spanish tennis history, his triumph at Forest Hills made him a national hero. General Franco, the autocratic

Spanish ruler, decorated him with the coveted Medal of Isabella and, as if to justify the honour even further, he also led Spain to the final of the Davis Cup for the first time that year. He played 120 Davis Cup singles and rubbers matches and won a record 13 singles rubbers during 1967 – since equalled by Ilie Nastase. He remains a Spanish hero as their Davis Cup captain.

Dick Savitt

Born: *March 4, 1927*
Bayonne, NJ, USA

Turning to tennis after a basketball injury in 1949, this solidly powerful American is the last to have won the men's singles at Wimbledon at the first attempt. It was in 1951, when he beat Ken McGregor in straight sets in the final to continue a fantastic year which had started with an earlier defeat of McGregor which made him the first American to win the Australian title. Only four Americans have won the Australian and Wimbledon in the same year. The others are Don Budge 1938, Jimmy Connors 1974 and Pete Sampras 1994.

The key to his Wimbledon triumph was the semi-final when he controlled his often inflammable temperament to beat Herbie Flam 1–6, 15–13, 6–3, 6–2, despite trailing 1–5 in the second set. He enjoyed success too at the Italian, on clay. Despite that and after playing in earlier rounds against Japan and Canada, the big-serving Savitt, second in the world rankings, was omitted from the United States team which failed to win back the trophy in the Challenge Round, losing 3–2 to Australia in Sydney. He made only one other European Tour, in 1952, when he lost to Mervyn Rose in the quarter-finals.

Frederick Schroeder

Born: *July 20, 1921*
Newark, NJ, USA

This muscular, often taciturn, competitor with a monstrously effective volley was another American who won Wimbledon on his first visit. And in his case it was his only attempt. A refrigeration engineer, who is now also

GABRIELA SABATINI – *beauty in motion*

MONICA SELES *reigned supreme until being stabbed in Hamburg*

a tennis radio broadcaster, he was a worthy, resilient and popular champion in 1949. His success was adventurous. He was two sets down against Gardnar Mulloy in the first round and match point down against Frank Sedgman in the quarter-final. Yet, despite being foot-faulted on his first serve, he was not deterred from racing in to the net behind his second, to put away a volley.

Most of Schroeder's individual success came during the war. In 1942 he became only the second player to win the NCAA and US Championships in the same year. Don McNeil, in 1940, was the first. He also won the doubles at Forest Hills three times. When the Davis Cup resumed after the war in 1946, he beat Jack Bromwich in five sets in the opening rubber of a 5–0 defeat of the Australians as the United States retained the trophy and he maintained his unbeaten Davis Cup singles record as the Americans kept the trophy for another three years, always against the Australians.

Richard "Dick" Sears

Born: *October 16, 1861*
Boston, MA, USA

At least one of the records Dick Sears set as the original US champion will surely be everlasting. He played in the tournament, originally staged on the lawns of the Newport, Rhode Island, Casino, seven times and won it seven times. He had played 18 matches by the time this former Harvard graduate retired from tennis in 1887. Even that stood as a record until after the Challenge Round had been abandoned when Bill Tilden's success in reaching the semi-finals in 1922 was his 19th consecutive match win.

In those days many of the players still served underarm but not Sears. His original slightly lop-sided racket, similar to those used in real tennis, was replaced in the last four years he won the singles and US doubles by one presented to him by Willie Renshaw, the seven-times winner of Wimbledon singles' titles. His older brother Frank is credited, with James Dwight, whom Dick beat in the 1883 US final, as hav-

ing played the first competitive tennis match in America. In 1892 Sears won the US real tennis title and went on to become president of the USTA.

Frank Sedgman

Born: *October 29, 1927*
Mount Albert, Victoria, Australia

A natural athlete, with a fine physique, speed and stamina, Frank Sedgman won 22 major singles and doubles titles, three less than fellow Australian John Newcombe and six behind the all-time leader, Roy Emerson. His achievement was all the more remarkable because those titles were won within only four years before he turned professional in 1953. A fine mover and deft volleyer, who was just as much at home in doubles as singles, his first major triumph came in 1949 when he hit John Bromwich off the court in the Australian final. He retained the title a year later before starting to demonstrate his prowess just as emphatically elsewhere.

In 1951 he overwhelmed Art Larsen for the loss of only four games to win the US title and, together with Ken McGregor, scored the only calendar year Grand Slam in doubles. His Wimbledon glory came in 1952 when, in addition to beating Jaroslav Drobny in the singles final, he won the doubles with McGregor and the mixed with Doris Hart to become the last man to win the triple crown there. In 1950, when he upset Tom Brown and Ted Shroeder in singles and won the doubles with Bromwich to end four successive defeats by the Americans, he became the first Australian since Norman Brookes in 1911 to win three rubbers in a Davis Cup final.

Pancho Segura

Born: *June 20, 1921*
Guayaquil, Ecuador

With the possible exception of the other Pancho, Gonzales, few were missed more because of the game's refusal to acknowledge professionals, until there was no alternative, than this diminutive (5ft 6in), bow-legged South American who remains one of the most charismatic characters in the game – and certainly one of the finest judges of talent. A victim of rickets as

a child, hence the deformity of his legs, he more than compensated with enormous energy, willpower and a rugged cheerfulness which, together with his endless enthusiasm, made him an outstanding crowd-pleaser. Although he made little impact during two Wimbledon visits before he turned professional in 1947, he was enormously impressive in later years when he returned to England in professional tournaments at Wembley. The only player this century to win the inter-collegiate title in the United States for three consecutive years, he was consistently a semi-finalist at the US Championships, 1942–46, and went on to win the US indoor and clay-court titles. Even before retiring as a veteran player, Segura was already being called up for coaching advice by several of the leading modern players.

Vic Seixas

Born: *August 30, 1923*
Philadelphia, PA, USA

Vic Seixas was one of the game's great match-players, with an indomitable fighting spirit – qualities which remained long after he reached the peak of success by winning Wimbledon in 1953, a few weeks after finishing runner-up to Ken Rosewall at the French, and the US singles and doubles a year later. As late as 1966, at the age of 42, he battled for almost four hours on the Philadelphia grass to beat the up-and-coming 22-year-old Australian, Bill Bowrey. The struggle, although only over three sets, lasted a staggering 94 games. He lost the first set 32–34! He won as top seed, but it was a tough fortnight. He was taken to five sets by Lew Hoad in the quarter-finals and had to battle through another, even tighter five-setter against Mervyn Rose in the semis before running away with the final against the unseeded Kurt Neilsen.

That year also brought him the first of four consecutive mixed doubles titles at Wimbledon, the first three partnered by Doris Hart, with whom he also won the US mixed, 1953–55, and the French, 1953. When he won the US singles in 1954, it was at his ninth attempt and completed the triple crown. He played at Forest Hills a record 28 times between 1939 and

1969 and won the most Davis Cup matches, 38 of 55 singles in 19 ties, until John McEnroe did even better.

Monica Seles

Born: *December 2, 1973*
Novi Sad, Yugoslavia

In what until then had been a routine quarter-final in Hamburg on Friday, April 30, 1993, Monica Seles, firmly established as number one in the world rankings, was just leaving her chair in a change-over against Magdalene Maleeva, when a deranged 38-year-old German, Guenter Parche, darted on to the court and stabbed her just below the left shoulder-blade. Tennis has never been the same since. At many leading events top players now have to be protected by armed bodyguards and Seles, despite occasional glimpses of her old form, has never fully recovered psychologically from the attack.

Until then, the girl who had won eight of the previous nine Grand Slam tournaments and become the youngest number one-ranked player in tennis for men or women (a record since taken by Martina Hingis) looked set to reign supreme for the foreseeable future. Double-handed off the ground on both flanks, with the power off the forehand side of a natural left-hander, she could be as ferocious and sometimes as intimidating as her renowned grunt. Although she was immediately triumphant when eventually persuaded to return to the game in August 1995, Recurring shoulder problems since then, although not directly related to the stabbing, may mean we will never know how good a player she might have been. She began 1998 as world No. 5 and showed glimpses of her old form when she finished runner-up in the 1998 French Open.

In addition to her 9 majors, she won 53 singles and 6 doubles titles in a career which earnt her $14,891,762 in prizemoney.

Maria Sharapova

Born: *April 19, 1987*
Nyagan, Siberia, Russia

Not many players have burst on to the scene in such a dramatic style as Maria Sharapova did in 2004. She first came to the public notice when she won the Wimbledon warm-up event at Edgbaston, and then surprised the public by actually reaching the final of The Championships themselves. Still only 17, the runner-up of the previous year's Junior event at Wimbledon faced the defending champion, Serena Williams, and calmly took the crown off the powerful American.

With that victory, Maria Sharapova, the long legged Russian beauty, arrived and captured the hearts of a million testosterone filled youngsters but unlike her countrywoman, Anna Kournikova, this Russian is a true winner, very much dedicated to her sport, despite having signed up with the IMG Model Agency and being featured heavily in advertising and promotional material.

She proved that her debut Grand Slam title was not a flash-in-the-pan by claiming the end-of-season WTA Championships and ending 2005 with 10 titles to her name having made a brief visit to the top of the world rankings in August of that year and then collecting her second Grand Slam title at the US Open.

She developed her talent in the hot house of the Nick Bollettieri Tennis Academy in Florida having been spotted when just six, by non other than the legendary Martina Navratilova.

Pam Shriver

Born: *July 4, 1962*
Baltimore, MD, USA

Pam Shriver became the youngest women's singles finalist at the US Open in only the second Grand Slam tournament of her career in 1978 when aged 16 years 2 months, an amateur and still at school. Yet although she went on to be a semi-finalist three times at the Australian Open, twice at Wimbledon and twice more at Flushing Meadows, her most indelible success was achieved in doubles, especially in partnership with Martina Navratilova. Between 1981 and 1990 they won 20 major titles, equalling the record held by Louise Brough and Margaret du Pont. This included a Grand Slam in 1984.

In all they won 79 titles in harness, during which they had one unbroken record run of 109 matches from

April 1983 until they lost the 1985 Wimbledon final to Kathy Jordan and Elizabeth Smylie. Shriver also won Olympic gold with Zina Garrison in Seoul in 1988. Between 1980 and early 1989 this rangy six-footer, best when able to serve and volley on faster surfaces, was constantly in the top 10, despite the diversion of campaigning for the Republicans in a presidential election. Her best ranking was reaching number three on six separate occasions between 1984 and 1988. Unafraid to express her forthright, sometimes controversial views, she is now a member of the USTA Board.

Stan Smith

Born: *December 14, 1946*
Pasadena, CA, USA

While at 6ft 3in not so tall as some of the top modern players, this very epitome of an all-American male, straight-backed, with fair hair and good looks, was nicknamed the "leaning tower of Pasadena" because of the way he used to lean into his serve – and thereby on his opponents. His 1972 victory over Ilie Nastase in the Wimbledon final, just one year after qualifying for The Championships, was, thanks to the weather, the first to be staged on a Sunday. It was also one of the best of the decade. A year earlier this model sportsman had figured in another piece of tennis history by beating Jan Kodes in the first US Open final decided by a tie-break.

During a remarkable 11-year Davis Cup record, starting in 1968, he was on the winning side in 22 out of 24 matches and 16 times won the point which clinched the tie: three times in singles and 13 with Bob Lutz, with whom he also won the US Open four times. His serve-and-volley game naturally flourished most consistently on grass, although his most rewarding triumph was probably in the 1972 Davis Cup final in Bucharest when he won the decisive third point the United States needed. "I had to concentrate so hard I got a headache", he said after a three-day ordeal amid a noisily partisan crowd which match officials, before the appointment of neutral umpires, described as "over-patriotic".

MICHAEL STICH – *the ultimate achievement. Wimbledon champion, 1991*

Harold Solomon

Born: *September 17, 1952*
Washington, DC, USA

Now a successful coach and eager competitor, when time allows, on the Seniors' Tour, "Solly" was an accurate clay-court specialist who won 22 singles and one doubles title on the circuit and was consistently in the top 10 between 1976 and 1980, but never quite made the breakthrough to the very top. He helped the United States win the Davis Cup in 1972 and 1978 and six times qualified for the year-ending Masters tournament.

His principal successes, though, were confined to the French Open where he had a 36–12 record and, although beaten by Adriano Panatta in the 1976 final, was still the first American to reach that stage for 21 years. He also reached the semi-finals at Roland Garros in 1974 (losing to Bjorn Borg after beating Ilie Nastase)

and 1980, when he was allowed only four games in six sets by Borg, and the semi-finals of the US Open in 1977, the last year it was played on Har-Tru (green clay) at Forest Hills.

Michael Stich

Born: *October 18, 1968*
Pinneburg (Hamburg), Germany

The day after Michael Stich beat Tim Henman to reach the semi-finals at Wimbledon in 1997 and declared "I didn't come here to retire, I came to win The Championships", his loss of a five-set classic against 46th-ranked Frenchman Cedric Pioline became his retirement from major tennis after all. Although he had stayed in the top 20 of the world rankings for most of his career and usually in the top 10 in the years when he was free from injury, Stich never fully regained the peak he reached in the summer of 1991 when he beat an astonished Boris

Becker in the final at Wimbledon. It was the culmination of seven matches in which Stich, who also beat Jim Courier and defending champion Stefan Edberg, not only proved himself the master of tie-breaks, but demonstrated the value of hitting second serves with just as much variety and almost as much stinging authority as the first. He also captured the Wimbledon men's doubles title a year later, partnered by John McEnroe, in one of the most memorable matches in the tournament's history.

When he reached the final of the French Open in 1996, he became one of only seven active players on the men's Tour to reach three different Grand Slam Tour finals. He reached a career-best second place in the world rankings in 1993 by winning the ATP Tour Championship. Despite that and his pivotal role in leading Germany to victory in the Davis Cup final against Australia in Düsseldorf a week later, Stich, who for most of his teenage years seemed more likely to concentrate on soccer than tennis, never matched Becker's popularity. The off-court rivalry between them remains intense.

Dick Stockton

Born: *February 18, 1951*
New York, NY, USA

The winner of 20 US national junior titles and then the NCAA champion, 6ft-2in Dick Stockton went on to a career-best fifth in the world rankings in 1977 when he won the US Pro Indoor Championships in Philadelphia and finished runner-up in the WCT Finals in his adopted home town of Dallas. Yet barely a year later, after reaching the semi-finals of the US Open, he was struck by a succession of debilitating back injuries from which he never fully recovered and which meant that thereafter he seldom appeared on court without wearing a spinal brace.

He had been a semi-finalist at Wimbledon in 1974 and won mixed doubles titles at first the US Open, with Rosie Casals in 1976, and then the French Open, with Anne Smith in 1984, as he fought determinedly to keep his tennis career alive.

Fred Stolle

Born: *October 8, 1938*
Hornsby, NSW, Australia

Fred Stolle remains one of the best-known and most-loved personalities on the tennis scene as a respected television commentator for companies in America and his native Australia. "Fiery Fred", as he is known for his outspoken competitiveness, was one of the most successful players in the 1960s, except in one important respect – Wimbledon. There he was runner-up three years in succession, 1963–65, a fate also shared only by Baron Gottfried von Cramm, 1935–37. On the other hand he won the French – a major achievement for a grass-court specialist – in 1965 and the US title in 1966.

In addition, together first with Bob Hewitt and then with Roy Emerson, who invariably proved too resourceful for him in singles, he proved himself an outstanding doubles player. With Hewitt he won the Australian, 1963–64, and Wimbledon, 1962, 1964. With Emerson he won the French and US titles in 1965 and the Australian a year later. He won a total of 16 major doubles titles, including the mixed doubles at Wimbledon with Ann Jones the day after she had won the singles in 1969. He was also a member of three winning Australian Davis Cup teams, winning 13 of his 16 singles rubbers.

Betty Stove

Born: *June 24, 1945*
Rotterdam, Netherlands

The only Dutch woman to reach the final at Wimbledon, she had the painful disappointment in 1977 of losing all three finals, singles, doubles and mixed. Still the most successful Dutch woman player there has been, winning 20 singles and eight doubles titles, Stove, whose career spanned the amateur and professional days of the game, beat Martina Navratilova in the quarter-finals and Sue Barker in the semi-finals before losing the final of the Centenary Wimbledon to Virginia Wade in 1977.

At least she had some compensation for her mixed doubles defeat the following year when she and Frew McMillan won the title and again, when she was 36, in 1981, by which time

she had also started to coach Hana Mandlikova. In addition, she won the US Open doubles three times, with three different partners: 1971, Françoise Durr; 1977, Martina Navratilova; and 1979, Wendy Turnbull. She represented the Netherlands in the Federation Cup for 11 successive years, finishing with a 20–4 record in singles and 20–8 in doubles, before going on to captain their team.

Vera Sukova

Born: *June 13, 1931*
Prague, Czechoslovakia

Helena Sukova

Born: *February 23, 1965*
Prague, Czechoslovakia

They are the only mother and daughter to have both been in the finals of Grand Slam tournaments. Vera, a solid baseliner with strong passing shots, was a semi-finalist at the French Championships before losing to the eventual champion, Shirley (Bloomer) Brasher in 1957, but it was five years later that she really came into her own. Unseeded, she upset defending champion Angela Mortimer and former champion Maria Bueno before losing to Karen Susman in the final after being unlucky enough to damage her ankle in practice on the morning of the match. She reached the last eight of the US Championships the same year.

Helena, a brilliant serve-and-volleyer, one of the tallest (6ft 2in) and certainly one of the most enduring leading players in the women's game, broke into the top 10 in 1984, stayed there for five years, and has continued to be one of the most adventurous players in both singles and doubles on the Tour, reaching the quarter-finals or better at all four of the Grand Slams. By beating Navratilova in the semi-finals of the 1984 Australian Open, she ended the world champion's record 74-match winning streak, but then lost to Chris Evert. Two years later the situation was reversed. She beat Evert at Flushing Meadows in the semi-finals, but then lost to Navratilova. She won the Wimbledon doubles four times, most notably with Martina Hingis in 1996. In the same year she

and her brother, Cyril Suk, won the mixed doubles title that they retained in 1997, six years after they also became the first brother-and-sister team to win the mixed at Roland Garros.

Karen Susman

Born, *December 11, 1942*
San Diego, CA, USA

Just like Maureen "Little Mo" Connolly and Alice Marble, Karen (née Hantze) Susman, who won Wimbledon in 1962, was coached by Teach Tennant. She was also the forerunner in some respects of the many American youngsters so precociously gifted at an early age that, long before they move into adult tennis, the expectations on them are enormous. Karen was the US 18-and-under junior champion when she was only 14, and on her first visit to Wimbledon in 1960 she not only won the junior title but reached the quarter-finals of the main event before losing to Britain's Christine Truman.

The following year, three months before she was married, she won the doubles with Billie Jean Moffitt (later King), but her most memorable performances were recorded in 1962. Despite a blood disorder which meant she often became quickly exhausted and accounted for what many regarded as her infuriating habit of barely strolling between points, she won the singles by defeating Vera Sukova, who had beaten Maria Bueno and then damaged her ankle while practising, and also retained the doubles title. She did not defend her title and, after winning the US doubles in 1964, again with Billie Jean, largely faded from the international scene.

Roscoe Tanner

Born: *October 15, 1951*
Chattanooga, TN, USA

This powerful left-hander had one of the hardest, fastest serves in the game, delivered off a short toss. It was once timed (though not with the sophisticated systems available today) at 153mph, using a wooden racket. He won his lone Grand Slam title at the Australian Open in 1977 when he beat the veteran Ken Rosewall in the semifinals and then Guillermo Vilas 6–3, 6–3, 6–3 in the final.

Twice before that he had been a semi-finalist at Wimbledon, in 1975 and 1976, but it was his heroic attempt to break Bjorn Borg's three-year reign as champion in the 1979 final which brought him the most recognition. He pushed the Swede to 6–4 in the fifth set before being forced to yield. On the other hand, two months later, when he reached the semi-finals of the US Open for a second time, he took full advantage of Borg's dislike of having to play under floodlights to reach the final, but then lost to Vitas Gerulaitis despite holding a two-set lead. The winner of 15 singles and nine doubles titles, this former NCAA doubles champion also won the French Open doubles title with Heinz Guenthardt.

Unable to settle in retirement, he was convicted on various charges, resulting in a two year jail sentence for violation of probation terms in connection with a 2003 grand theft conviction.

Roger Taylor

Born: *October 14, 1941*
Sheffield, Yorkshire, UK

The last British man to reach the semifinals at Wimbledon, a feat he achieved three times: 1967, 1970 (when he beat defending champion Rod Laver in the fourth round, from a set down) and 1973, the year of the ATP boycott, when he beat Bjorn Borg. The Swede was competing in the men's singles for the first time. Taylor won over five gruelling sets but then lost, also in five, to eventual champion Jan Kodes. A month earlier the strong left-hander with a match-winning serve reached the quarter-finals of the French Open, the first Briton to do so for a decade.

The same year, Taylor, one of the original "Handsome Eight" when he turned professional in 1967, became the first British player to qualify for the WCT Finals in Dallas, where he

ROGER TAYLOR, *adored in Britain for his looks as well as his tennis*

lost the finest match of the tournament, 6–4 in the fifth set, to Ken Rosewall. Brought up in tennis the hard way, the rugged son of a steelworker, Taylor spent his apprenticeship living a Spartan existence in the Wimbledon YMCA, so that he could train regularly at the All England Club. An outstanding doubles player, he won the US Open with John Newcombe in 1971 and retained the title with Cliff Drysdale a year later. He won 17 of his 23 Davis Cup singles for Britain.

Bill Tilden

Born: *February 2, 1893*
Philadelphia, PA, USA

Some rate William Tatem Tilden as the greatest player of all time. He certainly had every shot in the book, including a cannonball serve, tremendous pace, accuracy and conviction off his baseline driving and a firm temperament. As one contemporary wrote, "He has no weakness of any sort and can successfully oppose any style of play."

His first notable success came at Wimbledon in 1920 when he won seven rounds in the All-Comers event and then beat defending champion Gerald Patterson in the Challenge Round. Between then and February 1926, when Jean Borotra upset him, he was unbeaten in any significant singles match – and that despite having to change his grip after needing to have part of a finger removed in 1922. In that invincible spell he won Wimbledon twice, the US title six times and played 15 Davis Cup singles, 12 in the Challenge Round, without loss. All told he won 34 out of 41 singles rubbers in the competition. A third Wimbledon title came in 1930. He was then 37 and the oldest champion since the abolition of the Challenge Round. He turned professional in 1931. A recluse in later years, he died in 1953.

Tony Trabert

Born: *August 16, 1930*
Cincinnati, OH, USA

An outstanding athlete and an exceptional champion, Marion Anthony Trabert's record lists, among others, one Wimbledon singles title in 1955, two at the French, 1954–55, and two at the US, 1953 and 1955. What makes those five triumphs so special, though, is that all but those at Roland Garros were achieved without him dropping a set. His performances throughout 1955 were then the best ever recorded by an American. He won 18 out of 23 tournaments to finish with a 106–7 record, which included an unbeaten stretch of 36 matches. He also won 12 doubles titles with Vic Seixas, including the French, which was a third-time success in that event.

He was the world number one in 1953 and 1955, and his Davis Cup playing career lasted from 1951 to 1955, when he turned professional and became ineligible. He had won 27 out of 35 rubbers, and after the advent of Open tennis returned in 1976 to become Davis Cup captain. He led the team to success in 1978 and 1979. Still a major figure on the international scene, he is a leading television commentator in the United States and for several years has acted as MC for trophy presentations at the US Open.

Christine Truman

Born: *February 16, 1941*
Loughton, Essex, UK

Christine Truman took Wimbledon crowds on so many emotional roller-coaster rides to success and failure that she became the most adored British woman player both before and after she became Mrs Janes (in 1967) and started to raise her now grown-up family. An outstanding junior, she saw her original request to compete at Wimbledon in 1956 rejected because she was 15 and the minimim age was 16, but a year later she made a spectacular debut, reaching the semi-finals unseeded before losing to the eventual champion, Althea Gibson. Although a series of equally spectacular Wimbledon setbacks followed, there were other triumphs abroad. When she won the French title, two weeks after the Italian, in 1959 at the age of 18 years 4 months, she beat Maureen Connolly's record as the youngest Roland Garros champion by four months. Although that record has since been lowered by Steffi Graf in 1987, Arantxa Sanchez Vicario in 1989 and is now held by Monica Seles, who was 16 years 6 months when she won for the first time in 1990, Christine remains the youngest amateur champion in Paris.

She reached the Wimbledon final in 1961 but, hampered by a strained leg, was beaten by Angela Mortimer. Christine, who won the Australian doubles with Maria Bueno in 1960, linked with her sister, Nell, for Wightman Cup doubles. A transparently honest, lovable and frank personality, she played a game which thrived on a big forehand and unorthodox volleys. Such traits remain delightfully evident today in her role as a tennis analyst on matches for BBC radio.

Wendy Turnbull

Born: *November 26, 1952*
Brisbane, Queensland, Australia

Nicknamed "Rabbit" because of her fleetness of foot, she was a latecomer to professional tennis for, after leaving school aged 15, she worked in a bank for four years before turning what had been a sporting love into a career. She made her first appearance at the Australian Open in 1970, and over the next 19 years reached the final of all the Grand Slam tournaments bar Wimbledon and won nine Grand Slam doubles titles including three in mixed doubles, two at Wimbledon and one at the French, with John Lloyd. She also won Wimbledon in 1978 with Kerry Reid, and the US with Rosie Casals (1982) and Betty Stove (1979) with whom she won the French in the same year. To reach her first Grand Slam singles final at the US Open in 1977, the last time the event was held on clay and at Forest Hills, she upset reigning Wimbledon winner Virginia Wade and Martina Navratilova, but lost to her constant nemesis, Chris Evert. She lost the 1979 French final also to Evert and the 1980 Australian final to Hana Mandlikova.

Lesley Turner Bowrey

Born: *August 16, 1942*
Sydney, NSW, Australia

Bill Bowrey

Born: *December 25, 1943*
Sydney, NSW, Australia

1968, the year they married, proved to be a magical one for them both. Bill, Australia's leading amateur at the time, who six years earlier had been the first winner of the now-defunct British 21-and-under Championship at Manchester, won the Australian Open. Lesley, already well established and more accomplished on slow European clay than the grass courts at home in Australia, retained the Italian title she had won for the first time in 1967 after three times finishing as runner-up.

Lesley established the stronger record. She won 12 Grand Slam tournament titles, including winning the French twice, beating Ann Jones in 1963 and Margaret Court in 1965. She was also runner-up in two other years and runner-up at the Australian in 1964 and 1967. She succeeded in the doubles at all four of the Slams. Judy (Tegart) Dalton twice partnered her to success at the Australian, the French twice and Wimbledon once with Margaret Court and the US in 1961 with Darlene Hard. She was ranked number two in the world in 1963.

Arantxa Sanchez Vicario

Born: *December 18, 1971*
Barcelona, Spain

Winner of 29 singles titles since joining the Tour in 1987, the "Barcelona Bumblebee", as she is known, has stung virtually all of the other top players during her time, including Martina Navratilova, Steffi Graf and Monica Seles, and often on major occasions. One of the most momentous was in 1989 when, in her first Grand Slam final, she beat the then seemingly insuperable Steffi Graf and became, for one year only, the youngest winner of the French Open, as well as the first Spaniard to win the women's singles title.

She went on to win the French and US Open titles in 1994, making her one of only nine women in the Open era to win two or more Grand Slam singles titles in the same year. The diminutive Arantxa, whose elder brothers Emilio and Javier have both been successful on the men's Tour, is one of the fastest retrievers the game has known. Fluent in four other languages apart from Spanish, she was number one in the world for several months in 1995, since when most of her major successes have come in doubles. In 1995 she won doubles at Wimbledon with Jana Novotna, while in 1996, she retained the Australian doubles with Chanda Rubin. She also won the French singles for the second time in 1998.

Guillermo Vilas

Born: *August 17, 1952*
Mar del Plata, Argentina

Although Guillermo Vilas never went further than the quarter-finals in his 11 visits to Wimbledon between 1970 and 1986, his failure to do so was actually somewhat disappointing. For while this "Young Bull of the Pampas", as he was dubbed when he first burst on the scene with his swarthy, stocky appearance, was naturally more at home on clay courts, he still had notable successes on grass. In 1974, for instance, he won the Masters on grass in Melbourne, from a field which included Bjorn Borg (though before his first Wimbledon title), Ilie Nastase and John Newcombe. Then, in 1978–79, he won the Australian Open twice, albeit from depleted entries.

With his chestnut hair flowing below his shoulder, the burly left-hander exuded fitness and strength, especially during 1977–78 when he

won 46 consecutive matches. In 1977 alone he played 159 matches, winning 145 of them, and among his 15 titles that year was the French Open when for once he escaped having to face Borg, who beat him in two of the three other finals he played there. The third was in 1982 when, astonishingly, even he was worn down by 17-year-old Mats Wilander, who won the senior title the year after finishing as junior champion at Roland Garros. At the US Open, Vilas was the winner in 1977, one of the 62 singles and 14 doubles titles which put him fourth equal with Bjorn Borg in the Open era.

Ellsworth Vines
Born: *September 28, 1911*
Los Angeles, CA, USA

Of the nine men who have won Wimbledon at the first attempt, few have looked more impressive than this rangy Californian, who came to his peak in 1932. He was only 20 and two years earlier had suffered considerable self-doubts about his tennis after what for him was a demoralizing defeat when he was unable to fathom the seemingly innocuous game of Sidney Wood. Helped by a ferocious and risky forehand, devastating control and power overhead and impressive volleying, he pulled himself round and in that summer of 1932 was in superb form as he completed a 6–4, 6–2, 6–0 defeat of Bunny Austin in the Wimbledon final with a cannonball delivery which the Englishman agreed he never saw.

Two months later he retained the US title, but in 1933 when he again reached the final at Wimbledon the spark of genius had faded just a little. He lost a classic contest with Jack Crawford, was beaten by Fred Perry and Austin in the Davis Cup, and was so upset after losing to Bitsy Grant in the fourth round of the US Championships that he cut the gut out of his rackets, declared his amateur days were over and decided to turn professional. His first match against Bill Tilden attracted 14,637 fans. In 1939 he also became a professional golfer and became one of America's leading players.

ARANTXA SANCHEZ VICARIO *wins the French Open title in 1989*

Virginia Wade

Born:, *July 10, 1945*
Bournemouth, UK

The date was Friday July 1, 1977, the year of Wimbledon's centenary celebrations and the Silver Jubilee of Queen Elizabeth II. The place was the Centre Court at the All England Club. How fitting it was, therefore, that, watched by Her Majesty, Virginia Wade, nine days away from her 32nd birthday, finally won the women's singles title at the 16th attempt. Her 4–6, 6–3, 6–1 victory over Betty Stove was by no means a high-quality contest – the pressure of the occasion was too much for that. But the emotion within the arena was overflowing as the winner of the very first Open tournament for women at Bournemouth in 1968, the first and so far only British winner of the US Open in 1968, the Australian Open champion in 1972 and the leader of so many British Federation Cup and Wightman Cup teams achieved her lifetime ambition. Grown men wept as Wade, after winning the last point, charged to the net in much the same gloriously extravagant manner as she had often advanced to put away volleys. When she eventually retired in 1987, having played in The Championships for 26 years, she had competed in 212 singles, doubles and mixed doubles matches, placing her fourth on the all-time list. Her record of 64 victories in singles matches is exceeded only by Billie Jean King. She was the first woman to be elected to the All England Club committee.

Maud Watson

Born: *October 9, 1864*
Harrow, Middlesex, UK

Maud Watson will always retain a place in tennis history as the inaugural Wimbledon women's singles champion, a title she won on Saturday July 19, 1884. There were only 13 competitors and the event did not begin until after the men's singles had been completed. In the final Maud, aged 19, beat her 26-year-old sister, Lilian, after losing the first set. In 1885, before the Challenge Round was introduced for the women, she won again, but this time there were only 10 entries and, as she was given a bye in the first round, the final in which she defeated the soon-to-be-invincible Blanche Bingley on the Worple Road courts was only the third match she had to play. It was her last victory at the tournament. Bingley gained revenge in 1886, and three years later, with singles titles from Ireland and Wales also against her name, she retired from the sport. She died in 1946.

Mal Whitman

Born: *March 15, 1877*
New York, NY, USA

Winner of the US Championships three years in succession, 1898–1900, an equally significant claim to fame for this Harvard graduate who, always fascinated by the history of the sport, went on to write Tennis Origins and Mysteries in 1931, is that he played in the first rubber of the first Davis Cup match. It was his 6–1, 6–3, 6–2 defeat of Arthur Gore, who had lost the Challenge Round at Wimbledon that year, which spearheaded the 3–0 victory for the United States over the British Isles in 1900. He also won his two singles the only other time he played in the Davis Cup, two years later.

Mats Wilander

Born: *August 22, 1964*
Vaxjo, Sweden

When Mats Wilander won the French Open aged 17, in 1982, outlasting Guillermo Vilas in the final, a Swedish journalist leapt up in the press box at Roland Garros and cried, "There is life after Borg." Just when Swedish tennis was trying to come to terms with Borg's decision to quit, along came this quick, diligent teenager, with relentless top spin on a single-handed forehand and tortuous accuracy off a double-handed backhand, to take over at the helm. The following year, on grass, he won the Australian Open, beating first John McEnroe and then Ivan Lendl. He retained the title 12 months later. Wilander won the French again in 1985, by which time he was already into his fourth year in the top 10.

His greatest success, though, was in 1988 when he won three of the four Grand Slam tournaments, but missed out on the chance for a Grand Slam when he was remorselessly outwitted by Miloslav Mecir in the quarter-finals. His victory that year at the US Open also lifted him to the world number one ranking, ending the 156-week reign of Lendl. He won 33 singles and seven doubles titles, including Wimbledon with fellow Swede Joakim Nystrom in 1986. Three times in winning Davis Cup teams, 1984, 1985 and 1987, he had a 36–14 singles and 7–2 doubles record in 26 matches over 10 years. In 1997, after a lengthy legal dispute, and by which time he had retired, he accepted that positive drug tests on him and Karel Novacek at the 1995 French Open were correct, but claimed he had taken the substances unknowingly.

Tony Wilding

Born: *October 31, 1883*
Christchurch, New Zealand

This handsome Wimbledon champion, 1910–13, who lived most of the time in England, rather than returning to New Zealand after coming down from Cambridge, lived and died a hero. He had originally planned to compete in the US Championships for the first time in 1914, immediately after the Davis Cup at Forest Hills, where he won the opening rubber as Australasia, as it was then, beat the United States 3–2. But he returned to Europe instead, determined to enlist as soon as possible in the armed forces, for the 1914–18 war had just started. He joined the Royal Marines, and on May 19, 1915 was killed in action at Neuve Chapelle in France.

A daring and brilliant stroke-

VIRGINIA WADE, *the 1977 Centenary champion at Wimbledon*

SERENA AND VENUS WILLIAMS, *credited with transforming the women's game*

maker, which was in keeping with his whole dashing style, appearance and approach to life, he was adored by crowds wherever he played, especially at Wimbledon. He and Australian Norman Brookes were inextricably linked, not only because they won the Davis Cup together three times in succession, but because on the two occasions Brookes won the title, 1907 and 1914, he beat the partner with whom he won the doubles that year (and in two others) along the way. In 1907 it was in the second round, in 1914, the Challenge Round.

Serena Williams
Born: *September 26, 1981*
Saginaw, Michigan

Venus Williams
Born: *June 17, 1980*
Lynwood, California

The Williams sisters were unleashed on an unsuspecting public in the mid-nineties by father Richard who had forewarned the tennis world that his daughters, at the time still juniors, would dominate the women's game. His forecast proved correct, first with Venus and then, a year later, with the younger of the two siblings, Serena. The two topped the rankings for 68 weeks, Serena with 57 and Venus with 11.

At the turn of the century fans could expect both sisters to be contesting the finals of all the majors and as a result the two feature strongly on the respective championship rolls of the four Grand Slams, especially those of the US Open and Wimbledon.

Both sisters play an aggressive power game, with Serena probably the stronger of the two. In Grand Slam terms, Serena has proved the more successful having collected seven titles in comparison to Venus' five, a fact also reflected in the number of finals they have both lost, Serena two and Venus six. In fact in 2002 Serena won the French, Wimbledon, US Open and the following year's Australian Open to score a non-calendar Grand Slam which she described as a 'Serena Slam'.

On the circuit itself Venus has been the more successful winning 33 tournaments to Serena's 26 though again Serena's total includes the 2001 WTA Championships, surprisingly the only occasion a Williams has won the prestigious end of season bash.

To say the two changed the women's game would not be overstretching the matter. There is no doubt that their style of play precipitated an end to interminable rallies as players were forced to not only counter their powerful approach, but find ways of beating them which meant growing stronger!

The pro game can also thank the two for raising the profile of their sport as they became icons for the young and in many ways, the disadvantaged. And having established themselves on the tennis circuit, they broadened their horizon by establishing separate business operations, Venus in interior design and Serena pursuing a second career in films.

Injuries and an element of off-court distractions has resulted in both players not being so dominant in recent years though Venus came through to win her third Wimbledon title in 2005.

The pair are also accomplished doubles players being the only sisters to have won a doubles Grand Slam title. They in fact won three. They also won the gold medal at the Sydney Olympics in 2000, again the only sisters to have achieved that distinction.

The list of accomplishments and accolades they have received from the sport and their admirers would fill pages. They have always entertained from the days they first burst on the scene with their beaded hairstyle and continue to do so, especially Serena with her extravagant tennis outfits.

Helen Wills Moody

Born: *October 6, 1905*
Berkeley, CA, USA

Known for hitting the ball harder than any woman, and one of the greatest women amateur champions, Helen Wills Moody, who died on January 1, 1998, aged 92, won 19 Grand Slam singles titles between 1923 and 1938 – four at the French, seven at the US, where she was only 17 the first time and eight at Wimbledon in only nine visits between 1927 and 1938. That lasted as a record until Martina Navratilova won her ninth and last title in 1990. Known as "Little Miss Poker Face", because of her totally focused and determined approach to every match she played, she lost the only match she ever played against Suzanne Lenglen in Cannes in 1926 but, with the exception of one occasion at Forest Hills, always beat her greatest rival, Helen Jacobs, in major tournaments. In one amazing six-year period she did not lose a single set in the French, Wimbledon or US Championships and also won 21 of her 30 Wightman Cup matches against Britain between 1928 and 1938.

Moody, whose white eyeshades became her trademark, learned the game mainly from her physician father and from watching others, especially visiting Australian players, at the Berkeley Tennis Club where membership was her 14th birthday present. Helen Wills, who remarried and took the name Helen Wills Moody Roark in 1939, won an Olympic gold medal in Paris in 1924, the last time tennis was a full medal sport in the Games until it returned in Seoul in 1988.

Sidney Wood

Born: *November 1, 1911*
Black Rock, CT, USA

It was ironic that in 1931 Sidney Burr Beardslee Wood, who had been subject to serious boyhood illnesses, should become the only player to receive a walkover in a Wimbledon final. Having beaten Fred Perry in the semi-finals, he should have played his higher-seeded Davis Cup team-mate Frank Shields. The latter, though, had injured his ankle, so it was felt it would be more sensible for him to rest to ensure being fit for a Davis Cup Inter-Zone final against Britain in Paris two weeks later. How times have changed! And, as it happened, Britain still won the match in Paris. So without having to play the final, Wood, then 19 years 8 months, became the second-youngest champion at the time after Wilfred Baddeley who had been 81 days younger when he won the first of his three titles in 1891.

Despite a poor physique, Wood, who had a wonderful backhand and potent volleys, astonished the Centre Court crowd at Wimbledon on his first visit when still only 15 in 1927, by wearing plus-fours for his match against René Lacoste. Perry, who also lost to him at the US Championships in 1932, took his revenge in a dramatic Wimbledon semi-final in 1934. Wood was runner-up to Wilmer Allison at Forest Hills in 1935.

SIDNEY WOOD, *a brilliant volleyer, in full flight at Eastbourne's Devonshire Park in 1932*

THE GREAT

From Australia to Argentina, Wimbledonto the West Indies, there are tennis stadiums large and small which togetherprovide facilities for thousands of touring tennis players at different times of the year. Between them, whether the game is being played outdoors or indoors, they all have their place in the game's atlas of adventure.

The game of tennis is blessed with some of the most historic sporting arenas in the world, some more ancient than others, some naturally admired more than others, but all contributing to the continuing development of a sport now well into its second century.

At the top of the list, of course, are the homes of the four Grand Slam tournaments – The All England Club at Wimbledon, where the ancient has been moulded so effectively into the modern; Roland Garros in Paris, where evidence of typical French elegance and pride is easy to find; and the two newest stadiums – Flushing Meadows in New York and Melbourne Park.

More about them and the venues they replaced will follow, but there are many others with equally impressive characteristics, some traditional, some even futuristic, which add to the overall colour and atmosphere of the men's and women's tours.

There can be very few, who do not

fall in love with the Monte Carlo Country Club from the moment they first step into this tiered paradise on the Côte D'Azur; especially if they climb through the steep, neatly kept gardens from the coastline at the bottom of the cliffs. On a sunny afternoon, the view across the courts and the beach below, into the blue Mediterranean where small sailing boats mingle between millionaire's yachts and even the occasional cruise liner, is certainly one to be cherished.

It is one of the first steps on the annual European clay court tour, which two weeks later stops in Hamburg, where facilities for the German Open in the tree-lined Rothenbaum Club have undergone such major changes in recent years. The wonderful old, largely wooden pavilion may be no more and some of the replace-

THE IDYLLIC *view over the Mediterranean from the Monte Carlo Country Club*

ARENAS

THE TREE-LINED *outside courts at the Foro Italico, home of the Italian Open in Rome*

ment structures functional rather than elegant, but the unveiling in 1998 of the spectacular new umbrella-style tented roof to protect players and spectators when wintry blasts still strike in early May – which in recent years has been an all-too-frequent occurence – is a perfect example of tournaments keeping pace with progress.

Halle, of course, pioneered covered outside courts – and grass courts at that – in 1995, and there are other pre-Wimbledon grass-court tournaments other than in Britain, Holland and Austria. Did you know, though, that the German Open also used to be played, albeit in mid-summer, on grass? The tournament, which began in 1892, had three earlier homes before settling at Rothenbaum in 1923, one of which was at nearby Vordem Dammtor from 1894–1897 and again from 1902–1922, on a lawn area which used

to be flooded in winter to transform it into an ice rink.

After Wimbledon and Roland Garros, however, the most famous of all European tennis venues is probably the Foro Italico in Rome, a lasting, extravagant reminder of the excesses of the dictator, Mussolini, in 1935. Set amid the pines close to the Tiber, the recent introduction of a new centre court has made it possible to restore to full view the marble splendour of the original arena, surrounded by statues depicting nude warriors ready for battle.

Bournemouth, on the South Coast of England, is another tennis centre which will forever be enshrined in tennis history. For it was there, in 1968, that the very first tournament involving professionals and amateurs, was staged. Further East along the British coastline Eastbourne's Devonshire Park is another picturesque tennis centre, full of

charm and history, but it would be wrong to suppose that Europe has a monopoly in such matters. The White City in Sydney has an equally historic background, which, until recent changes, provided an easy reminder of how Eastbourne also used to look. In the United States, where so many fine new arenas have been built in recent years, the magnificent new permanent home which has enabled the Nasdaq-100 Championships to put down its roots after Delray, Boca Raton and then a decade of temporary accomodation at Key Biscayne, has also set standards for others to follow.

WIMBLEDON

Wimbledon arrived at the new millenium almost at the halfway stage of a 20-year, multi-million pound development plan designed to maintain the supremacy, as well as the traditions of The Championships in the

21st century. By now some of the major improvements have already been completed – the magnificent new No. 1 Court, the spectacular flagship of the whole enterprise, which was opened in time for the 1997 tournament, together with a purpose-built, modern broadcasting centre. In 2000, a handsome new facilities centre became home to the players, the media and members of The All England Club during the fortnight. And even the historic clubhouse is now undergoing the most extensive revamp since it was built in 1922 as the club administration and Wimbledon Tennis Museum are moved to make way for a sliding roof over Centre Court, the latter a major development due to be completed in 2009.

It is part of an on-going policy to move with the times, whilst maintaining the best of what has served the game so well in the past. It sustains a policy that began almost as soon as the

A VISION *of Wimbledon in the twenty-first century*

journalists and spectators regarded as the most homely and intimate, albeit physically uncomfortable, at any major tournament, was opened with 2,500 seats and room for 750 standing. By adding bits here, there and then almost everywhere, there was seating for 6,500 when the demolition men moved in soon after Britain's Davis Cup victory over Egypt in 1996.

Incidentally, when the old No. 1 court was about to be pulled down, the club thought that some people might be interested in purchasing some of the bench seats as a sentimental reminder of many happy years there. Arrangements were made for them to be auctioned after members of The All England Club had had the chance to buy them at the reserve prices which had been set. Such was the response that the members, including some former leading players, snapped up everything and the auction was cancelled. When they were refurbishing Centre Court some years earlier, Martina Navratilova arranged for three of the old metal seats to be shipped to her home in the United States, where they were given pride of place on the verandah.

Circular in plan, the 11,000-capacity, all-seated, new No. 1 court, was based, to a large extent, on Stan-

first tournament was held about two miles or so away at Worple Road, in 1877. To get there, other than on foot or by bicycle, most spectators would have to walk along what was often a muddy lane or along the footpath which ran from Wimbledon Station. Initially there were no stands, and as the Championships began to grow in popularity, there are tales of enterprising youngsters offering building bricks at a half-penny each for late-comers to stand on so that they had a better view over those in front of them.

A selected few, though no more than 30, were able to sit in a three-row mini stand to watch the first final. By 1881, there were larger temporary stands on three sides of the centre court and three years later, by which time nearly 3,000 attended the final, the first permanent, covered structure was provided. By 1919 it was obvious that the tournament needed a larger home and the late Edwin Fuller, who was to become head groundsman, recalled how the secretary asked him, "If I knew of a piece of ground which was level, with a lake or stream nearby from which the courts could be watered." Eventually someone heard about a 13-and-a-half acre site, much of it a farm, in Wimbledon Park

Road (now Church Road) and in 1922, at a cost of £140,000, the move was completed – although some might argue that the work was only just beginning.

The new centre court provided seating for 9,989 and standing room

for 3,600. Now the standing room, steadily reduced anyway to prevent crushing to 2,000, has gone, a victim of the Safety of Sports Grounds legislation and the number of seats has increased to 13,120. Two years later the old No. 1 court, which many players,

A VIEW *over the courts on the South side of the grounds*

ley Peach's original design for Centre Court – although it was extended to incorporate a whole range of other spectator and marketing facilities which no one would ever have considered in 1922.

While it is common knowledge among tennis followers that The All England Lawn Tennis and Croquet Club has not only changed its home during its lifetime, but also the club name, which was originally The All England Croquet Club, fewer realize that its famous and distinctive colours of dark green and purple were not introduced until 1909, or that in 1913, the tournament was also called The World Championships after the newly created International Tennis Federation awarded the title to the British Isles in perpetuity. However, it has never been a title that has been given great prominence.

Over the years the number of courts in use for The Championships have grown from nine, in 1877, to 13, when the tournament first moved to Church Road, and in recent years to 18. During the late 1970s in particular, when attendances rose by about 25 per cent in a decade, it was not unusual to hear the complaint that Wimbledon had become too cramped for comfort and getting to some of the outside courts was a battle. However, by taking over the grounds of Aorangi Park, the number of match and practice courts on the North side of the ground has grown and this has largely solved that problem – except perhaps when a British player is on course to achieve a major upset on one of the outside courts!

As anyone who has queued for hours just to saunter round the outside courts will tell you, the gates often have to be closed for a few hours at the peak of the afternoon until those leaving early make room for others still waiting to get in. What is not generally appreciated is that, over and above Centre and No. 1 Courts, there are at least another 8,000 seats, the large majority of them unreserved, round the other 17 courts.

The Association of Wimbledon Honorary Stewards, some of them hitherto associated with The Championships in various ways, such as umpires or service personnel, is responsible for crowd management, acting as hosts to the crowd. The practice of using them began in 1927, but it was not until 1950 that they formed their own association. Apart from giving directions and general help, they also help marshal the queues inside and outside the grounds, together with volunteer servicemen and women.

One other feature of Wimbledon, of course, is the immaculate nature of the gardens, hedges and since 1997, the waterfall leading down from the new No. 1 Court, which itself has been sunk deep into the ground so that the roof is at exactly the same level as the roof of Centre Court. During The Championships, the grounds are awash with glorious colours from about 21,000 petunias, 13, 000 geraniums and 3,500 hydrangeas, all of which play their part in making the end product what it is supposed to be – tennis in an English country garden.

ROLAND GARROS

There are few principal venues in the world of tennis where the enormous growth in the popularity of the game as a major spectator sport has been more graphically demonstrated, or where the character of the host nation has been more obviously preserved in an increasingly cosmopolitan game than at Roland Garros. And why not? French, after all, is one of the three official languages of the game,

ROLAND GARROS, *where umbrellas provide popular cover from either the sun or the rain, pictured in 1989*

along with English and Spanish, so it is appropriate that after so many years of scores being given in both English and French, *égalité* and *jeu décesif*, as well as the term *reprise*, are as commonly used as their English counterparts.

Roland Garros took its name from one of France's most famous aviators – an airman shot down during aerial combat in October 1918, just five weeks before the Armistice which ended the First World War. The City of Paris decreed that his memory should be marked in a manner fitting for future generations of sporting high flyers, and when tennis administrators set about designing an area of land close to the Porte D'Auteuil to stage France's first home defence of the Davis Cup in 1928, the name Roland Garros was the obvious choice for the new grounds. In the three years before players from other countries, or those not resident in France, were allowed to compete in the French Championships, they had been played alternately at the Racing Club, at Croix-Catelan, and the Stade Française at the Faisanderie. However, as the official guide to Roland Garros now relates, "these two clubs were soon caving in under the weight of the throngs of spectators."

The stadium was built in less than a year thanks to reinforced concrete set in the "art deco" style so much in fashion at the time. Curiously enough, Lenglen apart, women's tennis never drew the same crowd response at Roland Garros as the men until the days of Chris Evert and Martina Navratilova, even though the women were first to set foot on the now-famous red clay, in a match between France and Britain which the visitors won 8–4.

Over the next 35 years there were few significant structural changes, although the advent of Open tennis in 1968 was clearly a turning point in terms of rapidly increasing crowds; even though the student riots and a transport strike that year made it so difficult for most people to reach Roland Garros – and even harder to get back to their homes or hotels, when everyone was on the road together. Even so, it was not until 1976 – the year that the best of five sets for all rounds

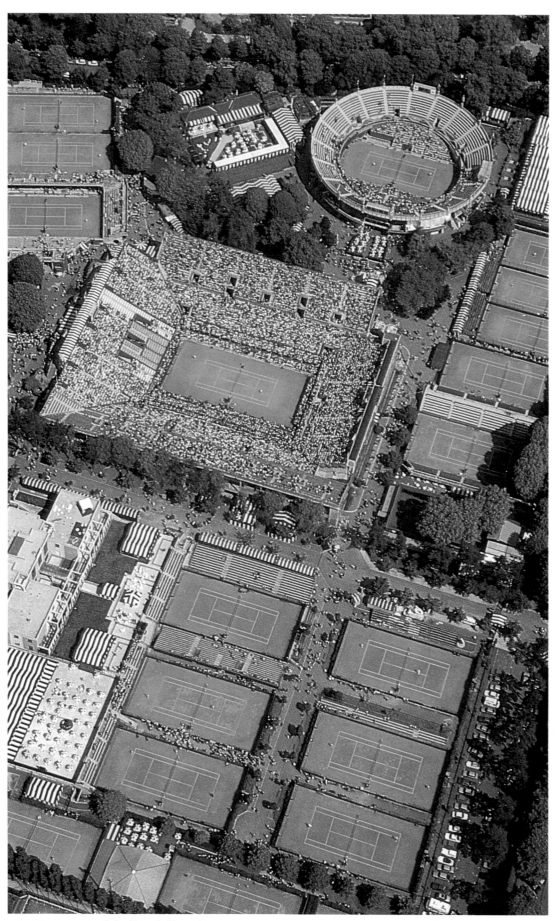

AN AERIAL VIEW *of the French Open in progress*

161

in the men's singles was reinstated – that the attendances for the fortnight exceeded 100,000. Just three years later it was already more than 200,000 and now the 400,000-mark is on the horizon.

Back in the late 1960s and early 1970s, there was no sign of the ticket touts who now mingle with the crowds wending their way from the Porte D'Auteuil subway to the first main entrance at Ave. Gordon Bennett, desperate to find anyone with a spare ticket to sell for the eager market of those waiting to buy. All this is a far cry from the year in which the first of the women's singles quarterfinals in the early 1970s involving Britain's Virginia Wade, began on the centre court at 11a.m. with only 71 spectators in the stadium – and they included 12 British journalists.

The French Championships, which take place in the last week of May and the first week of June, are considered to be the unofficial World Championships on clay courts, with players most accustomed to the surface from childhood tending to be the most successful, at least so far as the men's singles have been concerned. In recent years, especially since a firmer base has been installed beneath the clay and faster balls have been introduced, the pace of the play at Roland Garros has certainly quickened.

Serve and volleyers now believe that they have a better chance of winning at Roland Garros than at almost any time in the past. However, despite the spirited, attacking performance which brought Brazil's unseeded Gustavo Kuerten the title out of the blue in 1997, one has to go back to 1983, when France's own Yannick Noah became champion, to find the last time that victory was influenced more at the net than from the baseline.

The upsurge in interest and support has naturally meant the provision of new facilities and extensions to some of the old ones, including the Centre Court, where major renovations and the provision of much more seating was completed in 1984, when the Porte de Suzanne Lenglen lane, or alley as it was called, became a street between the main stadium and the new courts. Four years earlier there had been the inauguration of Court 1, as a second centre court with a capacity for 4,500, although this intimate circular arena, housing administrative and hospitality areas underneath, was reduced to only the third court in terms of importance when the new Court de Suzanne Lenglen, with room for 10,000 as well as a new media restaurant and overflow work areas, was inaugurated in 1994.

This and seven new practice courts now occupy land which was once part of the old Fond des Princes stadium, and because of legal problems, three years elapsed between the beginning of construction and the day that Chrstian Bimes, the current president of the French Tennis Association, supported by the presidents of many other French tennis clubs, performed the opening ceremony.

As at Wimbledon, where the qualifying competition, which has been described by some as "the toughest tournament in the world"other than a Grand Slam, and where the difference between making it into the main draw or not can mean so much, qualifying for the French Open used to be staged away from the main arena. However, since 1997, thanks to all the additional facilities in recent years, it too has been played at Roland Garros.

Walking round the grounds, one senses the same feeling of tradition as at Wimbledon, and there is a glorious reminder every year of just how great a history there has been at the French Open when the new singles champions receive their trophies. The winner of the men's title receives the "Coupe des Mousquetaires"and it is sad that none of them are any longer there to make the presentation in person. As for the winner of the women's singles, she is the recipient of the "Coupe Suzanne Lenglen"– what else could it possibly be called!

FLUSHING MEADOWS

Officially, the US National Tennis Center at Flushing Meadows – not Flushing Meadow, singular, as so many still refer to it – was first opened in 1978. It was then that the tournament moved from its ancestral venue five miles away at Forest Hills and the brief experiment with green clay courts after the grass had been dug up in time for the tournament in 1975, was abandoned. In many ways, though, the original facilities within the original 21.6-acre site containing a centre court which was merely the old Louis Armstrong site from the World Trade Fair, adapted as best they could, and quickly became the holding operation for a much more extravagant and impressive redevelopment which came into being 19 years later for the 1997 tournament. In a sense the real opening came on Monday August 25, 1997 when a host of former champions from Don Budge to those of the present day, came to mark both the opening of the new Stadium Court and the champion after whom it was named, Arthur Ashe.

The Louis Armstrong Stadium which served as the centre court, had 20,000 seats and an adjoining grandstand with seating for a further 5,000 people. In 1998, seating on the old centre court was reduced to 10,000 by removing the top tier of some 20 or more rows which some felt provided a better view of the magnificent Manhattan skyline than the tennis way down below.

Depending on your affinity with

FLUSHING MEADOWS, *with its commanding view of the Manhattan skyline*

THE MAGNIFICENT *Arthur Ashe stadium, opened at Flushing Meadows for the US Open in 1997*

architecture, the Arthur Ashe Stadium is either a modern masterpiece, with its wonderfully clear sight lines of the court and easy access for spectators or a confusing mix of styles and ideas. Gino Rossetti, the architect for Rosetti Associates, describes the design concept as one of "tennis in the park". Fair enough, and for once bigger really is more beautiful for after what many regarded as a site which was little more than a concrete jungle, with little character and even less charm, the home of the US Open has been transformed into a truly equal partner with the other Grand Slams.

The facility has more than doubled in size to 46.5 acres and most of it has been put to use in a most attractive as well as a practical fashion, even though most purists might suggest that the Arthur Ashe centre court would be even more admirable if, instead of holding 23,000 people, the capacity was reduced by a third. Apart from

needing a sturdy head for heights, for those trying to follow the play intently from the higher echelons of the arena, perfect vision is also required, even in some cases to be sure of the players in action, let alone to appreciate the power, tactics and subtle nuances of the shots being played.

The old facility had 28 outdoor courts, over and above the two principal arenas and nine indoor courts. Now there is a total of 45 courts, including 11 new practice courts. Even without the obvious difference, hard courts instead of grass, it is worlds apart from the West Side Club at Forest Hills, with its typical 1920s-style clubhouse. It was a private club which only opened its doors and grounds to the tennis community from all round the world for two weeks of the year. Before the arrival of Open tennis, Forest Hills was adequate enough, but as tennis began to devel-

op in such a dramatic fashion, everything reached bursting point and there was a severe limit to how much had to be done to provide the extra space needed for everything concerned, not least car parking.

Yet those who were fortunate enough to have covered the US Championships in the Forest Hills days will retain fond memories of the place, especially the "happy hours" on the club verandah, with its always-busy bar which overlooked one of the most popular courts from the spectators point of view. To get to the centre court in those days, members and many of those with centre court seats would have to walk through the clubhouse itself, past the women's dressing rooms and then down the walkway between two rows of courts to the main stadium. Here, for the first ten days of the tournament, there would be two centre courts side by side within the one

arena. For the last few days, by which time the wear and tear on both was usually considerable, a new centre court would be marked out in the middle, overlapping both of them.

The whole arena was surrounded by white geraniums, although one year the grime in the air over the district of Queen's left its mark in such a way that the plastic nature of the flowers became apparent to everyone who looked at them. They were sprayed with red dye to spruce them up for the finals and more than one innocent newcomer who left Forest Hills with the grass a burnt brown on the second Friday night, was astonished to find the court a rich green again the next morning after it too had been sprayed back to life.

Wonderful memories without doubt, but tennis and the US Open outgrew Forest Hills and it would be wrong to look back with anything more than fond nostalgia. The record

MELBOURNE PARK, *home of the Australian Open, with the sliding Centre Court roof open*

crowd for a day's play at Forest Hills was just under 17,000 in 1976. Nowadays, day and night crowds well in excess of 40,000 are a daily occurence and with approximately that total number of seats in the show courts and outside courts, the only time when the arena feels over-crowded is when the day session over-runs to such an extent that a huge night crowd is then kept waiting for admission.

Americans are great sports lovers and avid believers in statistics, including tennis, but the United States Tennis Association, for the open-ing of the Arthur Ashe Stadium, did not merely confine itself to making sure the world's media were fed all the facts and figures relating to the matches. They came up with other vital information such as the number of toi-lets within the grounds (411), and the fact that they had quadrupled the num-

ber of women's toilets since 1996. With-in the Arthur Ashe and Louis Arm-strong stadiums alone there are 35 food concession stands, while for the players between 12 and 15 racket stringers are on duty in shifts from 7a.m. to 11p.m. every day. If that was not enough, the press handout reported that about 500 construction workers had been involved in the two-and-a-half years it had taken to build the Arthur Ashe stadium, five per cent of whom were women.

What matters most, though, is that the new stadium, which has been pri-vately funded by bonds issued by the City of New York, is one which all can admire. There have been complaints that too many of the box seats closest to the court have been sold to corpo-rate customers, but that sadly is becoming a commercial fact of life in most sports, not just tennis, as ever ris-ing costs have to be recouped some-

how. The US Open, perhaps because it makes it more obvious than the oth-ers, is a prime example of how tennis has long since left behind the garden-party style and has now become a big business. But they haven't forgotten their stars and the contributions they make and, in acknowledgement of one great American player's record and her fight for women's rights in sports, the complex was renamed in 2006, the 'Billie Jean King National Tennis Centre'.

MELBOURNE PARK

Once a name becomes firmly estab-lished in the mind, it is not always easy to remember when it has been changed. Just as it took a good decade for some players to stop referring to Forest Hills after the US

Open moved to Flushing Meadows, so the decision, taken under pressure from the government of Victoria, to change the name of Flinders Park to Melbourne Park in time for the 1997 Australian Open, is sometimes diffi-cult to remember.

Not though the arena itself, sur-rounded on one side by the Yarra River and the other by the MCG, the Melbourne Cricket Ground, another of the finest venues for any sport in the world. It was impressive enough when it was first opened in 1988, but the extensions and improvements since then have helped to make the Australian Open what on most days is one of the most comfortable destina-tions on the tennis circuit. The excep-tion concerns those days when the heat is too much for almost anyone to bear. More about that later.

The thing which strikes you most when you first enter Melbourne

Park, apart of course from the sliding roof which can cover the centre court in the event of extreme weather conditions – a first for the sport – is the space, particularly since the land reclaimed from the no-longer-needed adjoining railway yards have been transformed into additional courts and a magnificent, fully landscaped picnic area, when one can lounge and either keep an eye on events on the centre court from a huge outdoor screen at one end, or merely glance over the ever-changing skyline of this bustling city. Even before one gets into the arena, there is a feeling of grandeur as from the roadside you walk along avenues surrounded by grassland for about 50 yards before going through the turnstiles and then climb the 30-or-so steps to the main concourse which surrounds the mid-level height of the stadium.

As discussed in the feature outlining the history of the Australian Open, there was much heartache in some quarters over the decision to transfer the tournament from the old country club atmosphere at Kooyong – and even more so over the change from grass to Rebound Ace, a moderately fast hard court surface. Now there are few who look back with sadness. Nostalgia perhaps, but the reality is that the Australian Open could neither have grown in the way it has done since 1988, nor achieved such increased international praise, had the change not been made. Apart from anything else, there simply was not the room for the developments which were essential for the Australian Open to keep pace with the advances being made everywhere else in the world, not least Wimbledon, Roland Garros and, for all the complaints at the time, Flushing Meadows.

Now among the major tennis venues round the world, Melbourne Park takes some beating, whether you are a player, spectator or representative of the media, providing you remember to take a hat and sunscreen with a high enough factor with you. Oh yes, and a map of the courts. For while Courts 13 and 14 at Wimbledon are almost as far away from each other as one can imagine, there is some logic to that inasmuch that 13 is the highest numbered court on the south side of the grounds and 14 starts another sequence of numbered courts on the north side. In Melbourne showcourts 1, 2 and 3 are on one side of the grounds, together with courts 5, 6 and 7 etc. But to reach Court 4, which is surrounded by courts 13, 14, 15, 16 and 17, you have to walk through the covered marketplace where sporting goods manufacturers ply their wares, to the other side of the ground.

Not that this is a major problem. Indeed a trip to Melbourne Park in January, is an inspiring way to begin the tennis year and after the record crowds in 1998, plans are already afoot for the building of another 8–10,000 show court which could also double up as a home for other sports at other times in the year. As mentioned earlier, the one drawback can be the heat. While, as artifical surfaces go, Rebound Ace is probably one of the most acceptable, because it tends to give clay courters and serve and volleyers an almost equal chance to play their best tennis, there can be serious problems in days of extreme heat. The way the heat is reflected, to the extent that many players have talked of feeling the heat burning their feet through their shoes, is an obvious difficulty, but some players have found that the elasticty of the surface, while kinder on the limbs in normal conditions, can become sticky and make it harder for them to twist or turn quickly on the hottest days.

Although it was not introduced with that specifically in mind, the Australian Open is the only Grand Slam which has a specific policy as to when the roof over the centre court should be closed in the case of extreme heat and, despite opposition from some of the players, this was strengthened in 1998. Basically if a match has already started on the centre court with the roof open it will have to be completed with the roof open whatever the temperature reaches in the meantime. On the other hand, if during that time the referee has decided not to allow any more matches to start on any of the outside courts, then the centre court roof will be closed before the next match is allowed to begin. This is a health and safety measure designed to help not only the players – several of whom have needed intensive medical treatment after completing matches in extreme heat – but also officials, spectators and stewards. There was criticism during the 1997 Open when although the centre court was deemed too hot for play to continue without the roof being closed, even junior matches were being allowed to continue on the outside courts as no rules governed that situation at that time.

While Melbourne Park is principally known round the world as the home of the Australian Open, to Victorians, it is much more than that for, thanks to the roof and all the other built-in facilities, it could rapidly be transformed into anything from a conference centre, to the venue for a pop concert, a boxing arena or a Torvill and Dean ice dance extravaganza, as the photographs along the walls of the corridor which leads the players from the main entrance to their locker rooms demonstrates.

Most of the entertainers who fill the arena in the other 11 months of the year, though, are transient visitors. For the two weeks of the Open, the date of which, incidentally, is frequently being reviewed by those who would like it to be two or three weeks later to offer players a longer period of preparation, the stars are those who return year after year hoping to add their names to the roll of honour dating back to 1905.

A MODERN IMAGE *of the Centre Court in Melbourne, as tennis keeps up with the times*

THE GREAT MATCHES

There are occasions in any sport that will be remembered by thousands for many years to come. Tennis is no different and certain encounters are now part of tennis legend.

From time to time there are some contests which either because of the impact they made at the time or because of the particularly dramatic way in which they were recorded, have become part of tennis legend handed down to each succeeding generation.

The classic confrontation between Suzanne Lenglen and Helen Wills on the French Riviera in 1926, the only time these two giants of women's tennis met, is one such example. More than 70 years on there are few people still alive who can recall this remarkable occasion but most modern chroniclers of the game have heard enough to realize that this was far more than just an ordinary challenge match. Here was a match which had all the intriguing ingredients worthy of a modern television soap opera, not least jealous rivalry, so it is only natural that it warrants inclusion among the choice of momentous contests recalled on the following pages.

Bjorn Borg's fifth and last victory in a Wimbledon final when he beat John McEnroe in 1980 is worthy of tennis legend. It was the year of the most famous as well as one of the most compelling tie-breaks ever played. It lasted 23 minutes and offered Borg five match points in addition to two he had already missed before the American took it on the 34th point – still the longest in any Wimbledon sin-

gles final, 18–16. Borg still won the match, but it is the tie-break which was later packaged into a 30-minute television special of its own.

For someone who rarely lifted the curtain on his own feelings while he was on court, Borg certainly figured in a huge number of highly emotion, top-quality clashes, with his 1977 semi-final against Vitas Gerulaitis still regarded by many as the best match they have ever seen. Others might just as easily put the classic women's singles final at the French Open in 1985 between Martina Navratilova and Chris Evert into that category. The way in which at 30, Evert who had lost all but one of their 16 previous encounters, produced a performance of such epic quality to maintain the fascination surrounding what for so long was the game's greatest on-court rivalry.

The extremes of human emotions involved make some matches catch the imagination more than others. Pancho Gonzales versus Charlie Pasarell, for instance. That extraordinary Wimbledon first round contest in 1969, which was almost won by Pasarell before bad light stopped play but was dramatically turned round by the veteran Gonzales, then 41, the next day. It was not just the dramatic turn in the path of the match, though, it was the quality of play, the courage and the astonishing stamina employed by them both. It lasted 5 hours 12 minutes, a record for a Grand Slam tour-

nament, which lasted until 1992 when Stefan Edberg outlasted Michael Chang in the semi-finals of the US Open.

At other times human frailty can make the occasion all the more poignant. The photograph of Jana Novotna sobbing on the shoulder of a compassionate Duchess of Kent after going so close to beating Steffi Graf in the 1993 Wimbledon final, was featured all round the world. It captured the moment when, if anything, the collapse of Novotna's challenge became all the more painfully vivid than when it was actually happening. It is not often that the winner of a Grand Slam title is so obviously sorry for her opponent as Graf was on that day.

Others are treasured for the breathtaking tennis which was produced, such as the wonderful final of the WCT Championships in Dallas between Ken Rosewall and Rod Laver in 1972. Professional tennis was still in its infancy but here were two seasoned competitors, whose ability was already deeply enshrined in tennis history. Even though the pace of that match flagged occasionally for the most part it was the most enthralling and inspired tennis.

Rosewall was so completely overcome that he was near to tears during the presentation ceremony. And he remained in such a high mood of euphoria that when he went back

to his hotel he forgot to take the winners cheque for $50,000 with him and a friend had to drive back to the arena to find it.

Arthur Ashe felt equally elated when he won Wimbledon in 1975. Taking the title was glorious enough for a man who, in his childhood, must have wondered if someone from his background would even be allowed a decent opportunity to play tennis, let alone scale such heights. But to succeed by devising a game plan which reduced Jimmy Connors, the unrivalled world number one at the time, was straight out of a schoolboy adventure story.

The superb US Open final between Steffi Graf and Monica Seles in 1995 was particularly noteworthy for also being the first meeting between them after Seles's comeback from her stabbing in Hamburg two years earlier, while Pete Sampras versus Boris Becker in the final of the ATP Tour Championships in 1996, was equally befitting of the reputations and record of these two giants of the game on a fast indoor court. Picking just one match from the 98 completed years of the Davis Cup, was a near impossibility but the match-winning fifth rubber in Malmo in 1996 when Arnaud Boetsch won the trophy for France against Sweden's Nicklas Kulti in five sets had everything anyone could wish for.

Cannes, 1926

The Battle of the Century

SUZANNE LENGLEN VS. HELEN WILLS SPECTATORS WITHOUT TICKETS CLIMBED NEARBY BUILDINGS FOR A GLIMPSE OF THE BATTLE BETWEEN THE GREATEST PLAYERS OF THEIR TIME. THE WINNER WAS TO END UP WITH MORE BRUISES THAN THE VANQUISHED

No match, outside the framework of the Grand Slams, the Olympic Games or international competition, not even Billie Jean King vs. Bobby Riggs, aroused such passions as the one and only meeting, in a Challenge match on the French Riviera in early 1926, between Suzanne Lenglen and Helen Wills. The setting was the Carlton Club in Cannes. Journalists from all over the world poured in for what humorist James Thurber called "the battle of the century". Few realized that it would turn out to be the last really great match Lenglen was to play.

The build-up beforehand was extraordinary. The intense rivalry between the two, at a time when Wills, 21, had already won the US national championship three times, as well as collecting Olympic gold in singles and doubles, was far more significant in the French camp. Indeed, Lenglen's reported observation to a friend – "This girl must be mad. Does she think she can come and beat me on my home court?" – merely added spice to the occasion.

Lenglen was the reigning Wimbledon and French triple champion in singles, doubles and mixed at the time but Wills, with her persistent, accurate driving, which contrasted wonderfully with the flouncing flair of her opponent, was known to be a threat to the French player's status as the best woman player in the world.

The pre-match pressure on Lenglen was enormous. She was, nat-

THE SHOWDOWN *between Helen Wills (foreground) and Suzanne Lenglen in Cannes*

urally enough, the favourite, regarded as invincible, except on the rare occasions that her health was a problem. Monsieur Lenglen, who had such a powerful influence on his daughter, did not help matters. Both he and Madame Lenglen were said to have gone to such pains to impress upon Suzanne how much in terms of pride and prestige rested upon her shoulders the next day that she did not retire to bed until 2.30 a.m.

The front row of the main stand was reserved for dignatories such as the former King Michael of Portugal, Prince George of Greece, the Grand Duke Michael of Russia, the Rajah and Ranee of Pudukota and Britain's largest landowner, the Duke of Westminster. Their arrival was met with the sort of ovation associated with a Hollywood first night.

Such was the public interest that every spare inch of space in the stands and elsewhere round the court was filled by 4,000 spectators, and people living nearby sold space in their homes overlooking the club to those who could not get closer. These are said to have been the first tennis tickets to fetch black-market prices. Lenglen won the first set 6–3, but in the second, when the length of the rallies and the strength of her opponent's resistance began to test her nerve, she was seen to be taking frequent sips from her silver brandy flask. Wills, hitting her groundstrokes as hard and true as at any time in her career, looked capable of levelling the match, but somehow Lenglen's artistry prevailed, although only after the most extraordinary climax.

With Lenglen leading 6–5, Wills hit another stunning forehand crosscourt shot so close to the line that it was thought to have been out. Indeed the match was awarded to Lenglen and spectators began to swarm around the players until Lord Charles Hope, the linesman involved, pushed his way to the umpire's chair to insist that he certainly had not called the shot "out". When it was announced that Wills' shot had been declared "in" after all and that the point had therefore been given to her, there was pandemonium.

Lenglen, not surprisingly, lost the game. She broke serve again in the 13th and took the match, but drained of emotion and sobbing she looked more the vanquished than the victor. In a way she was. She sensed her reign was ending and, after her controversial departure from Wimbledon, she turned professional. Wills had lost the match, but gained a husband in Frederick Moody. She went on to win Wimbledon eight times.

The Longest in Wimbledon History

PANCHO GONZALES VS. CHARLES PASARELL THE AMAZING STORY OF HOW THE PASSION, COURAGE AND SKILLS OF A PLAYER DENIED ACCESS TO THE CENTRE STAGE FOR SO LONG, OVERCAME ALL ODDS TO DEFEAT A FORMER PUPIL YOUNG ENOUGH TO HAVE BEEN HIS SON

It still stands as the longest match ever played at Wimbledon, a total of 112 games, 19 more than the previous record in the match between Jaroslav Drobny and Budge Patty in 1953. It began late in the afternoon of the first Tuesday and extended into Wednesday before Gonzales, then 41 – and having saved seven match points, including twice escaping sensationally from 0–40 in the final set – finally beat an opponent no less than 16 years younger.

The match lasted 5 hours, 12 minutes, but it was not until the light was fading fast on the first evening and Gonzales, as the first set looked like going on for ever, was trying in vain to get play postponed overnight that it started to become one of the finest, most emotional matches in the history of The Championships.

Pasarell, who two years earlier had been the first player to defeat a defending champion (Manuel Santana) in the first round, had ample chances in the first set. Indeed, by the time he moved ahead 23–22, he had already missed or seen Gonzales save 11 set points, the last of them when the veteran nonchalantly ignored what most thought would be a set-winning drive, but did eventually turn to make sure it had dropped inches out after all. On his 12th set point, though, Pasarell hoisted a lob which not even Gonzales could reach – and this one landed in.

Most people, especially Gonzales, presumed that play would then stop for the day and there was a look of angry disbelief on his face when he appealed to the umpire to call a halt, only for the referee, Captain Mike Gibson, standing almost out of sight in the corner below the left-hand side of the Royal Box, to order them to "play on". Gonzales was livid

and the crowd started to boo at various stages in the second set when he kept complaining, slinging his racket towards the umpire's chair and saying, "You can't see the ball." He did little more than go through the motions as the set ran away from him 6–1 in less than 15 minutes.

PANCHO GONZALES
takes a brief rest as he wipes away the perspiration

Yet it was not long on the second day before the boos turned to cheers, especially when Gonzales, clearly having benefited from the overnight rest, persisted to survive the third set and then clearly began to dominate in the fourth. By now the crowd was fully behind the older man. The tension seemed to be getting to Pasarell and two double faults at 14–15 to decide the third set told their own story. Gonzales, who had coached the Puerto Rican-born Pasarell as a junior, realized that his opponent's confidence had gone. But his own body was suffering painful fatigue in an amazing fight to the finish. With Pasarell leading 5–4 in the fifth, he had his first three match points. Yet just when the lob had been starting to work again, two crucially missed thus helping Gonzales to escape. At 6–5, Pasarell held three more match points, but Gonzales hit three winners, a smash, a volley and a serve.

Another misplaced lob cost Pasarell his seventh match point at 8–7, but at 9–9 he finally cracked. He dropped his serve to love and Gonzales, poised like a tiger, went for the kill. He won 10 consecutive points to reach match points of his own at 40–0, but needed only one. Yet another Pasarell lob went out.

There was nothing but joy over the way Gonzales won, but it was tinged with sadness; it was a poignant reminder of how much the game had lost during all the years he had not been allowed to play.

FACTS

June 23 & 24
Wimbledon first round
Gonzales defeats Pasarell from two sets down
22–24, 1–6, 16–14, 6–3, 11–9

WCT Finals, 1972

A Tennis Treat in Dallas

KEN ROSEWALL VS. ROD LAVER THE SPECTATORS PACKING THE HALL ON THE CAMPUS OF SMU UNIVERSITY SENSED FROM THE FIRST POINT THAT THEY WERE WATCHING A TENNIS MASTERPIECE AND WATCHED IN AWE AS THE TWO AUSTRALIANS DID BATTLE

It was the second time within seven months that Ken Rosewall, already 37 years old but still one of the top six players in the world, met his long-standing rival, fellow Australian Rod Laver, for what was then a staggering first prize of $50,000. To put that into perspective, the prize money for the men's singles champion at Wimbledon two months later was little more than $10,000.

The previous meeting, at the inaugural WCT Finals in Houston, had been exciting enough, "so thrilling that the strain of watching it, never mind playing in it, became almost unendurable", according to Rex Bellamy, the correspondent of *The Times*. This second clash, after Rosewall had beaten Arthur Ashe 6–4, 6–3, 7–6 in one semi-final and Laver had outlasted a brilliantly resilient and durable Marty Riessen in five sets, earned even greater accolades. In addition to the capacity 9,300 crowd in Moody Coliseum, what was then a record television audience estimated at 22 million tuned in to, and became totally enthralled by, this 3-hour 34-minute classic. Indeed it was the first time that NBC Television stayed with a tennis match instead of giving way to advertised programmes as the match long outlasted the time originally allocated for its transmission.

Laver, who started brilliantly, won the first set 6–4, but suddenly the match dramatically swung the other way, with Rosewall delivering one

KEN ROSEWALL *was overcome with emotion as he collected the trophy and a cheque for $50,000*

majestic winner after another as he not only romped through the second set 6–0 but also took the third 6–3. With Laver 1–3 down in the fourth set, his hopes looked slim but then, principally by taking some of the stinging pace off his serve, which had been playing into the hands of Rosewall's ability to turn such tactics to his own advantage, he drew level by winning the fourth set tie-break 7–3.

By now the tension in the arena was again almost too much to bear for those privileged to have been there. It was not just the uncertainty of the outcome as Laver again fought back, this time from 1–4 to force yet another tie-break, but the sustained quality of the tennis was extraordinary and a tribute to the fitness, as well as the skill, of two of the game's greater players.

The first match point fell to Rosewall at 5–4, but his attempted lob was just out and suddenly it looked as if exhaustion would consume him. Not for the first time, however, the little

warrior found reserves of energy and inspiration as another tie-break loomed. Laver struck the first blow, earning a mini-break to lead 3–1 and sustained it until he was 5–3 ahead, just two points from victory. At 5–4 he had two serves for the money, the diamond ring and the gold cup, not to mention the Lincoln Continental car which went with the title.

Amid growing excitement, a hush eventually fell over the arena. Laver's serve at 5–4 was challenging enough – but not good enough to prevent Rosewall pouncing with a brilliant backhand cross-court return. Laver, who had spent almost a lifetime expecting and then trying to cope with such counter-attacks by Rosewall, spotted it quickly enough to get his racket to the ball, but was unable to control his volley which flew over the baseline. At 5–5 Laver again attacked the Rosewall backhand with an even stronger first serve, but once more the little master was

ready for it and struck another vintage outright winner, which left the red-haired left-hander stranded in mid-court.

So Rosewall held match point for a second time at 6–5 and Laver had nothing left to give. His attempted return of the serve went looping into the net. Both players looked fit to drop, but the crowd was on its feet stamping and cheering their approval and appreciation. As Mike Davies, the executive director of WCT, told them, "Tennis was the real winner today", before echoing the thoughts of many when he added, "That was the greatest match I've ever seen."

FACTS

WCT Finals
Moody Coliseum, Dallas, Texas
Rosewall beats Laver in five sets
4–6, 6–0, 6–3, 6–7, 7–6 (7–5)

Wimbledon, 1975

A Case of Mind over Matter

ARTHUR ASHE VS. JIMMY CONNORS IT IS THOUGHT THAT SUCCESS IN TENNIS DEPENDS MORE ON THE MESSAGES THE BODY RECEIVES FROM THE MIND THAN THE ENERGY PROVIDED BY THE MUSCLES. THAT WAS THE CASE AS ASHE TROUNCED CONNORS

Arthur Ashe was only five days away from his 32nd birthday and it was seven years since he had carried off the US Open when he met his fellow American Jimmy Connors, almost 10 years his junior and the favourite to retain the title he had won so emphatically for the first time 12 months earlier. Yet what was to unfold on the tennis court was one of the most remarkable examples of intellect succeeding against youthful muscle and bold but brash talent being put in its place by the most astutely crafted skills. The crowd loved it. Watching the modest but highly intelligent and respected Ashe, as the underdog, take on and tame the ebullient young champion Connors, who many felt should be taken down a peg or two, was something to be relished by all but Connors's fans.

What many in the crowd probably did not fully appreciate was the intriguing background to the contest. Connors was suing those he held responsible for barring him from the French Open in 1974 because he had signed a contract with what was regarded as the rebel World Team Tennis organization. Three individuals were named in the action, one of whom was Ashe, as president of the Association of Tennis Professionals.

Ashe, however, despite losing to Connors in the final in Johannesburg in 1973, remained confident that he was the best player in the world at that time on grass who had never won Wimbledon. Ken Rosewall followers

ARTHUR ASHE *turns to friends and celebrates his epic victory*

might have disagreed but, recalling what he had written in his diary after that defeat in South Africa, he was certain that, with the right strategy, he could and would win. For all that, even he was beginning to have doubts after the awesome display from Connors which had destroyed Roscoe Tanner in the semi-finals. That night, though, in conversation by transatlantic telephone with his Davis Cup coach, Dennis Ralston, and his close friend and manager, Donald Dell, he worked out a plan of campaign which was risky inasmuch as it called upon Arthur to play in a manner entirely foreign to him. But they felt there was nothing to lose.

Essentially Ashe had to be as error-free as possible while at the same time, and at all costs, denying Connors the one thing he hungered for most of all – pace. Maybe Connors felt that, after the ruthless manner in which he

had shot down Tanner, Ashe would be a pushover but, as the player who was to become the first black man to win the men's singles at Wimbledon was to say later, "Watching his match against Roscoe showed me how not to play him. I knew he had to be restrained." From the start the contest became more like a game of chess than a regular tennis match, with Connors increasingly made to look like a pawn, and the world number one found himself with little to hit – and none of the pace off which he could generate his fiercely hit winning shots.

Ashe broke for the first of many times in the third game. A smash from Connors was well out. There was no call, but with the crowd bellowing their annoyance the linesman eventually indicated that he was unsighted and the umpire, who at that time had no automatic right to overrule, rightly gave Ashe the point. From then on

there was growing amazement within the crowd as Ashe patiently, relentlessly and with increasing confidence dismantled Connors's game piece by piece. He was like a puppet master controlling the strings as, with a mixture of delicately chipped returns, which regularly made Connors lunge and miss on the forehand, frequent perfectly weighted lobs which added to his opponent's frustration and a great deal of courage, he tormented the man who was supposed to have been tormenting him.

When Connors tried counter-lobs, Ashe was devastating overhead, while he was always in the right place at the right time around the net to volley better than at any other time in his career. "Come on Connors", came a cry from the standing enclosure, as from holding in the first game, he lost the next nine to be 0–3 down in the second set. "I'm trying, for Christ's sake", was the bellowed response from the court. Ashe meanwhile allowed nothing to distract him, shutting his eyes as if meditating on his chair at changeovers. He broke for 3–2 in the third, but then lost his own serve for the first time, which encouraged a more urgent style from Connors, who not only snatched the set but reached 3–0 and held a point for 4–1 in the fourth.

"I wasn't worried. It was only one break", mused Ashe later after quickly recovering the break and earning another when Connors let go a ball which landed inside the baseline and was caught by yet another service return to his feet. All that was necessary then was for Ashe to serve out for the title. He did so with a swinging serve to the backhand. A desperate Connors return floated back to him which needed only an easy forehand volley. "When I walked on court I felt I was going to win. I felt it was my destiny", said Ashe. Without doubt on that day he was in control of his own destiny.

FACTS

July 5
Wimbledon final
Ashe defeats Connors in four sets
6–1, 6–1, 5–7, 6–4

Wimbledon, 1977

Perfect Way to Mark a Centenary

BJORN BORG VS. VITAS GERULAITIS THE CONTRAST BETWEEN THE UNFLAP- PABLE SWEDE, DEFENDING HIS WIMBLEDON CROWN FOR THE FIRST TIME, AND THE AMERICAN WHO LIVED UP TO HIS REPUTATION AS A PLAYBOY, WAS THE PERFECT MIX FOR A GREAT MATCH

Although the Wimbledon Centenary Championships will best be remembered for Virginia Wade's triumph in the women's singles, the finest of all among a host of notable match-

es was this semi-final in which the defending champion and the American full of extravagant flair faced each other. In this match, whose quality was worthy of the anniversary celebrations, there were endless extended rallies in which almost every shot was a marvel of pace and accuracy.

Gerulaitis, who never played with greater ambition, commitment or control, was prepared to take risks by the score which led him into producing volleys, which made it easy to remember that here was a flamboyant sportsman who was the owner back in New York of two Rolls-Royces. For his part, Borg delivered passing shots which sped like bullets to their target, more often finding the outside rather than the inside of the lines, as he too called upon his unfailing ability to use every inch of the court to full advantage.

There were times when both players carried tennis on to previous-

ly unattained levels of magnificence, not least on the last point of the second game as Borg broke to lead 2–0. In another lengthy rally, both men played just about every shot in the game. Borg, having delivered a near-perfect lob, then had to chase one which was every bit as good before he hoisted yet another which proved to be even more telling.

Here was more than just a match for the connoisseur. Two games later Gerulaitis, a lean, long-haired right-hander who had won the Italian Open two months earlier, was hard-pressed to hold his serve again as Borg six times fought his way to break point in a game of 22 points and eight deuces before the American prevailed. Then in the last game of this mouth-watering set, the rally which took Borg to set point was another interchange of thrust and counter-thrust of lob, passing shots and volleys during which each seemingly impossible

shot was matched by another that was even more so.

Borg, cool as ever as he walked from one gloriously played point to another, had the basic advantage all through in that he won the opening set which, like the next three, was decided on just one service break. Gerulaitis had to play like a saint to pull himself level, but every time he looked ready to launch a serious bid for control, the Swede succeeded in producing something even more extraordinary in response.

Only those who were there on that Thursday afternoon could fully appreciate the magnitude of a match which warranted far more than the "Oh I say!" excitement in the voice of BBC Television commentator Dan Maskell, who forever after listed this as one of the finest matches he had seen anywhere, let alone at Wimbledon.

The tension in the fifth set, which was as exhausting to watch as it must have been to play, was incredible. Virtually every point was a gem as the conflict reached a pitch of quickfire expertise. Borg almost lost it. In the fifth game of the fifth set he was broken to love and in the game which followed Gerulaitis held a point for 4–2, except that the top seed rescued it with another backhand return, rifled down the line and went on to break back. Once again Borg had demonstrated his ability to survive in moments of acute pressure. The end eventually came in the 14th game when, after more than three hours in which one could count the unforced errors by both men on one hand, one crucial loss of concentration on a return allowed Borg to pounce like a leopard on its prey. Not even Gerulaitis, who produced one of the most remarkable Davis Cup escapes of all time when he came back from two sets and 7–8, 0–40 down to beat Mark Edmondson in Australia, could fight his way free.

BJORN BORG *(left) and Vitas Gerulaitis in a cool, contemplatory mood before an epic battle*

FACTS
June 30
Wimbledon semi-final
Borg defeats Gerulaitis in five sets
6–4, 3–6, 6–3, 3–6, 8–6

GRIM CONCENTRATION *from John McEnroe (left) and Bjorn Borg as they arrived on court for the 1980 Wimbledon final*

Wimbledon, 1980

Tennis from Another Planet

BJORN BORG VS. JOHN McENROE EVEN THOSE BOOING AT THE START GAVE JOHN McENROE A MIGHTY OVATION AT THE END AFTER HE HAD WON WIMBLEDON'S MOST MEMORABLE TIE-BREAK, BUT BJORN BORG HAD STILL WON HIS FIFTH CONSECUTIVE TITLE

This was more than a great Wimbledon final. It was a clash of the young titans, two players who with their vastly different playing styles and temperaments were leading tennis to a new world. It produces a magnificent climax to the dampest and one of the most disappointing Championships anyone could remember. Yet the way Borg's courage and endurance brought about his victory created arguably the greatest Wimbledon final of modern times.

Certainly, those with memories stretching back almost half a century found it more impressive even than Jack Crawford's classic win over Elsworth Vines in 1933, Stan Smith's breathtaking defeat of Ilie Nastase in 1972 or even Bob Falkenburg's saving of two match points at 4–5 in the final set on his way to beating John Bromwich in 1948.

Measured in games it was three short of Jaroslav Drobny's defeat of Ken Rosewall, an emotional four-set final of 58 games in pre-tie-break days in 1954, but in time on court it was 3 hours 53 minutes, exceeding the 1954 match by more than an hour. After the extraordinary first set in which McEnroe was brilliant and Borg warily shaky, the contest became a treasure trove of memorable moments, highlighted most of all by the fourth set tie-break which became a match of its own, within a great match.

The set spanned 34 points. Borg had lost two match points in the set when leading 5–4, with diffident approach shots which were dismissed contemptuously by the American. In the tie-break, Borg had five more, four on his own serve, but McEnroe kept his chances alive with wonderfully challenging passing shots. Eventually Borg's nerve cracked and McEnroe took the set on his seventh set point.

So to the final set. In the first game McEnroe led 30–0 on Borg's serve and it looked as if Borg's dismay at losing the tie-break might be continuing. But, as in the crucial first game of the second set when he saved four break points, as McEnroe looked poised for a runaway triumph, the Swede's response was as cool as it was formidable.

He dropped only one more point on serve in the match as he held on, so that once again he could drop to his knees and kiss the trophy even more passionately than he had done before in celebration of winning the closest and most momentous of his five finals.

"I still thought the match could have slipped away from me when he recovered from 0–4 to 4–4 in the final set. Certainly, if he'd then gone ahead 5–4, I'd have been in big trouble", said Borg. "I've never felt so tired on a tennis court before."

One year later, Borg's reign was ended appropriately enough by McEnroe, but it was their 1980 final which showed both men at their best. It was also another occasion when McEnroe transformed those Centre Court boos, as he again started to question calls, once more into cheers.

FACTS

July 5
Wimbledon men's singles final
Borg beat McEnroe in five sets
1–6, 7–5, 6–3, 6–7 (16–18), 8–6

The Queen Regains Her Crown

CHRIS EVERT VS. MARTINA NAVRATILOVA THE WOMEN'S SINGLES AT THE FRENCH OPEN IN 1985, HAD NOT BEEN ONE OF THE BEST. ALL THAT CHANGED WHEN THE WORLD'S TWO BEST PLAYERS, NEITHER OF WHOM HAD DROPPED A SET, REACHED THE FINAL

Few would disagree that the greatest women's rivalry since the advent of Open tennis in 1968 has been between Chris Evert and Martina Navratilova. It began on an indoor court in Akron, Ohio, in 1973 when Evert won 7–6, 6–3, and continued for another 79 matches until their last meeting in the Virginia Slims of Chicago in 1988. Of them all, though, none matched that wondrous French Open singles final in 1985 which delighted the tennis world and gave Evert's distinguished career a fresh lease of life.

Evert was then 30. Navratilova was two years younger, but she had certainly established the upper hand in their saga after trouncing Evert on her favourite slow red clay 6–3, 6–1 a year earlier and won 15 of their previous 16 encounters. Although it did not seem quite so relevant at the time as it does today, Evert, on her way to the final in Paris that year, had beaten two supremely gifted teenagers both aged 15: Steffi Graf and then, in the semi-finals, Gabriela Sabatini.

The last time Evert had beaten Navratilova when they met in a Grand Slam had been two years earlier, before the Czech exile had served and volleyed her way to six consecutive Grand Slam tournament titles in singles and seven in doubles. Despite the odds against her, Evert, who had taken notice of Navratilova's dedicated fitness routines and stepped up her own training, was convinced that she could win,

especially if Navratilova's serve, which had appeared tentative in her semi-final against Claudia Kohde-Kilsch, was anything but at its peak.

With the help of her estranged husband, John Lloyd, with whom she was still on good terms, she worked out tactics designed to break up the attacking rhythm in Navratilova's game and then begin to plant doubts in the mind of a champion always at her best as a front runner. Basically what John advised was that Chris should hit more looping balls to the forehand, rather than hitting them flat, and give Navratilova the opportunity to chip and charge.

A gusty wind added to the pressure on Navratilova. Evert moved into a 3–0 first set lead and, although the scores were levelled at 3–3, the American's consistency and control as her number of backhand winners mounted enabled her to take the set 6–3. While the conditions and the occasion meant nerves were ragged at

times on both sides of the net and the quality of the tennis far from classic, it nevertheless steadily became a contest of epic proportions, particularly in terms of excitement. Playing in the most inspired fashion, Evert led 4–2 in the second set, with points for 5–2, but Navratilova fought back to force a tie-break which she won 7–4 helped by a crucial double fault from her opponent.

The third set became what Navratilova later called, "the closest, most suspenseful final we've ever played", as first one and then the other found added resilience, courage and skill when it was most needed. Evert led 3–1, with two points for 4–1, but was caught at 3–3. She led again at 5–3 with a brilliant running forehand pass. Yet seemingly on the point of victory, she lost 11 of the next 12 points, so that it was 5–5 and 0–40 on her serve. "I thought I'd blown it", Evert said. "There was only one thing in a situation like that. Go for a winner." In fact

Navratilova missed a forehand volley – and with it, effectively, the match. For having extricated herself from the third break point by outnerving Navratilova in a volley duel, Evert held for 6–5, reached match point one game later and unleased one of those ripping double-handed backhand passes down the line which were so often her trademark.

The players embraced warmly. Even Navratilova was able to take some comfort from her own verdict that it was, "one of the most incredible matches you can ever imagine. It had everything."

FACTS

June 8
French Open women's singles final, Roland Garros, Paris
Evert beats Navratilova in three sets
6–3, 6–7, 7–5

MARTINA NAVRATILOVA *stretches at the net during her epic encounter with Chris Evert.*

US Open, 1995

Steffi Graf Has a Point to Prove

STEFFI GRAF VS. MONICA SELES FOR ALMOST AN HOUR AFTER BECOMING THE US OPEN CHAMPION FOR THE FOURTH TIME IN SEPTEMBER 1995, STEFFI GRAF NEVER STOPPED SMILING, SOMETHING AT THE TIME SHE HAD NOT BEEN GIVEN OCCASION TO DO VERY OFTEN.

Against all expectations, Graf provided the perfect riposte to those who had hinted darkly that there was something bogus about the six Grand Slam tournament titles she had won, while Monica Seles had tried to shake off the nightmare of being stabbed during a match in Hamburg, almost two and a half years earlier.

On a day when the vast majority of the 18,000 crowd at New York's Flushing Meadow seemed ready and eager to celebrate a second coronation for Seles, they ended up instead admiring Graf for her resourcefulness, as well as her courage, as she took her chances for a 7–6, 0–6, 6–3 victory.

It had been desperately close, 96–95 for Graf in points and, as Seles observed in trying to mask the disappointment of the first defeat in her comeback, "it might have been very different" had a serve which she was convinced was an ace and would have given her the first set tie-break 8–6 not been called out.

Still fuming over the decision, Seles, who had saved five break points in the seventh game of the set and then rallied from 1–3 in the tie-break, double-faulted on the second serve and overhit two forehands to lose the tie-break 8–6. It was the first set she had dropped in the 12 matches she had played since returning to the circuit, and if Graf thought that her opponent might then crumble she was very much mistaken. Seles won every game of the second set so that 27 minutes after the first set ended the match was level.

After the first game of the final set Graf left the court to change her saturated shirt and socks. It gave her the chance she needed to gather her thoughts at a time when Seles was starting to struggle from the pressure of not having played a match so full of emotion for so long. Seles double-faulted again and made three unforced errors in being broken to 1–3 and, hard though she fought, there was little more she could do than generously applaud the stunning drives which swept her opponent on to a joyous triumph.

It was not until some considerable time later that Graf realized she had just become the first person to win all four of the Grand Slam titles at least four times. "I'm going to celebrate tonight", she said … "Very big!"

For Graf, it was her 18th Grand Slam singles title, taking her above two of the former champions she had admired most, Chris Evert and Martina Navratilova. For Seles, though, there was much over which she could rejoice. Less than a month after emerging from what had become a psychological prison to return the tour, there were signs that she had not only regained her old appetite for the game but had taken advantage of her enforced absence to improve her sometimes costly serve. Sadly there were other problems on the horizon.

FACTS

September 9
US Open final, Flushing Meadow, New York
Graf beats Seles in three sets
7–6 (8–6), 0–6, 6–3

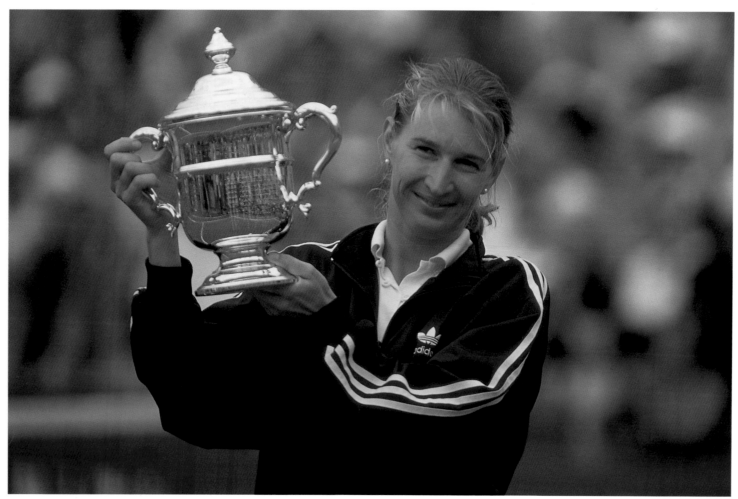

STEFFI GRAF, *triumphant at the US Open in 1995*

Boris Finds Sampras in the Mood

PETE SAMPRAS VS. BORIS BECKER IT WAS THE SHOWDOWN WHICH THE PUBLIC HOPED FOR WHEN THE ATP TOUR TOOK ITS END OF THE YEAR CHAMPIONSHIPS TO HANOVER FOR THE FIRST TIME IN 1996 – THE GERMAN HERO AGAINST THE WORLD NUMBER ONE

The inner strength which has so often saved the situation as Pete Sampras has registered his crucial victories came to his aid again with perfect timing as he beat Boris Becker in this pulsating final. Just when it looked as if the world champion would pay an enormous price for producing so many of his weaker shots at the most critical moments, the American kept his nerve and served his way out of trouble to another fine success.

Victory came at exactly four hours, on his fourth match point, and 53 minutes after his first in what he called "one of the greatest indoor matches I've ever been part of". Even in defeat Becker echoed that observation. Three days earlier in the round-robin group matches in this event bringing together the eight most successful players on the circuit in 1996, Becker had beaten Sampras in another classic contrast which was decided by two tie-breaks. It was, incidentally, the fifth time in six years that they had met in the round-robin stage of this competition and every time the loser had gone on to win the title.

There was so much to savour and remember from the way Becker, urged on by more than 15,000 spectators determined to give their hero every support, began the final with four aces, progressed to an incredible match-winning point, during which the ball crossed the net 23 times with ever-quickening pace in the longest rally of the contest before breaking down on the 24th shot when the German netted a forehand. The pace of the court meant service velocity would be a major factor and both players revelled on such a surface.

The atmosphere electric from the moment the combatants, both of whom thrive in such circumstances, appeared in the spotlight 100 steps up in the stand before slowly parading like heavyweight boxers, between a phalanx of bodyguards, down to the court. The scream of delight from Sampras when he won the second set emphasized how much the occasion meant to him. So did the way he pounced after a Becker double fault to hit an ace and then an immaculate backhand pass to win the third-set tie-break, 7–4.

Even that, though, paled alongside the fourth-set tie-break, by which time Becker, serving superbly and volleying with all his old flamboyant flair, had only conceded 18 points in 22 service games. In probably the most thrilling tie-break in any contest of this importance since John McEnroe's 18–16 success against Bjorn Borg at Wimbledon in the 1980 final, mini-breaks abounded. Becker led 5–3, but lost the next three points. Then Sampras gifted his first match point with two errant forehands and a poor serve, which was followed by a careless backhand.

No less than 10 of the first 14 points in this gripping tie-break went against the serve. Sampras survived set points at 6–7, 7–8, 9–10 and 10–11 and overhit a forehand volley after he had earned his second match point at 9–8. Then on the 24th point the American, who was struggling to overcome the pressure of the crowd's backing for his opponent, missed an easy backhand volley so that Becker won it 13–11 and they were all square at two sets each.

As at Wimbledon in 1980, however, the winner of an epic tie-break failed to win the match. One had to feel sympathy for Becker, who had missed three months of the year after rupturing a tendon in his wrist at Wimbledon. He hit far more aces (32–15), one more outright winner (75–74) and even won 12 more points (178–166) than Sampras, who finally produced the quality of returns necessary to break the German's serve for the first time in the match in the penultimate game and then served out, complete with one leaping "slam dunk" overhead, for the title and the $1.34m winner's cheque which went with it.

Becker, the winner a year earlier, when the tournament bade farewell to Frankfurt's elegant Festhalle and moved to this larger but purely functional exhibition arena, summed up a marvellous occasion as well as a superb match when he said, "That's the way tennis goes sometimes. It's an amazing sport." It was the response you had come to expect from one of the game's most flamboyant characters

CONGRATULATORY *smiles from Boris Becker after a brilliant display by Pete Sampras*

FACTS
ATP Tour Championships final
Hanover, Germany
Sampras defeats Becker in five sets
3–6, 7–6, 7–6, 6–7, 6–4

Davis Cup, Sweden, 1996

Davis Cup Drama Down to the Wire

NICKLAS KULTI VS. ARNAUD BOETSCH MANY EXPECTED THE 1996 DAVIS CUP FINAL TO FIZZLE OUT ONCE EDBERG WAS INCAPACITATED BY AN ANKLE INJURY IN THE OPENING RUBBER. INSTEAD IT WAS TO BECOME ONE OF THE MOST REMARKABLE IN THE EVENT'S HISTORY

MATCHWINNER, *Arnaud Boetsch chaired by his team-mates*

At the end of a final day's play which prompted the Swedish captain Carl-Axel Hageskog to declare, "Hitchcock couldn't have done it better", France triumphed 3–2 after the most thrilling and astonishing climax to any Davis Cup final in the 96-year history of the event. The final day's play, as Sweden kept the match alive so heroically, lasted a marathon 10 hours. It began with Thomas Enqvist recovering from two sets down to make the score 2–2 with his 3–6, 6–7, 6–4, 6–4, 9–7 defeat of Cedric Pioline.

Yet even that gripping contest paled into insignificance compared with the decider between Arnaud Boetsch and Nicklas Kulti, brought in as a substitute for Stefan Edberg, whose hopes of a fairytale and triumphant ending to his distinguished career were cruelly destroyed by the twisted right ankle he suffered in the sixth game of what became a straight-sets defeat against Pioline in the opening rubber.

The decider had everything – great winners, a fair number of nerve-ridden blunders, total commitment and determination and so many frequent changes in apparent supremacy that the neutrals among the crowd in this cramped arena on the site of an old boatyard almost hoped that there would not have to be a loser. In the end, almost 20 minutes after he had bravely saved three match points with bold serving in the 14th game of the final set, fresh-faced Boetsch became the match winner of this first Davis Cup final not to be decided until the fifth set of the fifth rubber.

Sweden had been hoping against hope that, with almost 48 hours to rest his ankle, Edberg might have been fit to play and win the crucial last rubber, as he had been when they narrowly defeated what was then West Germany in 1985. It was not to be. Yet although Kulti had registered only one singles win on the Tour since June – and that, ironically, had been the one which ended Edberg's tournament career at the Stockholm Open a month earlier – he played the match of his life against a much higher-ranked opponent.

On a court which helped Kulti's heavy hitting more than the clay on which he had lost both previous matches to Boetsch, the Swede was a shade fortunate to survive a blistering first set and take it 7–2 in the tie-break. Undeterred, Kulti snatched the next two sets 6–2, 6–4 and at the changeovers one could see French team captain Yannick Noah working hard to keep his man focused. The fourth set, like the first, went to a tie-break where a superb backhand which clipped the back of the line gave Boetsch a mini-break to lead 4–3. One point later Kulti cramped badly. He limped to the umpire's chair and sought assistance, but was reminded by referee Ken Farrar that although the ATP Tour by then allowed treatment for cramp, neither the Slams nor the Davis Cup had adopted such a fundamental rule change.

Kulti battled on. Boetsch levelled the match by taking the tie-break 7–5, but more drama followed. At 6–7 in the fifth set the Frenchman, who some years earlier had expressed the desire to play for Switzerland after he and his Swiss wife began living there, found himself at 0–40. Kulti, still limping between many of the points had somehow produced two of his biggest forehand winners of the match. Instead of then making sure, Boetsch had to find a way of winning every point. Kulti continued to go for broke not just on one of the break points but all three – and he missed three times. Boetsch escaped.

Kulti hit an ace to lead 8–7, but the cramp was returning with a painful vengeance and three games later, with the match into its fifth hour, it was his turn to defend three match points. He saved two but, swinging wildly, more in hope than judgement, overhit the third. It was all over, but there was one memorable gesture to come. Noah, the hero in particular of France's 1991 triumph in the final against the United States, ran over to where the Swedish players were consoling Kulti and then hoisted up Edberg and carried him round the court on his shoulders. There was no loser on this day, only winners, especially the credibility of the Davis Cup competition itself.

FACTS

Davis Cup final
Malmö, Sweden
Boetsch beats Kulti in five sets
7–6, 2–6, 4–6, 7–6, 10–8

Wimbledon, 2001

Wild Card Wimbledon Winner

GORAN IVANISEVIC VS. PAT RAFTER THERE CAN'T BE A MORE INCREDIBLE GRAND SLAM FINAL VICTORY THAN THIS, BETWEEN A TOP SEED AND THE WILD CARD ENTRY WHO'S CHANCES OF WINNING A WIMBLEDON TITLE APPEARED TO HAVE LONG SINCE PASSED.

Most assumed Goran Ivanisevic, who had been struggling with his fitness and confidence, had received a wild card into the 2001 Championships as a sympathy gesture in acknowledgement of his three previous unsuccessful final appearances.

What then unfolded over the coming fortnight was the stuff of fairy tales as the popular Croat went on to upset all the odds to not only reach his fourth singles final but also make history by defeating the favourite, the equally popular third seeded Pat Rafter.

The score line shows how the fortunes of the players twisted and turned as the match unfolded in front of a packed Centre Court of 13,370 spectators made up of two very partisan groups of friendly supporters proviing an atmosphere more akin to a rugby match.

The match itself was played on a third Monday, the Championships having been forced into that extension by the demands of the weather, Ivanisevic arriving for the championship round following a five-set victory over the home favourite, Tim Henman, in a semi-final which had stretched over three days.

The two protagonists then delivered a match filled with emotion, courage, brilliant tennis and a nail-biting finish. The first four sets were very much decided by brief bursts of inspiration and the odd careless shot at critical moments. The first three were won on single service breaks

GORAN IVANISEVIC *never slow in showing his emotions.*

whilst the fourth saw Ivanisevic drop his serve twice as he struggled to control his temperament. A foot-fault on a first serve followed by a double fault when he thought he had struck an ace, didn't help his demeanour.

Fortunately for all concerned he managed to calm down sufficiently for the vital fifth which Rafter, now on a roll, opened, sticking to his well established and effective serve and volley game.

Ivanisevic, playing catch up throughout the final deciding set with some steely play, came within two points of defeat on three occasions but his nerve wavered somewhat as, having broken the Australian to 15 with two glorious passes, he then double faulted twice, the second time on his first match point having struck his 27th ace of the final to earn it.

Another service winner produced his second match point with the crowd going mad as they egged on their respective favourites. Again, Ivanisevic failed to convert the point with another double-fault and was forced to work his way to two more Championship points before Rafter, having saved the first with a brilliantly executed lob then netted a backhand return, to concede the final.

That error released all the tension within Ivanisevic who burst into tears as the reality of the occasion and the incredibleness of his achievement, nine years after his first appearance in a Wimbledon final, sank in. For the crowd the occasion proved just as emotive as they rose to acknowledge a classic encounter between two great entertainers, one described as a lovable rogue and the other, one of the finest and fairest sportsmen ever to grace a tennis court.

Ivanisevic, who had climbed into the players' box to embrace his family, described those moments with the memorable 'everybody going nuts' phrase, whilst Rafter, defeated in the final for the second successive year, had nothing but praise for his victor, declaring "I'm happy for you, mate."

The victory, the Croat's only Grand Slam title, was just reward for Ivanisevic's perseverance, especially this year when his ranking, at 125, only guaranteed him a place in the Roehampton Qualifying competition. As history now records, he is the first player to lift the Wimbledon crown thanks to a wild card entry, and there could not have been a more popular victory in the annals of The Championships. There might have been better matches, but non could have matched this one for its thrills and inspiration.

FACTS

**Wimbledon final
Ivanisevic defeats Rafter
in five sets
6–3, 3–6, 6–3, 2–6, 9–7**

THE BUSINESS OF TENNIS

Just as the sport has grown out of all proportion since the advent of the Open era in 1968, so has the commercial aspect of the game. From tennis commercials, to clothing endorsements, from prize money to corporate hospitality, tennis has transcended the notion of being just a popular pastime. It has now evolved into a major business – and not just for the players.

Trying to evaluate the amount of money tennis generates in the world of business with any accuracy is virtually impossible. What one can surmise with reasonable confidence, however, is that in its own right it has become a multi-billion dollar industry and that there is at least another multi-billion dollar involvement in terms of ancillary activities.

Similarly, in terms of numbers alone, it is also impossible to state accurately how many people are involved, directly or indirectly, in the tennis business. Most believe it is at least as many as a million.

Yet a multitude of new organizations either totally or heavily involved in the financing, organizing, marketing, presenting, playing and officiating of tennis have sprung up since the green light was given for the game to be transformed from a sport into big business with the advent of Open tennis in 1968. And they in turn have spawned countless more money-making opportunities for existing industries, such as printing, catering, publishing, security and not least the design teams, architects and

construction companies involved in the countless new tennis stadiums that have been built in the last 40 years.

One indication of how the responsibilities of the International Tennis Federation have grown comes from the enormous growth in affiliated national associations, which now numbers around 140. Before Open tennis, the principal role of the ITF, apart from administering the Rules of Tennis, was overseeing the organization of the Davis Cup. Nowadays it not only plays a much more hands-on role in a Davis Cup which has more than doubled in entries over the past 25 years, but also plays a vital role in all aspects of the game from the worldwide training of officials to grass-roots opportunities in under-developed tennis nations.

Before Open tennis there were no trade associations for the men or women players to belong to. Nor was there a whole framework of employees to look after their interests from day-to-day matters, such as planning and operating the tours, to providing administrative officials, umpires, physiotherapy and other medical

staff in addition to providing support staff for the media and operating an increasingly significant information service on the internet.

One only has to consider the growth in prize money to begin appreciating just how much a business tennis has become. In 1968, when tennis became Open to all-comers (whether amateur or professional) for the first time, the total prize money at Wimbledon was £26,150 which at the dollar rate at the time was about $78,000. In 2005 it is over £10m ($17.5m). Add to that the prize money at the three other Grand Slam tournaments, the ATP Tour and the WTA Tour and you are already nearing the $200m mark.

Roger Federer, in seven years as a pro, entered the 2006 season with over $20m safely deposited in the bank from prize-money, not to mention commercial endorsements which are generally thought, at that level of the game, to at least double or triple the figure. Pete Sampras retired in 2003 having collected over $43m for his on court activities, while Boris Becker, Ivan Lendl and Stefan

Edberg earned more than $20m during their careers. Not all players make that sort of money, of course. Nevertheless there are already around 500 men and women who have become dollar millionaires from their prize money alone, so it is hardly surprising that there is also an army of commercial agents helping them to look after their money and maximize their success and popularity.

Bagnell Harvey in Britain was one of the first to realize the commercial opportunities in tennis. It was he who first persuaded Wimbledon in the early 1970s to dip their toes into the waters of corporate hospitality, which is now an enormous part of almost every event on the men's and women's tours.

One man, though, who did more than most to demonstrate, not least to the players themselves, that they were a commodity ready to be marketed aggressively, was American, Donald Dell, whose Pro-Serve organization,

AGASSI AND *and Federer promote a luxurious Dubai hotel by playing on its unique tennis court*

178

MARIA SHARAPOVA *wears a custom Nike court shoe as she prepares to serve at Wimbledon*

while no longer the leader of the pack, remains one of the three best-known in the field, along with Mark McCormack's huge International Management Group and Advantage International. Donald Dell and Arthur Ashe were close friends, as well as business partners. In 1968, after Ashe, then still an amateur, had won both the US amateur championships and the US Open, Dell was driving back to Manhattan in a taxi with Lamar Hunt, when the oil tycoon from Dallas asked him how much it would cost to persuade Ashe to turn professional and join his World Championship Tennis circuit. "A million bucks," Dell told him. Hunt gulped, for such a sum was unheard of at that stage. But the deal was done – and the bench mark set.

Nowadays the competition between management companies to sign the most promising juniors is almost as intense as the competition on court. The agents, in turn, live on the commissions they earn, not so much from a player's prize money, but from the additional earnings they can negotiate from companies who want their name to be associated with particular players or, indeed, tournaments. The more lucrative deals with players often lead to high-profile television commercials, such as those made by Andre Agassi, Pete Sampras and John McEnroe for Nike and Britain's Tim Henman for Adidas. This indicates another major branch of the tennis business – clothing and equipment, such as rackets and tennis balls.

Ion Tiriac, who has gone through the whole gamut of experiences in the world of tennis from being a player trying to make ends meet on a food allowance of $2 per day and free accomodation in private homes in the mid-1960s to one of the game's most adventurous and successful entrepreneurs, coaching and then managing players and organizing tournaments costing upwards of $15m to stage.

With the exception of Wimbledon which always announces what it calls "the surplus" (over £31m pounds in 1997 but down to 27m in 2005), rather

than the profit – all of which incidentally goes, by long-standing agreement, to the British LTA to plough back into the game in numerous ways – none of the other Grand Slams disclose their balance sheets. But Mr Tiriac says he would not be surprised if the actual turnover of a Grand Slam tournament was in the region of $400m.

Tiriac puts the average cost of staging a Masters Series tournament on the ATP Tour at between $10–15m with income generally between 20–30 per cent more than that. "All of them are making a good profit," he says. While the prize money of the next level of tournament, The International Series, is considerably less, that is often offset by the amount of appearance

money paid to attract the players who organizers feel will do most, in turn, to attract extra spectators and perhaps also extra courtside sponsorship. The going rate in that respect seems to range from $50,000 to a staggering $500,000 which a handful of the top box-office names can demand.

Tournament income is derived from a wide range of sources, over and above ticket receipts. Direct sponsorship, especially where a company or product name is included in the title of the event as, for instance, The NASDAQ-100 Championships, is usually one of the most significant. Although it may not be generally realized, sponsorship of tennis stretches back long before the advent of authorized

prize money. "Robinson's", is thought to have been the first product not directly linked to tennis, to have seen the commercial value of becoming associated with the sport. It was first made available to players on both the Centre and No. 1 Courts at Wimbledon in 1934. One of the first examples of a tournament itself being sponsored was in 1965, when the tobacco company, Rothmans, who went on to figure prominently in the field for the next decade or so, gave their support to the pre-Wimbledon international tournament at Beckenham, which, though more than 100 years old, was eventually killed off by the British LTA.

The cost of sponsorship natural-

DONALD DELL, *one of the pioneers in selling tennis*

ly varies according to the grade and appeal of the event concerned, though on the regular men's and women's tours, it is probably safe to suggest the figures range from $250,000 to upwards of $2m. Despite the ban on tobacco sponsorship, which at one time was expected to have hit the sport quite seriously, tennis, with its almost equal appeal among both sexes and across a wide spectrum of ages, can point to a long list of quality companies eager to be on board. From the motor industry alone one can think of Mercedes Benz, Opel, Peugeot, Rover and Ford. The computer industry, is equally represented by such companies as IBM, Compaq and Corel. In the past, Volvo, Commercial Union, Nabisco and of course Virginia Slims, pioneering sponsors of women tennis, are among the other giant companies who have made major investments in the game.

Marketing, in all its various forms, from souvenir programmes to package ticket and hospitality deals offered to travel companies, are also now an accepted and important part of the tennis business, so much so that at Wimbledon it is a worldwide, all-the-year-round activity. The Wimbledon Merchandising programme was started by The All England Club in 1979 with three main objectives: to increase awareness of The Championships throughout the world; to enhance further the image of The Championships; and to provide as broad an income base as possible for the one major tournament without direct major sponsorship.

It has 36 licensees in ten countries and until the economic recession in the Far East at the start of 1998, the Japanese market accounted for approximately 50 per cent of the total sales of merchandise, which, in 1997, totalled about $50 million. Among the principal products licensed are tennis and casual wear, footwear, tennis rackets, bags and balls. In addition the Club licenses a select, luxury range of items such as towels, leather goods, sunglasses, crystal, chinaware and jewellery. It has its own Wimbledon Shop in the Royal Arcade in London's Old Bond Street, "Shop in Shop" outlets in Harrods, Lillywhites and Duty Free

departments at the two main London airports, Heathrow and Gatwick. The trademarks of the Wimbledon crossed rackets and flying "W" are registered in more than 40 countries.

During 1998 there were several developments which demonstrated the staggering costs and rewards, depending on whether you are a giver or receiver, in tennis. As has already been mentioned, Wimbledon broke the £7 million barrier in prize money for the first time; the WTA Tour found a new overall sponsor willing to pay them their asking price of $2 million in return for having their name attached to all the Tour's activities for the next three years and the German Tennis Federation unveiled a new-style, umbrella roof which allows them more or less unbroken play on the Centre Court in Hamburg during tournaments and Davis Cup matches. The cost, a cool £6.5 million.

Television, not surprisingly, is a key player in the tennis business. One of the first tasks of any tournament organiser, especially those launching a new venture, is to ensure that the event receives as much exposure as possible in the markets regarded as those most important to the principal sponsor. On the other hand, Wimbledon with worldwide coverage every year in around 170 countries, does not have such concerns in that respect – indeed, it is the only professional event without advertising boards round the courts. And there are even occasions when tournaments would prefer not to have blanket worldwide exposure. That happened when tobacco sponsorship was still allowed, for there was one well known cigarette which, despite having the same name, was actually marketed by rival companies in different parts of the world.

Such a problem, though, is the exception rather than the rule. Once a television contract has been signed it makes the rest of the commercial package, such as attracting main and subsidiary sponsors, that much easier to slot into place. With the exception of the Grand Slams, income from television appears to have slipped from when German tennis ruled in the late 1980s and early 1990s.

In turn, though, television needs to know in advance that the tourna-

ment will have the support of a number of sufficient box-office players for them to attract enough viewers to make it worth their while and, even more importantly as far as commercial channels are concerned, sufficient advertising during the air time the tennis coverage is given. As such, there is virtually no end to the spread of the tentacles of the tennis business. Television coverage does not just help to fund the tennis itself, it also gives considerable employment to those who work for them, from commentators and researchers to a host of backroom staff.

Just as the game has grown beyond most people's expectations in the past 30 years, so too has the media circus which follows the game. At the US Open, for instance, where tennis does not enjoy the same degree of broad support which it does in many European countries, I recall that on my first visit to Forest Hills in 1971, there were about 70 full-time, accredited tennis writers, including 12 from Britain. In 1998, they were expecting close to 1,000 applications, including still, 12 from Britain.

ROGER FEDERER *answers questions from the media at an Australian Open press conference*

In turn, the cities which stage major events, such as Grand Slams and events such as the Nasdaq-100 in the Miami suburb of Key Biscayne, are also clear beneficiaries of the tennis business, as players, officials, the media and above all spectators, flock in to fill hotel rooms and restaurants.

While perhaps still not as comprehensive as in other sports, such as soccer, baseball and American football, the growing souvenir side of tennis is also big business and in recent years tennis memorabilia too has opened up a new, thriving market, as successful auctions in London just before Wimbledon, have illustrated.

What was once little more than a cottage industry, activated in different places at different times of the year according to where the leading tournaments were being played, tennis is now a multi-national business corporation, operating worldwide 365 days a year.

THE WIMBLEDON SHOP *in the Royal Arcade, Old Bond Street*

THE RULES OF TENNIS

Considering the major changes which have taken place in almost every other aspect of the game which can trace its roots back to 1859 when a Birmingham solicitor, Major Harry Gem and a friend marked out a lawn in Edgbaston to play a game they called tennis, the rules, once early problems were overcome, have changed surprizingly little.

Although the professional men's and women's tours both have their own rulebooks, differing slightly on what might be called ancillary matters, such as the time allowed for treatment during a match, the International Tennis Federation remains the principal architect and guardian of the Rules of Tennis.

It has its own rules committee, which is constantly examining ideas or formal proposals for changes, some of them minute, others reasonably significant as the game realizes that it is in its best interests to keep up with the changing needs of time, while simultaneously maintaining the true character of the sport.

That being so, once the fairly comprehensive alterations made to the original rules prepared by none other than the tennis committee of the Marylebone Cricket Club (MCC) in 1875 were carried out, there have been surprizingly few changes, save for the introduction of the tie-break and amendments to the foot-fault rule, for the last 100 years.

Initially, the idea was to retain the hour-glass shape of the court devised by Major Walter Clopton Wingfield, acknowledged as one of the founders of the game with the solicitor and magistrate, Major Harry Gem, 78ft long, 30ft wide at the baseline and 24ft wide in the middle. The net was to a height of 5ft at the sides and 4ft in the middle, with the service court extending 26ft from the net and the foot of the server kept outside the baseline. As in several other racket games, points (up to 15 to win a game) could only be won by the server, who continued to have "hand in" until he lost a rally.

By the time the first Wimbledon Championships were staged, the committee of The All England Club, seemingly without demur from the MCC, opted for major changes; the most significant of which was to have a rectangular court, 78ft x 27ft, as we do today, and scoring in general as it is now. In addition, the height of the net at the centre was reduced to 3ft 3in. Over the next five years various further changes were made, with the height of the net at the posts gradually being reduced by 1892 to its current level of 3ft 6in and 3ft at the centre (the latter was introduced in 1878).

In 1880 the service line was changed to 21ft from the line, just as it is today, while in the same year the "let" serve was introduced. Hitherto a ball touching the net but otherwise being good was allowed to stand. The modern wording of the Rules of Tennis illustrate how well most of them have stood the test of time.

The Court

The court shall be a rectangle 78ft (23.77m) long and 27ft (8.23m) wide. It shall be divided across the middle by a net suspended from a cord or metal cable of a maximum diameter of one-third of an inch (0.8cm), the ends of which shall be attached to, or pass over, the tops of the two posts which shall be not more than 6 inches (15cm) square or 6 inches (15cm) in diameter. These posts shall not be higher than 1 inch (2.5cm) above the top of the net cord. The centres of the posts shall be 3ft (0.914m) outside the court on each side and the height of the posts shall be such that the top of the cord or metal cable shall be 3ft 6ins (1.07m) above the ground.

When a combined doubles and singles court with a doubles net is used for doubles, the net must be supported to a height of 3ft 6ins (1.07m) by means of two posts called singles sticks, which shall be not more than 3ins (7.5cm) square or 3ins (7.5cm) in diameter. The centres of the singles sticks shall be 3ft (0.914m) outside the singles court on each side.

The net shall be extended fully so that it fills completely the space between the two posts and shall be of sufficiently small mesh to prevent the ball passing through [even though with the pace of today's serving that still does sometimes happen]. The rules go on to point out how the net should be maintained at 3ft in the centre in a taut condition by a strap of not more than 2 ins (5cm) wide and completely white in colour. There shall be a band covering the cord or metal cable and the top of the net of not less than 2ins (5cm) nor more than 2.5ins (6.3cm) in depth on each side and completely white in colour. There shall be no advertisement on the net, strap band or singles sticks.

However, as anyone who has regularly watched matches on the ATP Tour will realize, since Mercedes Benz became one of their major sponsors this is an aspect of the rule which they have not accepted, for the familiar logo of the

HOW *sponsorship has taken over*

German motor company is visibly displayed on both sides of the net within what would normally be the doubles court extension.

For those who remember the squiggly lines which one used to find on grass courts all over the country in the less sophisticated days when club members took it in turn to try, not always very neatly, to spot what was left from the last time the job had been done, the accuracy demanded today can come as quite a shock. The official wording says: "The lines bounding the ends of the court shall respectively be called the baselines and the sidelines. On each side of the net, at a distance of 21ft (6.40m) from it and parellel with it, shall be drawn the service lines. The space on each side of the net between the service-line and the sidelines shall be divided into two equal parts called the service courts, by the centre service-line, which must be 2ins (5cm) in width, drawn half-way between and parellel with the sideline. Each baseline shall be bisected by an imaginary continuation of the centre service line to a line 4ins (10cm) in length and 2ins (5cm) in width, called 'the centre mark', drawn inside the court at right angles to and in contact with such baselines. All other lines shall

be not less than 1in (2.5cm) nor more than 2ins (5cm) in width, except the baseline, which may be not more than 4ins (10cm) in width. All measurements shall be made to the outside of the lines. All lines shall be of uniform colour. If advertising or any other material is placed at the back of the court, it may not contain white or yellow. A light colour may only be used if this does not interfere with the vision of the players.

Permanent Fixtures

Most of the permanent fixtures on a tennis court are pretty obvious – the net, the posts etc., as mentioned in the rules governing the court. It is not always realized, though, that the list extends beyond the obvious. For instance, fixed or movable seats within the court and their occupants, such as the umpire, the net-cord judge and linespersons are all regarded as permanent fixtures. And so, too, are the ball boys and girls when in their respective places. So if a ball strikes any of them while it is still in play, the point continues. Similarly if a player collides with the net cord judge then it is just his or her bad luck if it proves impossible for them to play the shot.

There was a spectacular example of that at Wimbledon in 1993 when

Chris Bailey, who had a match point in the second round before losing to Goran Ivanisevic, raced in to meet an angled drop shot and despite trying to leap over the net cord judge, finished up in a heap on top of her. Similarly during the doubles in Britain's 1998 Davis Cup match against the Ukraine in Newcastle, Andrei Medvedev complained that he had been prevented from reaching another angled drop shot from Tim Henman because one of the ball boys, kneeling at the base of the net, was in his way. As the umpire explained, as the ball boy was in his correct position, he counted as a permanent fixture and therefore there was no case for ordering the point to be replayed.

Another more recent innovation has been the introduction of Hawk-Eye, the electronic line calling device, used over recent years during TV coverage of matches. Originally conceived as a visual aid for viewers, it has now developed into a drama enhancing feature at tennis matches, whilst aiding the umpire with close calls.

Players are now allowed two challenges per set and another during any tiebreak. Once the challenge is accepted, the video showing the

flight of the ball is shown on the big screens overlooking the courts allowing spectators and players to see the official result, in or out. If the player's challenge is proved wrong, he forfeits the challenge so he can challenge as often as he likes provided he gets it right! Two wrong in a set and the player can't query another call until the following set.

Hawk-Eye was first used at the 2006 Nasdaq-100 and is being seriously considered by the majors, though Roland Garros, with its easily marked clay courts, may not feel the investment to be necessary. However, the US Open became the first of the grand slam venues to adopt it on two of its showcourts. Currently the success rate of correct challenges is about one-third in favour of the player.

The Ball

Much has been said and written in recent years about the need to reduce the pressure in the balls to take some of the extra advantage the server has derived from modern rackets, which enable players to generate much more power without any extra physical effort. Each year the International Tennis Federation makes a list of the type of balls which have been approved and only these are allowed for use in a tournament, such as the Grand Slams, Davis Cup and Fed Cup, played under the Rules of Tennis.

Basically the ball shall have a uniform outer surface and shall be white or yellow in colour. If there are any seams they shall be stitchless. Yellow balls were first introduced in the mid-1970s by World Championships Tennis, the Dallas-based organization which began operating before Open tennis and ran its own tournament circuit for ten years. The idea for using yellow instead of the traditional white balls, which continued to be chosen at Wimbledon until 1986, was because it was found that once colour television took a hold, they were easier to see for the viewer at home.

A tennis ball has to weigh more than two ounces but less than two and one-sixteenth ounces and have a bounce of more than 53ins

(134.62cm) and less than 58ins (147.32cm), when dropped from 100ins (254cm) upon a concrete base. As for the other dimensions, unless you are a ball manufacturer or a ball tester for the ITF, they are too complicated to worry about in a journal such as this. Sufficient to say that in matches played over 4,000ft above sea level, what is called a pressurized ball may be used.

The Racket

Incredibly not until 1976 were there any rules governing the size, weight, shape or material used in the manufacture of a tennis racket. It was merely an implement with which to hit the ball. Even a dustbin lid could have been used. It was then, though, with the advent of first the steel racket pioneered by Jimmy Connors, the so-called Prince "jumbo racket" and the loosely strung "spaghetti racket", that the International Tennis Federation felt it was time to draw up specific rules for first rackets and then the stringing. With hindsight there are many who regret that a great opportunity was lost at that time to stipulate that only rackets made of wood should be allowed for use, at least in major competitions. Certainly it might have at least limited the increase in power play which some feel has taken too much of the skill factor out of matches in men's tennis.

Today's rules insist that: "The hitting surface of the racket shall be flat and consistent of a pattern of crossed strings connected to a frame and alternately interlaced or bonded where they cross; and the stringing pattern shall be generally uniform and, in particular, not less dense in the centre than in any other area. The strings shall be free of attached objects and protrusions other than those utilized solely and specifically to limit or prevent wear and tear or vibration and which are reasonable in size and placement for such purpose."

Even so, worried it seemed by the threat of legal action if they acted unilaterally, it was not until 1996, after lengthy consultations with all those affected, including the racket manufacturers and player agents, that a maximum size for a racket was approved to take effect on January 1,

1997. For professional play the frame of the racket shall not exceed 29ins (73.66cm) in overall length, including the handle, and the frame of the racket shall not exceed 12.5ins (31.75cm) in overall width. The string surface shall not exceed 15.5ins (39.37cm) in overall length and 11.5ins (29.21cm) in overall width. The rule governing the length of rackets does not affect non-professional players until January 1, 2000.

Server and Receiver

The Rules of Tennis, which one must remember have been drafted to help those who may never have seen tennis being played – and there are still some – just as much as to provide answers to queries which crop up from time to time, seem somewhat simplistic at times. For instance, "The players shall stand on opposite sides of the net; the player who first delivers the ball shall be called the Server and the other the Receiver."

On the other hand the addendums go on to answer some of the queries which often arise when beginners are playing in a local park, such as can the receiver stand where he likes on his side of the net to await the serve? The answer is "yes". Similarly in doubles, both the server and his partner may stand on the same side of the court if they so wish, a technique called "the Australian formation" because Australians were the first to use it, even if it does sometimes result in the server's partner being hit on the back of the

head by the ball. Just ask Mark Woodforde or Todd Woodbridge!

Choice of Ends and Service

The choice of ends and the right to be Server or Receiver in the first game shall be decided by the toss (usually nowadays with the use of a coin, although when only wooden rackets were used, one player would spin the racket and the other would guess rough or smooth, according to which face of the racket was upwards when it fell). The player winning the toss may choose or require his opponent to choose whether he/she wants to serve or receive.

If one player chooses the right to serve first the other shall then choose the end at which he wants to be when the match starts. Similarly if the first player opts for a particular end of the court then the opponent will decide which of them shall serve first. Incidentally, if for any reason a match is postponed or suspended before it has started then when it resumes the toss stands, but new choices may be made with respect to service and end.

The Service

The Server shall stand with both feet at rest behind the baseline and within imaginary continuations of the centre-mark and sidelines. The Server shall then project the ball by hand into the air in any direction and before it hits the ground strike it with his racket. The delivery shall be deemed to have been completed at the moment of impact of the racket and the ball. A player with the use of only one arm (this section was introduced in 1947 for the benefit of players like Austrian Davis Cup player, Hans Redl, who lost an arm in the 1939–45 war), may utilize his racket for the projection of the ball.

Foot Fault

This is a rule which has been changed more than most over the years, but which still causes enormous controversy. Originally, in addition to the clause that the server must not change his position, it stressed that the server had to "maintain contact with the ground" as well as keep both feet behind the baseline. In other words, no swinging of one foot over

PETE SAMPRAS *shows his perfect service action*

the lines in the follow through, which was first permitted in 1959, and none of what is effectively a jump into the court, providing there is no contact with the line or the court inside the line at the moment of impact, which was eventually approved in 1975.

Nowadays the rule reads: "The Server shall throughout the delivery of the service not change his position by walking or running. The Server shall not, by slight movements of the feet which do not materially affect the location originally taken up by him, be deemed to 'change his position by walking or running'. The Server shall not touch, with either foot, any area other than that behind the base-line within the imaginary extension of the centre mark and side-lines.

Hence the number of players who literally leap several inches off the ground when they deliver the serve, often with their body leaning forward in such a way that they can be half way to the net ready to volley a return, almost as soon as their serve is reaching the other player. The foot-fault is probably the most common offence in tennis but, judging by the number of arguments which occur, also the most difficult, in some cases, to pick out by officials. The look of disbelief on some players when they are called for foot-faulting raises a wry smile from those who have heard that same player (and there are many who fall into this cat-egory) later complain for the umpteenth time that he or she has never ever been foot-faulted before. At the same time line judges do make mistakes and Ion Tiriac, the former Romanian Davis Cup player who is now a major player in the international business world, once went to extreme lengths to point this out to an official who he sensed was making the call too early for him to have judged it accurately. The next time the cry of "foot-fault" was heard, instead of completing his service action, Tiriac checked, caught the ball and looked at the embarrassed offi-cial, as if to say, "I beg your pardon?"

Service Fault

In many cases, a faulty serve is obvi-ous – if the ball fails to cross the net,

lands outside the relevant service court on the Receiver's side of the net or if, as can happen among beginners, the Server goes through with the full service action but misses the ball in the attempt to strike it. What some beginners do not realize is that whereas a ball remains in play if it hits one of the various permanent fixtures, such as a net post in a rally, if it does so on a serve it is a fault, wherever it lands after that. The one exception is that if the serve hits the net itself and lands within the proper service court. In that case a let is called.

After a first fault on a point, the server shall serve again from behind the same half of the court from which he originally served. If the player then hit a second (or double) fault that point is lost. Serving underarm is per-fectly legitimate.

Order of Service

At the end of the first game, the Receiver becomes the Server and vice-versa. In doubles all four players take it in turns from alternating teams, to serve one game each in the same order until the end of a set when the order of serving within a team can be changed. Players change ends at the end after the first, third and every sub-sequent alternate game of each set and also at the end of each set unless the total number of games played in the set is even, in which case the next change is not until after the first game of the following set.

Scoring

The scoring within a game remains the same today as it was 100 years ago. A minimum of four points are need-ed to win a game, with the scoring going 15, 30, 40, game. In the event of a game reaching 40–40, or deuce, as it is called, then it is the first player who then established a lead of two points who wins the game. Tie breaks, which have become the norm in most events except in the fifth (or final) set of matches at Wimbledon, the French Open, Australian Open, Davis Cup and Fed Cup, were first used in the mid-1960s in the Prentice Cup, a bi-annual competition involving Oxford and Cambridge Universities against Harvard and Yale. In that instance a sudden death

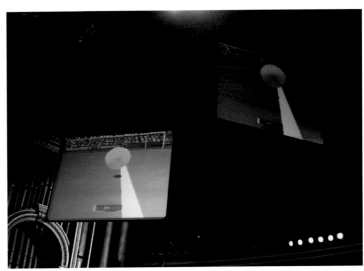

HAWKEYE *used to overule a line judge in a Masters match in 2005.*

best of nine points game was played so that at 4–4, both players were at set or match point. When the tie-break was introduced at Wimbledon in 1971, it was what was called the 8–8 tie-break, ie., the first player to reach nine points with a lead of two. In 1979, the tie-break in all but the final set was introduced when a set score reached 6–6, as is the case today.

However, in 2006 the ATP introduced scoring changes for their doubles events with the object of reducing time on court and increas-ing the profile of the disipline to improve public awareness and appeal. As a result, the matches are contested over two tie-break sets with games, should they reach deuce (40-40), being settled by the winner of the next point in a 'sudden death' move. Also, should the contestants split sets (i.e. one set-all) then the final third set is played out on a 'Champi-onship tie-break' basis, that is the first pair to reach ten with a two point advantage. At the time of writing these rules only apply to the ATP Tour events.

Miscellaneous

There is not room to reproduce in detail every Rule. In any case, sever-al tend to overlap others and to some extent are repetitive, but there are other matters worth noting. Although a ball remains in play if it hits anything regarded as a perma-nent fixture, that it not the case if it touches the player due to play the next shot or anything which he is

wearing. There was controversy during the US Open doubles final in 1985 when Ken Flach apparently did not feel the ball brush through his hair and won a crucial point he and Robert Seguso should have lost. A player also loses the point if he vol-leys the ball before it has passed the net or if he throws his racket at and hits the ball. It is the same if a play-er deliberately changes the shape of the racket during the playing of the point, although it is difficult to imagine that happening.

The shape of a racket is deliber-ately changed often enough when tempers become frayed, but that then becomes a disciplinary matter. That can be one of a series of offences, including verbal abuse, which can result in a player being warned. A sec-ond offence brings a point penalty, a third brings disqualification. How-ever, in 2006 the ATP introduced scor-ing changes for their doubles events with the object of reducing time on court and increasing the profile of the discipline to improve public aware-ness and appeal. As a result, the matches are contested over two tie-break sets with games, should they reach deuce (40-40) being settled by the winner of the next point in a 'sud-den death' move. Also should the con-testants split sets (i.e. one set-all) then the final third deciding set is played out on a 'Championship Tie-break' basis, that is the first pair to reach ten with a 2-point advantage. At the time of writing these rules only applied to ATP Tour events.

EQUIPMENT

The sales of tennis equipment, be it rackets, clothing or shoes, are often thought to provide a reliable guide to the overall health of the sport. Inevitably, as in any world trade, sales fluctuate, but the proliferation of companies which have joined the tennis market reflect the ever-growing, universal appeal of the game.

By far the biggest transformation in tennis equipment in recent years has involved rackets. Not only has the size, shape and materials used to make them changed dramatically, but compared with the pre-Open tennis era, one only has to walk into any major sports goods store to realize that the range of rackets now on offer, is enormous.

Older readers will recall how when they first played tennis, the choice of racket was limited to little more than six in most countries and in some cases not even as many as that. Almost all were made of wood and they had to be kept in presses to prevent them warping. Nowadays there are no commercial manufacturers of wooden rackets, although Grays of Cambridge, England, remains one of the very few companies that still has the equipment to make wooden frames for squash and Real Tennis rackets. Technology, coupled with new space-age and sturdier materials,

such as graphite, have banished almost all wooden rackets to lofts, as keepsakes, or to museums, such as those at Wimbledon, Newport Rhodes Island and, most recently, at Roland Garros in Paris. Various materials were tried by different companies, including titanium, which combines lightness, in terms of weight and strength, so well but it is extremely expensive. In the end, though, the graphite or composite rackets seem to have proved the most cost-effective and acceptable material used to make rackets.

Worldwide there are now probably close to 100 firms, large and small, which make tennis rackets, although the number of major international players in the field are no more than 15–20, with the most recent surveys at tournaments such as the Grand Slams indicating that the six most pop-

A TREASURED COLLECTION *of some of the earliest rackets*

HUNDREDS *of wooden racket frames awaiting distribution in bygone days*

ular among both professional and recreational players are Prince, Wilson, Head, Dunlop, Pro-Kennex and Slazenger – although, it must be said that this can vary considerably from country to country.

Curiously enough, until 1975, there were neither rules governing the size, shape or weight of rackets, nor the materials from which they could be made. There were also no rules on stringing. Now, however, there are specific rules applying to both. It was not until new methods of manufacturing rackets and in a few cases the growing number of pioneers eager to take extravagant advantage of new opportunities came into being, that it

became apparent that the time for the International Tennis Federation had arrived. Although over the previous 100 years the method of construction and the choice of materials had occasionally changed, the size seldom varied from 25–27ins long (63.5cm to 68.6cm) and a weight range between 12.5oz–16oz (354.4–467.8gms).

Yet, just as today, some broke away from traditional shapes and sizes. One of the most striking was the Donnisthorpe, a huge, loosely-strung racket which F.W. Donnisthorpe built for his own use at Wimbledon in the early 1920s, but apart from attracting enormous publicity, it never caught on, except that tales about it became relevant again almost 50 years on with the arrival of the short-lived, double-strung "Spaghetti" racket. Back in the 1920s

one could also find a limited number of square-shaped rackets; some were completely round, while also about that time, one company incorporated a small pointed gadget on the end of the handle which could be turned after each point so that the player could keep the score.

Metal frames, which had initially been made with wire stringing some 40 years earlier, started to become popular in the late 1960s and early 1970s, but many of the more fundamental changes had started to take place during the 1930s. Racket shafts began to be slimmer. Instead of one-piece frames, laminated frame construction began to give rackets the extra strength they needed to cope with the stresses on them as harder balls were introduced into the game. It was also around then that rackets,

which hitherto had mostly been produced with a natural timber finish, started to be painted, with the designs and motifs accentuating the growing competition between manufacturers.

One man who did much to launch what was to become the tennis racket revolution, was the American, Howard Head, already renowned as the founder of the Head Ski company. When he switched his attention to tennis and joined forces with the company making Prince ball machines to produce the first "jumbo" racket, as it was called, it was the most talked about change in racket design and manufacture since Wilson had introduced their steel T-2000 in 1967. Nowadays rackets with an oversized head are quite common. In 1976, though, they were a sensation and only

THE CONTRAST *with the modern racket is clear to see*

ANDRE AGASSI *taking off in Nike footwear illustrates how shoes have become a major fashion item*

speeded up the demands on the ITF to lay down rules for the future.

The Prince Classic largely succeeded because of the benefit it clearly offered to the average club or recreational player. In time, virtually every other racket manufacturer followed in this direction and if you look around the courts at Wimbledon or any of the other Grand Slam tournaments, it is doubtful if you will find many not using a racket which at least falls into the midsize or oversize category.

Different players look for different things in a racket and that does not always mean that the most expensive one – or even the one for which they will be paid the most money to use – is necessarily the right one for them. It has to be a question of which one suits each individual the player the best, i.e. the one with which they feel most comfortable and in which they have the most confidence. At the same

time almost everyone is looking for a racket which combines the right strength with the right weight and degree of stiffness and vibration dampening for them, to reduce the risk of undue strain on ligaments or muscles in the arm. And because of the modern materials, many of today's rackets, while larger than 20–30 years ago, do indeed weigh less than some of their cherished heirlooms.

In fact one of the most recent new models from Head, although 28.5ins long, weighs only 8oz and the average weight these days is between 10oz and 12oz, a reduction of around 20 per cent since the days of wooden rackets.

Andrew Coe, former technical manager for the International Tennis Federation, says: "What happened when graphite came in was that it allowed racket manufacturers to become a lot more adventurous in fundamental designs. For a start the new lighter material allowed for rackets

with larger heads, which has easily been the biggest single improvement in racket technology over the last 30 years."

Scientists have played an increasingly vital role in the production of almost all sports equipment, especially tennis, for they can now prove how tennis power essentially comes from a property within the racket called stiffness. "Stiffer rackets are by definition more powerful because they don't absorb as much energy as wooden rackets used to do," Coe points out. "Ideally you want the racket to absorb as little energy as possible so that the energy is then transferred back to the ball."

Much of that added stiffness has been provided by increasing the cross-section of the frame, which in turn accounts for the description "wide bodies". The contrast with the past is immense. "In the days of wooden rackets, a typical Dunlop Maxply Fort was 70 square inches. Today it is

very difficult to find a racket of a size below 90 square inches and most of the professionals use rackets of 100 square inches. Over and above that there are even some rackets on the market covering 135 square inches though most of these are only for recreational use."

As for the added length of rackets, these are now restricted in professional tennis to 29ins which has applied to all tennis since 2000. "Again, this extra length has only been made possible by the new techniques and materials which give you more hitting power with less racket weight," adds Coe. "In the old days if you had a racket which was 29ins long I doubt if anyone would have been able to wield it properly let alone win matches. What the new technology has done is push the boundaries of what is possible, way back."

For almost as long as anyone can remember, even in the earliest days, racket manufacturers have used players to help them popularize their wares. The Renshaws, the Dohertys and Arthur Gore, Wimbledon champion for the first time in 1901, all had rackets named after them, while in more modern times, the Jack Kramer Wilson racket was a fine example of the same policy. Although Open tennis did not begin until 1968, under-the-counter payments to persuade star players to use their rackets were commonplace long before that. Slazenger, for instance, were paying Fred Perry through Slazenger Australia in the 1930s. It was just a case of the companies finding the best way in the pre-computer age to make the payments without anyone finding out. Plenty of other players had similarly clandestine deals.

It was not only the star players who benefitted. Dunlop-Slazenger were pioneers when it came to giving players of varying standards what were quaintly named "terms" whereby, depending on what was thought to be their commercial advertising value, the players would either be on the free list for rackets and clothing, the half trade-price list or the trade-price list.

Since Open tennis, of course, it has been a case of "open sesame" so far as payments to players are concerned for endorsing rackets, shoes and almost anything else, with usually reliable sources indicating three-year contracts worth around $25m paid by Nike to their clothing clients such as André Agassi and Pete Sampras. Among the most successful in terms of racket promotion has been the marathon association Jimmy Connors had with Wilson to promote the Wilson T2000 steel racket. Yet although Wilson had the license to market it under their name in the United States, it was actually made by Lacoste.

John McEnroe, who was the last player to win Wimbledon using a wooden racket in 1981 and the first to win it using a graphite racket two years later was one of the sponsoring pioneers of the Dunlop Max 200G, along with Steffi Graf, while for most of his major tournament career, Bjorn Borg was involved with Donnay. Indeed it was often thought in Belgium that the success of the factory there fluctuated according to the amount of success that the Swedish player was enjoying at the time.

In terms of tennis balls, as explained in the section on the Rules of Tennis, there are strict guidelines as to their size and weight, with variations allowed to take account of where they are being used, for altitude can obviously have a considerable affect on how fast a ball flies when it is struck. There are far more recognized manufacturers of tennis balls round the world than there are racket makers, with much of the production now coming from China, India and the Far East. As for the most popular name brands, Penn, in 1998, was the biggest seller according to information held by the International Tennis Federation, with Wilson, Dunlop, Slazenger (their tennis balls have been used at Wimbledon since before the First World War) and Nassau among the others manufacturers with the biggest market share.

Tennis shoes, which should also be classified as tennis equipment, have also undergone major changes in design, quality and indeed colours. Compared with pre-Open days, they often look much bulkier, but in many instances they are so well cushioned and offer a better tread that they feel lighter. The important thing is to choose the right type of footwear for specific surfaces, especially on grass. At Wimbledon, for instance, players can only use what are approved as grass court shoes not only for their own benefit but because of the damage other shoes might cause to the courts. Needless to say, they have become major fashion item.

NEW BALLS PLEASE! *Traditional white balls are now consigned to history*

POLITICS

It has often been suggested by many of the game's keenest observers, paricularly since money started pouring into the sport, that tennis needed its own commissioner, someone who could ensure that the many talents and the various, sometimes competing groups vying for them, were channelled in the most profitable manner for the game as a whole. It is easier said than done.

The principal cultural and political changes which the world of tennis has undergone since its formation, particularly over the last 50 years, have almost all, with the exception of apartheid in South Africa – infinitely more than just a sporting issue – involved the struggle for control of the game. It remains the same today, except that now more than ever, the degree and range of control equates to the breakdown in the way money is distributed in the game. Increasingly that is the only thing which seems to matter.

Before the First World War tennis generally retained its reputation as being essentially a recreational sport for the upper classes and their families, with many a court to be found on vicarage lawns. Steadily, though, pioneered by shrewd and extravagant personalities such as Suzanne Lenglen, one of the first to realize how much money she was generating for others, and champions such as Fred Perry from far humbler backgrounds, everything began to change.

It was as early as the mid-1930s, when Perry was so dominant and there were already hints that it would only be a matter of time before he accepted professional offers, that the idea of Open tennis was first mooted, by a member of The All England Club at the annual meeting of the British LTA. Yet it was not until

1958 that the ten-year campaign needed to bring it about first attracted serious attention. The LTA accepted guidelines from the International Lawn Tennis Federation, aimed at finding a compromise between amateurism, in the true sense, and modern circumstances, which acknowledged that international players at least, had to be paid enough to live, as well as to travel. Among other things the new rules limited expense-paid play abroad to 150 days a year.

Already, though, there were more far-sighted observers who realized that it would only be a matter of time before the best players, as in the 1930s, would start flocking to the professional ranks if they were not able to make a reasonable living all the year round. As A.D. Knight, father of British Davis Cup player, Bill Knight, was recorded as asking at the time, "If the players are only allowed to receive expenses for 240 days a year at home or abroad, who employs them for the other three or four months?"

Two years later Britain, United States, France and Australia, supported moves at the annual meeting of the ILTF in Paris that Open tennis should be permitted. The motion for reform was passed by 135–75, but was five votes short of the required two-thirds majority. The disappointment and anger was not molified when it became known why the move failed.

It transpired that one delegate bearing three votes which would have been in favour, missed it because he was organizing an excursion on the Seine, another because the delegate was asleep and a fifth because he was in the lavatory.

Seven years on, by which time Texan oil millionaire, Lamar Hunt, was beginning to emerge from the shadows as the banker for one of two professional tours annually luring the best amateurs into their ranks, John Newcombe, the 1967 Wimbledon champion and Tony Roche decided it was also time for them to join them. Herman David, chairman of The All England Club, who had already demonstrated his growing exasperation by expressing fear for the long-term credibility of major championships if no established names took part, decided it was time to act. He prompted Wimbledon to stage a professional championship on the Centre Court and publicly denounced amateur tennis at the highest level as "a living lie". Furthermore, he stated that no matter what any other tournament might do, Wimbledon would accept entries from amateur and professionals alike in 1968.

In the months leading to an extraordinary meeting of the ILTF, there was much heart-searching among many of the nations as to whether they could bow to what some of them viewed as an ultimatum from

Wimbledon which was soon to have full support from the British LTA, even though it left them open to expulsion from both the ILTF and the Davis Cup if things went wrong. Two crusading speeches by Derek Penman – framed handwritten copies of which are now in the Wimbledon Lawn Tennis Museum – helped swing the LTA decision. The second, at the annual meeting in December, stressed that the fight for Open tennis was not to enable Wimbledon to stage an Open tournament, but "that we should remove sham and hypocrisy from the game". He went on: "For too long now we have been governed by a set of amateur rules which are quite unenforceable. We know the so-called amateur players bargain for payments grossly in excess of what they are entitled to but without which they cannot live. We know that tournaments connive at this else there would be no players at their tournaments. We feel we owe it not only to ourselves but to our players to release them from this humiliating and hypocritical situation and that the players should be able to earn openly and honestly the rewards to which their skill entitles them."

Getting the Americans on their side was obviously of major importance and it was fortunate that the president of the USLTA at the time was the equally progressive minded, Bob Kelleher, who also favoured the introduction of Open tennis and was determined to do everything possible to convince the many and often vocal opponents within the United States that at least a start should be made to widening the opportunities for all full-time players, whether they were professionals or so-called amateurs.

Penman and fellow cohort, Derek Hardwick, a future president of the ILTF, repeated their strident views, which many did not want to hear, wherever they went on a worldwide crusade for Open tennis, which took in Australia, New Zealand and also the United States, where at least the principal of self-determination by nations on the issue, was passed by 102,064 votes to 9,978. Hardliners within the ILTF were still implacably opposed, but steadily, as more and more examples of hypocrisy within the game were revealed, such as when the Italians were forced to admit they had paid the best players not to turn professional, they knew their resistance would fail. Their face-saving act was a compromise, whereby "authorized" (or registered players as they were to be called) would be allowed to accept prize money at certain designated tournaments, while still remaining under the jurisdiction of their national association. They, unlike professionals under contract to other organizations, would also be allowed to continue playing in the Davis Cup. It did for the moment, but was the recipe for fresh conflict in the not too distant future.

Although few would have guessed it from the general jubilation when the first Open tournament was held at Bournemouth that spring, with Ken Rosewall taking the title, there were already new ominous dark clouds of conflict on the way. The continuing hypocricy of the situation was highlighted at the first US Open in 1968 when Arthur Ashe, still an amateur because he wanted to play in the Davis Cup, got nothing for winning the title but Tom Okker, the runner-up, was allowed to take home his $14,000 because he had agreed to be an authorized player with the Dutch LTA.

The section devoted to the Davis Cup in this book outlines the damaging impact the continuing ban on professionals being allowed to compete had on the event. Meanwhile the row between the establishment, whose members could see their influence ebbing away, and the enterprising World Championship Tennis organization, was brewing. Much of the blame for the ILTF decision to ban players contracted to WCT from January 1972 – and by then there were 32 of them – was placed on men such as Lamar Hunt, the paymaster for the rapidly expanding WCT Tour. Just as much to blame were those amateur administrators who, having opened Pandora's Box, had absolutely no idea how to respond to the outcome. With hindsight there were weaknesses on both sides. Some like former British Davis Cup player, Mike Davies, a fiery Welshman working for Hunt, did little to calm the fears that his intention was to buy up the whole tennis world, including Wimbledon. And, on the face of it, Hunt's demand, that in return for not organizing his own tournaments which would clash with the Grand Slams, he should receive 13 per

LAMAR HUNT, *the Texan oil millionaire who pioneered the modern presentation of tennis*

R.J. "BOB" KELLEHER, *USTA president at the right time*

cent of their gate receipts and have the right to negotiate their television contracts, tended to give that impression.

Hunt, in fact, was no ogre. He was a hard-headed businessman, but he was also a genuinely modest American multi-millionaire, who felt that everyone could benefit from tennis being promoted and marketed in the high-profile manner which the product deserved. That though, was not the message which came across. Hunt, as was sharply evident during a heated press conference at Wimbledon in the summer of 1971, did not appreciate how much even such a perceived threat would have British traditionalists, in particular, manning the barricades.

The 1972 ban went ahead, even though in April, Hunt and Allan Heyman, president of the ILTF, reached an agreement that in 1973, WCT would be free to organize their events through to May, with the ILTF's Grand Prix circuit, including the four Grand Slams, filling the rest of the year

unhindered. It was too late to save the French Open or Wimbledon. It had to be ratified at the ILTF annual meet-

ing in July and Heyman, a barrister, refused to pre-empt the decision. The US Open escaped the ban, but several of the most prominent WCT players, including Laver, Rosewall, Emerson and Cliff Drysdale withdrew. Both sides were continuing to score own goals.

Although, as the financial rewards in the game grew, it was only going to be a matter of time before the male players followed the women in forming their own organization to represent them on political and other issues which affected their livelihood, it was probably the agreement to co-operate between the ILTF and WCT more than anything which concentrated minds in this direction. WCT had agreed that there would be no more long-term, guaranteed contracts so that, some players feared, would leave them relying too heavily on the whims of their national associations. During the US Open in 1972, the Association of Tennis Professionals was formed with 40 inaugural members.

Even so no-one could have guessed how swiftly or dramatically they would become embroiled in their first major battle. The following spring, Niki Pilic was requested to play for Yugoslavia in their Davis Cup tie against New Zealand. Pilic agreed, though subject to several provisos. The

president of the Yugoslavian Tennis Association, who was also related to Pilic's wife, did not see it that way and when Pilic did not play, he suspended him for nine months.

Under ILTF rules, the ban had to be recognized by all other national associations, but Heyman agreed under pressure that Pilic would be allowed to compete in the forthcoming French Open while he and two other leading ILTF representatives, Walter Elcock of the United States and Robert Abdesselam of France, reviewed the case. Pilic was supported at the hearing by Donald Dell, his agent, and Jack Kramer, honorary executive director of ATP. They produced a copy of the letter Pilic had sent to his Federation in which he stated that if he and the Australian Allan Stone qualified for the WCT Doubles finals in Montreal – which they did – he would not be able to play in the Davis Cup match because the two dates clashed.

The ban was reduced from nine months to one month ... but that meant Pilic would not be able to play at Wimbledon. The seeds for what was to become the greatest *cause célèbre* in tennis since Suzanne Lenglen was supposed to have snubbed Queen Mary at Wimbledon in 1926, were being sown. During the Italian Open, more than 40 players indicated

ALLAN HEYMAN, *president of the ITLF during the Wimbledon boycott*

THE DEBONAIR *and eloquent Cliff Drysdale, first president of the Players' Union*

under their rules, to suspend the Yugoslav left-hander. On the grounds that Mr Justice Forbes had not ruled whether Pilic should have been suspended – partly it seemed, because he did not feel a British court should intervene in a case which had already been dealt with abroad – the ATP announced that the boycott of Wimbledon by their members would go ahead.

What they conveniently played down was the fact that Mr Justice Forbes had nevertheless gone through the case put forward by the ATP point by point and intimated that had he been allowed to do so, he would have found against them almost point by point. Things moved on apace. The Minister for Sport, Eldon Griffiths, called in Drysdale and Heyman for separate talks, urging them to make one more attempt the next day to find a solution. Drysdale agreed. Heyman said the issues were now so broad that all he could offer was that the revision of possibly outdated rules could be considered after The Championships.

There was one last hope. A late night meeting of the ATP board was held at the Westbury Hotel, London, on the Thursday evening. A compromise was proposed – if the ILTF agreed in writing that members of the ATP owed their first allegiance to their own association rather than their national association, then they would accept Pilic's offer to withdraw voluntarily, which in turn would make it possible for the Wimbledon boycott to be lifted. Drysdale had invited three non-board members, Ken Rosewall and two recognized militants on the issue, Charlie Pasarell and Cliff Richey to join the talks, though without a vote. It soon became clear that any compromise proposal had little chance of being accepted and, like the failure to accept at least the moral verdict handed down by Mr Justice Forbes, that cost the ATP many of the friends they might otherwise have had.

Had they thrown the ball back into the ILTF's court, then at least they could never have been blamed had the ILTF rejected the get-out clause and had the boycott then gone ahead. Instead they were left looking the villains. That was not helped by the out-

to Cliff Drysdale, the first president of the ATP, that as a matter of principle they would be willing to boycott any tournament, including Wimbledon, which refused Pilic permission to play because of the Davis Cup affair. Over the next couple of weeks, the level of support swelled and positions on both sides hardened.

However reluctant he may have been, Herman David, chairman of Wimbledon, said they had to uphold a suspension imposed by the ILTF. After days of fruitless negotiation, with Allan Heyman rejecting the ATP's suggestion of setting up yet another arbitration panel, the players eventually accepted advice that Pilic should seek an injunction against the ILTF which would at least prevent the

suspension taking affect until after a full judiciary hearing.

But a hearing took place in the High Court chambers of Mr Justice Forbes on the Monday before The Championships were due to begin. Three days later and 24 hours after the draw had been made, he rejected the application for an injunction on the grounds that the ILTF had the right,

HERMAN DRAVID, *chairman of the All England Club in years when epic decisions were necessary*

The public, almost to a man, sided with Wimbledon. To them here was a British institution under attack from a power-crazy organization dominated by Americans. The standing ovation led by the Duke and Duchess of Kent when Taylor walked out to play his opening Centre Court match, summed up the Dunkirk mood of the nation. In the end, 93 players stayed away, including some who were not ATP members, but the crowds quickly found a new hero in Bjorn Borg who, at 17, was not old enough be an ATP member and the crowd total for the year was the second highest on record.

In the aftermath of the boycott, the Men's International Professional Tennis Council, consisting of three members of the ILTF, three from ATP and three tournament directors, was formed, despite last ditch efforts by some ILTF delegates for them to retain control. It existed until the ATP broke away to form the ATP Tour in 1990. Not that there was peace in the meantime. Far from it.

There were not only disputes between the various factions within the Council, but also within ATP. There was also another battle between the MIPTC and Lamar Hunt, which led to the formation in the mid-1980s of a 22-tournament rival WCT circuit, much wasting of money by both sides on lawsuits and Ivan Lendl, one of the few top players who enthusiastically committed himself to WCT, winning most of the events offering $100,000-a-week prize money. Some of the principals were also playing musical chairs. Owen Williams, a former South African player and promoter, who had been a member of the Pro Council, not only took over at WCT when Mike Davies left them to join the ATP, but found himself fighting the Pro Council over decisions they had taken while he was still with them.

After two years, WCT effectively ceased operating, except for their continuing support for the World Doubles, but the family members of the Pro Council were still arguing, with varying degrees of seriousness, among themselves. There were some measures of universal agreement, such as the appointment of the

rageous antics of some of their more militant members at the qualifying tournament in Roehampton on the afternoon of that fateful final meeting, in threatening young British players, including John Lloyd, that unless they supported the boycott they would make sure they would never be allowed to play in any tournaments in the United States.

When it came to a straightforward vote on whether the boycott decision the night before should be ratified or overturned, Stan Smith and two Englishmen, John Barrett and Mark Cox, voted in favour of playing. Arthur Ashe, Kramer and Jim McManus voted for the boycott. The casting vote went to Drysdale, but he stunned the meeting by deciding to abstain.

It was well after 2 a.m. that a shaken Drysdale, with Kramer at his side, emerged from the meeting room to break the news to almost all of the leading British tennis writers and other reporters who had been fortifying themselves for hours with coffee, that without a majority either way, the original decision stood. Almost without exception, every major national newspaper made it their main story on the front page that morning. The next test, as Wimbledon decided for the only time in the tournament's history to re-make the men's singles draw, was if the ATP members would follow their Board's decision. Several leading European players were ordered by their national association's to play. Most defied the instruction, though not Ilie Nastase, while Britain's Roger Taylor, acknowledged by the ATP as a special case, decided at the last moment that he too had to play.

game's first three full-time umpires, Richard Kauffman of the United States, Gerry Armstrong from Britain and Richard Ings of Australia. Curiously enough, though, if only to satisfy the accusations from outside the sport, by the end of the 1980s, by which time Ilie Nastase, John McEnroe and Jimmy Connors had retired or calmed down, there was more pressure for uniformity in keeping the sport clean from drug taking than stronger action against ill-disciplined competitors.

In the background, though, there was the persistent mistrust between the ATP and the ITF, although with the three tournament representatives apparently taking the side of the players on the majority of issues which were discussed, it was hard to understand why the players felt so aggrieved that moves began for them to breakaway, other than because they felt the game was not making financial

headway at a pace they felt was possible. Enter Hamilton Jordan, the new chief executive officer for ATP and a man credited as having played a major role in the election of Jimmy Carter as president of the United States.

Matters came to a head during the US Open in 1989. ATP called a press conference in a parking lot outside the main gates of Flushing Meadows where Jordan announced that the players "wanted to have a bigger say in their own destiny" and from the following January, what was now the Grand Prix, would effectively become the ATP Tour, scheduled round the Grand Slams, which would remain independent, and the Davis Cup. Making such a newsworthy declaration in such surroundings was an enormous publicity coup. "We had to hold it here because they wouldn't let us do it inside," was the explanation.

That was not entirely true. The

ATP had originally asked if they could hold a press conference to announce a new sponsorship. "Does it involve one of the sponsors on site?" the USTA asked. It was only because the reply was in the negative that ATP's request was refused. By the time the USTA discovered the real reason for the conference and lifted their objection, ATP said it was too late, even though it would only have meant moving everyone less than 100 metres.

Since then relations between the ATP Tour, which set up its own management structure, the Player Council, and the ITF, have been warmer in public than in private, with something of a major hiccup for a while when it became known that the ITF was ready and, it seemed, eager to set up its own ranking system and circuit, in 1995. The introduction of the Compaq Grand Slam Cup, initially offering a staggering $2m to the winner in

1990, which the ATP Tour saw as a wilful attempt to overshadow their own end-of-year climax to the circuit, has remained a controversial issue, all the more so in 1998 with the introduction of a Grand Slam Cup for women as well – a natural evolution.

In late 1997, as they started to look seriously towards how best to guarantee tennis growth in the new millenium, Mark Miles, who succeeded Jordan as CEO of the ATP Tour in 1991, talked of plans which he said he hoped would lead to all the various groups within the game, not just the men and women, but the ATP, WTA and ITF all coming together again. A case of what goes round, comes around? Maybe, but one can certainly assume that there will be many more political manoevres before that happens. Why? For one very simple reason. All of the parties concerned want the most money. For with the money comes the power.

RICHARD KAUFMANN, *one of the first professional umpires using one of the first service-line monitors*

SCANDALS
AND CONTROVERSIES

According to many in the entertainment business, there is no such thing as bad publicity. Judging by the public fascination with some players who are famous for what could be called the wrong reasons, it is also true in tennis.

Tennis has been fortunate in some ways inasmuch that it has not really been hit by the sort of scandals which have so seriously blighted the reputation and credibility of other sports. Over the years, for instance, there have been proven, as well as several other suspected bribery cases round the world in soccer, doping in horse racing plus, of course, the now well publicized abuses in some of the former Eastern bloc countries involving track and field athletes, gymnasts and swimmers

In gymnastics, for instance, outstanding schoolgirl performers, were treated medically to prevent them developing physically until as late as possible, apparently without any major concern for their long-term welfare, so that they would remain light and agile enough to continue competing at the highest international level.

While it is true that there have been a handful of cases in tennis where players have proved positive when tested for drugs, mainly most notably former world No. 1 Mats Wilander and his doubles partner at the time, Karel Novacek, during the French Open in 1995, they have mainly been for social use. That scenario changed dramatically in 1998 when Petr Korda became the first player to be banned for testing positive with performance enhancing drugs. Further cases followed during the ensuing years involving in the main, five players from Argentina with Mariano

KAREL NOVACEK *tested positive for drugs at the French Open in 1995*

Puerta receiving the biggest penalty consisting of an eight year ban. Only one woman has fallen foul of the drug testing authorities, Bulgaria's Elena Likhovtseva, 16, who, at the time of writing was appealing against her two year banishment from the circuit. For the record, Puerta is also appealing against his own ban.

Many of the so-called scandalous tales etched into tennis history which caused enough outrage and indignation at the time, can now be viewed, with hindsight, as having an amusing side to them, while there are others which though obviously significant at the time, judging by the furore they caused in the media, leave modern followers of the game wondering what all the fuss was about.

Some of those are also part of the story of tennis fashions. One prime example was the concern expressed at Wimbledon in 1949 when, unable to use even the pastal colours allowed within the "predominately white rule" still demanded today, Ted Tinling, the fashion designer, who for so long was also the "call boy" for women's matches at The Championships, provided Gertrude Moran, "Gorgeous Gussy" as she was called, with half an inch of lace trim round her panties.

The matter became world news from the moment Gussie, who had asked Tinling to produce something a little more flamoyant than usual to match her personality, was seen wearing them for the first time at the pre-Wimbledon tennis garden party at Hurlingham. Questions were asked in Parliament. "Queen Mary (an avid Wimbledon visitor, then aged 84) might not like it," anxious Wimbledon officials told her when, together with her partner, Pat Todd, Moran reached the women's doubles final on the Centre Court, which Her Majesty was due to attend.

Uncertain about what to do, Moran remained in her hotel as long as possible, regularly phoning The All England Club to see if Queen Mary had arrived. As it happened, because of the excessive heat, her visit was cancelled, so the dilemma was solved. The next morning, almost every newspaper carried photographs of the winners, Louise Brough and Margaret du Pont walking behind Gussy with what Tinling called "unabashed and unconcealed curiosity".

Writing in his book *White Ladies* Tinling told how Clement Attlee, the Prime Minister, complimented him on Moran's outfit and Duncan Macaulay, secretary of The All England Club had confided that, "The Duchess [the late Princess Marina, Duchess of Kent] had thought it 'great fun'." When though, in a speech to all the leading players and officials at one of the post-Wimbledon parties, club president Louis Greig thundered, "I will never allow Wimbledon to become a stage for designers' stunts," Tinling's formal association with the tournament ended. It was 20 years before he returned, this time more in the role of a cultural ambassador representing the views of the club to the players and, even more importantly, the increasingly independent and rebellious views of the players, to the club.

In 1926, Suzanne Lenglen, very much the Queen of the courts in her day, was supposed to have snubbed Queen Mary and King George V by arriving late for a doubles match with her partner, Diddie Vlasto, against Elizabeth Ryan, her usual doubles partner and Mary K. Browne. Lenglen, who was already emotionally upset after having been ordered by the French Federation to play with another French player instead of Ryan, had sent word to the

JEFF TARANGO *and his wife, Benedicte, at Wimbledon in 1995*

referee's office that she did not want to play singles on that day as well. Somehow the message did not get through. When Lenglen arrived at the club and discovered there was a singles to be played first, she refused to play at all.

Anyone else would have been scratched, but the committee was sympathetic. The doubles was re-scheduled for the following day. Lenglen and Vlasto lost a fierce contest 3–6, 9–7, 6–2. Two days later, by which time the "snub to the Queen" story had become a major public talking point, Lenglen found the hostility within the press had extended to the public, when she walked out to play in the first round of the mixed. That evening an overwrought Lenglen withdrew

from the singles and mixed, returned to Paris and never played at Wimbledon again.

What most might regard as the real scandals in tennis, have either been covered up, brushed aside or not been more then generally discussed because of the legal implications which might otherwise have been involved. The sort of things which fall into this category could include:

Accepting a huge appearance fee, some as high as $250,000 or more, from a tournament but then either not turning up or doing so in body but hardly in mind or spirit and giving such a pathetic, unprofessional performance in losing his or her first match that it looking like a case of "take the money and run".

Deliberately not trying, or at least giving the public that impression, without appearance money being involved, as quite a number of top ten players holding top ten status in the 1980s and 1990s have done, with no disciplinary action being taken against them.

Pushing the letter of the tennis law to such a limit in a way that in countries without strict libel laws, the offender might reasonably have been accused of deliberate cheating.

The allegations in 1995 by no less a figure than Boris Becker that drug taking and even blood doping, had spread to tennis. He even went so far as to point an accusing figure at the super-fit Austrian, Thomas Muster, for which he was disciplined and forced to issue a written apology.

It was in that same year that the volatile American, Jeff Tarango, who had convinced himself that the highly regarded French umpire, Bruno Rebeuh, was less than even-handed in his dealing with any player other than French-speaking ones, catapulted himself into a worldwide fame which his then world ranking of 80 barely deserved, by storming off court at Wimbledon just as he was about to be disqualified.

During the uproar which followed, Tarango, 26 at the time, accused Rebeuh of being corrupt, while his French wife, Benedicte, caught up with the official on his way back to report the incident and slapped him before slipping past security guards to join her husband in the interview room, where journalists, not normally fazed by events, listened with a mixture of glee and astonishment as the tirade continued.

Standing alongside her husband, Mrs Tarango said he had slapped the umpire because "this guy deserves a lesson", at which point Tarango himself, hardly a newcomer in a controversial starring role, told her, "I'm glad you did that."

The drama on Court 13 began to unfold during the second set of his third round match against Germany's Alexander Mronz. Tarango, a student of philosophy, began arguing over a line call. As the crowd became restless and started to barrack him, he shouted something at them which promoted umpire Rebeuh to issue a warning for an audible obscenity. From that moment the blue touchpaper was alight. Tarango, who claimed he had only told spectators to shut up, raged "I'm not having that" at the umpire, demanded to see the supervisor and then added, "I have a big beef."

Stefan Fransson, the supervisor, a tall, strapping fellow from Sweden, with a calm, but firm demeanour, arrived, listened to both sides, but insisted that the warning should stand, at which point Tarango, looking at Rebeuh, roared, "You're the most corrupt official in the game." Rebeuh then called a point penalty against the Californian, who promptly shouted, "That's it. I'm not playing – no way." He threw down the

two balls he was still holding, collected his things and stalked off amid a fresh storm of boos and jeers.

The press conference which followed was not just one of the best attended but one of the most extraordinary ever to take place at Wimbledon, on a par with one in 1981 when a fight broke out between an American radio reporter and the tennis correspondent for the British newspaper, the *Daily Mirror*, about whether John McEnroe was being fairly treated by the London tabloids.

For Tarango (who was suspended from his next Grand Slam tournament

TIM HENMAN *says "Sorry" with flowers*

and also Wimbledon the following year, but later had his $15,000 fine put on hold subject to him offering a written apology), it was the latest in a long line of occasions in which he had clashed spectacularly with officials.

One of the most memorable was in Tokyo in October 1994 when, after losing his serve in the third set of a match he was to lose against Michael Chang, he dropped his shorts to the crowd. His explanation for this mooning incident? "I thought people were concerned because tennis isn't entertaining enough. People complain that tennis is boring. I played my heart out against Chang and after losing my serve against a guy I'd been a set and a break up against maybe four times I just lost my head. My shorts came down. And that was that. The gig was up."

After more than 100 Wimbledons without even one player being disqualified, that year there were three. Three days before the Tarango incident, Britain's Tim Henman, distraught with embarrassment and full of apologies, became the first, though in vastly different circumstances. Hitting a ball away in anger, he accidentally struck a ball girl during a late-night men's doubles match and as referee Alan Mills explained later, "even though accidental, that is an automatic disqualification under the rules." Henman was also fined $2,000. Tarango, ironically, was one of his opponents. Then two days after Tarango's departure, another American, Murphy Jensen, went missing when he should have been playing a mixed doubles match and was also disqualified and fined $1,000.

It has frequently been suggested that had Fred Hoyles, the Wimbledon referee at the time, taken sterner action against John McEnroe on that infamous occasion in 1981, the year of his first Wimbledon title, when phrases such as "pits of the world" and best loved of all "You cannot be serious" became part of not just tennis but sporting legend, then perhaps the fiery American would not have found himself in so much trouble and had to pay so much in fines in later years.

Hoyles, a farmer in the lowlands of Lincolnshire, has often asked the question of himself. In his defence, though, there was no code of conduct for him in those days to offer him the statutory support, which even those in the crowd egging on the easily tempted American, would have understood.

McEnroe, it is not always appreciated, had trouble excusing what he saw as shortcomings on the part of others, especially match officials, well before making his debut at Wimbledon in 1977 when, even during the qualifying rounds, umpires were suggesting to the referee's office that perhaps someone needed to have a quiet word with him for his own good.

Justice on the court finally caught up with the tennis genius with his own inbuilt self-destruct button, when he was thrown out of the Australian Open during a fourth round match against Mikael Pernfors in Melbourne in January 1990. He had the dubious privilege of becoming the first player to be disqualified for misbehaviour in a Grand Slam tournament since Open tennis began in 1968.

The act of disqualification was carried out by British umpire, Gerry Armstrong, though it was on the instructions of chief supervisor Ken Farrar for what he called "the worst abuse directed at me in 11 years". For the next 15 minutes thousands in the Centre Court crowd, apparently as stunned as the offender by the sentence, first booed loudly, then cheered the former world champion, chanting, "We want McEnroe" in between directing abuse at the officials.

What they presumably had not heard were the four-letter utterances by McEnroe which provoked floods of telephone calls to the television station which had been broadcasting the match and to Australian newspaper offices. Although McEnroe had once defaulted himself from a tournament in Dusseldorf in 1987, this was the first time during a career that was as illustrious as it was tempestuous, that he had been thrown out. The last time any player had been disqualified from a Grand Slam match for bad behaviour was the Spaniard, Willie "Pato" Alvarez, at the French Open in 1963.

In 1950, the American, Earl Cochell, was defaulted at the US Championships. During a four-set defeat to Gardner Mulloy in the

fourth round, he frequently argued with the umpire and spectators over line calls. At one time he tried to climb the umpire's chair and grab his microphone to lecture the crowd. In the end, after blatantly throwing several games and even underlining his contempt by playing left-handed, when he was a right-hander, he launched into a furious abusive verbal tirade against the referee, Dr Ellsworth Davenport. Whereas McEnroe, as stipulated in the rules, was fined $6,500, and had a right of appeal, Cochell was suspended for life. And although the ban was lifted some

years later, it was too late for him to restore his career.

In McEnroe's Melbourne affair, one sensed the Jekyll and Hyde of tennis beginning to boil early when he was leading 2–1 in the third set. After the changeover he walked up to a lineswoman who had made a call which upset him while he was at the other end two games earlier and stared at her in such an intimidatory fashion than he was warned for unsportsmanlike conduct. At 2–3 in the fourth set, when he was leading by two sets to one, he was so furious about an error which put him break point

down that he smashed his racket on the court for at least the fourth time and it cracked. The mandatory point penalty made the game score 2–4.

McEnroe unsuccessfully put it to Mr Farrar and the referee the ingeious but specious argument that it was only a small crack. He implied that as he had every intention of continuing to use the racket how could be considered to be broken? It was as he walked away that the verbal obscenities flowed. "This is a long story," said McEnroe later, when he admitted swearing but claimed that he did not know that the disciplinary rule had

ILIE NASTASE *often crossed the dividing line between having fun and giving offence*

MARTINA NAVRATILOVA'S *lifestyle cost her millions in lost sponsorship*

been changed on January 1 from three warnings before disqualification to only two! "It [the disqualification] was bound to happen sometime. I don't feel good about it, but I can't say I'm totally surprised."

His mitigating pleas only underlined the complex nature of the man. He agreed he swore but said, "They could have let me off by saying it was in the heat of the moment." He also asked, "Should I have got a warning for going up to that lady and just looking at her because she had made a terrible call?" Perhaps not, but nor should he have got away with much worse so many times before, not least when during the Masters in Madison Square Garden one year, angry over a baseline call by a lineswomen he had encountered many times before in that part of the United States he told her, "You've been screwing me over calls since I was 13."

Fourteen years before umpire Gerry Armstrong's name was written into tennis history as the man who disqualified McEnroe, his father, George (also an international umpire, though in the days before they were rewarded with much more than lunch vouchers), was in the chair at Forest Hills for one of the most tempestuous Open-era matches in the old

stadium. It involved Ilie Nastase and the German, Hans-Joachim Pohmann, now a leading television commentator. Nastase might easily have been disqualified for his outrageous gamesmanship and obscene language, not least when Pohmann was suffering from cramps. The ill feeling evident between the players was reported to have carried over into the locker rooms. Nastase was fined $1,000 and because that took his total for a 12-month period over $3,000, it triggered off an automatic 21-day suspension. What made this even more scandalous was that it applied only to Grand Prix tournaments. Nastase was able to laugh all the way to the bank as he earned more than $50,000 for exhibition and other non-Grand Prix events during the period in which he was supposed to be punished.

Almost every umpire taking charge of a match in either a Grand Slam or some other major tournament today is a highly qualified, full-time official, who can usually be sure that he has the backing of the tournament organisers. It was not always the case in the days of George Armstrong and even Fred Hoyles, while even in the late-1980s there was the scandal of British umpire, Jeremy Shales, being dropped as a full-time official on the

Grand Prix circuit, apparently under pressure from one particularly influential player. "Not so," said the Grand Prix hierarchy, who suggested

his umpiring had fallen below the required standard. Somehow that did not tie in with the fact that they made no effort to downgrade him from the gold badge top standard.

Two classic, scandalous examples of umpires not being supported, involved the Americans, Jack Stahr and Frank Hammond. Stahr, the doyen of American officials at the time, had disqualified the Mexican Raul Ramirez during his match against Brian Gottfried in the round-robin section of the Grand Prix Masters in Houston and was astonished to discover while he was holding a press conference to explain what led him to taking such drastic action, that the match had been allowed to continue with another umpire in the chair.

At the US Open three years later, in a match played under the Flushing Meadows floodlights, Hammond, whose booming voice made him a personality in his own right, had the challenging task of trying to control a tempestuous contest between McEnroe and Nastase. An advertisement in the *New York Post* that evening, urged fans to "Come see the

RENEE RICHARDS, *the first trans-sexual in major tennis*

fight of the century" – so the provocative mood was already set before a match in which both players appeared to be trying to psyche the other out, began. Hammond, who at one time was heard to ask the constantly stalling and protesting Romanian, "What are you trying to do to me, Ilie?," could eventually take it no longer and having already docked him a point, gave Nastase a penalty-game punishment as well.

Nastase's raged response led Hammond to tell him he would be defaulted. There was uproar for 15 minutes. Beer cans, plastic popcorn buckets and various other objects rained down and continued until the tournament director over-ruled Hammond, who was replaced in the chair by umpire-emeritus, Mike Blanchard.

It is not only in the United States, though, that tennis fans show their fury. For decades it was commonplace during Davis Cup matches in South America, for the mood of the crowd to reach such a level of deliberate antagonism that in some cases visiting players and officials became afraid for their safety. As a result, the International Tennis Federation had to introduce a rule whereby the umpire can invoke the warning, point penalty and disqualification ruling against home crowds as well as players, if their enthusiasm becomes deliberately intimidating.

Crowd passions can also sometimes run high at Wimbledon, even for a women's doubles match. On the second Tuesday of the 1981 Championships, a Centre Court contest between Britain's Sue Barker and the American, Ann Kiyomura, against another American, Jo Anne Russell and the Romanian, Virginia Ruzici, was stopped at 9.35p.m. at 5–5 in the final set (for which there would be no tie-break) because of bad light. The crowd was furious. First there were boos and jeers. Then cushions, programmes and other objects were hurled on to the court. This, too, provoked editorial comment in the British press, with one of them calling it "game, set and match for common sense, not just in tennis but in sport".

Sex, in whatever walk of life, is often portrayed as scandal, as Billie Jean King and later Martina Navratilova discovered when admitting their lesbian lifestyles. Indeed in Navratilova's case, it became something of a long-running serial for gossip columns and the tabloid media as her various partners came and went.

Few incidents, though, attracted more attention at the time than when Richard Raskind, a 41-year-old ophthalmic surgeon – married with a son – who had played at Wimbledon and Forest Hills 20 years earlier, underwent a sex-change operation in August 1975 and the following year began competing in Californian tournaments as a woman. Despite opposition from the Women's Tennis Association, the ITF and the USTA, who ruled that women, as in track and field, would have to pass an Olympic-style chromosome test before being allowed to play in national or international championships, Raskind, now Renee Richards, won a court order allowing her to compete unhindered within the United States.

Most WTA members withdrew from the first Tour event in which Richards played in South Orange, New Jersey, where amid huge newspaper and television publicity she was beaten in the semi-finals by 17-year-old American, Lea Antonoplis. At the US Open, Richards was promoted to the Centre Court in the first round and was beaten by Virginia Wade, the reigning Wimbledon champion.

Pictures of a teenage Bjorn Borg, his clothing apparently in disarray, while canoodling with a girlfriend in a London park, were also given the scandal treatment, as was the still-unanswered puzzle as to whether the American player Linda Siegel's bra had slipped to the extent photographers and the stories beneath their blurred pictures suggested, in the middle of a match on an outside court at The Championships.

More recently there was the mass invasion of photographers on Court 2 at Wimbledon when it was learned that Anne White was playing in a full length all-white leotard, which was never to be seen in public again. Then there was the Centre Court streaker which broke the tension for Richard Krajicek and MaliVai Washington while they were warming up for the 1996 men's singles final. Also the pin-up poses featuring Gabriela Sabatini, Anna Kournikova and for the girls, Patrick Rafter and 1998 heartthrob, Jan-Michael Gambill.

This though is fun sometimes dressed up as scandal. No publicity is bad publicity.

THE ALL-WHITE *leotard was banned after one appearance*

THE ODDITIES OF TENNIS

Now that one tennis season seems to run into the next, barely a day goes by without the sport filling space in most major newspapers. Often, it is not so much the matches themselves as the events which have a major impact on them, which demand the most attention.

An event which stunned not only the world of tennis but had instant repercussions throughout most sports, happened on the centre court of the Rothenbaum Club in Hamburg on Friday April 30, 1993. Monica Seles was just leaving her courtside chair to go out to serve at 3–4 in the first set of her WTA Tour quarter-final match against Magdalena Maleeva, when a 38-year-old German, Gunther Parche, suddenly emerged from the crowd behind her and stabbed the world No. 1 in the back, just below the left shoulder blade.

While the injury itself was not life threatening, it had a devastating affect, particularly on Seles, who was only 19 at the time, but already in line, having won six of her previous Grand Slam tournaments, to become one of the best players of all time. With the psychological harm far more severe than the physical damage, which had led one of the doctor's who treated her to say, "She should be fully recovered in time for Wimbledon (eight weeks hence) and with a little bit of luck might even be able to play in the French," it was not until August 1995, when she reappeared at the Canadian Open, that Seles felt rehabilitated enough to return to major competition.

The mentally deranged Parche was such an obsessed supporter of Steffi Graf, that he was prepared to do anything to try and make sure she would be able to regain her place at the top of the world rankings. The suffering for Seles and her family was exacerbated when Parche was not given a custodial sentence, for there was the constant fear in their minds that perhaps he might try to strike again. But as the examining judge pointed out, the failure of those acting for Seles to produce medical evidence about the extent of the injury, meant that under German law, the sentencing options were reduced.

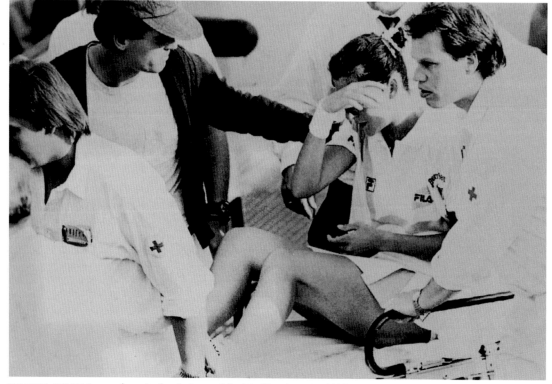

MONICA SELES *is comforted after being stabbed in Hamburg in 1993*

TWO POLICEMEN *arrest a streaker who ran across Centre Court before the Wimbledon Tennis Championships' men's final in 1996*

On the wider issue, the security of players suddenly became a key problem for the organisers of all tournaments, which is why today you will often find security men sitting behind the players at the side of the court, with one facing the court to prevent any intrusion from the front and the other sitting facing the spectators behind the player. In addition, there are often two or three other security guards strategically positioned in the corners, ready to pounce if necessary.

There have been plenty of other court invasions before and since, though happily none so serious as the one in Hamburg. But even the security checks carried out in recent years at Wimbledon, because of terrorist threats, are nothing new. As far back as 1913, spectators carrying bags or parcels into the grounds underwent what at the time was called "close scrutiny" by the doormen following a raid on the grounds earlier in the year

by suffragettes. Nowadays tight security at The All England Club is maintained all the year round. For decades it was hardly thought necessary for there to be any security present other than on the main gates at Church Road and Somerset Road.

It was a view which had to be reconsidered after the night of January 14, 1976, when vandals broke into the grounds and damaged the Centre Court. In the morning, groundstaff found five holes in the turf, the largest about 9ins long, while there were also concentrated splashes of red and white paint on the grass plus windows and doors surrounding the court. Wimbledon was not the only major sporting venue hit around that time. A cricket Test match had to be abandoned at Headingley, Leeds, after campaigners for the release of convicted Londoner, George Davis, dug up the wicket and slogans appeared all over London claiming,

"George Davis is innocent, OK."

In 1969, Britain's Davis Cup match at the Redland Club in Bristol against South Africa in 1969 was interrupted when demonstrators outside the ground were hurling bags of flour over the low roof of the stand on to the court. Other forms of protest have been made by simply holding up large slogans to attract the attention of other spectators and, of course, the television cameras. Andrew Castle, the British Davis Cup player, now a prominent television journalist, caused consternation among officials of the British LTA by placing a notice on his chair during the British Championships in Telford, in full view of the cameras, expressing what he felt about the introduction in Britain of a Poll Tax.

One of the most well-publicized on-court intrusions, though, came just as Richard Krajicek and MaliVai Washington were preparing to begin the men's singles final at Wimbledon

in 1996. Suddenly from the north-west corner of the arena, a female streaker appeared, "swinging her way" as one tabloid newspaper put it, past the two players who watched with huge grins on their faces. The official statement is worth recalling: "We have never had a streaker on the Centre Court before so I suppose it was inevitable. Whilst we do not wish to condone the practice, it did at least provide some light amusement for our loyal and patient supporters who have had a trying time during the recent bad weather."

The history of tennis is, not surprisingly, full of stories about freak weather conditions and occasionally, the drastic measures taken to overcome them. In 1969, officials of the US Open needed the help of a helicopter hovering over the Centre Court at Forest Hills to try and dry the court after torrential rain which had delayed the staging of the finals for

WIMBLEDON'S *great flood in 1985 made the notice superfluous*

ing at 12.30 p.m., when the first players should have been making their way to the outside courts on the first Monday, ugly black clouds and ominous rumblings of thunder made it too much of a risk to remove the court covers. The precautions, though disappointing, were wise. The rain began and then at 12.50 p.m. there was a terrific bang as the corner of the new building was struck by a thunderbolt. Small pieces of masonry fell from the building, one of which is now on show in the Wimbledon Lawn Tennis Museum. It was not until late in the afternoon that the skies brightened, but although John McEnroe eventually began his defence of the title at 6.24 p.m., he and Peter McNamara skidded about for only 18 minutes before the referee, Alan Mills, decided it was too dangerous for them to continue.

If that was bad enough, the second Friday was infinitely worse, prompting Alan Chalmers, who apart from being the owner of the Tennis Bookshop in England oversees the competitors stand at The Championships, to write in his annual Wimbledon diary, "A mini tornado hit Wimbledon at 1.50 p.m., provoking panic and chaos. It was probably the most frightening moment of my life."

Diana, the Princess of Wales, had just arrived when the All England Club was deluged by a downpour of one-and-a-half inches of rain, three quarters of the average July rainfall, in just 20 minutes. Such was the ferocity of the rain that for a while those finding protection by sitting close to the back of the South Stand could not see the North Stand. Water overflowed from gutters and drains, sweeping down steps in a torrent, turning more than one tunnel entrance to the Centre Court into makeshift pools. One lady, in response to a bet and to the delight of the equally soaked newspaper photographers, jumped in and briefly swam around.

The impact and the delay would have been infinitely greater but for a warning from the London Weather Centre which prompted officials to leave the tented cover over the Centre Court in position until the storm passed. In the event only 90 minutes after the rain began and a mere 40

three days. The Italians have, from time to time, had their own novel way of drying out a waterlogged clay court; especially when it makes the difference between playing the final of the appointed day or not. They pour petrol all over the clay – and then set light to it!

Wimbledon has had its fair share of weather problems, although not so many as people assume, with barely a dozen completely washed out days since 1914. One of the worst years was 1985, when officials were proudly showing off the completed extensions on the East side of the Centre Court; complete with a fine new media complex. Although it was not actually rain-

minutes after it stopped, the first of the men's singles semi-finals was able to begin. With a masterpiece of understatement, which still seems so totally appropriate at Wimbledon, Christopher Gorringe, the chief executive apologized for the delay caused by what he called "that little shower". In one sense, though, a second violent storm was on the way. With the help of 17 aces over the first 92 minutes of play, Kevin Curren, who had beaten John McEnroe in the quarter-finals, proved that lightning can strike twice by destroying Jimmy Connors for a place in the final, 6–2, 6–2, 6–1, although Boris Becker then beat him to become the youngest champion.

Ten years on it was the turn of the Australian Open to suffer the wrath of Mother Nature, also on men's semi-finals day. Again there was advance warning and again precautions had been taken, with the sliding roof over the Melbourne arena firmly in place before the rain began. Then, suddenly, while Andre Agassi, the eventual champion, was playing fellow American, Aaron Krickstein, a trickle of water began seeping up from beneath the court. Soon the trickle became a flood, as water seemed to be pouring in from all directions as the players padded to safety. Pressure on the storm water system from the nearby River Yarra, became so great that a drain burst. It was not only the court which was flooded. A tidal wave of water swept down a pathway straight into the media work room and on into the locker rooms, with electricity having to be shut off as a safety measure, especially as most journalists were by then trying to retrieve items from their desks in bare feet.

Umpires have a habit at times, usually inadvertently, of figuring in unusual incidents, quite apart from the much-more-frequently publicized controversies when players do not approve of their decisions. There are many times when the umpire's lot, as Gilbert and Sullivan said of policemen, is not a happy one. Those who have taken crash landings out of their chairs when gale force winds have suddenly blown up, as in Lee on Solent in England, will testify to that. British professional umpire, Jane Tabor's feet and legs had become so rigid with cold at one event that she had to be lifted back down to the ground.

Similarly Georgina Clark, now European director for the WTA Tour, discovered that what goes up does not always necessarily come down, when she was one of the first to use a hydraulic umpire's chair during the Benson & Hedges tournament at Wembley, and she too had to be rescued. On a far more sombre note, an American linesman died after being struck by a ball during a junior boy's singles final at the US Open. He was taking the centre line and suffered what proved to be fatal injuries, not from being hit by the ball but by hitting his head on a concrete base as he fell.

There are also plenty of tales of umpires and linesmen losing patience with argumentative players – and even at times, fellow officials. During a Centre Court match at Flushing Meadows involving Ilie Nastase, the official on the sideline, was clearly so incensed by twice having his calls over-ruled by the chair umpire that the next time a decision was demanded of him, he was to be seen still in his chair but with his back to the court, taking no notice. Italian umpire, Luigi Brambilla, simply walked off and left Ivan Lendl and Todd Witsken to it when they disagreed with him over the score and began calling it themselves when they were playing at the Lipton Champi-

THE ROOF *protects the Australian Open from rain, but not when flood water seeps in from below, as in 1995*

onships. Similarly on the Centre Court at Wimbledon in 1969, when umpires and linesman were still very much unpaid volunteers, whose training basically only came from the experience they picked up as they went along, one umpire of long-standing argued for a while with the two players as to whether a score should be 15–15 or 30–0 and then told them, "All right, have it your own way," and carried on quite happily.

One of the most extraordinary tales was the case of the ice-cream seller and a linesman at the Italian Championships which led to Tony Pickard losing a match to New Zealander, Ian Crookenden, in five sets, which everyone watching agreed he had won in four. The problem was that the one person not watching, who should have been at the crucial moment, was the official on the baseline. On match point to Pickard, Crookenden, a big left-hander, sent the ball at least 9ins out. But there was no call. Everyone turned to look at the linesman, only to see that he was leaning over the fence, buying an ice cream.

As Pickard, who went on to coach Stefan Edberg through most of his outstanding career and then began coaching Greg Rusedski after being Britain's Davis Cup captain for a spell, recalls, "In those days you couldn't appeal. That was the end of it and so I ended up losing a match I'd won." When asked later to explain what had happened, the umpire apparently told officials that before punishing the linesman (though not that they could in those days, other than drop him from future use) they should remember that it was a very hot day. It had been a very long match. He was tired and hot. He needed something to quench his thirst. He heard the ice-cream seller behind him and couldn't resist.

One of the common complaints among modern players is that they are expected to play too much. Before Open tennis, though, they played far more. Most international tournaments would involve the best of five sets in all rounds of men's singles and

doubles and the players were also expected to play in the mixed. Pickard remembers at the British Hard Courts in Bournemouth finishing a five sets singles and then being told by the referee Colonel Johnny Legg. "Pickard, you may as well stay on the court because I'm putting your doubles on here now." At the same tournament in another year, Australian Don Candy, who went on to coach Pam Shriver, played three best-of-five set singles in one day to help the tournament catch up after rain – and was rewarded with a pint of beer from Colonel Legg.

Just occasionally

DAVID LLOYD, *never afraid to state his case, both on and off the court*

tennis players attract considerable unfavourable publicity for events off the court. The conviction of Bill Tilden on charges involving homosexuality in 1951, was just one example. More recently, of course, there were the shoplifting and drug-related charges against Jennifer Capriati, whose difficulties in coping with fame and fortune so early in life, helped prompt the re-introduction of age eligibility rules. Nothing though quite compares with the case of Vere Thomas St. Leger Goold, an Irishman of noble descent from Waterford, County Cork, who, at the age of 25, won the men's singles title at the first Irish Championships held at Fitzwilliam Square, Dublin in 1879 and went on a month later to make his one and only appearance at Wimbledon. He won through four rounds before receiving a bye into the All-Comers final which, due to the absence of the holder, P.F. Hadow, was also The Championship final. Goold was beaten 6–2, 6–4, 6–2 by the Reverend John Hartley, but won the play-off against C.F. Parr for second place.

In 1883, Goold left Dublin for Monte Carlo. He was not heard of again until 1907 when, following a tip off from a porter, disturbed by a smell coming from luggage, including a trunk which had been left with him, Goold and his wife were charged with murdering Mme Emma Liven, a Danish subject, whose decomposing body had been found in the trunk. Liven had reportedly gone to the Goolds to reclaim a loan. A furious row broke out and she had been struck. Goold confessed to the murder was sentenced to penal servitude for life, while his wife who had protested her innocence, was condemned to death, although that was later reduced to life imprisonment.

An incident which proved to be less serious than first thought but still with a twist in the tale, happened during the US Open in 1977 when John McEnroe, then still a junior, was playing Eddie Dibbs in a match under floodlights the last year the tournament was held at Forest Hills. Suddenly there was the sound of a gunshot and considerable turmoil up in one of the stands as stewards and then first aid staff ran to help a man who had been shot in the thigh. The players, understandably enough, were taken off for safety. Was there a madman somewhere inside the arena, people were asking? In the end it turned out that the pellet, rather than a bullet, as first feared, had come from someone who had casually discharged an air gun into the air from outside the arena. No serious damage was done, except that the victim doubtless had some explaining to do when he arrived home. In refusing to provide his name and address, Queens' district police, not noted for such reticence, explained, "The poor guy was here with someone else's wife, so we don't want to do anything which might mean he gets an even more serious injury when he faces his own wife."

Over the years there have also been plenty of examples of feuds between players spreading way beyond the courts. During the Rothmans International at the Royal Albert Hall in London in 1972, Clark Graebner was not amused when Ilie Nastase protested loud and long against the umpire's decision to play a let, quite properly, after the American had been prevented from making a return because a ball boy was in the wrong place. As Graebner pointed out, to have tried to play a shot could easily have meant hitting the lad on the head. Graebner, with his patience exhausted, eventually summoned Nastase to the net and told him, "You're not going to get away with it like you did against Cliff Richey," referring to an earlier incident. "Try anything else and I'll crack this racket over your head," basically summed up

TONY PICKARD, *beaten by an ice-cream seller in Rome*

Graebner's message to the Romanian, who not too long after went to the umpire and told him, "I can't play, I'm too scared to continue."

Nastase also figured in a stormy Davis Cup incident in Bucharest when he and Ion Tiriac were playing the doubles in what became a winning 3–0 lead against the Lloyd brothers, David and John, playing for Britain. David Lloyd, like Nastase, has a short fuse and with the British pair leading 2–0 in the second set after losing the first, he ended up on the Romanian's side of the net after speedily chasing a ball which was travelling well wide of the court. Nastase, as was – and still is – his tendency, made what he thought was a funny remark. David had not heard what was said, but presumed it must have been derogatory. He bristled and snapped, "What was that you said?" Nastase's response was clearly provocative, but David

pretended he had not heard it properly and goaded his opponent to repeat the insult. Nastase could not resist, at which point David announced: "That's it, I'm off. I'm not taking any more of that." He made as if to walk off, but then changed direction and the next thing one saw was David and Nastase walking towards each other, wagging fingers. Tiriac and Spanish referee, Jaime Bartroli, stepped in between them, but Nastase appeared to tap David on the head, prompting accusations later from the British player that Nastase had hit him with his racket.

David was frogmarched to the back of the court by Bartroli and Constantin Nastase, the Romanian captain, but it was a full ten minutes before order was restored sufficiently for Bartroli to issue Nastase with a public warning for insulting behaviour. The match over, the problems

continued, with the British players arguing heatedly among themselves over the dinner table about whether to forfeit the two remaining rubbers the next day in protest at Nastase's behaviour. David threw out what seemed to be an ultimatum, "You guys can do what you like, but I'm on the first flight out of here in the morning," and when Richard Lewis, the former national director of tennis at the LTA who became chief executive of Rugby League, urged team loyalty, saying, "How can you bugger off now just because you're upset?" Lloyd called him gutless.

"If you're going to call me gutless, you can step outside and we'll see whose gutless," said a now blisteringly angry Lewis. "No-one's ever called me that before." Lewis then slammed down the spoon he was holding, stood up and grabbed David by the collar, as if trying to haul him to his feet. In the end team captain, Paul Hutchins, succeeded in calming everyone down. Nastase, when he learned what had happened, just laughed.

There have been other well documented flare-ups, with Britain's Roger Taylor and South African, Bob Hewitt, once coming to blows in a locker room at Queen's Club, but it is not always a case of one player trying to put one across the other. Sometimes there has been joint, mutual action against broader targets. In the last year of the John Player International at Nottingham in 1976, Corals, the bookmakers, were given permission to operate a betting shop within the tournament grounds. As none of their staff were particularly familiar with tennis, let alone the current form of players, they took on two non-playing British players to advise them about the odds. Whether anything underhand took place only those who were most intimately involved will ever know – and they haven't said. In any case there were no rules governing what players could or could not bet on at the time. Suffice to say that long before the week was over the betting shop closed down with stories that on one day it had even run out of money. Most of it had been paid out in winnings to the players who knew more than anyone about current form.

TENNIS RECORDS

The pinnacle of tennis remains the four annual Grand Slam events, where the world's best players convene to battle it out over the course of two weeks. Here is a list of those whose names will live forever in the annals of the sport.

AUSTRALIAN CHAMPIONSHIPS

1. Held as the Australasian Championship from 1905 to 1926. **2.** In 1927 became the Australian Championships to coincide with the opening of the Kooyong Stadium in Melbourne. **3.** The Championships became open in 1969. **Venues:** Since 1905 there have been 83 Championships held in the following cities (there were two Championships in 1977 (Jan and Dec) and from then until 1985 the event was staged in December. In 1986 there was no Championship so that the Jan date could be resumed in 1987): Melbourne (50): 1905, '14, '24, '27, '30, '33, '35, '39, '48, '50, '53, '57, '61, '65, '68, 1972–2006 (1927–1987 at Kooyong; since 1988 at the National Tennis Centre, Melbourne Park. Sydney (17): 1908, '19, '22, '25, '28, '31, '34, '37, '40, '47, '51, '54, '58, '62, '66, '70, '71. Adelaide (14): 1910, '20, '26, '29, '32, '36, '38, '46, '49, '52, '55, '59, '63, '67. Brisbane (8): 1907, '11, '15, '23, '56, '60, '64, '69. Perth (3): 1909, '13, '21. Christchurch, NZL (1): 1906. Hastings, NZL (1): 1912

Men's Singles

	Champion	Runner-up	Score				
1905	R.W. Heath	A.H. Cutis	4–6	6–3	6–4	6–4	
1906	A.F. Wilding	F.M.B. Fisher	6–0	6–4	6–4		
1907	H.M. Rice	H.A. Parker	6–3	6–4	6–4		
1908	F.B. Alexander	A.W. Dunlop	3–6	3–6	6–0	6–2	6–3
1909	A.F. Wilding	E.F. Parker	6–1	7–5	6–2		
1910	R.W. Heath	H.M. Rice	6–4	6–3	6–2		
1911	N. E. Brookes	H.M. Rice	6–1	6–2	6–3		
1912	J.C. Parke	A.E. Beamish	3–6	6–3	1–6	6–1	7–5
1913	E.F. Parker	H.A. Parker	2–6	6–1	6–3	6–2	
1914	A.O'Hara Wood	G.L. Patterson	6–4	6–3	5–7	6–1	
1915	F.G. Lowe	H.M. Rice	4–6	6–1	6–1	6–4	
1916–1918 *Not held*							
1919	A.R.F. Kingscote	E.O. Pockley	6–4	6–0	6–3		
1920	P.O'Hara Wood	R.V. Thomas	6–3	4–6	6–8	6–1	6–3
1921	R.H. Gemmell	A. Hedeman	7–5	6–1	6–4		
1922	J. O. Anderson	G.L. Patterson	6–0	3–6	3–6	6–3	6–2
1923	P. O'Hara Wood	C.B. St John	6–1	6–1	6–3		
1924	J.O. Anderson	R.E. Schlesinger	6–3	6–4	3–6	5–7	6–3
1925	J.O. Anderson	G.L. Patterson	11–9	2–6	6–2	6–3	
1926	J.B. Hawkes	J. Willard	6–1	6–3	6–1		
1927	G.L. Patterson	J.B. Hawkes	3–6	6–4	3–6	18–16	6–3
1928	J. Borotra	R.O. Cummings	6–4	6–1	4–6	5–7	6–3
1929	J.C. Gregory	R.E. Schlesinger	6–2	6–2	5–7	7–5	
1930	E.F. Moon	H.C. Hopman	6–3	6–1	6–3		
1931	J.H. Crawford	H.C. Hopman	6–4	6–2	2–6	6–1	
1932	J.H. Crawford	H.C. Hopman	4–6	6–3	3–6	6–3	6–1
1933	J.H. Crawford	K. Gledhill	2–6	7–5	6–3	6–2	
1934	F.J. Perry	J.H. Crawford	6–3	7–5	6–1		
1935	J. H. Crawford	F.J. Perry	2–6	6–4	6–4	6–4	
1936	A.K. Quist	J.H. Crawford	6–2	6–3	4–6	3–6	9–7
1937	V.B. McGrath	J.E. Bromwich	6–3	1–6	6–0	2–6	6–1
1938	J.D. Budge	J. E. Bromwich	6–4	6–2	6–1		
1939	J.E. Bromwich	A.K. Quist	6–4	6–1	6–3		
1940	A.K. Quist	J.H. Crawford	6–3	6–1	6–2		
1941–45 *Not held*							
1946	J.E. Bromwich	D. Pails	5–7	6–3	7–5	3–6	6–2
1947	D. Pails	J.E. Bromwich	4–6	6–4	3–6	7–5	8–6
1948	A.K. Quist	J.E. Bromwich	6–4	3–6	6–3	2–6	6–3
1949	F.A. Sedgman	J.E. Bromwich	6–3	6–2	6–2		
1950	F.A. Sedgman	K. McGregor	6–3	6–4	4–6	6–1	
1951	R. Savitt	K. McGregor	6–3	2–6	6–3	6–1	
1952	K. McGregor	F.A. Sedgman	7–5	12–10	2–6	6–2	
1953	K.R. Rosewall	M.G. Rose	6–0	6–3	6–4		
1954	M.G. Rose	R.N. Hartwig	6–2	0–6	6–4	6–2	
1955	K.R. Rosewall	L.A. Hoad	9–7	6–4	6–4		
1956	L.A. Hoad	K.R. Rosewall	6–4	3–6	6–4	7–5	
1957	A.J. Cooper	N.A. Fraser	6–3	9–11	6–4	6–2	
1958	A.J. Cooper	M.J. Anderson	7–5	6–3	6–4		
1959	A. Olmedo	N.A. Fraser	6–1	6–2	3–6	6–3	
1960	R.G. Laver	N.A. Fraser	5–7	3–6	6–3	8–6	8–6
1961	R.S. Emerson	R.G. Laver	1–6	6–3	7–5	6–4	
1962	R.G. Laver	R.S. Emerson	8–6	0–6	6–4	6–4	
1963	R.S. Emerson	K.N. Fletcher	6–3	6–3	6–1		
1964	R.S. Emerson	F.S. Stolle	6–3	6–4	6–2		
1965	R.S. Emerson	F.S. Stolle	7–9	2–6	6–4	7–5	6–1
1966	R.S. Emerson	A.R. Ashe	6–4	6–8	6–2	6–3	
1967	R.S. Emerson	A.R. Ashe	6–4	6–1	6–4		
1968	W.W. Bowrey	J.M. Gisbert	7–5	2–6	9–7	6–4	
1969	R.G. Laver	A. Gimeno	6–3	6–4	7–5		
1970	A.R. Ashe	R.D. Crealy	6–4	9–7	6–2		
1971	K.R. Rosewall	A.R. Ashe	6–1	7–5	6–3		
1972	K.R. Rosewall	M.J. Anderson	7–6	6–3	7–5		
1973	J.D. Newcombe	O. Parun	6–3	6–7	7–5	6–1	
1974	J.S. Connors	P. Dent	7–6	6–4	4–6	6–3	
1975	J.D. Newcombe	J.S. Connors	7–5	3–6	6–4	7–6	
1976	M. Edmondson	J.D. Newcombe	6–7	6–3	7–6	6–1	
1977 (Jan)	R. Tanner	G. Vilas	6–3	6–3	6–3		
1977 (Dec)	V. Gerulaitis	J. M. Lloyd	6–3	7–6	5–7	3–6	6–2
1978 (Dec)	G. Vilas	J. Marks	6–4	6–4	3–6	6–3	
1979 (Dec)	G. Vilas	J. Sadri	7–6	6–3	6–2		
1980 (Dec)	B. Teacher	K. Warwick	7–5	7–6	6–3		

	Champion	Runner-up		Score			
1981 (Dec)	J. Kriek	S. Denton	6–2	7–6	6–7	6–4	
1982 (Dec)	J. Kriek	S. Denton	6–3	6–3	6–2		
1983 (Dec)	M. Wilander	I. Lendl	6–1	6–4	6–4		
1984 (Dec)	M. Wilander	K. Curren	6–7	6–4	7–6	6–2	
1985 (Dec)	S. Edberg	M. Wilander	6–4	6–3	6–3		
1986 *Not held*							
1987 (Jan)	S. Edberg	P. Cash	6–3	6–4	3–6	5–7	6–3
1988	M. Wilander	P. Cash	6–3	6–7	3–6	6–1	8–6
1989	I. Lendl	M. Mecir	6–2	6–2	6–2		
1990	I. Lendl	S. Edberg	4–6	7–6	5–2	ret'd	
1991	B. Becker	I. Lendl	1–6	6–4	6–4	6–4	
1992	J. Courier	S. Edberg	6–3	3–6	6–4	6–2	
1993	J. Courier	S. Edberg	6–2	6–1	2–6	7–5	
1994	P. Sampras	T. Martin	7–6	6–4	6–4		
1995	A. Agassi	P. Sampras	4–6	6–1	7–6	6–4	
1996	B. Becker	M. Chang	6–2	6–4	2–6	6–2	
1997	P. Sampras	C. Moya	6–2	6–3	6–3		
1998	P. Korda	M. Rios	6–2	6–2	6–2		
1999	Y Kafelnikov	T Enqvist	4–6	6–0	6–3	7–6	
2000	A Agassi	Y Kafelnikov	3–6	6–3	6–2	6–4	
2001	A Agassi	A Clement	6–4	6–2	6–2		
2002	T Johansson	M Safin	3–6	6–4	6–4	7–6	
2003	A Agassi	R Schuetler	6–2	6–2	6–1		
2004	R Federer	M Safin	7–6	6–4	6–2		
2005	M Safin	L Hewitt	1–6	6–3	6–4	6–4	
2006	R Federer	M Baghdatis	5–7	7–5	6–0	6–2	

Women's Singles

	Champion	Runner-up	Score			
1922	Mrs M. Molesworth	Miss E.F. Boyd	6–3	10–8		
1923	Mrs M. Molesworth	Miss E.F. Boyd	6–1	7–5		
1924	Miss S. Lance	Miss E.F. Boyd	6–3	3–6	8–6	
1925	Miss D. Akhurst	Miss E.F. Boyd	1–6	8–6	6–4	
1926	Miss D. Akhurst	Miss E.F. Boyd	6–1	6–3		
1927	Miss E.F. Boyd	Mrs S. Harper	5–7	6–1	6–2	
1928	Miss D. Akhurst	Miss E.F. Boyd	7–5	6–2		
1929	Miss D. Akhurst	Miss L.M. Bicerton	6–1	5–7	6–2	
1930	Miss D. Akhurst	Miss S. Harper	10–8	2–6	7–5	
1931	Mrs C. Buttsworth	Mrs J.H. Crawford	1–6	6–3	6–4	
1932	Mrs C. Buttsworth	Miss K. Le Messurier	9–7	6–4		
1933	Miss J. Hartigan	Miss C. Buttsworth	6–4	6–3		
1934	Miss J. Hartigan	Mrs M. Molesworth	6–1	6–4		
1935	Miss D.E. Round	Miss N.M. Lyle	1–6	6–1	6–3	
1936	Miss J. Hartigan	Miss N.M. Wynne	6–4	6–4		
1937	Miss N.M. Wynne	Mrs V. Westacott	6–3	5–7	6–4	
1938	Miss D.M. Bundy	Miss D. Stevenson	6–3	6–2		
1939	Mrs V. Westacott	Miss H.C. Hopman	6–1	6–2		
1940	Mrs G.F. Bolton	Miss T. Coyne	5–7	6–4	6–0	
1941–45 *Not held*						
1946	Mrs G.F. Bolton	Miss J. Fitch	6–4	6–4		
1947	Mrs G.F. Bolton	Mrs H.C. Hopman	6–3	6–2		
1948	Mrs G.F. Bolton	Miss M. Toomey	6–3	6–1		
1949	Miss D.J. Hart	Mrs G.F. Bolton	6–3	6–4		
1950	Miss A.L. Brough	Miss D.J. Hart	6–4	3–6	6–4	
1951	Mrs G.F. Bolton	Mrs M.N. Long	6–1	7–5		
1952	Mrs M.N. Long	Miss H. Angwin	6–2	6–3		
1953	Miss M. Connolly	Miss J. Sampson	6–3	6–2		
1954	Mrs M.N. Long	Miss J. Staley	6–3	6–4		
1955	Miss B. Penrose	Mrs M.N. Long	6–4	6–3		
1956	Miss M. Carter	Mrs M.N. Long	3–6	6–2	9–7	
1957	Miss S.J. Fry	Miss A. Gibson	6–3	6–4		
1958	Miss A. Mortimer	Miss L. Coghlan	6–3	6–4		
1959	Mrs S.J. Reitano	Miss R. Schuurman	6–2	6–3		
1960	Miss M. Smith	Miss J. Lehane	7–5	6–2		
1961	Miss M. Smith	Miss J. Lehane	6–1	6–4		
1962	Miss M. Smith	Miss J. Lehane	6–0	6–2		
1963	Miss M. Smith	Miss J. Lehane	6–2	6–2		
1964	Miss M. Smith	Miss L.R. Turner	6–3	6–2		
1965	Miss M. Smith	Miss M.E. Bueno	5–7	6–4	5–2	
1966	Miss M. Smith	Miss N. Richey	w.o			
1967	Miss N. Richey	Miss L.R. Turner	6–1	6–4		
1968	Mrs L.W. King	Mrs B.M. Court	6–1	6–2		
1969	Mrs B.M. Court	Mrs L.W. King	6–4	6–1		
1970	Mrs B. M. Court	Miss K. Melville	6–1	6–3		
1971	Mrs B.M. Court	Miss E. Goolagong	2–6	7–6	7–5	
1972	Miss S.V. Wade	Miss E. Goolagong	6–4	6–4		
1973	Mrs B.M. Court	Miss E. Goolagong	6–4	7–5		
1974	Miss E. Goolagong	Miss C.M. Evert	7–6	4–6	6–0	
1975	Miss E. Goolagong	Miss M. Navratilova	6–3	6–2		
1976	Mrs E. Cawley	Miss R. Tomanova	6–2	6–2		
1977 (Dec)	Mrs G. Reid	Miss D. Fromholtz	7–5	6–2		
1977 (Jan)	Mrs E Cawley	Mrs H. Gourlay	6–3	6–0		
1978 (Jan)	Miss C. O'Neil	Miss B. Nagelsen	6–3	7–6		
1979 (Jan)	Miss B. Jordan	Miss S. Walsh	6–3	6–3		
1980 (Jan)	Miss H. Mandlikova	Miss W.M. Turnball	6–0	7–5	6–6	
1981 (Jan)	Miss M. Navratilova	Mrs C. Evert Lloyd	6–7	6–4	7–5	
1982 (Jan)	Mrs C. Evert Lloyd	Miss M. Navratilova	6–3	2–6	6–3	
1983 (Jan)	Miss M. Navratilova	Miss K. Jordan	6–2	7–6		
1984 (Jan)	Mrs C. Evert Lloyd	Miss H. Sukova	6–7	6–1	6–3	

	Champion	Runner-up	Score		
1985 (Jan)	Miss M. Navratilova	Mrs C. Evert Lloyd	6–2	4–6	6–2
1986 *Not held*					
1987 (Dec)	Miss H. Mandlikova	Miss M. Navratilova	7–5	7–6	
1988	Miss S. Graf	Miss C. Evert	6–1	7–6	
1989	Miss S. Graf	Miss H. Sukova	6–4	6–4	
1990	Miss S. Graf	Miss M. J. Fernandez	6–3	6–4	
1991	Miss M. Seles	Miss J. Novotna	5–7	6–3	6–1
1992	Miss M. Seles	Miss M. J. Fernandez	6–2	6–3	
1993	Miss M. Seles	Miss S. Graf	4–6	6–3	6–2
1994	Miss S. Graf	Miss A. Sanchez Vicario	6–0	6–2	
1995	Miss M. Pierce	Miss A. Sanchez Vicario	6–3	6–2	
1996	Miss M. Seles	Miss A. Huber	6–4	6–1	
1997	Miss M. Hingis	Miss M. Pierce	6–2	6–2	
1998	Miss M. Hingis	Miss C. Martinez	6–3	6–3	
1999	Miss M Hingis	Miss A Mauresmo	6–2	6–3	
2000	Miss L Davenport	Miss M Hingis	6–1	7–5	
2001	Miss J Capriati	Miss M Hingis	6–4	6–3	
2002	Miss J Capriati	Miss M Hingis	4–6	7–6	6–2
2003	Miss S Williams	Miss V Williams	7–6	3–6	6–4
2004	Mrs J Henin-Hardenne	Miss K Clijsters	6–3	4–6	6–3
2005	Miss S Williams	Miss L Davenport	2–6	6–3	6–0
2006	Miss A Mauresmo	Mrs J Henin-Hardenne	6–1	2–0	ret'd

FRENCH OPEN CHAMPIONSHIPS

1. From 1891 to 1924 the Championships, restricted to members of French clubs, were played at the Stade Français ground at the Faisanderie in St. Cloud Park. It included the title "World Clay Court Championship" between 1912 and 1924 when the title was abolished. **2.** Up to 1924 entry was restricted to members of French clubs. International from 1925, the Championships were played for three years alternately at the Racing Club at Croix-Catelan in Paris and the Stade Français at the Faisanderie. Since 1928 the Championships have been played continuously at the Stade Roland Garros, Porte D'Auteuil, Paris. The Championships became "Open" in 1968.

Men's Singles

Year	Champion	Year	Champion
1891	H. Briggs	1903–04	M. Decugis
1892	J. Schopfer	1905–06	M. Germot
1893	L. Riboulet	1907–09	M. Decugis
1894–96	A. Vacherot	1910	M. Germot
1897–1900	P. Ayme	1911	A.H. Gobert
1901	A. Vacherot	1912–14	M. Decugis
1902	M. Vacherot	1915–19	*Not held*
		1920	A. H. Gobert
		1921	J. Samazeuilh
		1922	H. Cochet
		1923	P. Blanchy
		1924	J. Borotra

	Champion	Runner-up	Score				
1925	R. Lacoste	J. Borotra	7–5	6–1	6–4		
1926	H. Cochet	R. Lacoste	6–2	6–4	6–3		
1927	R. Lacoste	W.T. Tilden	6–4	4–6	5–7	6–3	11–9
1928	H. Cochet	R. Lacoste	5–7	6–3	6–1	6–3	
1929	R. Lacoste	J. Borotra	6–3	2–6	6–0	2–6	8–6
1930	H. Cochet	W.T. Tilden	3–6	8–6	6–3	6–1	
1931	J. Borotra	C. Boussus	2–6	6–4	7–5	6–4	
1932	H. Cochet	G. de Stefani	6–0	6–4	4–6	6–3	
1933	J.H. Crawford	H. Cochet	8–6	6–1	6–3		
1934	G. von Cramm	J.H. Crawford	6–4	7–9	3–6	7–5	6–3
1935	H. Henkel	H.W. Austin	6–1	6–4	6–3		
1936	G. von Cramm	F.J .Perry	6–0	2–6	6–2	2–6	6–0
1937	H. Henkel	H.W. Austin	6–1	6–4	6–3		
1938	J.D. Budge	R. Menzel	6–3	6–2	6–4		
1939	W.D. McNeill	R.L. Riggs	7–5	6–0	6–3		
1940–45 *Not held*							
1946	M. Bernard	J. Drobny	3–6	2–6	6–1	6–4	6–3
1947	J. Asboth	E.W. Sturgess	8–6	7–5	6–4		
1948	F.A. Parker	J. Drobny	6–4	7–5	5–7	8–6	
1949	F.A. Parker	J.E. Patty	6–3	1–6	6–1	6–4	
1950	J.E. Patty	J. Drobny	6–1	6–2	3–6	5–7	7–5
1951	J. Drobny	E.W. Sturgess	6–3	6–3	6–3		
1952	J. Drobny	F.A. Sedgman	6–2	6–0	3–6	6–4	
1953	K.R. Rosewall	E.V. Seixas	6–3	6–4	1–6	6–2	
1954	M.A. Trabert	A. Larsen	6–4	7–5	6–1		
1955	M.A. Trabert	S. Davidson	2–6	6–1	6–4	6–2	
1956	L.A. Hoad	S. Davidson	6–4	8–6	6–3		
1957	S. Davidson	H. Flam	6–3	6–4	6–4		
1958	M.G. Rose	L.Ayala	6–3	6–4	6–4		
1959	N. Pietrangeli	I.C. Vermaak	3–6	6–3	6–4	6–1	

Year	Champion	Runner-up	Score				
1960	N. Pietrangeli	L. Ayala	3–6	6–3	6–4	4–6	6–3
1961	M. Santana	N. Pietrangeli	4–6	6–1	3–6	6–0	6–2
1962	R.G. Laver	R.S. Emerson	3–6	2–6	6–3	9–7	6–2
1963	R.S. Emerson	P. Darmon	3–6	6–1	6–4	6–4	
1964	M. Santana	N. Pietrangeli	6–3	6–1	4–6	7–5	
1965	F.S. Stolle	A.D. Roche	3–6	6–0	6–2	6–3	
1966	A.D. Roche	I. Gulyas	6–1	6–4	7–5		
1967	R.S. Emerson	A.D. Roche	6–1	6–4	2–6	6–2	
1968	K.R. Rosewall	R.G. Laver	6–3	6–1	2–6	6–2	
1969	R.G. Laver	K.R. Rosewall	6–4	6–3	6–4		
1970	J. Kodes	Z. Franulovic	6–2	6–4	6–0		
1971	J. Kodes	I. Nastase	8–6	6–2	2–6	7–5	
1972	A. Gimeno	P. Proisy	4–6	6–3	6–1	6–1	
1973	I. Nastase	N. Pilic	6–3	6–3	6–0		
1974	B. Borg	M. Orantes	2–6	6–7	6–0	6–1	6–1
1975	B. Borg	G. Vilas	6–2	6–3	6–4		
1976	A. Panatta	H. Solomon	6–1	6–4	4–6	7–6	
1977	G. Vilas	B.E. Gottfried	6–0	6–3	6–0		
1978	B. Borg	G. Vilas	6–1	6–1	6–3		
1979	B. Borg	V. Pecci	6–3	6–1	6–7	6–4	
1980	B. Borg	V. Gerulaitis	6–4	6–1	6–2		
1981	B. Borg	I. Lendl	6–1	4–6	6–2	3–6	6–1
1982	M. Wilander	G. Vilas	1–6	7–6	6–0	6–4	
1983	Y. Noah	M. Wilander	6–2	7–5	7–6		
1984	I. Lendl	J.P. McEnroe	3–6	2–6	6–4	7–5	7–5
1985	M. Wilander	I. Lendl	3–6	6–4	6–2	6–2	
1986	I. Lendl	M. Pernfors	6–3	6–2	6–4		
1987	I. Lendl	M. Wilander	7–5	6–2	3–6	7–6	
1988	M. Wilander	H. Leconte	7–5	6–2	6–1		
1989	M. Chang	S. Edberg	6–1	3–6	4–6	6–4	6–2
1990	A. Gomez	A. Agassi	6–3	2–6	6–4	6–4	
1991	J. Courier	A. Agassi	3–6	6–4	2–6	6–1	6–4
1992	J. Courier	P. Korda	7–5	6–2	6–1		
1993	S. Bruguera	J. Courier	6–4	2–6	6–2	3–6	6–3
1994	S. Bruguera	A. Berasategui	6–3	7–5	2–6	6–1	
1995	T. Muster	M. Chang	7–5	6–2	6–4		
1996	Y. Kafelnikov	M. Stich	7–6	7–5	7–6		
1997	G. Kuerten	S. Bruguera	6–3	6–4	6–2		
1998	C. Moya	A. Corretja	6–3	7–5	6–3		
1999	A Agassi	A Medvedev	1–6	2–6	6–4	6–3	6–4
2000	G Kuerten	M Norman	6–2	6–3	2–6	7–6	
2001	G Kuerten	A Corretja	6–7	7–5	6–2	6–0	
2002	A Costa	J C Ferrero	6–1	6–0	4–6	6–3	
2003	J C Ferrero	M Verkerk	6–1	6–3	6–2		
2004	G Gaudio	G Coria	0–6	3–6	6–4	6–1	8–6
2005	R Nadal	M Puerta	6–7	6–3	6–1	7–5	
2006	R Nadal	R Federer	1–6	6–1	6–4	7–6	

Women's Singles

1887–99	Mlle F. Masson	1906	Mme F. Fenwick	1913–14	Mlle M. Broquedis
1900	Mlle Y. Prevost	1907	Mme de Kermel	1915–19	*Not held*
1901	Mme P. Girod	1908	Mme F. Fenwick	1920–23	Mlle S. Lenglen
1902–03	Mlle F. Masson	1909–12	Mlle J. Matthey	1924	Mlle D. Vlasto
1904–05	Mlle K. Gilou				

Year	Champion	Runner-up	Score		
1925	Mlle S. Lenglen	Miss K. McKane	6–1	6–2	
1926	Mlle S. Lenglen	Miss M.K. Browne	6–1	6–0	
1927	Mlle K. Bouman	Mrs G. Peacock	6–2	6–4	
1928	Miss H.N. Wills	Miss E. Bennett	6–1	6–2	
1929	Miss H.N. Wills	Mme R. Mathieu	6–3	6–4	
1930	Miss F.S. Moody	Miss H.H. Jacobs	6–2	6–1	
1931	Frl C. Aussem	Miss B. Nuthall	8–6	6–1	
1932	Mrs F.S. Moody	Mme R. Mathieu	7–5	6–1	
1933	Miss M.C. Scriven	Mme R. Mathieu	6–2	4–6	6–4
1934	Miss M.C. Scriven	Miss H.H. Jacobs	7–5	4–6	6–1
1935	Mrs H. Sperling	Mme R. Mathieu	6–2	6–1	
1936	Mrs H. Sperling	Mme R. Mathieu	6–3	6–4	
1937	Mrs H. Sperling	Mme R. Mathieu	6–2	6–4	
1938	Mme R. Mathieu	Mme N. Landry	6–0	6–3	
1939	Mme R. Mathieu	Miss J. Jedrzejowska	6–3	8–6	
1940–1945	*Championships not held*				
1946	Miss M.E. Osbourne	Miss P.M. Betz	1–6	8–6	7–5
1947	Mrs P.C. Todd	Miss D.J Hart	6–3	3–6	6–4
1948	Mme N. Landry	Miss S.J. Fry	6–2	0–6	6–0
1949	Mrs W. du Pont	Mme N. Adamson	7–5	6–2	
1950	Miss D.J. Hart	Mrs P.C. Todd	6–4	4–6	6–2
1951	Miss S.J. Fry	Miss D.J. Hart	6–3	3–6	6–3
1952	Miss D.J. Hart	Miss S.J. Fry	6–4	6–4	
1953	Miss M. Connolly	Miss D.J. Hart	6–2	6–4	
1954	Miss M. Connolly	Mme G. Bucaille	6–4	6–1	
1955	Miss A. Mortimer	Miss D.P. Knode	2–6	7–5	10–8
1956	Miss A. Gibson	Miss A. Mortimer	6–0	12–10	
1957	Miss S.J. Bloomer	Miss D.P. Knode	6–1	6–3	
1958	Mrs Z. Kormoczy	Miss S.J. Bloomer	6–4	1–6	6–2
1959	Miss C.C. Truman	Mrs Z. Kormoczy	6–4	7–5	
1960	Miss D.R. Hard	Miss Y. Ramirez	6–3	6–4	
1961	Miss A.S. Haydon	Miss Y. Ramirez	6–2	6–1	
1962	Miss M. Smith	Miss L.R. Turner	6–3	3–6	7–5

Year	Champion	Runner-up	Score		
1963	Miss L.R. Turner	Mrs P.F. Jones	2–6	6–3	7–5
1964	Miss M. Smith	Miss M.E. Bueno	5–7	6–1	6–2
1965	Miss L.R. Turner	Miss M. Smith	6–3	6–4	
1966	Mrs P.F. Jones	Miss N. Richey	6–3	6–1	
1967	Mlle F. Durr	Miss L.R. Turner	4–6	6–3	6–4
1968	Miss N. Richey	Mrs P.F. Jones	5–7	6–4	6–1
1969	Mrs B.M. Court	Mrs P.F. Jones	6–1	4–6	6–3
1970	Mrs B.M. Court	Miss H. Niessen	6–2	6–4	
1971	Miss E. Goolagong	Miss H. Gourlay	6–3	7–5	
1972	Mrs L.W. King	Miss E. Goolagong	6–3	6–3	
1973	Mrs B.M. Court	Miss C.M. Evert	6–7	7–6	6–4
1974	Miss C.M. Evert	Mrs O. Morozova	6–1	6–2	
1975	Miss C.M. Evert	Miss M. Navratilova	2–6	6–2	6–1
1976	Miss S. Barker	Miss R. Tomanova	6–2	0–6	6–2
1977	Miss M. Jausovec	Miss F. Mihai	6–2	6–7	6–1
1978	Miss V. Ruzici	Miss M. Jausovec	6–2	6–2	
1979	Mrs C. Evert Lloyd	Miss W.M. Turnbull	6–2	6–0	
1980	Mrs C. Evert Lloyd	Miss V. Ruziki	6–0	6–3	
1981	Miss H. Mandlikova	Miss S. Hanika	6–2	6–4	
1982	Miss M. Navratilova	Miss A. Jaeger	7–6	6–1	
1983	Miss C. Evert Lloyd	Miss M. Jausovec	6–1	6–2	
1984	Miss M. Navratilova	Mrs C. Evert Lloyd	6–3	6–1	
1985	Mrs C. Evert Lloyd	Miss M. Navratilova	6–3	6–7	7–5
1986	Mrs C. Evert Lloyd	Miss M. Navratilova	2–6	6–3	6–3
1987	Miss S. Graf	Miss M. Navratilova	6–4	4–6	8–6
1988	Miss S. Graf	Miss N. Zvereva	6–0	6–0	
1989	Miss A. Sanchez Vicario	Miss S. Graf	7–6	3–6	7–5
1990	Miss M. Seles	Miss S. Graf	7–6	6–4	
1991	Miss M. Seles	Miss A. Sanchez Vicario	6–3	6–4	
1992	Miss M. Seles	Miss S. Graf	6–2	3–6	10–8
1993	Miss S. Graf	Miss M.J. Fernandez	4–6	6–2	6–4
1994	Miss A. Sanchez Vicario	Miss M. Pierce	6–4	6–4	
1995	Miss S. Graf	Miss A. Sanchez Vicario	7–5	4–6	6–0
1996	Miss S. Graf	Miss A. Sanchez Vicario	6–3	6–7	10–8
1997	Miss I. Majoli	Miss M. Hingis	6–4	6–2	
1998	Miss A. Sanchez Vicario	Miss M. Seles	7–6	0–6	6–2
1999	Miss S. Graf	Miss M Hingis	4–6	7–5	6–2
2000	Miss M Pierce	Miss C Martinez	6–2	7–5	
2001	Miss J Capriati	Miss K Clijsters	1–6	6–4	12–10
2002	Miss S Williams	Miss V Williams	7–5	6–3	
2003	Mrs J Henin-Hardenne	Miss K Clijsters	6–0	6–4	
2004	Miss A Myskina	Miss E Dementieva	6–1	6–2	
2005	Mrs J Henin-Hardenne	Miss M Pierce	6–1	6–1	
2006	Mrs J Henin-Hardenne	Miss S Kuznetsova	6–4	6–4	

Wimbledon Championships

From 1877–1921 the Championships were played at the Worple Road ground. Since 1922 they have been played at the present ground in Church Road. For the years 1913, 1914, 1919–1923 inclusive, these records include the World Championship on Grass granted to the LTA by the ILTF. This title was then abolished. Prior to 1922, the holder did not compete in the Championship but met the winner of the All-Comers singles in the Challenge Round. The Challenge Round was abolished in 1922 and the holder subsequently played through. Modified seeding was introduced in 1922. Full seeding as we know it today, was first practised in 1927. The Championship became open in 1968. There was a tie-break at 8-all in the years 1971–78. Thereafter the tie-break was played at 6-all.

Men's Singles

Year	Champion	Runner-up	Score				
1927	R. Lacoste	W.T. Tilden	6–4	4–6	5–7	6–3	11–9
1877	S.W. Gore	W.C. Marshall	6–1	6–2	6–4		
1878	P.F. Hadow	S.W. Gore	7–5	6–1	9–7		
1879	J.T. Hartley	V. St. L. Goold	6–2	6–4	6–2		
1880	J.T. Hartley	H.F. Lawford	6–3	6–2	2–6	6–3	
1881	W. Renshaw	J.T. Hartley	6–0	6–1	6–1		
1882	W. Renshaw	E. Renshaw	6–1	2–6	4–6	6–2	6–2
1883	W. Renshaw	E. Renshaw	2–6	6–3	6–3	4–6	6–3
1884	W. Renshaw	H.F. Lawford	6–0	6–4	9–7		
1885	W. Renshaw	H.F. Lawford	7–5	6–2	4–6	7–5	
1886	W. Renshaw	H.F. Lawford	6–0	5–7	6–3	6–4	
1887*	H.F. Lawford	E. Renshaw	1–6	6–3	3–6	6–4	6–4
1888	E. Renshaw	H.F. Lawford	6–3	7–5	6–0		
1889	W. Renshaw	E. Renshaw	6–4	6–1	3–6	6–0	
1890	W.J. Hamilton	W. Renshaw	6–8	6–2	3–6	6–1	6–1
1891*	W. Baddeley	J. Pim	6–4	1–6	7–5	6–0	
1892	W. Baddeley	J. Pim	4–6	6–3	6–3	6–2	
1893	J. Pim	W. Baddeley	3–6	6–1	6–3	6–2	

Year	Champion	Runner-up	Score				
1894	J. Pim	W. Baddeley	10–8	6–2	8–6		
1895*	W. Baddeley	W.V. Eaves	4–6	2–6	8–6	6–2	6–3
1896	H.S. Mahony	W. Baddeley	6–2	6–8	5–7	8–6	6–3
1897	R.F. Doherty	H.S. Mahony	6–4	6–4	6–3		
1898	R.F. Doherty	H.L. Doherty	6–3	6–3	2–6	5–7	6–1
1899	R.F. Doherty	A.W. Gore	1–6	4–6	6–3	6–3	6–3
1900	R.F. Doherty	F.L. Riseley	7–5	6–3	6–0		
1901	A.W. Gore	R.F. Doherty	4–6	7–5	6–4	6–4	
1902	H.L. Doherty	A.W. Gore	6–4	6–3	3–6	6–0	
1903	H.L. Doherty	F.L. Riseley	7–5	6–3	6–0		
1904	H.L. Doherty	F.L. Riseley	6–1	7–5	8–6		
1905	H.L. Doherty	N.E. Brookes	8–6	6–2	6–4		
1906	H.L. Doherty	F.L. Riseley	6–4	4–6	6–2	6–3	
1907*	N.E. Brookes	A.W. Gore	6–4	6–2	6–2		
1908*	A.W. Gore	H. Roper Barrett	6–3	6–2	4–6	3–6	6–4
1909	A.W. Gore	M.J.G. Ritchie	6–8	1–6	6–2	6–2	6–2
1910	A.F. Wilding	A.W. Gore	6–4	7–5	4–6	6–2	
1911	A.F. Wilding	H. Roper Barrett	6–4	4–6	2–6	6–2	ret'd
1912	A.F. Wilding	A.W. Gore	6–4	6–4	4–6	6–4	
1913	A.F. Wilding	M.E. McLoughlin	8–6	6–3	10–8		
1914	N.E. Brookes	A.F. Wilding	6–4	6–4	7–5		
1915–18 *Not held*							
1919	G.L. Patterson	N.E. Brookes	6–3	7–5	6–2		
1920	W.T. Tilden	G.L Patterson	2–6	6–2	6–3	6–4	
1921	W.T. Tilden	B.I.C. Norton	4–6	2–6	6–1	6–0	7–5
Challenge Round abolished							
1922*	G.L. Patterson	R. Lycett	6–3	6–4	6–2		
1923*	W.M. Johnson	F.T. Hunter	6–0	6–3	6–1		
1924	J. Borotra	R. Lacoste	6–1	3–6	6–1	3–6	6–4
1925	R. Lacoste	J. Borotra	6–3	6–3	4–6	8–6	
1926	J. Borotra	H. Kinsey	8–6	6–1	6–3		
1927	H. Cochet	J. Borotra	4–6	4–6	6–3	6–4	7–5
1928	R. Lacoste	H. Cochet	6–1	4–6	6–4	6–2	
1929	H. Cochet	J. Borotra	6–4	6–3	6–4		
1930	W.T. Tilden	W.L. Allison	6–3	9–7	6–4		
1931*	S.B. Wood	F.X. Shields	w.o.				
1932	H.E. Vines	H.W. Austin	6–4	6–2	6–0		
1933	J.H. Crawford	H.E. Vines	4–6	11–9	6–2	2–6	6–4
1934	F.J. Perry	J.H Crawford	6–3	6–0	7–5		
1935	F.J. Perry	G. von Cramm	6–2	6–4	6–4		
1936	F.J. Perry	G. von Cramm	6–1	6–1	6–0		
1937*	J.D. Budge	G. von Cramm	6–3	6–4	6–2		
1938	J.D. Budge	H.W. Austin	6–1	6–0	6–3		
1939*	R.L. Riggs	E.T. Cooke	2–6	8–6	3–6	6–3	6–2
1940–45 *Not held*							
1946	Y. Petr	G. Brown	6–2	6–4	7–9	5–7	6–4
1947	J. Kramer	T. Brown	6–1	6–3	6–2		
1948	B. Falkenburg	J. Bromwich	7–5	0–6	6–2	3–6	7–5
1949	T. Schroeder	J. Drobny	3–6	6–0	6–3	4–6	6–4
1950	B. Patty	F. Sedgman	6–1	8–10	6–2	6–3	
1951	D. Savitt	K. McGregor	6–4	6–4	6–4		
1952	F. Sedgman	J. Drobny	4–6	6–2	6–3	6–2	
1953	V. Seixas	K. Nielsen	9–7	6–3	6–4		
1954	J. Drobny	K.R. Rosewall	13–11	4–6	6–2	9–7	
1955	T. Trabert	K. Nielsen	6–3	7–5	6–1		
1956*	L.A. Hoad	K.R. Rosewall	6–2	4–6	7–5	6–4	
1957	L.A. Hoad	A.J. Cooper	6–2	6–1	6–2		
1958*	A.J. Cooper	N.A. Fraser	3–6	6–3	6–4	13–11	
1959*	A. Olmedo	R.G. Laver	6–4	6–3	6–4		
1960*	N.A. Fraser	R.G.Laver	6–4	3–6	9–7	7–5	
1961	R.G. Laver	C.R.McKinley	6–3	6–1	6–4		
1962	R.G.Laver	M.F. Mulligan	6–2	6–2	6–1		
1963*	C.R. McKinley	F.S. Stolle	9–7	6–1	6–4		
1964	R.S. Emerson	F.S. Stolle	6–1	12–10	4–6	6–3	
1965	R.S. Emerson	F.S. Stolle	6–2	6–4	6–4		
1966	M. Santana	R.D. Ralston	6–4	11–9	6–4		
1967	J.D. Newcombe	W.P. Bungert	6–3	6–3	6–1		
1968	R.G. Laver	A.D. Roche	6–3	6–4	6–2		
1969	R.G. Laver	J.D. Newcombe	6–4	5–7	6–4	6–4	
1970	J.D. Newcombe	K.R. Rosewall	5–7	6–3	6–2	3–6	6–1
1971	J.D. Newcombe	S.R. Smith	6–3	5–7	2–6	6–4	6–4
1972*	S.R. Smith	I. Nastase	4–6	6–3	6–3	4–6	7–5
1973*	J. Kodes	A. Metreveli	6–1	9–8	6–3		
1974	J.S. Connors	K.R. Rosewall	6–1	6–1	6–4		
1975	A.R. Ashe	J.S. Connors	6–1	6–1	5–7	6–4	
1976	B. Borg	I. Nastase	6–4	6–2	9–7		
1977	B. Borg	J.S. Connors	3–6	6–2	6–1	5–7	6–4
1978	B. Borg	J.S. Connors	6–2	6–2	6–3		
1979	B. Borg	R. Tanner	6–7	6–1	3–6	6–3	6–4
1980	B. Borg	J.P McEnroe	1–6	7–5	7–6	6–4	
1981	J.P. McEnroe	B. Borg	4–6	7–6	7–6	6–4	
1982	J.S. Connors	J.P. McEnroe	3–6	6–3	6–7	7–6	6–4
1983	J.P. McEnroe	C.J. Lewis	6–2	6–2	6–2		
1984	J.P. McEnroe	J.S. Connors	6–1	6–1	6–2		
1985	B. Becker	K. Curren	6–3	6–7	7–6	6–4	
1986	B. Becker	I. Lendl	6–4	6–3	7–5		
1987	P. Cash	I. Lendl	7–6	6–2	7–5		
1988	S. Edberg	B. Becker	4–6	7–6	6–4	6–2	
1989	B. Becker	S. Edberg	6–0	7–6	6–4		
1990	S. Edberg	B. Becker	6–2	6–2	3–6	3–6	6–4
1991	M. Stich	B. Becker	6–4	7–6	6–4		
1992	A. Agassi	G. Ivanisevic	6–7	6–4	6–4	1–6	6–4
1993	P. Sampras	J. Courier	7–6	7–6	3–6	6–3	
1994	P. Sampras	G. Ivanisevic	7–6	7–6	6–0		
1995	P. Sampras	B. Becker	6–7	6–2	6–4	6–2	
1996	R. Krajicek	M. Washington	6–3	6–4	6–3		
1997	P. Sampras	C. Pioline	6–4	6–2	6–4		
1998	P. Sampras	G. Ivanisevic	6–7	7–6	6–4	3–6	6–2
1999	P Sampras	A Agassi	6–3	6–4	7–5		
2000	P Sampras	P Rafter	6–7	7–6	6–4	6–2	
2001	G Ivanisevic	P Rafter	6–3	3–6	6–3	2–6	9–7
2002	L Hewitt	D Nalbandian	6–1	6–3	6–2		
2003	R Federer	M Philippoussis	7–6	6–2	7–6		
2004	R Federer	A Roddick	4–6	7–5	7–6	6–4	
2005	R Federer	A Roddick	6–2	7–6	6–4		
2006	R Federer	R Nadal	6–0	7–6	6–7	6–3	

Women's Singles

Year	Champion	Runner-up	Score		
1884	Miss M. Watson	Miss L. Watson	6–8	6–3	6–3
1885	Miss M. Watson	Miss B. Bingley	6–1	7–5	
1886	Miss B. Bingley	Miss M. Watson	6–3	6–3	
1887	Miss C. Dod	Miss B. Bingley	6–2	6–0	
1888	Miss C. Dod	Mrs G.W. Hillyard	6–3	6–3	
1889*	Mrs G.W. Hillyard	Miss H. Rice	4–6	8–6	6–4
1890*	Miss H. Rice	Miss M. Jacks	6–4	6–1	
1891*	Miss C. Dod	Mrs G.W. Hillyard	6–2	6–1	
1892	Miss C. Dod	Mrs G.W. Hillyard	6–1	6–1	
1893	Miss C. Dod	Mrs G.W. Hillyard	6–8	6–1	6–4
1894	Mrs G.W. Hillyard	Miss L. Austin	6–1	6–1	
1895*	Miss C. Cooper	Miss H. Jackson	7–5	8–6	
1896	Miss C. Cooper	Mrs W.H. Pickering	6–2	6–3	
1897	Mrs G.W. Hillyard	Miss C. Cooper	5–7	7–5	6–2
1898*	Miss C. Cooper	Miss L. Martin	6–4	6–4	
1899	Mrs G.W. Hillyard	Miss C. Cooper	6–2	6–3	
1900	Mrs G.W. Hillyard	Miss C. Cooper	4–6	6–4	6–4
1901	Mrs A. Sterry	Mrs G.W. Hillyard	6–2	6–2	
1902	Miss M.E. Robb	Mrs A. Sterry	6–0	6–3	
1903*	Miss D.K. Douglass	Miss E.W. Thomson	4–6	6–4	6–2
1904	Miss D.K. Douglass	Mrs A. Sterry	7–5	6–1	
1905	Miss M. Sutton	Miss D.K. Douglass	6–3	6–4	
1906	Miss D.K. Douglass	Miss M. Sutton	6–3	9–7	
1907	Miss M. Sutton	Mrs R. Lamb. Chambers	6–1	6–4	
1908*	Mrs A. Sterry	Mrs G.W. Hillyard	6–2	6–2	
1909*	Miss D.P . Broothby	Miss A.M. Morton	6–4	4–6	8–6
1910	Mrs R. Lamb. Chambers	Miss D.P. Boothby	6–2	6–2	
1911	Mrs R. Lamb. Chambers	Miss D.P. Boothby	6–0	6–0	
1912*	Miss D.R. Larcombe	Mrs A. Sterry	6–3	6–1	
1913*	Mrs R. Lamb. Chambers	Mrs R.J. McNair	6–0	6–4	
1914	Mrs R. Lamb. Chambers	Mrs D.R. Larcombe	7–5	6–4	
1915–18 *Not held*					
1919	Mlle S. Lenglen	Mrs R. Lamb. Chambers	10–8	4–6	9–7
1920	Mlle S. Lenglen	Mrs R. Lamb. Chambers	6–3	6–0	
1921	Mlle S. Lenglen	Miss E. Ryan	6–2	6–0	
1922	Mlle S. Lenglen	Mrs F. Mallory	6–2	6–0	
1923	Mlle S. Lenglen	Miss K. McKane	6–2	6–2	
1924	Miss K. McKane	Miss H.N. Wills	4–6	6–4	6–4
1925	Mlle S. Lenglen	Miss J. Fry	6–2	6–0	
1926	Mrs L.A. Godfree	Sta E. de Alvarez	6–2	4–6	9–7
1927	Miss H.N. Wills	Sta E. de Alvarez	6–2	6–4	
1928	Miss H.N. Wills	Sta E. de Alvarez	6–2	6–3	
1929	Miss H.N. Wills	Miss H.H. Jacobs	6–3	6–1	
1930	Mrs F.S. Moody	Miss E. Ryan	6–2	6–2	
1931*	Frl. C. Aussem	Frl H. Krahwinkel	6–2	7–5	
1932*	Mrs F.S. Moody	Miss H.H. Jacobs	6–3	6–1	
1933	Mrs F.S Moody	Miss D.E. Round	6–4	6–8	6–3
1934*	Miss D.E. Round	Miss H.H. Jacobs	6–2	5–7	6–3
1935	Mrs F.S. Moody	Miss D.E. Round	6–3	3–6	6–3
1936*	Miss H.H. Jacobs	Mrs S. Sperling	6–2	4–6	7–5
1937	Miss D.E. Round	Miss J. Jedrzejowska	6–2	2–6	7–5
1938*	Mrs F.S. Moody	Miss H.H. Jacobs	6–4	6–0	
1939*	Miss A. Marble	Miss K.E. Stammers	6–2	6–0	
1940–45 *Not held*					
1946*	Miss P.M. Betz	Miss A.L. Brough	6–2	6–4	
1947*	Miss M.E. Osbourne	Miss D.J. Hart	6–2	6–4	
1948	Miss A.L. Brough	Miss D.J. Hart	6–3	8–6	
1949	Miss A.L. Brough	Mrs W. Du Pont	10–8	1–6	10–8
1950	Miss A.L. Brough	Mrs W. Du Pont	6–1	3–6	6–1
1951	Miss D.J. Hart	Miss S.J. Fry	6–1	6–0	
1952	Miss M. Connolly	Miss A.L. Brough	6–4	6–3	
1953	Miss M. Connolly	Miss D.J. Hart	8–6	7–5	
1954	Miss M. Connolly	Miss A.L. Brough	6–2	7–5	
1955*	Miss A.L. Brough	Mrs J.G. Fleitz	7–5	8–6	
1956	Miss S.J. Fry	Miss A. Buxton	6–3	6–1	
1957*	Miss A. Gibson	Miss D.R. Hard	6–3	6–2	
1958	Miss A. Gibson	Miss A. Mortimer	8–6	6–2	
1959*	Miss M.E. Bueno	Miss D.R. Hard	6–4	6–3	
1960	Miss M.E. Bueno	Miss S. Reynolds	8–6	6–0	
1961	Miss A. Mortimer	Miss C.C. Truman	4–6	6–4	7–5

1962	Mrs J.R. Susman	Mrs V. Sukova	6-4	6-4
1963*	Miss M. Smith	Miss B.J. Moffitt	6-3	6-4
1964	Miss M.E. Bueno	Miss M. Smith	6-4	7-9 6-3
1965	Miss M. Smith	Miss M.E. Bueno	6-4	7-5
1966	Mrs L.W. King	Miss M.E. Bueno	6-3	3-6 6-1
1967	Mrs L.W. King	Mrs P.F. Jones	6-3	6-4
1968	Mrs L.W. King	Mrs J.A.M. Tegart	9-7	7-5
1969	Mrs P.F. Jones	Mrs L.W. King	3-6	6-3 6-2
1970*	Mrs B.M. Court	Mrs L.W. King	14-12	11-9
1971	Miss E. Goolagong	Mrs B.M. Court	6-4	6-1
1972	Mrs L.W. King	Miss E Goolagong	6-3	6-3
1973	Mrs L.W. King	Miss C.M. Evert	6-0	7-5
1974	Miss C.M.Evert	Mrs O. Morozova	6-0	6-4
1975	Mrs L.W. King	Mrs R.A. Cawley	6-0	6-1
1976*	Miss C.M. Evert	Mrs R.A. Cawley	6-3	4-6 8-6
1977	Miss S.V. Wade	Miss B.F. Stove	4-6	6-3 6-1
1978	Miss M. Navratilova	Miss C.M. Evert	6-4	6-4
1979	Miss M. Navratilova	Mrs C.M. Evert Lloyd	6-1	7-6
1980	Mrs R.A. Cawley	Mrs C.M. Evert Lloyd	6-1	7-6
1981	Mrs C.M. Evert Lloyd	Miss H. Mandlikova	6-2	6-2
1982	Miss M. Navratilova	Mrs C.M. Evert Lloyd	6-1	3-6 6-2
1983	Miss M. Navratilova	Miss A. Jaeger	6-0	6-3
1984	Miss M. Navratilova	Mrs C.M. Evert Lloyd	7-6	6-2
1985	Miss M. Navratilova	Mrs C.M. Evert Lloyd	4-6	6-3 6-2
1986	Miss M. Navratilova	Miss H. Mandlikova	7-6	6-3
1987	Miss M. Navratilova	Miss S. Graf	6-4	6-1
1988	Miss S. Graf	Miss M. Navratilova	5-7	6-2 6-1
1989	Miss S. Graf	Miss M. Navratilova	6-2	6-7 6-1
1990	Miss M. Navratilova	Miss Z. Garrison	6-4	6-1
1991	Miss S. Graf	Miss G. Sabatini	6-4	3-6 8-6
1992	Miss S. Graf	Miss M. Seles	6-2	6-1
1993	Miss S. Graf	Miss J. Novotna	7-6	1-6 6-4
1994	Miss C. Martinez	Miss M. Navratilova	6-4	3-6 6-3
1995	Miss S. Graf	Miss A. Sanchez Vicario	4-6	6-1 7-5
1996	Miss S. Graf	Miss A. Sanchez Vicario	6-3	7-5
1997	Miss M. Hingis	Miss J. Novotna	2-6	6-3 6-3
1998	Miss J. Novotna	Miss N. Tauziat	6-4	7-6
1999	Miss L Davenport	Miss S Graf	6-4	7-5
2000	Miss V Williams	Miss L Davenport	6-3	7-6
2001	Miss V Williams	Miss J Henin	6-1	3-6 6-0
2002	Miss S Williams	Miss V Williams	7-6	6-3
2003	Miss S Williams	Miss V Williams	4-6	6-4 6-2
2004	Miss M Sharapova	Miss S Williams	6-1	6-4
2005	Miss V Williams	Miss L Davenport	4-6	7-6 9-7
2006	Miss A Mauresmo	Mrs J Henin-Hardenne	2-6	6-3 6-4

US OPEN CHAMPIONSHIPS

1. A Challenge Round was introduced in 1884 and discontinued following the 1911 Championship. It was introduced in the women's singles in 1888 and discontinued following the 1919 Championship. In the years marked with an asterisk (*) the holder did not defend his/her title so the winner of the All-Comers Singles became the Champion. **2.** In 1917 a National Patriotic Tournament was held in all five events. The winners were not recognized as National Champions. **3.** During World War II (1942–1945) all five National Championships were staged together at the West Side Tennis Club, Forest Hills, NY. **4.** During the first two years of Open Tennis (1968, 1969) a National Amateur Championship was held for all five events at the Longwood Cricket Club, Boston, as well as an Open Championship at Forest Hills, New York (although there was no Open mixed in 1968). Thereafter the Amateur event was discontinued. 5. The "predominantly white" clothing rule was last enforced at the 1971 Championships. 6. Equal prize money for men and women was introduced in 1973. **Surfaces:** 1881–1973 grass; 1975–1977 American clay; 1978–present hard courts

MEN'S SINGLES Venues: 1881–1914 The Casino, Newport, RI; 1915–1920 West Side Tennis Club, Forest Hills, NY; 1921–1923 Germantown Cricket Club, Philadelphia, PA; 1924–1977 West Side Tennis Club, Forest Hills, NY; 1978– National Tennis Center, Flushing Meadows, NY
WOMEN'S SINGLES Venues: 1887–1920 Philadelphia Cricket Club, PA; 1921–1977 West Side Tennis Club, Forest Hills, NY; 1978– National Tennis Center, Flushing Meadows, NY

Men's Singles

	Champion	Runner-up	Score				
1881	R.D. Sears	W.E. Glyn	6-0	6-3	6-2		
1882	R.D. Sears	C.M. Clark	6-1	6-4	6-0		
1883	R.D. Sears	J. Dwight	6-2	6-0	9-7		
Challenge Round instituted							
1884	R.D. Sears	H.A. Taylor	6-0	1-6	6-0	6-2	
1885	R.D. Sears	G.M. Brinley	6-3	4-6	6-0	6-3	
1886	R.D. Sears	R.L. Beeckman	4-6	6-1	6-3	6-4	
1887	R.D. Sears	H.W. Slocum	6-1	6-3	6-2		
1888*	H.W. Slocum	H.A. Taylor	6-4	6-1	6-0		
1889	H.W. Slocum	Q.A. Shaw	6-3	6-1	4-6	6-2	
1890	O.S. Campbell	H.W. Slocum	6-2	4-6	6-3	6-1	
1891	O.S. Campbell	C. Hobart	2-6	7-5	7-9	6-1	6-2
1892	O.S. Campbell	F.H. Hovey	7-5	3-6	6-3	7-5	
1893*	R.D. Wrenn	F.H. Hovey	6-4	3-6	6-4	6-4	
1894	R.D. Wrenn	M.F. Goodbody	6-8	6-1	6-4	6-4	
1895	F.H. Hovey	R.D. Wrenn	6-3	6-2	6-4		
1896	R.D. Wrenn	F.H. Hovey	7-5	3-6	6-0	1-6	6-1
1897	R.D. Wrenn	W.V. Eaves	4-6	8-6	6-3	2-6	6-2
1898*	M.D. Whitman	D.F. Davis	3-6	6-2	6-2	6-1	
1899	M.D. Whitman	J.P. Paret	6-1	6-2	3-6	7-5	
1900	M.D. Whitman	W.A. Larned	6-4	1-6	6-2	6-2	
1901*	W.A. Larned	B.C. Wright	6-2	6-8	6-4	6-4	
1902	W.A. Larned	R.F. Doherty	4-6	6-2	6-4	8-6	
1903	H.L. Doherty	W.A. Larned	6-0	6-3	10-8		
1904*	H. Ward	W.J. Clothier	10-8	6-4	9-7		
1905	B.C. Wright	H. Ward	6-2	6-1	11-9		
1906	W.J. Clothier	B.C. Wright	6-3	6-0	6-4		
1907*	W.A. Larned	R. LeRoy	6-2	6-2	6-4		
1908	W.A. Larned	B.C. Wright	6-1	6-2	8-6		
1909	W.A. Larned	W.J. Clothier	6-1	6-2	5-7	1-6	6-1
1910	W.A. Larned	T.C. Bundy	6-1	5-7	6-0	6-8	6-1
1911	W.A. Larned	M.E. McLoughlin	6-4	6-4	6-2		
Challenge Round abolished							
1912	M.E. McLoughlin	W.F. Johnson	3-6	2-6	6-2	6-4	6-2
1913	M.E. McLoughlin	R.N. Williams	6-4	5-7	6-3	6-1	
1914	R.N. Williams	M.E. McLoughlin	6-3	8-6	10-8		
1915	W.M. Johnston	M.E. McLoughlin	1-6	6-0	7-5	10-8	
1916	R.N. Williams	W.M. Johnston	4-6	6-4	0-6	6-2	6-4
1917	R.L. Murray	N.W. Niles	5-7	8-6	6-3	6-3	
1918	R.L. Murray	W.T. Tilden	6-3	6-1	7-5		
1919	W.M. Johnston	W.T. Tilden	6-4	6-4	6-3		
1920	W.T. Tilden	W.M. Johnston	6-1	1-6	7-5	5-7	6-3
1921	W.T. Tilden	W.M. Johnston	6-1	6-3	6-1		
1922	W.T. Tilden	W.M. Johnston	4-6	3-6	6-2	6-3	6-4
1923	W.T. Tilden	W.M. Johnston	6-4	6-1	6-4		
1924	W.T. Tilden	W.M. Johnston	6-1	9-7	6-2		
1925	W.T. Tilden	W.M. Johnston	4-6	11-9	6-3	4-6	6-3
1926	R. Lacoste	J. Borotra	6-4	6-0	6-4		
1927	R. Lacoste	W.T. Tilden	11-9	6-3	11-9		
1928	H. Cochet	F.T. Hunter	4-6	6-4	3-6	7-5	6-3
1929	W.T. Tilden	F.T. Hunter	3-6	6-3	4-6	6-2	6-4
1930	J.H. Doeg	F.X. Shields	10-8	1-6	6-4	16-14	
1931	H.E. Vines	G.M. Lott	7-9	6-3	9-7	7-5	
1932	H.E. Vines	H. Cochet	6-4	6-4	6-4		
1933	F.J. Perry	J.H. Crawford	6-3	11-13	4-6	6-0	6-1
1934	F.J. Perry	W.L. Allison	6-4	6-3	1-6	10-8	
1935	W.L. Allison	S.B. Wood	6-2	6-2	6-3		
1936	F.J. Perry	J.D. Budge	2-6	6-2	8-6	1-6	10-8
1937	J.D. Budge	C. von Cramm	6-1	7-9	6-1	3-6	6-1
1938	J.D. Budge	G. Mako	6-3	6-8	6-2	6-1	
1939	R.L. Riggs	S.W. van Horn	6-4	6-2	6-4		
1940	W.D. McNeill	R.L. Riggs	4-6	6-8	6-3	6-3	7-5
1941	R.L. Riggs	F. Kovacs	5-7	6-1	6-3	6-3	
1942	F.R. Schroeder	F.A. Parker	8-6	7-5	3-6	4-6	6-2
1943	J.R. Hunt	J.A. Kramer	6-3	6-8	10-8	6-0	
1944	F.A. Parker	W.F. Talbert	6-4	3-6	6-3	6-3	
1945	F.A. Parker	W.F. Talbert	14-12	6-1	6-2		
1946	J.A. Kramer	T.P. Brown	9-7	6-3	6-0		
1947	J.A. Kramer	F.A. Parker	4-6	2-6	6-1	6-0	6-3
1948	R.A. Gonzales	E.W. Sturgess	6-2	6-3	14-12		
1949	R.A. Gonzales	F.R. Schroeder	16-18	2-6	6-1	6-2	6-4
1950	A. Larsen	H. Flam	6-3	4-6	5-7	6-4	6-3
1951	F.A. Sedgman	E.V. Seixas	6-4	6-1	6-1		
1952	F.A. Sedgman	G. Mulloy	6-1	6-2	6-3		
1953	M.A. Trabert	E.V. Seixas	6-3	6-2	6-3		
1954	E.V. Seixas	R.N. Hartwig	3-6	6-2	6-4	6-4	
1955	M.A Trabert	K.R. Rosewall	9-7	6-3	6-3		
1956	K.R. Rosewall	L.A. Hoad	4-6	6-2	6-3	6-3	
1957	M.J. Anderson	A.J. Cooper	10-8	7-5	6-4		
1958	A.J. Cooper	M.J. Anderson	6-2	3-6	4-6	10-8	8-6
1959	N.A. Fraser	A. Olmedo	6-3	5-7	6-2	6-4	
1960	N.A. Fraser	R.G. Laver	6-4	6-4	9-7		
1961	R.S. Emerson	R.G. Laver	7-5	6-3	6-2		
1962	R.G. Laver	R.S. Emerson	6-2	6-4	5-7	6-4	
1963	R.H. Osuna	F. Froehling	7-5	6-4	6-2		
1964	R.S. Emerson	F.S. Stolle	6-4	6-2	6-4		
1965	M. Santana	E.C. Drysdale	6-2	7-9	7-5	6-1	
1966	F.S. Stolle	J.D. Newcombe	4-6	12-10	6-3	6-4	

Year	Champion	Runner-up			Score		
1967	J.D. Newcombe	C. Graebner	6–4	6–4	8–6		
1968#	A.R. Ashe	R.C. Lutz	4–6	6–3	8–10	6–0	6–4
1969#	S.R. Smith	R.C. Lutz	9–7	6–3	6–1		
1968	A.R. Ashe	T.S. Okker	14–12	5–7	6–3	3–6	6–3
1969	R.G. Laver	A.D. Roche	7–9	6–1	6–2	6–2	
1970	K.R. Rosewall	A.D. Roche	2–6	6–4	7–6	6–3	
1971	S.R. Smith	J. Kodes	3–6	6–3	6–2	7–6	
1972	I. Nastase	A.R. Ashe	3–6	6–3	6–7	6–4	6–3
1973	J.D. Newcombe	J. Kodes	3–6	6–3	6–2	7–6	
1974	J.S. Connors	K.R. Rosewall	6–1	6–0	6–1		
1975	M. Orantes	J.S. Connors	6–4	6–3	6–3		
1976	J.S. Connors	B.Borg	6–4	3–6	7–6	6–4	
1977	G. Vilas	J.S. Connors	2–6	6–3	7–5	6–0	
1978	J.S. Connors	B. Borg	7–6	6–1	6–7	5–7	6–4
1979	J.P. McEnroe	V. Gerulaitis	7–5	6–3	6–3		
1980	J.P. McEnroe	B. Borg	7–6	6–1	6–7	5–7	6–4
1981	J.P. McEnroe	B. Borg	4–6	6–2	6–4	6–3	
1982	J.S. Connors	I. Lendl	6–3	6–2	4–6	6–4	
1983	J.S. Connors	I. Lendl	6–3	6–7	7–5	6–0	
1984	J.P. McEnroe	I. Lendl	6–3	6–4	6–1		
1985	I. Lendl	J.P. McEnroe	7–6	6–3	6–4		
1986	I. Lendl	M. Mecir	6–4	6–2	6–0		
1987	I. Lendl	M. Wilander	6–7	6–0	7–6	6–4	
1988	M. Wilander	I. Lendl	6–4	4–6	6–3	5–7	6–4
1989	B. Becker	I. Lendl	7–6	1–6	6–3	7–6	
1990	P. Sampras	A. Agassi	6–4	6–3	6–2		
1991	S. Edberg	J. Courier	6–2	6–4	6–0		
1992	S. Edberg	P. Sampras	3–6	6–4	7–6	6–2	
1993	P. Sampras	C. Pioline	6–4	6–4	6–3		
1994	A. Agassi	M. Stich	6–1	7–6	7–5		
1995	P. Sampras	A. Agassi	6–4	6–3	4–6	7–5	
1996	P. Sampras	M. Chang	6–1	6–4	7–6		
1997	P. Rafter	G. Rusedski	6–3	6–2	4–6	7–5	
1999	A Agassi	T Martin	6–4	6–7	6–7	6–3	6-2
2000	M Safin	P Sampras	6–4	6–3	6–3		
2001	L Hewitt	P Sampras	7-6	6-1	6-1		
2002	P Sampras	A Agassi	6–3	6–4	5–7	6–4	
2003	A Roddick	J C Ferrero	6–3	7–6	6–3		
2004	R Federer	L Hewitt	6–0	7–6	6–0		
2005	R Federer	A Agassi	6–3	2–6	7–6	6–1	
2006	R Federer	A Roddick	6–2	4–6	7–5	6–1	

US Amateur Championships

Women's Singles

Year	Champion	Runner-up	Score				
1887	Miss E. Hansell	Miss L. Knight	6–1	6–0			
1888	Miss B.L. Townsend	Miss E. Hansell	6–3	6–5			
1889	Miss B.L. Townsend	Miss L.D. Voorhees	7–5	6–2			
1890	Miss E.C. Rooseveldt	Miss B.L. Townsend	6–2	6–2			
1891	Miss M.E. Cahill	Miss E.C. Rooseveldt	6–4	6–1	4–6	6–3	
1892	Miss M.E. Cahill	Miss E.H. Moore	5–7	6–3	6–4	4–6	6–2
1893*	Miss A. Terry	Miss A.L. Schultz	6–1	6–3			
1894	Miss H. Hellwig	Miss A. Terry	7–5	3–6	6–0	3–6	6–3
1895	Miss J. Atkinson	Miss H. Hellwig	6–4	6–2	6–1		
1896	Miss E. H. Moore	Miss J. Atkinson	6–4	4–6	6–2	6–2	
1897	Miss J. Atkinson	Miss E.H. Moore	6–3	6–3	4–6	3–6	6–3
1898	Miss J. Atkinson	Miss M. Jones	6–3	5–7	6–4	2–6	7–5
1899*	Miss M. Jones	Miss M. Banks	6–1	6–1	7–5		
1900*	Miss M. McAteer	Miss E. Parker	6–2	6–2	6–0		
1901	Miss E.H. Moore	Miss M. McAteer	6–4	3–6	7–5	2–6	6–2
1902	Miss M. Jones	Miss E.H. Moore	6–1	1–0	ret'd		
1903	Miss E.H. Moore	Miss M. Jones	7–5	8–6			
1904	Miss M.G. Sutton	Miss E.H. Moore	6–1	6–2			
1905	Miss E.H. Moore	Miss H. Homans	6–4	5–7	6–1		
1906*	Miss H. Homans	Mrs M. Barger-Wallach	6–4	6–3			
1907*	Miss Evelyn Sears	Miss C. Neely	6–3	6–2			
1908	Mrs M. Barger-Wallach	Miss Evelyn Sears	6–3	1–6	6–3		
1909	Miss H. Hotchkiss	Mrs M. Barger-Wallach	6–0	6–1			
1910	Miss H. Hotchkiss	Miss L. Hammond	6–4	6–2			
1911	Miss H. Hotchkiss	Miss F. Sutton	8–10	6–1	9–7		
1912*	Miss M.K. Browne	Miss E. Sears	6–4	6–2			
1913	Miss M.K. Browne	Miss D. Green	6–2	7–5			
1914	Miss M.K. Browne	Miss M. Wagner	6–2	1–6	6–1		
1915*	Miss M. Bjurstedt	Mrs G.W. Wightman	4–6	6–2	6–0		
1916	Miss M. Bjurstedt	Mrs L.H. Raymond	6–0	6–1			
1917	Miss M. Bjurstedt	Miss M. Vanderhoef	4–6	6–0	6–2		
1918	Miss M. Bjurstedt	Miss E.E. Goss	6–4	6–3			
Challenge Round abolished							
1919	Mrs G.W. Wightman	Miss M. Zinderstein	6–1	6–2			
1920	Mrs F. Mallory	Miss M. Zinderstein	6–3	6–1			
1921	Mrs F. Mallory	Miss M.K. Browne	4–6	6–4	6–2		
1922	Mrs F. Mallory	Miss H.N. Wills	6–3	6–1			
1923	Miss H.N. Wills	Mrs F. Mallory	6–2	6–1			
1924	Miss H.N. Wills	Mrs F. Mallory	6–1	6–3			
1925	Miss H.N. Wills	Miss K. McKane	3–6	6–0	6–2		
1926	Mrs F. Mallory	Miss E. Ryan	4–6	6–4	9–7		
1927	Miss H.N. Wills	Miss B. Nuthall	6–1	6–4			
1928	Miss H.N. Wills	Miss H.H. Jacobs	6–2	6–1			
1929	Miss H.N. Wills	Mrs P.H. Watson	6–4	6–2			
1930	Miss B. Nuthall	Mrs L.A. Harper	6–1	6–4			
1931	Mrs F.S. Moody	Mrs F. Whittingstall	6–4	6–1			
1932	Miss H.H. Jacobs	Miss C.A. Babcock	6–2	6–2			
1933	Miss H.H. Jacobs	Mrs F.S. Moody	8–6	3–6	3–0	ret'd	
1934	Miss H.H. Jacobs	Miss S. Palfrey	6–1	6–4			
1935	Miss H.H. Jacobs	Mrs S.P. Fabyan	6–2	6–4			
1936	Miss A. Marble	Miss H.H. Jacobs	4–6	6–3	6–2		
1937	Miss A. Lizana	Miss J. Jedrzejowska	6–4	6–2			
1938	Miss A. Marble	Miss N. Wynne	6–0	6–3			
1939	Miss A. Marble	Miss H.H. Jacobs	6–0	8–10	6–4		
1940	Miss A. Marble	Miss H.H. Jacobs	6–2	6–3			
1941	Mrs E.T. Cooke	Miss P.M. Betz	7–5	6–2			
1942	Miss P.M. Betz	Miss A.L Brough	4–6	6–1	6–4		
1943	Miss P.M. Betz	Miss A.L Brough	6–3	5–7	6–3		
1944	Miss P.M. Betz	Miss M.E. Osbourne	6–3	8–6			
1945	Mrs E.T. Cooke	Miss P.M. Betz	3–6	8–6	6–4		
1946	Miss P.M. Betz	Miss P.C. Canning	11–9	6–3			
1947	Miss A.L. Brough	Miss M.E. Osbourne	8–6	4–6	6–1		
1948	Mrs W.D. du Pont	Miss A.L. Brough	4–6	6–4	15–13		
1949	Mrs W.D. du Pont	Miss D.J. Hart	6–3	6–1			
1950	Mrs W.D. du Pont	Miss D.J. Hart	6–4	6–3			
1951	Miss M. Connolly	Miss S.J. Fry	6–3	1–6	6–4		
1952	Miss M. Connolly	Miss D.J. Hart	6–3	7–5			
1953	Miss M. Connolly	Miss D.J. Hart	6–2	6–4			
1954	Miss D.J. Hart	Miss A.L. Brough	6–8	6–1	8–6		
1955	Miss D.J. Hart	Miss P.E. Ward	6–4	6–2			
1956	Miss S.J. Fry	Miss A. Gibson	6–3	6–4			
1957	Miss A. Gibson	Miss A.L. Brough	6–3	6–2			
1958	Miss A. Gibson	Miss D.R. Hard	3–6	6–1	6–2		
1959	Miss M.E. Bueno	Miss C.C. Truman	6–1	6–4			
1960	Miss D.R. Hard	Miss M.E. Bueno	6–4	10–12	6–4		
1961	Miss D.R. Hard	Miss A.S. Haydon	6–3	6–4			
1962	Miss M. Smith	Miss D.R. Hard	9–7	6–4			
1963	Miss M.E. Bueno	Miss M. Smith	7–5	6–4			
1964	Miss M.E. Bueno	Mrs C. Graebner	6–1	6–0			
1965	Miss M. Smith	Miss B.J. Moffitt	8–6	7–5			
1966	Miss M.E. Bueno	Miss N. Richey	6–3	6–1			
1967	Mrs L.W. King	Mrs P.F. Jones	11–9	6–4			
1968#	Mrs B.M. Court	Miss M.E. Bueno	6–2	6–2			
1969#	Mrs B.M. Court	Miss S.V. Wade	4–6	6–3	6–0		
1968	Miss S.V. Wade	Mrs L.W. King	6–4	6–2			
1969	Mrs B.M. Court	Miss N. Richey	6–2	6–2			
1970	Mrs B.M. Court	Miss R. Casals	6–2	2–6	6–1		
1971	Mrs L.W. King	Miss R. Casals	6–2	2–6	6–1		
1972	Mrs L.W. King	Miss K. Melville	6–3	7–5			
1973	Mrs B.M. Court	Miss E. Goolagong	7–6	5–7	6–2		
1974	Mrs L.W. King	Miss E. Goolagong	3–6	6–3	7–5		
1975	Miss C.M. Evert	Mrs R.A. Cawley	5–7	6–4	6–2		
1976	Miss C.M. Evert	Mrs R.A. Cawley	6–3	6–0			
1977	Miss C.M. Evert	Miss W. Turnbull	7–6	6–2			
1978	Miss C.M. Evert	Miss P. Shriver	7–5	6–4			
1979	Miss T.A. Austin	Miss C.M. Evert	6–4	6–3			
1980	Mrs C. Evert Lloyd	Miss H. Mandlikova	5–7	6–1	6–1		
1981	Miss T.A. Austin	Miss M. Navratilova	1–6	7–6	7–6		
1982	Mrs C. Evert Lloyd	Miss H. Mandlikova	6–3	6–1			
1983	Miss M. Navratilova	Mrs C. Evert Lloyd	6–1	6–3			
1984	Miss M. Navratilova	Mrs C. Evert Lloyd	4–6	6–4	6–4		
1985	Miss H. Mandlikova	Miss M. Navratilova	7–6	1–6	7–6		
1986	Miss M. Navratilova	Miss H. Sukova	6–3	6–2			
1987	Miss M. Navratilova	Miss S. Graf	7–6	6–1			
1988	Miss S. Graf	Miss G. Sabatini	6–3	3–6	6–1		
1989	Miss S. Graf	Miss M. Navratilova	3–6	7–5	6–1		
1990	Miss G. Sabatini	Miss S. Graf	6–2	7–6			
1991	Miss M. Seles	Miss M. Navratilova	7–6	6–1			
1992	Miss M. Seles	Miss A. Sanchez Vicario	6–3	6–3			
1993	Miss S. Graf	Miss H. Sukova	6–3	6–3			
1994	Miss A. Sanchez Vicario	Miss S. Graf	1–6	7–6	6–4		
1995	Miss S. Graf	Miss M. Seles	7–6	0–6	6–3		
1996	Miss S. Graf	Miss M. Seles	7–5	6–4			
1997	Miss M. Hingis	Miss V. Williams	6–0	6–4			
1999	Miss S Williams	Miss M Hingis	6–3	7–6			
2000	Miss V Williams	Miss L Davenport	6–4	7–5			
2001	Miss V Williams	Miss S Williams	6–2	6–4			
2002	Miss S Williams	Miss V Williams	6–4	6–3			
2003	Mrs J Henin-Hardenne	Miss K Clijsters	7–5	6–1			
2004	Miss S Kuznetsova	Miss E Dementieva	6–3	7–5			
2005	Miss K Clijsters	Miss M Pierce	6–3	6–1			
2006	Miss M Sharapova	Miss J Henin-Hardenne	6–4	6–4			

US Amateur Championships

TENNIS CHRONOLOGY

1872 The first lawn tennis club in the world was formed in Leamington, Warwickshire.

1875 First rules for tennis published.

1877 The All England Club Club staged a men's singles championship at Wimbledon for the first time.

1881 US Tennis Association formed. Championships introduced at Newport, Rhode Island, though only for American citizens until 1885.

1884 Women's singles introduced at Wimbledon.

1895 Wimbledon lost £33 on the staging of The Championships.

1896 Tennis included in the first staging of the modern Olympics.

1900 Davis Cup introduced, but entries only from Britain and the United States.

1905 British born May Sutton becomes first overseas player to win singles title at Wimbledon.

1913 International Lawn Tennis Federation founded in Paris, with 12 nations.

1920 Suzanne Lenglen first player to win a hat-trick of titles at Wimbledon.

1923 Inauguration of Wightman Cup, annual challenge match between Britain and the United States. New Forest Hills stadium for US Championships opened at West Side Club, New York.

1924 Bill Tilden resigned from US Davis Cup team after being refused permission to write about tennis for a newspaper. Ballot for Wimbledon tickets first introduced.

1925 French Championships open to non-French citizens or residents for the first time. French players win both singles titles, men's doubles, women's doubles and one half of mixed doubles title in a Wimbledon clean sweep. Lenglen dropped only five games in five matches in women's singles.

1926 Suzanne Lenglen wins the only match she ever played against Helen Wills. The Duke of York, later to become King George VI, lost in first round of men's doubles at Wimbledon.

1927 French break the USA, Britain and Australia stranglehold on the Davis Cup.

1928 New home for the French Championships at Roland Garros. Ruth Tapscott of South Africa first woman to compete at Wimbledon without wearing stockings.

1930 Bill Tilden wins Wimbledon for a third time aged 37, but at the US Championships lost to another American, Californian left-hander John Doeg, for the first time in 11 years and retired at the end of the year.

1931 Sidney Wood becomes the only player to win a singles title at Wimbledon on a walk-over when American Frank Shields pulled out with injured leg muscle.

1933 Britain win Davis Cup back from France. Bunny Austin first man to wear shorts at Wimbledon.

1935 Fred Perry's victory at the French Championships makes him the first player to win all four of the Grand Slam titles.

1936 Fred Perry wins third successive Wimbledon, helps Britain to fourth consecutive Davis Cup triumph.

1937 Wimbledon the first tennis tournament to be televised.

1938 Don Budge becomes first man to win the Grand Slam and achieve the triple crown at Wimbledon.

1940 Stick of five 500-lb bombs hits All England Club and grounds, destroying 1,200 Centre Court seats.

1947 Jack Kramer becomes the first men's singles champion to wear shorts.

1948 Britain's Joy Gannon barred from wearing "bits of colour" on the frock Ted Tinling designed for her a year earlier, when she wanted to wear it in the Wightman Cup.

1949 "Gorgeous" Gussy Moran shocked Wimbledon with her lace-trimmed panties.

1949 Louise Brough played 117 games over five hours when competing in three matches on the final day.

1951 Frank Sedgman becomes the first Australian to win the US men's singles championship.

1953 Maureen Connolly ("Little Mo"), aged 18, won Grand Slam for the loss of only one set in 22 matches and finished year with a 61–2 record.

1954 Jaroslav Drobny beat Hoad, Patty and Rosewall to win one of Wimbledon's most emotional finals.

1955 The rules were changed, so that instead of new balls after each set, new balls were introduced after the first seven games and then after each subequent nine.

1956 BBC Television stayed on live after midnight for the first time to see the finish of Pancho Gonzales's classic 4–6, 11–9, 11–9, 9–7 win against Frank Sedgman at Wembley.

1957 Althea Gibson, who learned the game playing paddle tennis on the streets of Harlem, wins Wimbledon for the first time.

1960 Hurricane Donna delays finals of US Championships for a week. United States, beaten by Italy, fail to reach Davis Cup Challenge Round for first time since 1936. Proposal to allow Open tennis defeated at ILTF annual meeting by five votes.

1961 Angela Mortimer beats Christine Truman in first all-British final at Wimbledon since 1914 in the 75th anniversary staging of The Championships.

1962 Rod Laver wins Grand Slam for the first time and turns professional.

1963 Wimbledon introduces rule that players must be dressed in predominately white throughout.

1964 Australians win Davis Cup for the 11th time in 14 years.

1965 Manola Santana becomes the first Spaniard to win a Grand Slam titles on grass.

1966 Britain's Roger Taylor beats Wieslaw Gasiorek in the longest singles match on record in major international event, 27–29, 31–29, 6–4 in a King's Cup match on wood in Warsaw.

1967 Wimbledon, with a Championships attendance of more than 300,000 for the first time, also stages a tournament just for professionals and calls for tennis go "Open". British LTA defies the threat of expulsion by voting to remove the distinction between amateurs and professionals at all their tournaments, including Wimbledon, the following year.

1968 Emergency meeting of ITF in Paris in February approved 12 Open tournaments during the year. First Open tournament staged at Bournemouth in England in April with £2000 for winner of men's singles and £700 to winner of women's singles.

1969 Rod Laver becomes only player to win the Grand Slam twice.

1970 US Open introduced sudden-death 9-points tie-break. Margaret Court wins the Grand Slam. WCT announce $1.5m dollar tournament circuit in competition with ITF approved tournaments. Publisher, Gladys Heldman, leads breakaway by women players in protest at prize money disparity.

1971 Rod Laver becomes first player to win more than $1m in prize money. ITF banned WCT "contract professionals" from all tournaments under its jurisdiction in 1972.

1972 Peace agreement between ITF and WCT came too late to allow WCT players to compete at the French Open or Wimbledon.

1973 Billie Jean King beats Bobby Riggs before a tennis record crowd of 30,472 in the "Battle of the Sexes" in Houston. Men players boycott Wimbledon in protest at suspension of Niki Pilic.

1974 Jimmy Connors, 21, and Chris Evert, engaged to be married at the time, both win singles at Wimbledon. Davis Cup final decided by default for only time when Indian government refused to allow its team to play in the final as a protest against apartheid.

1975 Arthur Ashe outwits defending champion Jimmy Connors in the Wimbledon final. US Open switches from grass to all-weather synthetic clay surface, allowing night play for first time.

1977 Wimbledon centenary. Queen Elizabeth II sees Virginia Wade win women's singles title for Britain. Renee Richards, formerly Richard Raskind, becomes the first to compete in the US Championships as a man (1954) and a woman.

1978 French Open golden jubilee. US Open moves from Forest Hills to Flushing Meadows.

1980 John McEnroe wins 18–16 tie-break but loses Wimbledon final to Bjorn Borg.

1981 McEnroe ends Borg's five-year reign at Wimbledon, but was denied his Wimbledon membership for 12 months because of his behaviour.

1982 Mats Wilander wins French Open title aged 17 years, 10 months, one year after being boy's singles champion at Roland Garros.

1984 Martina Navratilova's unbeaten streak of 74 matches ended.

1985 Boris Becker, 17 years 227 days, youngest men's singles winner at Wimbledon.

1986 Martina Navratilova, who had helped Czechoslovakia win the Federation Cup for the first time in 1975, returned to Prague as an American and was again on the winning side.

1987 Australian Open staged at Kooyong for last time.

1988 Steffi Graf wins Grand Slam and the gold medal in Seoul when tennis returns to the Olympic Games as a competitive sport for the first time in 64 years. Australian Open moves to Flinders Park and unveils the first tennis arena with a sliding roof.

1989 Michael Chang, 17 years 3 months, wins French Open to become youngest winner of a Grand Slam men's singles title.

1990 ATP Tour launched. John McEnroe first to be defaulted at a Grand Slam tournament in Open tennis.

1991 Monica Seles wins $2.4m prize money, a record one-year total for any player.

1992 Monica Seles becomes first player to win three consecutive women's singles titles at Roland Garros for 55 years.

1993 Arthur Ashe dies from AIDS contracted from blood transfusions while undergoing surgery in 1988, on February 6. Jana Novotna weeps on the Duchess of Kent's shoulder after losing the Wimbledon

final she should have won against Steffi Graf. Monica Seles stabbed in the back while playing in Hamburg by a fanatical fan intent on restoring Steffi Graf to world No. 1.

1994 Andre Agassi wins the US Open unseeded.

1995 Tim Henman becomes first player to be disqualified at Wimbledon after he unintentionally struck a ballgirl with a ball hit away in anger. Four days later Jeff Tarango was disqualified for bad behaviour.

1997 Martina Hingis wins Australian Open to become the youngest player this century (16 years and 4 months) to win a Grand Slam title. New 11,000-seat No. 1 Court opened at Wimbledon. Arthur Ashe stadium with seats for 23,000 opened at the US Open.

1998 Record 131 entries for Davis Cup. Marcelo Rios from Chile becomes first South American to attain world No. 1 ranking.

1999 Steffi Graf retires after 17 years on the Tour with 22 Grand Slam single titles.

2000 The ATP Champions Race is launched and the Tennis Masters Series is established.

2001 Wild card entry Goran Ivanisevic wins Wimbledon on his fourth appearance in the singles final.

2003 Serena Williams wins Australia and scores a non calendar Grand Slam which she names a 'Serena Slam'.

2004 Russians dominate the women's Grand Slam singles, first Anastasia Myskina lifts the Roland Garros trophy, then Maria Sharapova claims Wimbledon and finally Svetlana Kuznetsova annexes the US Open.

2006 Hawk-Eye, the electronic line calling system, is used for the first time on the Tour at the Nasdaq-100 event in Miami.

INDEX

PICTURE CREDITS

The publishers would like to thank the following sources for their kind permission to reproduce the pictures in this book:

Allsport UK Ltd/Al Bello, Howard Boylan, Clive Brunskill, Simon Bruty, Tony Duffy, Stephen Dunn, Stu Forster, John Gichigi, Mike Hewitt, Hulton Getty, Trevor Jones, Bob Martin, Steve Powell, Craig Prentis, Gary M.Prior, Pascal Rondeau, Dan Smith; **Michael Cole Camera Work**; **Colorsport**; **Corbis**; **Justin Downing**; **Mary Evans Picture Library**; **Popperfoto**/Dave Joiner, Reuters; **Professional Sport**; **Sporting Pictures (UK) Ltd**; **Paul Zimmer.**

Additonal pictures courtesy of: **Corbis Images**: /Eric Lalment/EPA: 69; **Empics:** /S&G/Alpha: 100; **Getty Images:** 113, 159; /David Ashdown /Keystone: 71; /Clive Brunskill: 25, 40, 177; /David Cannon: 179; /Adrian Dennis/AFP: 180; /Don Emmert/AFP: 72; /Julian Finney: 187; /Focus on Sport: 101; /Sean Garnsworthy: 164; /Jean-Loup Gautreau/AFP: 207; /David Hancock/AFP: 15; /Mike Hewitt: 6; /Robert Laberge: 4, 82; /Nick Laham: 56; /Alex Livesey: 154; /Christophe Simon/AFP: 49; /Jamie Squire: 35, 39; /David Teuma: 183; /Ian Walton: 22.

Every effort has been made to acknowledge correctly and contact the source and/or copyright holder of each picture, and Carlton Books Limited apologises for any unintentional errors or omissions which will be corrected in future editions of this book.